Australian**Broadcast
Journalism**

Australian Broadcast Journalism

Second Edition

Gail Phillips and Mia Lindgren

OXFORD
UNIVERSITY PRESS

OXFORD

UNIVERSITY PRESS

253 Normanby Road, South Melbourne, Victoria 3205, Australia

Oxford University Press is a department of the University of Oxford.
It furthers the University's objective of excellence in research, scholarship,
and education by publishing worldwide in

Oxford New York

Auckland Cape Town Dar es Salaam Hong Kong Karachi
Kuala Lumpur Madrid Melbourne Mexico City Nairobi
New Delhi Shanghai Taipei Toronto

With offices in

Argentina Austria Brazil Chile Czech Republic France Greece
Guatemala Hungary Italy Japan Poland Portugal Singapore
South Korea Switzerland Thailand Turkey Ukraine Vietnam

OXFORD is a trade mark of Oxford University Press
in the UK and in certain other countries

National Library of Australia
Cataloguing-in-Publication data:

Phillips, Gail, 1947– .
Australian broadcast journalism.

2nd ed.
Bibliography.
Includes index.
For tertiary students.

ISBN 9 78019551 7552.
ISBN 0 19 551755 5.

1. Broadcast journalism—Australia. 2. Journalists—
Australia—Case studies. I. Lindgren, Mia. II. Title.

070.190994

Typeset by Linda Hamley
Printed in China by Golden Cup Printing Co. Ltd

Contents

Part II   Radio Craft Skills

Part III   Radio Production Formats

Part IV Radio and Television News

Part VI A Broadcast Journalist's Guide to Law and Ethics

Preface

This is a book by journalists for journalists: this is how we started the first edition of this book and it holds as true for the second edition. Once again the information here is firmly grounded in the practice of broadcast journalism as recounted by the experienced journalists with whom we have had the pleasure of collaborating across all broadcast media: radio, television, and online. The aim remains to give new recruits to broadcast journalism a firm grounding in the core skills that all the media have in common, and then showing how these are customised to specific formats ranging from live and pre-produced radio through to radio and television news reporting and beyond to the evolving online services.

Modern-day broadcast journalism is less medium-specific than it used to be: whereas it was easy in the past for broadcast journalists to spend their entire careers within a single medium, now they are encouraged to be as multiskilled as possible and are likely to find themselves working in radio, television, and online at some time or another as they rise up the journalism ladder. This book mimics this career pathway, taking journalistic skills as the starting point and tracking their application across the different broadcast media, just as broadcast journalists will have to adapt their own practice in a convergent, multiple-media working environment.

Most importantly, the book is firmly located in Australia, giving students the chance to relate what they are being taught to their own domestic context, rather than having to extrapolate from the British or American experience on which many of the classic journalism textbooks are based. Through 'day in the life' segments students can experience industry practice first-hand, sitting alongside a talkback radio producer, going on the road with a television news reporter, and following the development of an online news story from headline to full-blown Web feature.

Part I locates Australian broadcast journalism within the history of radio, television, and online media in this country, pointing out how the Australian media industry of today very much bears the imprint of its past in terms of its structure, regulatory framework, and value system.

Part II moves on to the baseline production skills, using radio as the starting point. Radio is the most accessible medium for audiences and students alike, and more often than not is the stepping-stone for broadcast journalists into other media. In this book we use it as the setting for the learning of basic journalism skills that can then be applied elsewhere. In this section, students are introduced to the craft skills of voice production, writing, interviewing, and sound production techniques.

In Part III, the challenges of story selection and story development are discussed in the context of different radio formats, both pre-recorded and live. This allows us to examine the hunting-and-gathering production process of putting together radio stories and radio promotion packages. We then look in some detail at live talk radio production and the unique journalistic challenges this format poses to production staff working without a safety net in the live-to-air radio environment.

In Part IV, the focus shifts to the broadcast newsroom and we look first of all at how news is defined and how the editorial and reporting processes function in this environment. We examine first the role of the radio news reporter, and see how the radio journalism skills discussed in previous chapters are adapted to the specific task of radio news production.

The television newsroom comes next, and students are able to explore the impact on journalism practice of working with vision as well as sound. The complex process of gathering material on the road and crafting a story in the editing suite is analysed in detail and illustrated with the real-life example from a typical reporter's day.

We then examine the production challenges of putting the news bulletins to air, and the roles of the radio and television newsreaders in this process.

In Part V we look at the production processes in the online environment and the particular journalistic and technical challenges posed by a globalised 24/7 medium with no deadlines and an ever-open maw for new information.

No one working in journalism can afford to ignore the laws and regulatory codes that govern journalistic practice, and throughout the book we note the legal and ethical minefields that broadcasters may encounter in different situations. In Part VI we provide a more detailed summary of the legal and ethical frameworks for broadcast journalism. The relevant sections of the regulations and codes of practice are included at the back of the book.

As previously noted, a key feature of this text is its industry focus. Insights from practising journalists are incorporated into each chapter to illustrate key points, while the companion CD provides an opportunity not only to hear samples of their work, but also to hear them talking about how they do what they do.

As we have already said, this book was very much a collaborative venture involving media practitioners from all facets of the broadcasting industry. The authors wish to thank the ABC, Channel Nine, Channel Seven, 2GB, and 3AW for allowing us to access their facilities and use their content. The authors also wish to thank the following people for their enthusiastic support, for their good-humoured participation, and for their patience in dealing with what were often time-consuming requests:

- ABC Radio: Bill Bunbury, Steve Cannane, Geraldine Doogue, Adam Sallur, Ron Sims, Margaret Throsby
- ABC News and Current Affairs: Alison Caldwell, Tony Clough, Katy Cronin, Scott Holdaway, Sally Sara
- ABC Online: Kerrin Binnie, Brett Bugg, Bob Johnston, David O'Sullivan, Martin Southgate, Col Wotherspoon
- The Age Online: Libby Chow, Simon Johanson
- BBC Online: Peter Clifton
- Channel Seven News, Perth: Shaun Menegola
- National Nine News, Perth: Richard Allen, Marianne Ellis, Trent Nind

- 2GB, Sydney: Selby-Lynn Bradford, Philip Clark, Justin Kelly
- 3AW, Melbourne: Clark Forbes, Neil Mitchell
- 6PR, Perth: Howard Sattler.

We also wish to give special thanks to Leo Murray for his advice and help in the production of the CD, and Chaz Jones and Dominique Pratt for lending us their voices.

We are grateful to Lucy McLoughlin of Oxford University Press for her patient guidance through the process of preparing this second edition. Once again our families have been the source of unstinting comfort and support and we dedicate this book to them.

Abbreviations

ABA	Australian Broadcasting Authority
ABC	Australian Broadcasting Corporation
ABCB	Australian Broadcasting Control Board
ABT	Australian Broadcasting Tribunal
ACMA	Australian Communications and Media Authority
AJA	Australian Journalists Association
APRA	Australian Performing Rights Association
ARIA	Australian Recording Industry Association
BBC	British Broadcasting Corporation
CBAA	Community Broadcasting Association of Australia
CRA	Commercial Radio Australia
FACTS	Federation of Australian Commercial Television Stations
FTA	free-to-air
ISP	Internet service provider
MEAA	Media Entertainment and Arts Alliance
SBS	Special Broadcasting Service

PART I

Radio, Television, and the Web in Australia

Radio in Australia

The radio services that we have in Australia are very much a product of their origins in the earliest years of the twentieth century.

A short history

The technology that became radio emerged in 1896 when the Italian Guglielmo Marconi worked out how sound could be converted into electronic impulses and transmitted through the air without the need of electronic wires. This opened up the prospect of person-to-person long-distance communication, and the early dabblers took to this new technology in much the same way as the computer buffs of today have taken to the Internet. Where the modern radio audience listens to material that others provide, in those early days radio was a medium that the listeners were involved in themselves as originators and transmitters of their own messages to other like-minded enthusiasts.

In Australia, the first use of two-way radio transmission occurred in 1906 with a link between Victoria and Tasmania. During the subsequent two decades the popularity of radio grew, and by the 1920s interest was shifting from point-to-point wireless telephony to **broadcasting**—the transmission of material from a single source to multiple recipients.

As the competition for radio spectrum heated up the government became involved, and by 1923 it began to introduce regulations governing the use of the airwaves. In 1924 it created the concept of 'A' and 'B' class stations, the former government-sponsored and funded by licence fees and some advertising, and the latter funded by commercial revenue alone.

In 1932 the *Australian Broadcasting Commission Act* brought together the eight 'A' class stations in the Australian capital cities as a single federal **broadcaster** with similar aims and aspirations to the British Broadcasting Corporation (BBC) in the United Kingdom. In this way the two strands of mainstream Australian radio—the public broadcaster and commercial radio—were born. It was only in 1974 that a third strand emerged, when the Whitlam government legislated for the introduction of local community radio stations. (The Special Broadcasting Service, or SBS, was set up by the government in 1978 as a separate entity with the specific brief of offering multilingual broadcasting directed at Australia's diverse ethnic communities.) So what distinguishes these three strands?

Commercial radio

Section 14 of the *Broadcasting Services Act* defines commercial broadcasting services as services:

a that provide programs that, when considered in the context of that service being provided, appear to be intended to appeal to the general public; and

b that provide programs that:

i are able to be received by commonly available equipment; and

ii are made available free to the general public; and

c that are usually funded by advertising revenue; and

d that are operated for profit or as part of a profit-making enterprise; and

e that comply with any determinations or clarifications under section 19 of the Broadcasting Services Act 1992 in relation to commercial broadcasting services.

Broadcasting Services Act 1992

So we can expect commercial radio services:

- to be profit-driven and funded by advertising
- to appeal to a mass audience
- to reflect popular culture of wide appeal.

According to Commercial Radio Australia, the sector's industry peak body, there are 257 commercial radio stations in Australia, with the list continuing to grow. Commercial radio is driven by the prime imperative of generating its own revenue. This means it has to attract advertisers willing to pay for station time, and to do this it has to promise them a mass audience to which to deliver their advertising messages. This has implications for **formats** and programs since inevitably the stations are pulled towards content of high appeal and high entertainment value. From the very start, therefore, commercial radio's realm has been that of popular culture and its aim has been to give the public programming with mass appeal.

① Comparision with Newspaper

For many years metropolitan commercial radio was dominated by three players: Austereo, Southern Cross Broadcasting, and ARN (Australian Radio Network). When the federal government created ten new FM licences under the 1988 National Radio Plan, the subsequent feeding frenzy grossly inflated the licence value; that put the whole radio market under considerable strain. To relieve the pressure, regulations were relaxed to enable licensees to run up to two stations in the market. The Big Three were in the best position to benefit from the relaxation of the rules, and quickly snapped up their quota to build formidable national **networks**. However, at the same time foreign ownership restrictions were lifted and the UK-based Daily Mail Group was quick to take advantage of the opportunity this presented. Since 1999 DMG Radio Australia has been on a spending spree, snapping up FM licences in the capital cities for its network of Nova stations, and creating ripples throughout the industry with its appeal to the 18-24 audience. As an example of the ownership spread, the major metropolitan commercial radio markets now look like this:

Capital City	ARN	Austereo	DMG	Southern Cross
Adelaide	Mix 102.3 FM 5DN 1323 AM	SA FM Triple M FM	5AA AM Nova 91.9 FM	
Brisbane	4KQ AM 97.3 FM	B105 FM Triple M FM	97.3 FM 106.9 new licence not yet operating	4BC AM 4BH AM
Canberra	Mix 106.3 FM (joint with Austereo) FM 104.7 FM	Mix 106.3 FM (joint with ARN) FM 104.7 FM		
Melbourne	Gold 104.3 FM Mix 101.1 FM	Fox FM Triple M FM	Nova 100 FM 91.5 new licence not yet operating	3AW AM Magic 693 AM
Perth		Mix 94.5 FM 92.9 FM	Nova 937 FM	882 6PR AM 96.1 FM
Sydney	WS FM Mix 106.5 FM	2DAY FM Triple M FM	Nova 969 FM 95.3 new licence not yet operating	2UE AM

Metropolitan networks

Source: Commercial Radio Australia, http://www.commercialradio.com.au

The network strategy has been either to cover two different music markets (for example Austereo in Melbourne) or to combine an AM talk station with an FM music station (for example Southern Cross in Perth). There are also substantial networks covering the regions, the major players being Macquarie Regional Radioworks, with stations in forty-four locations nationwide; Super Network, covering sixteen locations in New South Wales; and Grant Broadcasting, covering nine locations in various states.

Community radio

According to section 15 of the *Broadcasting Services Act*, community broadcasting services are services that:

- are provided for community purposes, and
- are not operated for profit or as part of a profit-making enterprise; and
- provide programs that:
  - are able to be received by commonly available equipment and
  - are made available free to the general public.

Broadcasting Service Act 1992

So, in contrast to the commercial sector, community radio stations are:

- non-profit
- alternative
- local.

The sector may have started modestly with the first licensed station beginning operations in 1975. However, growth has been rapid, with fifty-six stations by 1985, 120 in 1992, and 265 in 2004. There are fifty-eight aspirant broadcasters waiting in the wings, and a further eighty radio licences covering remote Indigenous communities (Department of Communications, Information Technology and the Arts, http://www.dcita.gov.au/broad/radio/community_radio).

Running on shoestring budgets, relying on donations and government grants, and staffed mostly by volunteers, community radio has the brief of providing an intimate local service to the immediate community. Here members of the general public can do their own thing, often gearing themselves towards niche audiences that are ignored by mainstream radio with its broader public service or commercial imperatives. It is community radio that has therefore been used as a vehicle for religious, ethnic, and indigenous broadcasting, and for minority groups (such as gays and lesbians). It has also attempted to fill gaps in regional coverage.

The public broadcasters

The *Broadcasting Services Act 1992* doesn't contain a specific definition for the public broadcasters, the Australian Broadcasting Corporation and the Special Broadcasting Service. Instead, in Part 2 Section 13 ('National broadcasting services'), it refers us to their respective acts, the *Australian Broadcasting Corporation Act 1983* and the *Special Broadcasting Service Act 1991* (*Broadcasting Services Act 1992*). These acts contain the charters that set out the brief for each service and we discuss them in detail below. But let's consider first what gave rise to the concept of public broadcasting in the first place.

When radio was starting up, governments quickly sought to involve themselves not only to provide appropriate regulation of a valuable and restricted resource, but also to ensure that at least part of the service was reserved for what was deemed the public good. Radio was seen as a means of informing as well as entertaining. So when the government brought the old Class A stations under its domain as what was then called the Australian Broadcasting Commission the aim was to create a service that would:

- be government-funded
- provide 'quality' broadcasting
- be a repository for 'high' as opposed to popular culture.

While the commercial stream focuses on 'what the public wants', the Australian public broadcaster, like the BBC in Britain, has from its inception aspired to provide listeners with something 'better than they want', as the BBC's first Director-General Lord Reith put it.

Government money, initially through a licence fee and later by direct appropriations, was committed to an editorially independent service dedicated to quality broadcasting that would enshrine public values and help define the national culture. The ABC's freedom from commercial pressures meant that quality rather than audience size was the determining force behind programming. Its focus on high arts rather than low culture gave it an elitist image, although in recent years the need for the public broadcaster to deliver value for money has seen it joining in the race for audience numbers itself.

The ABC provides the following services:

- *Local radio*. This is the name given to the network of stations based in state and regional centres that deliver locally generated programming to their respective communities. Although there is some networked material, the aim of this service is to provide programming geared to the specific needs of individual regional populations.
- *Radio National*. In contrast to the local service that varies from location to location, Radio National is a nationally networked talk service that delivers a single format all around Australia. Its brief is to provide specialist, well-researched programs across a wide range of subjects including politics, social affairs, science, religion, and the arts. Although production teams are based in different states, the nerve centre of the network is in Sydney.
- *Triple J*. This is the ABC's youth network and aims to provide a mix of youth-oriented music and talk, extending beyond the bounds of the commercial music stations. Like Radio National, it is based in Sydney, although program teams around Australia contribute to its output.
- *Classic FM*. This is the ABC's classical music network, again centrally networked, this time out of Adelaide.
- *NewsRadio (Parliamentary and News Network)*. This service, based in Sydney, broadcasts Parliament when it is in session, and otherwise provides a rolling news service in real time across the nation.
- *Radio Australia*. This is the ABC's international arm, which broadcasts to the Asian region in English and other languages.

In 1978 the Fraser government established a second public broadcaster, the Special Broadcasting Service (SBS), to cater for the specific needs of Australia's diverse multicultural audience via a network of multilingual radio stations. Starting from the modest base of two stations, 2EA in Sydney and 3EA in Melbourne, it now broadcasts in sixty-eight different languages, a diversity not replicated anywhere else in the world, aiming, in its own words, to meet:

the settlement, information and communication needs of Australians of non-English speaking backgrounds. It provides cross-cultural links and information lifelines to Australia's diverse cultural groups, allowing them to adjust and participate fully in Australian life and maintain their cultural identities as well.

http://www20.sbs.com.au/sbscorporate/index.php?id=373

Regulating radio

Freedom to access the airwaves comes at a price, although the hand of government is felt more heavily in some areas than in others. Regulation of the sector began with the *Wireless and Telegraphy Act 1905*, where the main concern was to ration access to the airwaves to avoid overload.

The first regulation specific to the broadcasting industry was the *Australian Broadcasting Act 1942*, which signalled the beginning of government attempts to balance service delivery with measures to limit over-concentration of ownership. This resulted in the creation in 1948 of the first independent body to oversee broadcast regulation in Australia—the Australian Broadcasting Control Board (ABCB). The ABCB proved a rather ineffectual guardian and the Fraser government replaced it in 1977 with the Australian Broadcasting Tribunal (ABT), which had a brief to be more assertive in ensuring the protection of the public interest.

The pendulum had swung back to a more laissez-faire approach by the time the 1942 Act was replaced by the *Broadcasting Services Act 1992*, whereby the ABT was replaced in its turn by the Australian Broadcasting Authority (ABA), which would take the role less of enforcer than of overseer as the industry was left to regulate itself as far as programming was concerned. The change in approach from government-as-regulator to government-as-market-facilitator is confirmed as the way of the future in the most recent reappraisal of broadcast regulation in Australia. The Productivity Commission's Broadcasting Inquiry in 2000 advocated even fewer controls over cross-media ownership and entry into the broadcast industry in the face of the dual challenge of new technology and globalisation.

On 1 July 2005 the ABA and the Australian Communications Authority were amalgamated to form the new super regulator the Australian Communications and Media Authority whose brief includes

- promoting self-regulation and competition in the telecommunications industry, while protecting consumers and other users
- fostering an environment in which electronic media respect community standards and respond to audience and user needs
- managing access to the radiofrequency spectrum, including the broadcasting services bands
- representing Australia's communications and broadcasting interests internationally

ACMA, http://www.acma.gov.au

So what is the situation today?

Commercial radio

Commercial radio is overseen by the ABA (now ACMA), which administers the *Broadcasting Services Act* and has the power to grant or withdraw licences. Until 2000, the industry was given considerable latitude to self-regulate via voluntary codes supervised by its industry body, the Federation of Australian Radio Broadcasters (FARB), now rebadged as Commercial Radio Australia. Although the ABA was often called in to adjudicate over transgressions such as the broadcasting of racist language or inappropriate advertising, it has resorted to its ultimate power of withdrawing a broadcasting licence on one occasion only, in November 2003 when it refused to renew the licence for the 6GS Wagin Radio service on the grounds that the licensee was deemed not suitable. Its apparent weakness as a regulator was exposed by the 'cash-for-comment' affair in the late 1990s where a number of commercial **talkback** hosts were revealed to have taken money from advertisers, independently of any advertising agreement with their radio stations, in exchange for favourable coverage on air. Even with this level of provocation no licences were threatened. Instead the ABA, while still subscribing to the principle of industry self-regulation, introduced stricter guidelines for broadcasters and station owners alike in dealing with such conflicts of interest. (This is discussed further in chapter 17. The Commercial Radio Codes of Practice and the ABA's new Broadcasting Services Standards introduced following the 'cash-for-comment' affair are reproduced in the *Regulations and Codes of Practice* appendix at the back of this book).

Community radio

Community radio, which also includes the indigenous and ethnic stations, also comes under the regulatory umbrella of the ABA (now ACMA), which in this case ensures the stations keep to their brief of remaining strictly non-profit and non-commercial in nature. This sector has its own code of practice drafted and monitored by its representative body, the Community Broadcasting Association of Australia (CBAA). This code enshrines the key values for community broadcasters in terms of equity and access. The *CBAA Code of Practice* is reproduced at the back of this book.

The ABC

The brief for the operations of the ABC is contained in the *Australian Broadcasting Corporation Act 1983* under which the old Australian Broadcasting Commission became a corporation. The Act defines the ABC as a Commonwealth Government Statutory Authority and, in Section 6 (1) and (2), sets quite specific parameters for the operation of both ABC Radio and Television in what is known as the ABC's Charter.

The ABC Charter

The functions that Parliament has given to the ABC are set out in the Charter of the Corporation that is contained in section 6 of the *Australian Broadcasting Corporation Act 1983:*

6(1)   The functions of the Corporation are—

a. to provide within Australia innovative and comprehensive broadcasting services of a high standard as part of the Australian broadcasting system consisting of national, commercial and community sectors and, without limiting the generality of the foregoing, to provide:

   i.   broadcasting programs that contribute to a sense of national identity and inform and entertain, and reflect the cultural diversity of, the Australian community; and

   ii. broadcasting programs of an educational nature;

b. to transmit to countries outside Australia broadcasting programs of news, current affairs, entertainment and cultural enrichment that will:

   i.   encourage awareness of Australia and an international understanding of Australian attitudes on world affairs; and

   ii. enable Australian citizens living or travelling outside Australia to obtain information about Australian affairs and Australian attitudes on world affairs; and

c. to encourage and promote the musical, dramatic and other performing arts in Australia.

6(2)   In the provision by the Corporation of its broadcasting services within Australia:

a. the Corporation shall take account of:

   i.   the broadcasting services provided by the commercial and community sectors of the Australian broadcasting system;

   ii. the standards from time to time determined by the Australian Broadcasting Authority in respect of broadcasting services;

   iii. the responsibility of the Corporation as the provider of an independent national broadcasting service to provide a balance between broadcasting programs of wide appeal and specialised broadcasting programs;

   iv. the multicultural character of the Australian community; and

   v.   in connection with the provision of broadcasting programs of an educational nature—the responsibilities of the States in relation to education; and

b. the Corporation shall take all such measures, being measures consistent with the obligations of the Corporation under paragraph (a), as, in the opinion of the Board, will be conducive to the full development by the Corporation of suitable broadcasting programs.

> 6(3) The functions of the Corporation under sub-section (1) and the duties imposed on the Corporation under sub-section (2) constitute the Charter of the Corporation.
>
> 6(4) Nothing in this section shall be taken to impose on the Corporation a duty that is enforceable by proceedings in a court.
>
> Source: ABC, http://www.abc.net.au/corp/charter.htm

Four key areas are identified where the ABC can maximise its advantages as a broadcaster operating independently of commercial pressures:

1   Innovation: the ABC is expected to extend the boundaries of broadcasting, experimenting in challenging programming that opens up new areas of creativity.
2   Comprehensiveness: the ABC is expected to mix mass appeal programming with more specialist programs that appeal to a variety of different audiences.
3   National identity: the ABC is expected to be distinctly Australian, developing and enriching Australian culture through programs that reflect the regional and ethnic diversity of Australia.
4   Arts, cultural, educational, and international broadcasting: the ABC is expected to be an outlet for Australian arts and culture. It has an explicit brief to provide educational programming, and is also expected to have an international profile by presenting Australia to the world.

Although the activities of the Corporation are defined by law, the ABC Act also guarantees its editorial independence. Thus, while it is accountable to Parliament, the ABC has the power to make programming decisions on behalf of the Australian people.

The ABC Charter makes the ABC both more and less free than its commercial counterparts. It is more free to take risks, to experiment, or to shock because of its mandate to explore the boundaries of high quality broadcasting. It is more free to venture where commercial stations may fear to tread because it is independent of commercial influences. However, it is less free because its product is determined by government decree: it is required to provide a full spectrum of services to reflect Australian culture in all its diversity. It is less free because its funding imposes rigid limitations on what it can do, without the option of seeking additional funding from non-government sources. As far as ABC Radio is concerned, the six distinct services described earlier systematically address the key charter functions, ensuring that the ABC appeals to a range of different audiences both nationally and internationally with programming that reflects Australia's **demographic** and cultural diversity.

The Special Broadcasting Service

The SBS came into existence on 1 January 1978 as Australia sought to free itself of the negative image it had gained worldwide through the White Australia policy of the 1950s and 1960s. The idea of a specific multilingual and multicultural service was born out of the nation's growing desire to acknowledge rather than deny the diversity of its population mix. The Fraser government made the idea a reality in 1978 when the SBS was established as an independent statutory authority under the *Broadcasting Act* of 1942. Like the ABC, it subsequently became a corporation under the *Special Broadcasting Service Act* of 1991.

Like its mainstream counterpart, the SBS was set up with a particular brief, articulated in its own Charter as set out in Section 6 of the SBS Act. Its main focus was 'to provide multilingual and multicultural radio and television services that inform, educate and entertain all Australians, and, in doing so, reflect Australia's multicultural society'. The dual aim was to give the diverse communities of Australia access to programming in their own languages, and also to provide a multicultural showcase for the benefit of the community at large.

The SBS Charter

1. The principal function of the SBS is to provide multilingual and multicultural radio and television services that inform, educate and entertain all Australians, and, in doing so, reflect Australia's multicultural society.
2. The SBS, in performing its principal function, must:
   a. contribute to meeting the communications needs of Australia's multicultural society, including ethnic, Aboriginal and Torres Strait Islander communities; and
   b. increase awareness of the contribution of a diversity of cultures to the continuing development of Australian society; and
   c. promote understanding and acceptance of the cultural, linguistic and ethnic diversity of the Australian people; and
   d. contribute to the retention and continuing development of language and other cultural skills; and
   e. as far as practicable, inform, educate and entertain Australians in their preferred languages; and
   f. make use of Australia's diverse creative resources; and
   g. contribute to the overall diversity of Australian television and radio services, particularly taking into account the contribution of the Australian Broadcasting Corporation and the community broadcasting sector; and
   h. contribute to extending the range of Australian television and radio services, and reflect the changing nature of Australian society, by presenting many points of view and using innovative forms of expression.

Source: SBS, http://www20.sbs.com.au/sbscorporate/index.php?id=378

In radio this was done through a network of ethnic radio stations, based on 2EA in Sydney and later 3EA in Melbourne. This sector has not been without its problems—the national service has often been in competition with grassroots ethnic broadcasters who have used community radio as an outlet for product more responsive to local interests.

Further, there have been tensions as the population mix has changed and the service has had to accommodate new generations of migrants from other lands. This has challenged the domination over airtime of the longer-established communities.

The origins and nature of the three main strands of radio in Australia—community, commercial, and public sector—have important implications for program-makers. As we shall see, they define target audiences, **program formats**, program content, and program styles within each service, all of which broadcasting staff will have to take into account when crafting their on-air productions.

Exercises

Record a commercial, a community, and an ABC program.
1   Compare their content and presentation styles.
2   What do the programs tell you about their respective audiences?
3   How do they reflect their respective briefs as commercial, community, and public broadcasting services?

Further reading

Hawke, J. 1995, 'Privatising the Public Interest: The Public and the Broadcasting Services Act 1992', in Craik, J., Bailey, J.J. & Moran, A. (eds), *Public Voices, Private Interests: Australia's Media Policy*, Allen & Unwin, Sydney, pp. 33–50.

Inglis, K.S. 1983, *This is the ABC: The Australian Broadcasting Commission 1932–1983*, Melbourne University Press, Melbourne.

Johnson, L. 1988, *The Unseen Voice: A Cultural Study of Early Australian Radio*, Routledge, London.

Miller, T. & Turner, G. 2002, 'Radio', in Cunningham, S. & Turner, G. (eds), *The Media and Communications in Australia*, Allen & Unwin, Sydney, pp. 133–51.

Potts, J. 1989, *Radio in Australia*, NSW University Press, Sydney.

Thomas, J. 2000, 'It's Later Than You Think: The Productivity Commission's Broadcasting Inquiry and Beyond', *Media International Australia*, no. 95, May, pp. 9–18.

Web sites

ABA: http://www.aba.gov.au

ABC: http://www.abc.net.au

ACMA: http://www.acma.gov.au

Commercial Radio Australia: http://www.commercialradio.com.au/

CBAA: http://www.cbaa.org.au

Productivity Commission Broadcasting Inquiry Report: http://www.indcom.gov.au/inquiry/broadcst/finalreport/index.html

SBS: http://www.sbs.com.au

Television in Australia

Television arrived in Australia in 1956 and, as in other countries, has dominated the media landscape up to the present day. This domination is threatened now only because the traditional services, which viewers access for free, are under threat from the new opportunities afforded by pay and online delivery.

The development of Australia's television industry has been defined by an ongoing debate over ownership. As we saw in the case of radio, broadcasting is an area where governments have traditionally sought to balance commercial interests with the public interest. In the case of television, the Australian government has been particularly sensitive to pressure from the media owners. From the very start the Menzies government opted for a system that privileged the commercial sector. As with radio, there was to be a commercial and a public sector, but the ratio would be two commercial stations (channels Seven and Nine) to one public broadcaster in each of the major capital cities. Further, the commercial operators would own and operate the transmitters (in contrast to the UK, for example, where operators leased the transmission facilities from the state). As the sector has evolved, the government's concern has shifted away from the nature of the service and towards the creation of a viable broadcasting market.

Commercial television

Who are the commercial operators? In the mid 1950s, as now, television was an expensive business. This meant potential players needed substantial cashflow, and it was the local press barons with their newspaper 'cash cows' who became the pioneers in the budding television sector. Even at the time there was some disquiet in the general public about the impact this would have on media diversity, although the government did not object. Thus Frank Packer's Consolidated Press, John Fairfax, the Herald and Weekly Times group, and a consortium of the *Age* and *Argus* newspapers began the fledgling operations that would later consolidate into the Seven and Nine networks. The third commercial network (the 0 and Ten stations) began in the mid 1960s, and was the vehicle for News Corporation's entry into television in 1981. As with radio, the commercial sector was expected to finance its operations by selling advertising.

Key technological changes marked the progress of the industry over the next four decades:

- the introduction of colour television in 1975
- the arrival of cable and satellite technology in the mid 1980s

ABC News Online operations room.

- the advent of online **digital** technology in the 1990s
- the new delivery options via **broadband** in the 2000s.

Each decade also brought new challenges for government in relation to the ownership issues.

The 1970s

In the late 1970s, the power of the industry led to an attempt by the federal government to reintroduce some sort of social and cultural benchmarking. The original regulatory authority responsible for the awarding of broadcast licences, the Australian Broadcasting Control Board, was replaced by the Australian Broadcasting Tribunal. The aim was to bring greater rigour into the licensing process to ensure that public interest values such as Australian content were considered, in addition to the purely commercial brief. This was the last gasp for public interest standards—from now on commercial imperatives would be the primary defining factor in framing government media policy.

The 1980s

In the mid 1980s the Hawke government responded to pressures from the media owners by deregulating the market, relaxing ownership limits on the numbers of stations any one owner could have. The Keating government then introduced new cross-ownership rules, requiring media players to choose whether to be, in the prime minister's words, 'queens of the screen' or 'princes of print'. The end result was a major feeding frenzy as networks extended their tentacles into the regions and as new players sought to jump on to the gravy train. Many fell off again when the bubble burst with the stockmarket crash of 1987. Kerry Packer was there to pick up the pieces, buying back his Nine network from the disgraced Alan Bond at a fraction of the price he had sold it to him for in the boom. Rupert Murdoch opted for print, selling Channel Seven to another local print entrepreneur, Kerry Stokes. Channel Ten's owner, the Canadian Canwest Company, fell foul of the foreign ownership laws and took a back seat to the local company Telecasters North Queensland. In 2001 the network was bought by the Southern Cross Broadcasting group. Packer, Stokes, and Southern Cross continue to be the major players today.

The 1990s

The 1990s heralded further change. The pendulum swung even more towards commercial imperatives in the face of challenges on the global scale and, in 1995, the advent of Pay TV. *The Broadcasting Services Act* of 1992 replaced the ABT with the Australian Broadcasting Authority, which stepped back from the interventionist brief of its predecessor. With the exception of children's programming and Australian content levels, the industry was left to regulate itself on content, with the ABA overseeing the codes of practice that the industry's professional bodies crafted for themselves (these are reproduced in *Regulations and Codes of Practice* at the back of this book). In this new regime, listeners and viewers were customers, and the government saw the aim of legislation as facilitating the development of a profitable and successful private sector. There was less focus on diversity and localism, and more on maintaining a competitive broadcasting market.

The 2000s

In the new century regulators now have to contend with evolving digital delivery options that are exacerbating the trend towards media convergence, concentration of ownership, and globalised audiences. In Europe digital television has been available, although with disappointing uptake that has threatened the rather optimistic deadlines set for the close-down of **analog** Australia has gone against the global trend in choosing High Definition Television (HDTV) but here too regulatory uncertainties have threatened the timetable for switching off analog television, set for 2008. Digital technology promises better quality sound and pictures, different means of access via interactive services, and customised viewing schedules via personal recording devices like TiVo. Governments worldwide are struggling to balance the interests of existing players, eager for their reserved places in the new media world, with public interest and how it should be defined in this new arena. Should the Australian government act to protect the interests of the local media moguls, who could be swallowed in one gulp by the heavyweight players in the global marketplace? Relaxing cross-media ownership rules would give them scope to expand domestically, but at what cost to diversity? Should the government continue to protect the interests of domestic content producers by prescribing limits for Australian content? Up to now this has preserved at least a portion of the market for Australian product, but is it feasible in an era when the consumer has access to a global menu at the push of a button? Balancing the different and often contradictory interests of culture and industry is difficult for governments at the best of times, but free trade agreements, such as the one negotiated between Australia and the United States in 2004, make it more difficult for governments to place national interest above their global commitments. The amalgamation of the Australian Broadcasting Authority and the Australian Communications Authority into the Australian Communications and Media Authority in July 2005 created a unified super-regulator to help Australia navigate through this digital minefield.

Public broadcasting

Where the United States opted for the pure commercial paradigm in its broadcasting industry, Australia followed the British example of a mixed commercial/public sector model. So with television, as with radio, the idea was for the government-funded public broadcaster to fulfil a specific social and cultural brief.

The Australian Broadcasting Commission began its television services in 1956 in tandem with the commercial services. In accordance with the government's plan to have two commercial and one ABC television service in the capital cities, it set up services first in Sydney and Melbourne before extending to the other metropolitan centres. The same charter obligations that applied to radio also applied to television (see p. 9). Freed from the need to generate profits, the ABC was a repository for the nation's culture, offering quality independent programming that aimed to reflect Australia in all its diversity. The 'elitism' label that was attached to radio was also attached to television. Viewers associated commercial television with entertainment, while the ABC was seen as a source of information.

In 1980, the public sector was bolstered by the addition of the television arm of the Special Broadcasting Service (SBS), which focused specifically on multicultural and multilingual programming.

Community television

In contrast to the thriving community radio sector, community television has been slow to grow because of the expensive and labour-intensive nature of television itself. Starting with a trial in 1994 in Melbourne, the fledgling 31 network now comprises six full-time stations. The stations in Sydney, Melbourne, Brisbane, and Perth were granted permanent licences in 2004. Lismore and Adelaide were slated to follow in 2005. Like community radio, the operation is funded by sponsorship and staffed by volunteers. It aims to provide an outlet for local community-produced programming in niches ignored or neglected by the mainstream.

Challenges for television

Free-to-air services, whether commercial or public sector, face major challenges on two fronts: from Pay TV and from online delivery. With converging technology, these appear more like one mega-threat: viewer-generated scheduling.

Until now the public has been a prisoner to the network schedule. Viewers have had to access programs on a particular day, at a particular time. The advent of video did a lot to liberate them from the schedule, but the technology was rather cumbersome and still restricted them to the limited menu each television service had on offer.

Pay TV changed all that. In the United States an extensive network offers numerous niche services catering to all sorts of appetites. In Australia the subscription television sector has been slower to grow, held up by delays in formulating legislation that would accommodate the commercial interests of the main industry players while giving the public access to the range of services promised by new delivery formats. In the end, the satellite/cable alternatives may very well be overtaken by new communications technology that offers the promise of even greater viewer power. Set-top devices such as TiVo can be programmed to extract from the global ether, and to download into a combination television-computer, programs that suit viewers' personal tastes.

More worrying still for advertisers is the capacity of the new technology to allow audiences to by-pass advertisements altogether. Apart from anything else, this hits at free-to-air television's life-blood: if the FTA stations can't guarantee an audience, their revenue source will evaporate as advertisers seek alternative opportunities online. However, the new technology is also affording them alternative outlets for their creativity. Product placement allows them to integrate their wares into the very fabric of the television program. Interactive enhancements allow them to lure viewers away from the programs to their own sites for further information about the products displayed.

The 2000 and 2004 Olympics provide an interesting example of the impact new technologies are having on broadcasting. The US NBC television network, having spent millions securing the coverage rights for the 2000 Sydney Olympics, found the audience just wasn't there. With the arrogance of the old regime, it had stuck to the traditional way of doing things, eschewing live coverage that was out of prime time, and instead offering delayed programs that went to air eleven hours after the event. As a result, US viewers ignored it in droves, making it the least-watched Olympics since Mexico in 1968. Although NBC's exclusive contract with the International Olympic Committee prevented Internet services from accessing audio and video, the online sites were certainly where the public flocked for instant updates and backgrounders. By 2004 cross-platform coverage was the name of the game. Coverage of the Athens Olympics included extra widescreen high definition digital services, integrating pictures with statistical data and results, and web sites were actively maintained by all media to provide a wealth of background material in addition to up-to-the-minute reports. In the UK, the event also marked a breakthrough for interactivity—according to Greg Dyke, the ex-Director General of Britain's BBC, nearly ten million people chose to watch a different event to the one selected for broadcast by the BBC (Dyke 2004, p. 9)

In Australia the ABC is leading the way in experimenting with digital broadband delivery. In November 2004 it presented a program on Islamic terrorism that was in effect a bumper edition drawn from a wide range of previously broadcast *Four Corners* programs on the topic. The new technology allowed the producers to enhance this material with additional profiles of Osama bin Laden and Mohammad Atta, backgrounders on the Bali bombings, and the personal stories of the people involved, all available via Flash video streaming with viewers able to access material at their leisure in whatever order they desired (MacLean 2004, p. 20).

As well as the challenges posed by technology, Australian television faces a further challenge in relation to content. The new media marketplace is global rather than local. Further, new media services are content-hungry and expensive to feed. Australia's domestic television industry is tiny compared to the wealthy conglomerates in the United States and the UK, so the temptation will always be to buy product from those countries, which would always be cheaper than making our own. This trend might be counterbalanced by the capacity to make product to sell overseas; however, the Australianness of this product usually has to be watered down if it is exported abroad. For example, the full-blown Aussie culture as portrayed in the hit local film *The Castle* went way over the heads of American audiences and some of the more obscure slang words had to be altered for the US market, which still gave the film a rather lukewarm response.

There is a general worldwide concern about the threat to local cultures as a globalised culture dominates. Even the Productivity Commission, which in its Broadcasting Inquiry in 2000 made so many concessions towards commercial imperatives, acknowledges the importance of public interest tests to avoid a free-for-all in which Australia's consumers will come off worst (Productivity Commission 2000). We may very well see the pendulum, which has swung so far towards commercial interests in the past half century, swing back again as governments, including Australia's, step in to protect their nation's cultural heritage.

Exercise

Look at the program schedules for Channel Ten, SBS TV, and ABC TV.
1   What are the main points of difference?
2   What does the program selection tell you about each of the services?
3   What sort of audience do you think each is trying to attract?

Further reading

Flew, T. 2002, 'Television and Pay TV', in Cunningham, S. & Turner, G. (eds), *The Media and Communications in Australia*, Allen & Unwin, Sydney, pp. 173–87.

Given, J. 1995, 'Commercial TV: Bucks, Blokes, Bureaucrats and the Bird' in Craik, J., Bailey, J.J. & Moran, A. (eds), *Public Voices, Private Interests: Australia's Media Policy*, Allen & Unwin, Sydney, pp. 15–32.

Henningham, J. 1999b, 'Media' in Henningham, J. (ed.), *Institutions in Australian Society*, 2nd edn, Oxford University Press, Melbourne, pp. 274–97.

Inglis, K.S. 1983, *This is the ABC: The Australian Broadcasting Commission 1932–1983*, Melbourne University Press, Melbourne.

Thomas, J. 2000, 'It's Later Than You Think: The Productivity Commission's Broadcasting Inquiry and Beyond', *Media International Australia*, no. 95, May, pp. 9–18.

Web sites

ABA: http://www.aba.gov.au
ABC: http://www.abc.net.au
ACMA: http://www.acma.gov.au
CBAA: http://www.cbaa.org.au
Free TV Australia: http://www.ctva.com.au/control.cfm
Productivity Commission Broadcasting Inquiry Report: http://www.indcom.gov.au/inquiry/
    broadcst/finalreport/index.html
SBS: http://www.sbs.com.au

Australia has always been an early adopter of technology. Perhaps because of the vast distances separating us across the continent, perhaps because of our remoteness from the rest of the world, the Australian public has been quick to appreciate the benefits of advances in telecommunications. Even so, the statistics tell an amazing story. Given that the Web only really began to take off in the mid 1990s, according to the Australian Bureau of Statistics the proportion of households with a home computer increased from 44 per cent to 66 per cent between 1998 and 2003 (ABS 2003). This level of penetration put Australia fifth in the world behind Denmark, Sweden, Germany, and Switzerland, according to the OECD (Science, Technology and Industry Scoreboard, OECD 2003). During this period, access to the Internet also grew: from 16 per cent in 1998 to 53 per cent in 2003, ninth in the world according to OECD data, and showing just how exponential this growth is and continues to be.

The history of radio and television (chapters 1 and 2) took us back to the first half of the twentieth century. As far as online media are concerned, we are dealing with history in the making, and at a faster rate than ever before in the trajectory of technological progress. The spirit of adventure and discovery that fuelled the development of analog communications is alive and well today, and now fuels the push into digital communications. The amateur enthusiasts playing around with their crystal sets have been replaced by the modern computer buff. The world is in the middle of a revolution, and although we still don't know the final outcome, the parallels with radio may give us an idea of what lies ahead.

We can identify three stages in the development of radio. The first belongs to the amateur enthusiast, the second to the manufacturers, and the third to government. The technology that started as a gleam in Marconi's eye was adopted with alacrity by amateur enthusiasts who exploited the potential for one-on-one communication that the radio receiver offered. This didn't suit the manufacturers, who saw greater money-making potential in controlling both the construction of the receivers and the material broadcast on them. This led to the supplanting of one-to-one communication with one-to-many broadcasting, at which point the regulators became involved. With the airwaves seen as a public resource, and a money-making one at that, government intervened to exert control in the public interest and to get its share of the spoils.

A similar trajectory is apparent in online media. The talents of the individual enthusiasts are constantly being harnessed by the big business interests whose aim it is to control the market in both software and hardware. Governments are circling uneasily around the edges as they try to gain a foothold in this anarchic universe. Again their interests are twofold: first, they want to ensure the protection of the public interest generally and national cultural values specifically; second, they want a share in the economic windfalls. Unlike radio, the information technology industry is all the more elusive for being global and transnational, and therefore difficult to capture within the regulatory net of any one country.

Meanwhile, the revolution goes on, transforming the ways in which information is packaged, relayed, and received. Some see this revolution in cataclysmic terms—bringing in its wake the death of older media. The longer it goes on, however, the more it appears that the likely outcome will be the creation of a whole new hybrid medium, one that supplements rather than supplants print, radio, and television.

Example of new generation broadcast technology.

The new media structures

In his book *newmedia.com.au*, Trevor Barr compares the print, broadcasting, and information technology sectors and notes that while print publishing has been largely privately owned, and broadcasting has been a mix of commercial interests and public broadcasters, the growing information technology sector is dominated by transnational corporations (2000, p. 23). Not only is technology converging, but media businesses are likewise converging as they attempt to control the entire process from hardware and software to content generation through to transmission, not just within the confines of one country, but on a global scale. This is creating tensions on several different fronts.

Ownership tensions

Vertical integration, whereby single mega-corporations control the entire line of supply, is resulting in the consolidation of media ownership, limiting it to a few global super-players. This raises concerns about the reduction in media diversity, especially in relation to

reanlation

journalism: how do we know that we are getting the full story if newspapers, television stations, film companies, and satellite services are run by the same entity? In Australia there are controls on media ownership to prevent any one group gaining a cross-media monopoly in a given local market. There are also controls to limit the amount of foreign ownership of Australian media companies. However, the line is getting increasingly difficult to hold as convergence eliminates the old distinctions between media (print, radio, film, and television all come together online), and as globalisation wipes out the small local players.

Cultural tensions

The dominance of global super-players brings with it the threat of dominance by a global super-product. Countries around the world are worried that the preponderance of English-language programming generally, and US programming in particular, will swamp their local product.

Regulatory tensions

The extent of government control over the media has always been a thorny issue. Freedom of speech ideals have perennially been in conflict with government's desire to be an arbiter in terms of what we the public get access to. At one extreme, governments have wanted total control over the media so could be used as vehicles for their own propaganda. Even in more relaxed regimes, governments have been tempted to censor in relation to extreme violence, erotica, or child pornography.

Apart from censorship, countries have laws to protect people's reputations (defamation), and to protect the rights of content producers over their creative product (copyright). When there are no national boundaries, who sets the rules? We are only now beginning to see cases coming before the courts that are testing these principles in the online environment. For example, in April 2000 a British Internet service provider (ISP) was successfully sued by a man who accused the company of allowing defamatory material about him to be posted on one of its bulletin boards. Though the plaintiff came away with around A$600,000 in damages and costs, the case raised more questions than it answered, such as: in the online environment who is the 'publisher'? What liabilities does the ISP carry? How far can the ISP be responsible for the content it delivers? And does any of this make any difference, given that content providers can just take their material to any one of myriad alternative sites if they get into trouble? An even more high profile case concerns the Melbourne businessman Joe Gutnick, who in 2004 won a A$580,000 payout from Dow Jones for defamatory comments made about him in an article that appeared in the online version of Dow's *Barron* magazine. The case drew international attention for testing in the courts the principle that defamation occurs where articles are downloaded, not where they are uploaded. This opens up the capacity for potential plaintiffs to elect a country of choice from which to mount libel actions, raising concerns about the potential chilling effect on journalism with the standards being set by countries with the strictest defamation regimes.

Copyright is another minefield with particular challenges for the content producer. How can you protect your content from unlawful use by others? With the Web so difficult to monitor and police, the risk of undetected plagiarism is high. What about the issue of content ownership? Media companies now can use content in multiple media contexts, reaping corresponding financial rewards. Is this fair to the content creators, or should they get some of the spoils?

There are no answers to these questions yet, and resolving these issues will be a matter of years rather than months. In Australia, the amalgamation of the Australian Broadcasting Authority and the Australian Communications Authority into the Australian Communications and Media Authority created a super-regulator that now oversees this complex area.

What lies ahead?

Are we seeing the slow death of 'broadcasting'?

In 1995 Nicholas Negroponte foretold that computer technology might render broadcasting obsolete in favour of narrowcasting aimed at niche audiences. If information is thought of as bits, rather than as sound or pictures, these can be available in the ether at any place and at any time, ready to be pulled in and assembled by individual users at their convenience. David Docherty has given a neat summary of the trajectory so far, from a UK perspective:

> Ten years ago, we lived in BBC-world—a closed broadcasting system, advertising monopolies, programme-making priesthoods, and captured audiences. Then we had Murdochworld in which the consumer was given a choice from among (relatively) high quality content providers corralled into a walled garden with high barriers. Now we have Googleworld, in which the consumer is given a genuinely free choice of hundreds of millions of content providers, including other people like them (2004, p. 30).

Consumers now can use sophisticated compression and information-seeking technology to search for, download, and access the content they want at the time that they want it. They can even bypass the ads, a feature that is causing much consternation to the commercial media players and their clients. However, advertisers are adapting by themselves turning in ever increasing numbers to the Internet. In its 2004 forecast PricewaterhouseCoopers reported a 41.3 per cent growth in online advertising in Australia, among the fastest in the world, with the growth trend set to continue (Docherty 2004).

In the audio realm, the BBC, which has led the way in developing its Web presence, has conducted surveys that indicate that 'an increasing number of people are listening to radio via the web, but that the way they listen to it is also changing, with programmes being called up on demand several days after they were first broadcast' (Gibson 2004, p. 13). According to the BBC, online radio listening increased from 4.7 million to 6.1 million in the year 2003–04 (Gibson 2004). Between October 2003 and October 2004 the number of requests for on-demand radio programs online almost doubled from

4.5 million to 7.7 million, with Radio 4's adaptation of *Hitchhiker's Guide to the Galaxy* topping the list (Gibson 2004).

Technological advances are changing the nature of broadcasting. Here are two examples.

Podcasting

MP3 players like Apple's iPod are making it possible even for amateurs to bundle their own programs together as time-shifted 'podcasts' (Cook 2004, p. 21). Anyone with a computer and a microphone can become a broadcaster, with no deadlines, time limits, or government regulations. Listeners can download the audio files into a digital MP3 player, at no cost and without ads. Unlike traditional radio, shows can be rewound, fast-forwarded, or paused. Most importantly, the technology duplicates radio's portability—listeners don't have to be chained to their computers, the main drawback for most forms of Internet radio. And instead of having to trawl the Internet for the information they want, the software Really Simple Syndication, or RSS, automatically collects and sends the audio files to their computer for later download to a portable device. Podcasting only started in 2004 and while many programs at the moment are largely amateur radio, the industry is catching up quickly: the ABC now offers programs via podcasting on its web site. For the time being, podcasting poses no real threat to traditional broadcasting, but as the digital music player market grows—and more devices such as mobile phones become capable of playing audio files—it could snatch away advertising dollars, especially from commercial radio focusing on a young audience.

DAB

Digital Audio Broadcasting (DAB) is another example of how technological development is changing radio. Digital radio is often described as the next generation of radio. In analog broadcasting every radio station has its own **frequency**. Digital broadcasting uses so-called multiplex transmitters where each 'tower' can host several stations—how many depends on how much data rate each station is given (i.e. how good the audio quality is). In the UK each tower has nine or more stations; in Sweden the public broadcaster has settled on only six stations. DAB offers more services, clearer reception and sound quality, and a range of other features, including text information and graphics. Like online radio, it allows listeners to get text information about the broadcast as it happens. DAB receivers have displays where the name of artist and song can be shown or news headlines scrolled. The latest radio set even gives listeners the power to pause the radio program. Like online radio where niche stations can cater for specialist audiences, digital broadcasting allows broadcasters to set up temporary services easily without having to interrupt the radio schedule. The Danish Broadcasting Corporation used this option when it set up a digital channel broadcasting from Copenhagen during the Danish Crown Prince's wedding to his Australian bride. The station was on air for just two weeks.

After years of investing big money—with very few listeners—DAB is now fully established in Europe with the UK as a leader. Here in Australia, a consortium of the ABC and commercial broadcasters has been trialling digital radio in Sydney since 1999. These first trials have been primarily technical in nature. In 2004 the trials were expanded to include Melbourne in an attempt to assist broadcasters and the federal government in deciding what digital broadcasting standard to adopt in this country.

The liberated audience

The Web has liberated the audience from the mainstream media, making it possible for individuals to do their own thing with ready access to a broadcasting facility to take their message to the world. One such station is Resonance FM, broadcasting from tiny premises in London's Tottenham Court Road. Describing itself as 'London's first radio art station' (www.resonancefm.com) its station manager describes its mission as 'about providing a space for great stuff that doesn't fit anywhere else'. Its programs range from the arty and the ethnic to Xollob Park with its host Reverso Mondo where 'everything, including the DJ patter, runs backwards' (Katbamna 2004, p. 19). Live365, which proclaims itself to be 'the world's largest Internet radio network', claims to have more than 2.6 million listeners a month tuning in to 'do-it-yourself' radio services that anyone can set up with simply a computer and an Internet connection (http://www.live365.com/info/index.html).

Audience interactivity extends beyond this to much more sophisticated information exchange. For example, Wikipedia is 'a free-content encyclopedia in many languages that anyone can edit' (www.wikipedia.org). People-power is also extending into what was previously the province of professional journalists. An example of this is Indymedia.org, an independent media collective that grew out of the global protest movement against the power of the World Trade Organisation and whose aim is 'to empower people to become the media by present [sic] honest, accurate, powerful independent reports' (http://docs.indymedia.org/view/Global/FrequentlyAskedQuestionEn#what).

Webloggers (bloggers) have spawned a new genre of freelance Web reporting and have been responsible for some spectacular scoops that have trumped the traditional broadcasters or left them exposed and embarrassed. It was the blogger Russ Kirk who first published photographs of the flag-draped coffins of US soldiers being returned to the USA from Iraq. It was a blogger network that revealed that documents CBS news anchor Dan Rather had relied on for an exposé of President George Bush's National Guard Service were fakes, an event that led to the resignation of the American television icon. According to Dan Gillmor, a respected Silicon Valley journalist who has written a book on this new phenomenon, the Internet is changing journalism from a lecture to a conversation with what he calls the 'former audience' creating media for themselves (2004, p. xiv). Seventeen-year-old Sam Bear is an example of this. Four years ago he set up his own film review web site, www.Joecritic.com, as a space to air the views of 'the ordinary Joe' on the latest films. Now it is a site that the film industry keeps its eye on as a window on public opinion. Bloggers really come into their own in times of tragedy, providing eyewitness insights into war scenes or galvanising worldwide information networks to reunite families, as with the 2004 tsunami disaster in the Indian Ocean rim.

The Web and news broadcasting

By liberating the audience the Web has broken the monopoly of the traditional news broadcasters, spawning operations such as Global Radio News, 'an independent audio content distributor supplying material filed by journalists and reporters to radio stations and TV broadcasters worldwide'. With 400 freelancers in ninety countries it coordinates the work of a huge freelance network giving broadcasters large and small access to on-the-ground reporting that was previously beyond their budget (Gibson 2003, p.34). In the video realm, The Feedroom.com provides a broadband video news service sourcing material from a variety of news agencies. The rise of the independent operators has compelled the established news organisations to examine their role in the online universe. When information is so freely available *to* anyone *from* anyone, the reliability and trustworthiness of the source is crucial and this in the end is what can ensure their future. As Barrie Gunter notes, 'The major news organizations have reputations founded on many years of news provision, and citizens learn to know which news providers they can trust to supply accurate and unbiased accounts of events. Even in a world in which communications technologies open up greater choices for consumers, ordinary people will still need access to reliable news "brands"' (2003, p. ix).

Content production on the Web

What does all this mean for the content producers? The most exciting thing about working in the online media is that you are inventing the job as you go along. The formats are still evolving. As Negroponte points out:

> From a historical perspective, the incubation period of a new medium can be quite long. It took many years for people to think of moving a camera, versus just letting the actors move in front of it. It took thirty-two years to think of adding sound. Sooner or later, dozens of new ideas emerged to give a totally new vocabulary to film and video. The same will happen with multimedia (1995, p. 64).

We are at the equivalent stage now to the early years of television, when it was little more than radio with pictures. What we see in online media is mostly a repackaging of material prepared for other media. However, we are also seeing the beginnings of an idiom specific to the Web medium itself. Content producers are changing their technical protocols to suit the online format—shooting video, recording sound, writing **copy** for the Web in terms of style, length, layout, media mix, and download time. They are thinking about the creative opportunities and flexing their muscles to take advantage of the facilities this new medium provides.

So this online world, while holding out the promise of greater powers for media owners than they have ever had before, at the same time unhooks both audiences and content producers from the mainstream, bestowing on them the freedom to do what they want when they want.

Exercises

Do a tour of the web sites for the Age Online and the ABC News Online.
1   How do their front pages differ?
2   In what way do the sites reflect their origin within a newspaper and a broadcast
    operation respectively?

Further reading

Australian Broadcasting Corporation 2004, 'Music of the Blogospheres', *Background Briefing*,
    31 October.
Barr, T. 2000, *newmedia.com.au: The Changing Face of Australia's Media and Communications*, Allen
    & Unwin, Sydney.
Brown, A. 2000, 'Media Ownership in the Digital Age: An Economic Perspective', *Media
    International Australia*, no. 95, May, pp. 49–61.
Flew, T. 2002 (repr. 2003), *New Media. An Introduction*, Oxford University Press, Melbourne.
Gillmor, D. 2004, *We the Media: Grassroots Journalism By the People for the People*, O'Reilly,
    Sebastopol, Ca.
Given, J. 1998, *The Death of Broadcasting? Media's Digital Future*, University of New South Wales
    Press, Sydney.
Gunter, B. 2003, *News and the Net*, Lawrence Erlbaum Associates, Mahwah, New Jersey
Negroponte, N. 1995, *Being Digital*, Hodder & Stoughton, Sydney.
Tapsall, S. 2001, 'The Media is the Message', in Tapsall, S. & Varley, C. (eds), *Journalism Theory in
    Practice*, Oxford University Press, Melbourne, pp. 235–53.

Web sites

Global Radio News: http://globalradionews.com http://217.34.13.11/home/about.asp.
Indymedia: http://docs.indymedia.org/view/Global/FrequentlyAskedQuestionEn#what.
Live365.com: http://www.live365.com/info/index.html.
The Feedroom.com: http://www.feedroom.com/main_html_img/index.html.
Wikipedia: www.wikipedia.org.

PART II

Radio Craft Skills

Using the Voice

Margaret Throsby, radio presenter, ABC Classic FM

Margaret Throsby joined the ABC in 1969 as an announcer. She was the first female to be hired for many years by an organisation that had up till now been dominated by male voices. After starting in radio she broke new ground when in 1978 she became the first female television newsreader to broadcast nationally around Australia. Her radio experience spans current affairs and local radio magazine programs and she currently presents a 2-hour morning program on ABC Classic FM including a 1-hour segment where she interviews key national and international personalities about their lives and their music interests.

Photograph of Margaret Throsby by Greg Barrett, courtesy of ABC Classic FM

The voice in radio history

Margaret says: 'When I began working on radio and very shortly afterwards on television it was at a time when the voices that were heard on Australian radio belonged to people called announcers and nobody else's voice was heard—there was no journalist that was heard, there were no inserts from anyone else. The announcers were employed absolutely because they had voices which were passed at an audition. You had to have a good broadcast voice in order to get to first base. And then everything that went out on radio from newsreading to presentation of programs to narration of scripts—anything that was spoken by a human voice—belonged to an announcer. And in those days it was the voices of men with a medium BBC-style accent—that was what the ABC looked for.

'When I joined I was the first female for many years—there had been women during the war and women during the 1950s but then it became unfashionable. But they saw in me somebody who could talk about women's things like what the Queen was wearing when she came to Australia—and that was what I was employed for. The fact was that I also had a good voice which had been trained to a degree when I was studying acting, but it was an absolutely untrained voice really—I was just born with a good muscle in my throat and good vocal chords.

'But then fairly soon into the 1970s the whole idea of having only announcers broke down and, over a period of years, the old announcers one by one faded out and the voices that you began to hear on air were the voices of anybody— journalists, whoever, and that's the way it is today, and presenters of programs now don't particularly have to have beautiful voices. People who employ people for radio look for other things besides voice.'

Defining voice quality

'I was told that women's voices shouldn't be reading the news because "they lack authority" and I think a lot of women were told that. Nobody could ever tell me what that meant, and I think that a middle level—not too deep and not too high— female voice can sound far more authoritative than a high-pitched, reedy male voice. I think for women and men the aim is to be middle pitched—not too deep and not too high. A high or thin voice is hard to listen to. You need some mellow- ness there, some body in the voice, and that can be developed. You can apply the same analogy as to singing—some people are born with a good singing voice and then if they have it trained they get a beautiful singing voice. I think you have to be born with a good set of vocal chords to start with for the voice to become one that is attractive on air. It is the same as in life—you can hear what is a good voice to listen to, whether in a broadcast or in face-to-face contact.'

Voice maintenance

'I have a good muscular sort of voice that doesn't flag and it is strong—I don't lose my voice—which was lucky because I did a lot of reading on air and a lot of pres- entation of programs. I think your voice is part of your body and my friends think of me as a bit of a nut as far as health goes—I am a very keen runner, a gym junkie, and a yoga person, and I think that probably helps just as it helps the muscles of your legs and arms. I quit smoking soon after I started work as it was playing hell with my breathing and with the voice itself—it would get husky, a bit fractured, which doesn't sound good. If you have to clear your throat all the time it is not a good sound at all and not sustainable. And certainly you have to get enough sleep—if you are working on air nothing shows up more quickly in your voice than tiredness.'

Radio is the medium of sound, and voice is the radio broadcaster's principal tool. Just think about what you as presenter have to do through voice alone.

- Set a context—Radio is a disembodied medium. In contrast to newspapers and television there are no physical cues or clues that can help the listeners grasp what is going on. While each event has a beginning, a middle, and an end these aren't immediately obvious to the listeners who are effectively 'blind'. It is the radio voice that guides them, illuminating the structure and sequence that governs the radio experience.

- Set a tone—The voice alerts the listeners to the kind of experience they will have, be it serious and informative, or light-hearted and entertaining.
- Set a mood—The radio voice can set the mood, using the full dramatic range from profoundest grief to the heights of ecstasy.
- Give information—The radio voice is the purveyor of information; a never-ending stream of messages from innumerable sources that the listener has to grasp in a single hit, without the benefit of reruns or rewinds.

As a radio presenter, your voice is a tool. You have to control it absolutely to get the outcome you require, which means being aware not just of the mechanics of voice production, but also of the way the voice can be used quite deliberately to achieve particular effects.

It is worth noting that good voice production isn't just a question of technique. Experience comes into it too, and there can be no doubt that broadcasters improve with age. The way you present yourself at eighteen will be different from the way you present yourself at twenty-five or thirty-five when you have confidence born of life experience and maturity. Because your voice reflects your persona, it is a question of honing it over time rather than expecting it to emerge fully formed from the start.

The mechanics of the voice

I suppose the essence of it is you learn that your voice can be played with and remain authentically you and it's not to be terrified of. I think that's been a real journey I have made since my earliest days in television. I thought there was one way to speak—that's *me*! Well, it's not true.

Geraldine Doogue, radio and television presenter, ABC

The voice is like a musical instrument operating in much the same way as the bagpipes. With the bagpipes you have an inflated air sack (the 'lungs') and the air is gently forced out from the sack up through the reeds of the pipes. The different notes are formed by covering and uncovering the holes in the pipes. In a similar fashion, when we breathe in we take air into our lungs, and when we speak we force the breath over the vocal cords, or folds, and then out through the mouth. The amount of air and the speed of exhalation determines the loudness or softness of the sound we make, as well as the length of time we can hold the sound before needing to draw another breath. The shape of the mouth and the position of the tongue in relation to the teeth, palate, and lips determine the nature of the sound, giving us the vowels and consonants we combine into meaningful language. The nasal cavities also have a part to play in adding **resonance** and tone. The radio voice requires total control over this process, in terms of both breathing and articulation.

Breathing

It takes only one appearance in front of a microphone to appreciate the importance of breathing. When you are nervous your breathing tends to become rapid and shallow and you find you don't seem to have enough breath to say what you want to say. You find yourself literally gulping for air in the middle of words, and the microphone cruelly picks up every rasp and gasp. So, how do you acquire the measured pace and flow that even the most frenetic music jock has mastered? The answer is controlled breathing.

In normal life people tend to be lazy breathers, taking air in only as far as the lungs and upper throat. Actors, singers, and radio presenters learn to take in breaths as far as the diaphragm, using much more of the lungs' capacity. This not only results in quieter breaths that are less obtrusive over the microphone, but also gives you the ability to extend the intervals between pauses so that you can time your breaths to coincide with natural breaks in your speech.

Posture

Good breathing demands good posture. If you are hunched over, your lungs will have reduced capacity compared to when you sit straight up in the chair. Some presenters even prefer to stand in front of the microphone, to maximise the intake of air into the lungs. Make sure you move the microphone towards you, rather than moving towards it, so it adjusts to your position rather than the other way around. Your mouth should be 15–20 centimetres away from your mike.

Articulation

Just as many of us are lazy breathers, so too do we also tend to be lazy speakers. We mumble, we mutter, we speak too quickly, swallowing the ends of words and slurring sounds together. In radio, where the voice is the listener's lifeline, and where there are no second chances if something is missed, good articulation is essential. Again like actors, radio presenters need to master clear articulation where every sound is given its full value, where each word has a crisp beginning, middle, and ending, and where the end result is well defined and unambiguous.

CD TRACK 1: On this track, which starts with the voices of students attempting to read a news script without any training, former ABC newsreader Tony Clough talks about the ways of developing good voice production and script-reading skills.

Using the voice for meaning

One of my major problems when I did voiceovers was my voice was as flat as a tack—and I was someone who usually had a very expressive manner of speaking! Arch McKirdy [the ex-ABC Radio jazz presenter and in-house voice-trainer] helped me unravel all that and start to throw my voice around. He would get me to write a five-paragraph **intro** and then he'd sit in front of me and ask me to tell him that story. He would force me not to read those five pars to him, but to look at the first par and effectively *summarise* it—to tell him the story. I'd tell him the story and move on to the second par. By practising and practising I got the natural ebb and flow of the storytelling in my voice into the text. Of course I started to write differently as a result because in fact I was writing essays not pieces for speaking. Initially I hated it—I felt so artificial—and I think I just gradually got used to it.

Geraldine Doogue, radio and television presenter, ABC

The hardest thing I found about presenting was reading because it's not natural. Interviewing for me is really easy because I have been having conversations with people all my life, but reading is not a natural thing to do. One suggestion that was made to me was to read a page out of a book a day—that was a good tip.

Steve Cannane, radio presenter, Triple J

Once you have mastered the mechanics of voice production, you are then able to exploit the full potential of the voice to deliver meaning. How is this done?

Understanding your script

You can only convey meaning if you understand what you are reading yourself. All too often presenters fall into the trap of just reading the words on the page with their mouths disengaged from their brains. That may sound professional, but it will be devoid of personality. The words have to be processed by your brain AND your heart before coming out of your mouth.

Concentration

Whether reading from a script or **ad-libbing**, you are using your voice to say something. With or without script, as far as the listeners are concerned you are talking to them in an intimate one-on-one relationship. Scripts should be a totally invisible prop that don't impact on the naturalness of your delivery. As a radio presenter you therefore can't afford to go on automatic pilot, but need to remain focused on the meaning of what you are saying in order to convey its sense to the listener. If you switch off, the listener will too.

Pace

We have already talked about how radio doesn't give listeners a second chance. So that they can keep up with what is being said, presenters need to give listeners time to digest the message. During normal speech we can speak as quickly or slowly as we like in response to our mood and the emotion we wish to convey—we don't think consciously about pace at all. Radio speech is a much more self-conscious act in which you articulate more deliberately in order to use your voice as a pointer. For example, by slowing down you can draw the listeners' attention to a point you want them to focus on, while by speeding up you can allow them to skim over less important information. This doesn't mean you have to sound ponderous and stilted—it is remarkable how much scope we have to slow ourselves down and still sound quite natural and normal.

Stress

In singalongs and karaoke, the words to a song are highlighted for the audience to follow, and sometimes a bouncing ball is used to guide them through the tune. On radio, the voice is like this bouncing ball, highlighting the key words that the listener has to focus on in order to derive the full meaning of the message. This is why pre-reading is essential to ensure that the reader has absorbed the full meaning of the script and can convey it effectively to the audience. Some presenters mark up their scripts so they resemble a musical score with pauses and stress points clearly indicated. However, too many marks on a script can be distracting, and may lead to mistakes on air.

Tone

People are very good at absorbing the subliminal messages from tones of voice, and the radio voice is never neutral. Even the apparently neutral tones of the radio newsreader are deployed quite deliberately for specific effect, namely to convey credibility, authority, and impartiality. Similarly, radio broadcasters can, by the tiniest **inflexion**, suggest humour, compassion, or sorrow; they can make us laugh or cause us to reflect.

Pitch

Everyday speech is often conducted in a monotone, unless we are passionate or excited about something. We get away with this because we can use body language as a supplementary form of emphasis. On radio we don't have this dimension and have to rely on the voice alone. In this medium a monotonous drone can put listeners to sleep, so you need to learn how to exploit inflexion to inject colour and variety into your speech. Beginners may find that nerves restrict their vocal range; conversely, they may find that they overcompensate and trill up and down the octaves like a coloratura opera singer. To get it right you need to train your voice, and this may involve practising with a tape recorder to see just how far you can let yourself go. You will be surprised by what you can get away with—what might sound overblown in ordinary conversation will sound quite natural on air.

Breathing

We have already noted the importance of breathing when talking on air. Proper breathing ensures that you have enough air in your lungs to carry you from one natural breathing point to the next to make the intake of breath as unobtrusive an event as possible. When pre-reading any script, it is essential to note potential breathing points so you can pace yourself accordingly.

Pauses

Never underestimate the power of the pause. Too many presenters feel nervous about dead air, but it can be a friend as well as a foe. Pausation is a very important device in conveying meaning. Just as stress is used to highlight keywords, so pauses are used to draw the listeners' attention—signalling a detail that requires special emphasis, or a break between one item and another. They also give listeners time to reflect on and absorb what they have heard. It is important to make sure that pauses occur at natural breaks, reflecting the rhythm of normal speech, rather than popping up randomly in the middle of sentences. (Also see chapter 14 on newsreading skills.)

Talking into the microphone

Talking into a microphone (**mike**) is different from normal speech. Just as actors need to project their voices so they carry around the auditorium, so radio presenters need to use the quantity of air drawn into their lungs to project their voices into the microphone. The end result depends on three things:

Triple J presenter Steve Cannane at the mike.

- **Resonance**—This is the way the sound reverberates within the throat, chest, mouth, and head to gain richness and depth.
- Volume—This relates to the loudness or softness of your voice. Even though the listeners are some distance away, the microphone brings you up close to their ears. You need to speak the way you would to someone within normal conversational range.
- Microphone placement—This is often a matter of experimentation, working out what sounds best for you. Microphones aren't all the same and you will find different microphones react differently to your voice. Microphones aren't kind to high frequencies and to sibilant sounds (the hissing sound caused by 's' or 'c'). Light, breathy, sibilant voices sound scratchy and easily tire the ear. You can reduce **sibilance** and breathy quality by adjusting the position of the microphone so that you are slightly further away or off to one side. Another industry trick is to position the mike so that it points at your neck rather than your mouth as it will pick up more bassy tones that way. Beware of sitting too close to the microphone—this isn't necessary to get the right sense of intimacy and will pick up too much intake of breath.

Keeping your voice in trim

The broadcaster should look after his voice the way a concert pianist looks after his hands—very carefully!

Tony Clough, former radio newsreader, ABC

Summary of common problems of the voice

Problem	Solution
Reading too quickly	Beginners often speak too quickly on air, which can lead to on-air stumbles and stutters. Record yourself, listen back, and practice slowing down.
Croaky voice	Bad posture and bad breathing impact on voice quality especially towards the end of a sentence. By using your stomach muscles and breathing through your diaphragm you will have enough power in your voice to last for the whole sentence.
Popping	The plosive consonants 'b', 'p', and 't' often cause problems because they can cause a puff of air to be blown straight onto the microphone. This is avoided by moving the mike to one side of the mouth.
Sibilance	Some people pronounce 's' and 'c' sounds very sharply, which is further exaggerated by the mike. This can be avoided by moving the mike to one side and by using mouth movement to improve articulation.
Running out of breath	Novice presenters and newsreaders in particular often run out of breath caused both by nerves and by not breathing with the diaphragm. This can be relieved by improving posture to allow you to take full deep breaths. Pre-reading of the script can also alert you to possible trouble spots.
Wrong intonation	Inexperienced readers may sometimes stress the wrong words in a sentence, which obscures the meaning. This can be avoided by making sure you understand what you are reading. Underlining key words in each sentence may be helpful.
Singsong voice	Some readers go too far in trying to inject colour into their reading by over-stressing words and using a very limited range of inflections. You can avoid this by focusing on the rhythm, pace, and flow, and by training yourself to use the full range of your voice.
Flat voice	It is boring to listen to a monotonous, flat, or 'dead' voice where you sound as if you are reading at, rather than speaking to the listener. It can be fixed by using bullet points or memorising the script rather than following it word-for-word. It also helps to use your body as you do when speaking normally. Think about the listener as someone you want to tell a story to.

Because the voice is the radio broadcaster's principal tool, it needs to be nurtured and looked after. Many a broadcasting career has been cut short because of damage to the vocal folds through overuse or lack of appropriate care. As anyone who has barracked over-enthusiastically at a football match knows, too much shouting can cause you to lose your voice. Too long a newsreading shift may do the same sort of damage. Hoarseness and laryngitis can be an occupational hazard. Using your voice on air is not like normal speech—it requires effort and concentration, not only in controlling the elements listed above, but also in terms of projection into the microphone. You need to make sure recovery times are built in your shift to avoid putting too much strain on your voice.

Things we put in our mouths can affect our speech. As a general rule, what is bad for our general health can also impact on our vocal folds, for example cigarettes, caffeine, alcohol, and some drugs. Take hay fever medication for example: if it dries up your hay fever, it will almost certainly dry up your voice too. Some specific foods can make the mouth too liquid (milk or chocolate) or too dry (lemon juice), while gassy drinks can disrupt breathing.

Like any other part of the body, the voice benefits from exercise. Specific vocal callisthenics can help limber up lips, teeth, and tongue before starting an on-air shift. Others help improve pronunciation and articulation.

It is worth talking to a good speech therapist about voice care so that you build up good habits right from the start.

Exercises

Reading practice:
1 Monitor the way you breathe. Is the air coming from the throat and chest? Try taking a breath by drawing air in from your stomach. Put one hand on your chest and another on your stomach and note how the movement changes when you shift from drawing breaths high in the chest to breathing more deeply with your diaphragm, leading to your stomach moving in and out.
2 Try reciting the alphabet slowly. How far do you get on one breath? Practice breathing from your diaphragm and repeat the exercise several times seeing how much further you get.
3 Select a radio script and read it through noting your pattern of breathing. Record yourself reading the script with a frown on your face, and then record again reading with a smile. Do you note any difference in tone? Read again adding facial and hand movements as you would in everyday speech. Does this make a difference?
4 Listen to CD TRACK 1 and compare the voices of Tony Clough and the student readers.
   • What differences do you note in their style of delivery?
   • On the basis of Tony's advice, what regime would you set in place for looking after your voice?

Further reading

Ahern, S. & Brown, G. 2000, 'Radio Announcing', in Ahern, S. (ed.), *Making Radio: A Practical Guide to Working in Radio*, Allen & Unwin, Sydney, pp. 70–84.

Day, A., Pattie, M. & Bosly, N. 1998, *Presenting the News On Air: A Self-Paced Program to Develop Your Broadcast Voice*, University of Queensland, Brisbane.

Mills, J. 2004, *The Broadcast Voice*, Focal Press, Oxford.

Writing for Radio

The art of radio writing lies in its artifice. It is a type of writing in disguise, a means to an end; it is writing that will appear not to be writing at all when it is delivered on air. Writing for radio is an attempt to capture the style of live spontaneous speech, just as reading on radio is an attempt to replicate the delivery of live spontaneous speech on demand.

If you compare a radio script with a page from a novel or a newspaper story, the contrast is stark. The page from the novel is unbroken print, closely spaced and dense. The newspaper copy is easier on the eye through the use of pictures and varied layouts—but it too is closely spaced and information-heavy. By comparison there is a lot of blank paper in a radio script. The script itself consists of a bare few lines spread across the page. A story that is given a full-page spread in a newspaper can be summed up in three short paragraphs in its radio news equivalent.

So, what makes radio writing different?

- You are writing for the ears. Unlike readers of print, who have a physical text to rely on, or television audiences, who are helped by pictures, radio listeners are restricted to one sense only—hearing.
- You are writing for the voice. This means that what you write has to be said out loud. The words need to trip easily off the tongue, sounding like normal speech with all its rhythms, cadences, pauses, stresses, ebbs, and flows.
- You are writing for a one-off experience. The listener has one chance to grasp your meaning and this imposes all sorts of constraints on how you deal with information.
- You are painting pictures with words. Your script is taking the listener on a journey. If there are sights, sounds, and smells you need to describe for them what your senses are picking up.

These four elements are what define radio writing, and this becomes clearer when we look in a bit more detail at style, content, format, and structure for radio scripts.

The characteristics of a radio script

A journalist's workstation.

Style

> I think writing is really important—to work at getting your voice, because it is not a generic writing style for everyone, it has to sound right and be comfortable for you to read.
>
> Sally Sara, foreign correspondent, ABC News and Current Affairs

The style of a radio script will be conversational rather than literary. Having said that, there is no way a news bulletin sounds like a station ad, or a talkback script sounds like a Radio National think piece. In fact three clear styles can be identified:

- news—formal, correct, and neutral
- copywriting—colloquial and natural
- program scripts—normal speech.

Though scripts can range from a half-hour lecture to a 15-second promotional **grab**, with a similar range in the level of formality versus colloquialism, the writing style is aimed at live delivery rather than silent reading. This means that sentences will be similar to live speech—not overly complex, not overly long, not overly laden with facts and figures. The script will be addressing the listener—you as presenter will be talking to someone, not reading into a void. The style therefore has to be natural rather than stilted, friendly rather than formal, giving scope for the deployment of the full range of vocal pyrotechnics that enliven real speech.

Content

The content will be simple rather than complex. It often helps to identify the key words of a story and build your script around them. Again with the focus on your listeners, care will need to be taken to make sure that they aren't bombarded with detail that is difficult to grasp on a single hearing:

- Complicated numerals. If something is costing $15,133,000, round the figure off to 'just over $15 million'.
- Lengthy titles. 'Professor Jeff Bloggs, Pro-Vice Chancellor for Research for Pacific University', can be simplified to 'Professor Jeff Bloggs, research spokesperson for Pacific University.
- Professional jargon. This sort of language can often be cumbersome and also incomprehensible to non-experts. Why say 'the office is operationalised to help external clients' when you mean 'the office has been set up for the public'?

You will also need to be careful to avoid monotony—too lengthy a period of reading, unbroken by other sound, quickly leads listeners to lose concentration and to tune out, mentally even if not literally. Much more than two minutes of your unrelieved voice and you will have lost them. Content will therefore need to be digested and compressed, to be interlaced with other voices and other sounds to ensure as varied a mix as possible.

Format

The radio script's format is determined by the need for it to be easy to read. As a radio presenter, you need all your wits about you on air and any distractions in a script—typographical errors, scrawled corrections—can lead to stumbles that will destroy the illusion of effortless communication you are trying to build. Scripts therefore need to be:

- clearly typed, with as large a typeface as is comfortable for you to read
- double-spaced to ease the transition of the eye from line to line
- formatted on the page with one idea to a sentence and one sentence to a paragraph.

Each sentence will rarely exceed three lines. This is because longer sentences are not only more challenging to read in terms of retaining their sense from beginning to end; they are also likely to contain more information than the listener can realistically absorb. Breaking longer sentences into shorter ones is easier on reader and listener alike. However, variety is the name of the game in radio. Vary the length of sentences to avoid monotony.

It helps to have just one scripted **link** on each page rather than having a long unbroken script. This will make it easier for you to keep track of your place, and of what has, and has not, been read, greatly assisting your on-air housekeeping.

Structure

Radio scripts don't beat about the bush. The average reading speed is 150–180 words per minute. With so little time to gain the listener's attention and to impart information, you need to get to the point quickly. There is no such thing as the gradual build-up—you sock

SLUG		DCART	TALENT	DATE		COPY	
latham speaks 3 FLASH				18/01/2005 13:47:54		0:23	
Dest:	NICE	99:	Writer:	hawleys4g		Subbed:	hawleys4g
History:							
Headline:	grab to come						

```
EX-RN-CPH
latham speaks 3
hawley
```

Mark Latham has resigned as the federal Opposition Leader
saying he's too unwell to continue in the position.

Mr Latham broke his silence in Sydney a short time ago
after growing pressure from senior Labor figures to
resolve speculation about his future.

He's been suffering from a second bout of pancreatitis and
came under severe criticism after failing to make a
statement directly after the Boxing Day Tsunami disaster.

Sample of radio news script.

Source: ABC, 18 January 2005

INTRO – RON BAKIR   6.10pm

SCHAPELLE CORBY is back in a Bali courthouse tomorrow....

Gold Coast businessman RON BAKIR and lawyer ROBIN TAMPOE
flew out of Brisbane this morning in a last ditch attempt to clear
SCHAPELLE CORBY'S name and save her from a possible death
penalty....

We spoke to RON BAKIR and ROBIN TAMPOE before they left and
they were basically leaving on a wing and a prayer in the hope that a
letter will come through from a Minister in Indonesia to allow their key
witness to appear in court...

RON BAKIR joins me on the line live from BALI....

Questions:

- What is the process of the case?

- So you are now waiting for the government to receive a letter from
  the Indonesian government is that right?

- What will happen if the letter doesn't arrive?

- What sort of deadline are you running on?

Sample of radio program story script.

Source: Philip Clark Drive program, 2GB, 23 March 2005

it to them in the first line. This acts like the newspaper headline, grabbing attention, summing up the story, letting the listener know immediately what is going on. Subsequent paragraphs layer on more information, while the final paragraph provides closure, wrapping up the story in terms of where things will be likely to go from here.

These are the general rules that govern all radio writing. Having said that, scripts serve a variety of roles.

Types of radio scripts

The introduction is crucial to allowing people listening in to decide 'am I going to devote the next hour of my life to this?' I want the fishing line to go out and hook them in, so I spend a lot of time on the introduction working it out.

Margaret Throsby, radio presenter, ABC Classic FM

The *Morning Show* that I used to present was much longer and I could ad-lib a lot more because I had more room to move, but with *Hack* because it is so tight you are counting every second in every minute. You have just got to be really economical with what you say and you can't waste a word, so it's probably more scripted than the morning show— by scripted I mean we have intros and outros to stories and we pretty much stick to them because if I start waffling on about something else suddenly the story is going to crash into the 6 o'clock news. We have less room to move which I don't like so much because I would like to be able to ad-lib more.

Steve Cannane, radio presenter, Triple J

Link or lead-in

The **link** (or **lead-in**) is read by the presenter to introduce a program element that involves someone or something other than their own voice: an interview guest, a segment, a feature report. Its purpose is to set the piece up—to grab the listeners' attention and interest, to give background or content, and to prepare them for who or what they will be hearing next.

Listeners are easily puzzled by strange sounds they can't identify, and this very quickly turns to irritation if you let them go too long without telling them what the sound is— be it another person's voice on air, **location sound**, or even a piece of music. The link can be divided into three sections:

- The lead: introduces the story, almost like a newspaper headline
- The background: gives some additional information about the story and why it is relevant
- The **throw**: moves the listener from the presenter's voice to the beginning of the story.

Example (presenter's read): Have you ever wondered what fire tastes like? With the Fire-eaters Convention taking place in Albert Park today, reporter Jane Scoop took advantage of a perfect opportunity to get an answer to this burning question …

Story intro

The story intro is used by the interviewer or reporter to set up their story. If used with the link it will be designed to pick up where the link leaves off as the reporter takes up the baton from the presenter. Having grabbed the listeners' attention and curiosity in the link, the interviewer or reporter will use the intro to get in to the story proper, giving more information and setting up any other **talent** we will be hearing from.

Example—Intro to Jane Scoop's report (reporter's read): I have just arrived at Albert Park and there are fire-eaters on just about every corner. I am standing next to Joe Blow who has a burning torch in his hand ready to put into his mouth. Joe, what attracted you to the art of fire-eating?

Outro or back announce

After the story has finished the presenter needs to grab the baton back again from the reporter and the **back announce** or **outro** is a script read by the presenter to finish off the program event. It can be anything from a repetition of the track title and artist details of a piece of music to a reminder of the voices featured in a preceding report. It provides closure to one event in preparation for the beginning of the next, and helps to make sure that the listener is with you rather than lost in a maze of meaningless, directionless noise.

Example (presenter's read): That was our reporter Jane Scoop, taking a lesson in fire-eating from Joe Blow at the Fire-eaters Convention, which is on all day today in Albert Park.

Live liner

A **live liner** is used by the presenter to promote an upcoming event in the program or on the station, scripted to be punchy, concise, and persuasive to entice the listener to stay tuned.

Example (presenter's read): Barking dogs, broken fences, loud music—these are the sorts of things that can turn neighbours from friends into enemies. But what can you do about it? Ken Barney from the Newport Citizens' Advice Service will be joining us after the ten o'clock news to take your calls on neighbourhood nuisances.

News copy

This is the archetypal example of radio writing—information delivery that is pared down to the essentials in three or four one-sentence paragraphs; language that is factual, simple and clear; structure that is disciplined with a well-defined beginning–middle–end.

> **Example:** Fire-eaters have been banned from Albert Park in the wake of a fire earlier today which destroyed the Grand Bandstand.
>
> The bandstand, dating from Victorian times, was a much-loved landmark in the park and the local council says the bill for restoring it will run into the thousands of dollars.
>
> The fire-eaters, who are holding their annual convention in the park, blamed a freak wind for blowing a flaming baton onto the wooden roof during a juggling display.
>
> Spokesperson Joe Blow condemned the council ban as an over-reaction.

News writing is dealt with in more detail in chapter 12.

Promo copy

The **promo** script is used for promotional material, whether in the form of a paid advertisement or an in-house station announcement. While you still need to observe the usual radio writing rules in terms of spareness and structure, the style is much more relaxed and colloquial, often presenting mini-scenarios to encourage listener identification with the material. (See chapter 9, and p. 113 for a sample script.)

Voice reports

This is a longer script used by reporters to tell a story without the benefit of other voices or sound. It gives the radio broadcaster a larger palette to work with since more information needs to be conveyed. Once again, though, the usual rules governing style and structure will be observed. In this format you need to keep an eye on length since listeners tend to tire of the unbroken voice after a couple of minutes. Also, it poses a challenge for the reader since you need to retain your focus throughout—if you go into automatic pilot the listener will soon follow!

Commentaries and longer pieces

These vary from editorials and short opinion pieces, which often feature in talkback radio, to more specialist commentaries such as 'Ockham's Razor' (15 minutes, Radio National) or the full-blown lecture (such as the six half-hour talks comprising the annual Boyer lecture series on Radio National). The talkback editorials are scripted to suit the character of the presenter, their punchy style matched by a robust and lively delivery to ensure they achieve their aim of stirring the audience up. There is little chance of the listener falling asleep during this 2-to-3-minute address. The longer pieces are much more challenging—even though they are written for the voice, the format is demanding, requiring intense concentration from the listener for what is in radio terms a lengthy period of time .

Writing the radio script

If you are just talking you will naturally say whatever you think in your own style, but if you are reading a script it is difficult. You have got to read words you are comfortable with reading. You should write scripts yourself if you have got the time because it is more likely to be in your words. You can't sound natural if you are using other people's words and other people's style. If you've got a producer you have got to work with them and they'll know what you would say and what you wouldn't say, and they'll know also the style in which you would say it. I try and write most of my stuff.

Steve Cannane, radio presenter, Triple J

Writing for yourself

Because you are writing something that you will read out loud, you need to compose it for your voice and particular speech habits. The best way to test whether a script will work or not is to rehearse it as you write it—which is why radio production rooms can be noisy places. Read the script out loud to see whether the rhythm is right, whether the words flow, whether there are any awkward, difficult-to-pronounce words or groups of words. Rework it until you get it just right—this will help to ensure a trouble-free run on air.

Writing for someone else

Often you will be writing scripts for someone else, possibly the newsreader or the program presenter. This sort of writing is a singularly altruistic exercise. Here you are fashioning a script for another to perform. Just as you aim to reflect your own speech patterns in scripts you write for yourself, so those you write for others will be attuned to their speaking style. It should be their voice rather than your own that you hear in your head as you write: Do they use this sort of language? Do they have this sort of sense of humour? Do they favour this sort of inflexion?

Writing tips

- Write the words the way you say them: 'it's' rather than 'it is'.
- Simplify: say 'half a million' rather than '509,432'.
- Use phonetic spelling to ensure accurate pronunciation of difficult or unusual names.

- Don't be afraid to repeat key details. Listeners have short memories and may need reminding of who or what you are talking about.
- Paint word pictures that will be easy for listeners to understand.
- Avoid beginning scripts with numbers or crucial facts. Give listeners a lead-in time so they are prepared for difficult material: instead of '500 people died in a fire in the city centre' say 'A fire in the city centre has claimed the lives of 500 people'.
- If you are quoting someone, put their name and title before the quote rather than after as it allows listeners to understand the context of the statement: instead of 'Taxes are to rise next year, says Treasurer Peter Costello' say 'The Treasurer Peter Costello says taxes are due to rise next year'.
- Avoid jargon, including radio jargon: instead of 'Here is a segment on sex in the city' say 'Here is an interview on sex in the city' or, even better, ' Is there sex in the city? Reporter John Smith has the story'.
- Use abbreviations only after you have prepared the audience by using the complete word: 'The process is underway for Turkey to join the European Union. At last night's meeting of the EU governing body, members voted to allow negotiations to begin.' Some acronyms are in common usage and are acceptable: CSIRO, USA, UN.
- Use active rather than passive forms: 'Beckham scored the second goal' rather than 'The second goal was scored by Beckham'.
- Take care with the use of collective nouns that, while referring to groups of people (government, audience), nevertheless are treated as singular rather than plural entities ('The audience has given the thumbs up to the latest reality show on Channel Ten').
- Read aloud while you write. This way you can test-drive your words and see if they suit your way of speaking and don't pose any hidden problems for pronunciation.

Exercises

These exercises will help you understand the difference between spoken language, ordinary prose, and radio language, which sits between the two.

Go to a government web site and print out a media release. Use this as the basis for a radio script consisting of four one-sentence paragraphs.

1 Highlight the key words.
2 Re-write your own story based only on those key words (telling the story in your own words will give you ownership of it).
3 Practise reading it, noting any problems with language, sentence length, and rhythm, and revise the script accordingly.
4 Read the script to someone else to get their feedback on how well the content came across.
5 How does the finished product differ from ordinary conversational speech? How does it differ from the original written press release?

Further reading

Alysen, B. 2000, 'Writing and Narrating', in *The Electronic Reporter: Broadcast Journalism in Australia*, Deakin University Press, Geelong, pp. 73–99.

Boyd, A. 1997, 'Conversational writing', in *Broadcast Journalism: Techniques of Radio and TV News*, 4th edn, Focal Press, Oxford, pp. 39–51.

Day, A., Pattie, M. & Bosly, N. 1998, 'Writing Copy for Presentation', in *Presenting the News On Air: A Self-Paced Program to Develop Your Broadcast Voice*, University of Queensland Press, Brisbane, pp. 35–40.

McLeish, R. 2005, 'Writing for the ear', in *Radio Production*, 5th edn, Focal Press, Oxford, pp. 46–52.

Masterton, M. & Patching, R. 1997, 'Words', in *Now the News in Detail: A Guide to Broadcast Journalism in Australia*, 3rd edn, Deakin University Press, Geelong, pp. 87–118.

Web sites

Writing for Radio: http://www.newscript.com

Poynter Institute for Journalism Training: http://www.poynter.org

Interviewing

6

Geraldine Doogue, radio and television presenter, ABC

Geraldine Doogue's career has spanned all three media: print, radio, and television. After leaving university she joined the *West Australian* newspaper as a cadet, and then spent four years in London working as a print journalist before returning to Australia to work on the *Australian* newspaper. She then moved to television, presenting an early evening current affairs program on the ABC. From there she moved to radio and set up the *Life Matters* program on Radio National that under her stewardship was able to develop a unique niche in social affairs reporting. She has been able to extend that interest to her television work as presenter of the *Compass* program on ABC television, which explores

Geraldine Doogue, radio and television presenter, ABC. Photo: ABC.

modern social attitudes. Having moved on from *Life Matters* in 2003, Geraldine now presents Radio National's *Saturday Breakfast* program.

The job of interviewing

Geraldine says: 'I often find the first question's particularly difficult and then it seems to get a lot easier from there on in. I don't think there is an absolute rule about the way in which you go into an interview—they may become more definite rules after that, but at the start it's a very personal choice.

'The first few questions are truly almost a setting up of a conversation and it's like a bell curve effect so that you do ratchet up the "pressure" as the interview progresses. I must say I rather like proceeding in a sequential fashion—I like to move through almost topic headings and that's how I have tended to develop as an interviewer. However, sometimes, particularly with documentary work on television and radio, the producer needs you to produce certain key things, key bits of the interview to meet images they have, and you have to hop around. I actually don't like doing that because I feel it's disrespectful to the person's story and I have had to learn a way of explaining to the guest why we are doing this. I think it is quite destabilising for people actually, but often the form you are working in demands it.'

Framing the questions

'One of the simplest things I think is just that basic question "Tell me what struck you as most important in the experience you've just been through". If people are talking about an incredible incident that occurred, "Tell me the time you were frightened the most", "Tell me when you were most relieved"—in other words it's the secret of storytelling: "tell me a story". People often fail to use those words, but they open mouths like you wouldn't believe!

'Another one that sounds very formal but I have had great success with is: "What is your judgment about this?" It basically says to the person, "You are worthy of casting a judgment and I am going to listen to you" and I found it quite a technique that draws out people, often your least likely people, your inarticulate people: they feel they are being respected.

'And there's a third clever one which news and current affairs people don't use nearly enough, which is to say "what does all this amount to?" It's a sort of summary you are asking from people, which is often the very thing they are never asked. They are asked for little bits of episodes, usually to produce huge dollops of emotion about a particular episode, so that then the next person can be asked to produce huge dollops of emotion about their last dollop of emotion, and you go in this pathetically diminishing circle of emotion which I am bored by and I think bedevils a lot of news and current affairs reporting. I think a much more useful question which often gets you a headline and often takes the story further is that crucial question to people who are involved in the midst of controversy: "What does this amount to in your judgment?" and people come up with the goods because they actually have thought and have often got strong insights but they are never asked.'

Managing the talent

'Before I start the whole process I say to people "We are going to have, I hope, a great conversation, but it is not a floppy conversation where you feel super relaxed and you've got hours—this is a conversation such as you would have over a good dinner party where you're performing a bit and I want you to sit a little bit on the edge of your seat. I don't want the totally relaxed you, I want someone who's under a bit of pressure. I won't exploit that pressure, but I want you to be winning an argument that you care about at a dinner table." I say to people: "Can you give me the top 10 per cent of your energy—I don't want the bottom 50 per cent, I don't want a languid person"—and they actually perform differently.

'I do a lot of head nodding, I very much encourage them to speak. I suppose I try very hard to show them I'm fascinated—I am easily fascinated so that's helpful, in other words it's not artificial—but nevertheless, if anything, I do slightly exaggerate my responses that I'd give by comparison to those I would give over a good dinner party conversation.'

Playing to an audience

'I don't focus on the audience. I have to satisfy *me*. I think one of the key mistakes that you can make, and radio taught me this more than television, is that if you have the audience in mind it is too confusing. You have got to believe that you are the prism through which the audience is hearing things, and if *you* aren't satisfied with what you are hearing or you think it's dull, it's dull! I feel it's a very self-interested thing, this business about interviewing, and people confuse themselves by having some amorphous notion about satisfying the 30+ demographic or women in the west or men in the east—I think it mucks you up. I've tried it – it doesn't work. You've got to satisfy *yourself*. Now that means you've got to be satisfied you have a working knowledge of your audience and you've got to be well read enough and broad enough to allow yourself the arrogance of believing you are worth listening to, so there is a bit of work you've got to do, but I just think you've got to forget about the audience and think about yourself.

'My personal view is that still the best working method is to be genuinely interested in the person and the story they have to tell you, and to convey that to the person so that they start to lower their shoulders and sit back in the chair, and actually have their guard down so that they give you something fresh, different, from the heart, unguarded—I still think that's where the magic moments come from.'

Radio, especially talk radio, is the medium where the voice reigns supreme. Whether it be in talkback, in news grabs, in current affairs programs, or in lifestyle shows, radio allows us to hear a range of voices speaking about thoughts, views, feelings, activities, lifestyles, and customs. But we mustn't forget that what we hear is also a programmed event—people are talking on demand, and the vehicle for getting them talking is the interview. Before discussing the 'how' of doing interviews, it is worth asking some other basic questions: What is the interview? Why do we do them? Who are they for?

What is the interview?

A good interview to me is something that is revealing, entertaining, thought-provoking, and tells a good story as well—that's how I would describe a good interview.

Steve Cannane, radio presenter, Triple J

The interview is a planned chat—no matter how spontaneous an exchange may sound on air, the best interviews have been carefully engineered to ensure a specific outcome. They are intended to serve an editorial purpose—to suit an audience, a format, a program style, a mood. The interviewer has the goal of eliciting information from the interviewee (or '**talent**'), and must steer the interaction quite deliberately in order to get the required outcome.

Why do an interview?

The interview serves a variety of purposes. It can be used for seeking facts, for interpreting facts, for reacting to events. It can help us get to know someone better. It can sometimes expose secrets people may not want to reveal. It can sometimes catch people out in a lie or a subterfuge, as politicians have discovered to their cost! Radio in the end is disciplined gossip and through the interview listeners vicariously engage with the lives, emotions, and activities of people far removed from themselves.

Who is the interview for?

We have seen how speaking and writing, the other radio craft skills, involve doing an apparently straightforward activity for a more complex outcome. Radio speech sounds normal, but has actually been deliberately manufactured to get a specific on-air effect. Radio writing looks normal, but has actually been drafted to sound nothing like the written word when it is read. Similarly, the interview may seem like a natural conversation, but it is actually a clever artifice.

First, there is a third party involved—the unseen, silent, but omnipresent listener. The conversation between interviewer and interviewee may appear to be a private exchange, but is in fact directed at this absent third party—it is intended to be overheard. Even if the interviewee is lulled into forgetting the listener, the interviewer will never lose this awareness of the person the talk is really aimed at.

Second, the interview is designed to suit its context. News bulletins, current affairs shows, arts reviews, human interest profiles, lifestyle programs, and talkback segments will all contain interviews, but each format will require a different approach, a different balance in terms of information, entertainment, and emotion.

Having established the 'what', 'why', and 'who' of the interview, we can now go on to examine how you actually do one.

The technique of the interview

I've always taken the view that the key thing is to get the talent comfortable enough to actually open up to you. Now that is not necessarily what inspires a lot of people, I have come to see—some interviewers will consciously make the person feel as if they are on foreign territory and that they are on the edge of their seat and under pressure. So there are different strokes for different folks depending on where you are.

Geraldine Doogue, radio and television presenter, ABC

The most important thing is, while scene setting or subject setting for the audience, don't steal the story. If the talent's good enough to tell it, they'll tell it.

Howard Sattler, radio talkback presenter, 6PR Perth

Very often it doesn't go where I think it is going to go. It is like a tennis match: you serve a ball over the net and they return it to the backhand instead of the forehand, so you have to chase it, otherwise you don't get the shot back.

Margaret Throsby, radio presenter, ABC Classic FM

I think it is a real weakness within journalism where journalists broadcast and write for other journalists. They don't think about the audience, and they think they have got to ask really tough questions or they have got to ask certain questions, and they miss some very obvious ways and subtle ways of asking certain questions—like they have got to appear to be tough. Asking really straightforward questions in a relaxed manner can actually get the person to say more than they would if you asked them in an aggressive manner.

Steve Cannane, radio presenter, Triple J

A successful interview is the product of the right style, thorough preparation, and sensitive control.

CD TRACK 2: This track illustrates the process that interviewers go through when deciding on their topic, talent, and approach to an interview. Steve Cannane, presenter of Triple J's afternoon current affairs program *Hack*, takes us through an interview he did with Deputy Leader of the House of Representatives Peter McGauran on how the newly elected Howard government would be meeting its election promises in relation to the parliamentary agenda. He explains the reasons for doing the interview, the story angle he was following, and the rationale for his approach to his talent.

Style

Interviews serve different purposes in programs and the interview style will be determined by the effect you need to achieve on air. There are five basic interview types: informational, confrontational, inquisitorial, conversational, and confessional. Each requires the interviewer to fill a different role.

Informational interview—interviewer as facilitator

Used in news or general interest formats, the aim of this sort of interview is to extract facts, to get information in the most straightforward and emotionally neutral way. The exchange will be relatively unemotional and businesslike, with the talent simply a means to an end.

Confrontational interview—interviewer as adversary

Used most often in current affairs formats, this sort of interview puts the talent on the spot, with the interviewer filling the role of interrogator whose aim is to extract information that the talent may be reluctant to deliver. It makes particular demands on the interviewer who needs to be assertive without being aggressive (since aggression can put the audience offside), and forceful without getting angry (since real emotional involvement leads to loss of artistic control).

Inquisitorial interview—interviewer as prober

This is really a combination of the previous two interview styles—it is a rigorous attempt to explore an issue in some depth, but with less of the drama and grandstanding that tends to colour the confrontational interview. Terry Lane's interviewing style in Radio National's *The National Interest* program is a good example of this genre where, instead of verbal pingpong, the format provides enough space for in-depth discussion that can explore a topic beyond the headlines.

Conversational interview—interviewer as friend

This is a relaxed, friendly exchange, with the interviewer the benign listener who offers encouragement and reinforcement. Here the talent is wooed rather than attacked. This sort of interview is found in light entertainment formats.

Confessional interview—interviewer as confessor

This is a much more emotional experience where the interviewer is the sympathetic and empathetic witness to whom the interviewees bare their souls. This sort of interview is usually quite long and lends itself to formats such as slow-paced late-night talk shows where listeners have more time available for extended listening and are more likely to be in the mood for reflection. It is demanding on the interviewer who, having encouraged the outpouring of emotion, needs to make sure that the outcome isn't too uncomfortable for talent and listeners alike.

Preparation

You do have your strategy and you do have your tactics to achieve your strategy—the whole idea of planning an interview is something that I took years to learn. You do have to plan—especially if you are trying to get a particular answer or set of answers. It's very demanding work, particularly if you don't agree with the people you are interviewing and you are trying to restrain your own horror at what they are saying in order to draw them out. I think that you have to have a bit of the cross examiner about you. You have to lead people away from their self-protective measures and you have to spend a great deal of time with yourself first working out their psychology.

Geraldine Doogue, radio and television presenter, ABC

Usually I start out with a predetermined plan for the interview, but never ever just have a series of set questions where I just stick to those whatever. Usually I've got a starting point and then the rest of them are insurance policies—that's all they are.

Howard Sattler, radio talkback presenter, 6PR Perth

I don't believe in over-rehearsing things, like running through with talent the thing you're going to talk about, because you may get good 'talent' who then go bad on you in a sense in that they say 'Well, I told you all that' and of course the tape recorder wasn't running. So you tend to trust your luck on the day.

Bill Bunbury, radio feature producer, ABC Radio National

As with any performance, the more thorough your preparation, the better the result. As we have seen, in the interview you are not only directing a managed exchange with another individual—you are doing it for the benefit of a third party, the listener. This means that you have to view it as a proper production—something that will work on air— and consider the following elements.

Research

The purpose of research is to help you develop the best line of enquiry. You need enough information on the topic to give yourself confidence that you understand all the issues. Only then will you be able to ask intelligent questions, including playing devil's advocate when you need to make sure that the listener is aware of another side to the debate. Your research will involve not just reading relevant material but also, most importantly, it will involve talking to people, although the interviews you do at this research stage will be more wide-ranging and informal. The aim will be to get as much information as you need to be able to work out the format of the final product, as well as to identify potential talent.

Angle

Thorough research will help you decide on the **angle** for the story—the way you want it to develop on air in terms of information that needs to be brought out, the structure (beginning-middle-end), and your approach (interview style).

Choosing talent

It is very dangerous for interviewers to make assumptions about talent. You can have a hunch, but until you do the interview you don't know what the talent is capable of. There are as many different types of talent as there are people on the planet and as interviewer you have to calibrate your performance to suit the interviewee—you can't abandon someone who has been struck with nerves; neither can you allow an enthusiastic talent to go off on a tangent. And you can never anticipate who will rise to the occasion and who will fall flat. Talent can be unpredictable even if they are experienced and well known—on the day they might feel uninspired, or they might not want to be there, or they might really be sick of being interviewed having done many interviews before yours. My point is you can't make any assumptions. Sometimes the most unexpected things happen. As we have all learnt!

Margaret Throsby, radio presenter, ABC Classic FM

You need to select the appropriate person for the interview. This should be someone who not only knows the topic, but also will come across well on air. They should not only speak well, they should also be interesting to listen to. Try to get past public relations representatives or media spokespersons—aim for people who can talk about their real-life experiences. It may involve more work to track down the person whose house has burnt down, but an interview with them will have more impact than one with the fire department representative.

Briefing talent

If I am doing an interview with someone I will always tell them what is going to happen to the interview. If it's a pre-record, I'll say: 'This is a pre-record and we are going to edit it down' so they know that we are going to edit it and they're not at the end of it suddenly going to be surprised and think 'Oh, they've changed what I've said!' If it is going to be in a package, I will say 'We're going to use this and then someone is going to rebut what you've said and this is what they'll probably say so you've got an opportunity to respond to that'. So I will always make sure I put in the context of how it is going to be used so they don't have any surprises. That's a really important thing.

Steve Cannane, radio presenter, Triple J

Once you have decided on the talent, you need to make sure that they are properly briefed so they understand what the purpose of the interview is and what they can expect on air. Although interviewees have, sometimes notoriously, been ambushed on air and forced into situations for which they have not been prepared, this tactic is risky for your program (the outcome can't be guaranteed) and can be ethically questionable (the talent may never trust you again). We all perform better if we understand what is expected of us. The talent needs to know just what information you are looking for and how long they have to provide it. They need to know if other talent is involved and where their own comments fit in relation to what other people will be saying. They need to be made aware of the rules of broadcasting relating to defamation and other unsuitable material. They also benefit from knowing certain technical details such as how long the interview will be, whether it will be pre-recorded, and whether it will be edited.

Location

You need to decide when and where to conduct the interview. Will it be enhanced by being done on location, or should it be done in the studio or by telephone? Should it be live or pre-recorded? Each of these options will give a different result in terms of impact,

immediacy, and focus—for example if you are interviewing a vet about horse-doping, an interview in
the studio or by phone will focus attention on what
the talent says. The same interview done on location
will add a sound dimension that allows the listener
to picture a physical context as well.

Live versus pre-recorded

> Live interviews are a highwire act—you never
> know what is going to happen.
>
> Steve Cannane, radio presenter, Triple J

Doing a radio interview on location.

> When something is live there is a sense of rising to the occasion for the guest, and
> for me too when I know that what I am doing now is being heard as we do it. And
> there is some kind of authenticity that I think comes from a live interview because
> people listening know that it can't be edited so what they hear is what is happening.
> I like people to think that every day they can tune in and hear a guest who has made
> their way into the studio physically to sit with us and spend an hour, and that's why
> the program has that roll-on energy day after day.
>
> Margaret Throsby, radio presenter, ABC Classic FM

Live interviews are quite different from pre-recorded ones. When you are pre-recording
you have the luxury of more time to probe and prod, even if it takes you off on a tangent
for a time. You have the capacity to correct mistakes, and to jump backwards and forwards
if necessary to ensure all bases are covered. In a live interview you have just one shot at
getting it right. Your attention is inevitably split between the talent and the function of the
interview within the program. As interviewer you have to follow a linear path in your
questioning so the story is developed in a coherent way. Mistakes are difficult to correct,
there is no capacity to edit, and you have to keep to a strict timeframe. You also have to
cope with the adrenalin rush and nervousness that is an inevitable by-product of the red
mike light going on. Despite all this, live interviews can bring out the best in both interviewer and talent.

Control

> Those basics of interviewing come into play all the time—listening to what people
> say, which can be very hard when you are watching the clock; thinking about what
> you are going to ask next, but also wanting to listen to their reply because it might
> demand a further question. And making that split second decision: will I continue on
> that thread or is the clock getting around to time so I need to think about winding
> up? You have this split system happening in your brain. One part is very carefully

calculating and the other is listening and processing information and thinking what sort of question people might want me to ask next. I am very conscious that people might not want just what I want.

Margaret Throsby, radio presenter, ABC Classic FM

The outcome of the interview is very much dependent on how well you control your own performance as well as that of your talent.

Controlling your performance

Bridget Moore interviewing Claire Fletcher for community station Radio Fremantle 107.9FM, WA.

Being in control of your performance during an interview requires doing several things at once.

Keeping your focus on the content

This means having a clear idea of the outcome you want from the interview, and concentrating on how you develop the storyline to ensure a clear flow from introduction to conclusion.

Keeping your eye on the clock

This means pacing yourself according to the allotted time—a 3-minute interview will require quite different tactics from a 10-minute one.

Keeping your cool

This means retaining your objectivity—if you let your emotions rule you run the risk of losing the intellectual thread.

Keeping the listener in mind

This means remembering listeners' needs. Sometimes they may need extra help to keep up with the story, such as a reminder of the talent's name, or the restating of an important detail.

Controlling the performance of your interviewees

Being in control of the performance of your interviewees comes down to two things: keeping them comfortable and keeping them talking.

Keeping them comfortable

> I am physically as close to them as I can be without feeling I am invading their personal space. I think the body language from me is usually inclusive—I lean forward, I look at them, I don't look at notes.
>
> Margaret Throsby, radio presenter, ABC Classic FM

> You get bum ache a lot, often sitting in the dust talking to people because that is the best way to get a story, so you kind of merge there and people talk about things and forget that the microphone's on.
>
> Bill Bunbury, feature producer, ABC Radio National

The interview is a stressful situation for interviewees, not least because they aren't the ones in control. They are on your turf: in a studio setting, captured by your microphone, and with the unnerving sense of an audience 'out there' listening to their every word. However, they can be helped to relax simply by seeing that you are genuinely interested in them. If they sense you are really listening to them, they will tend to forget their nerves and concentrate on what they are saying. And they will gain this sense that you are listening through your body language.

When we are engrossed in conversation we tend to do three things: make eye contact; draw ourselves towards the other person, often mirroring their posture; and make noises indicating that we are following what they are saying. When you are doing an interview it is important to make sure that your body keeps up this sort of signalling. Even when you yourself may have to deal with studio distractions, such as the need to cue up a promo or follow an off-air instruction from your producer, you need to keep your eyes and body focused on the talent. Verbal reassurance is a different matter. This needs to be avoided on air as competing voices can be confusing for the listener. However, you can substitute smiles, nods, and other gestures to communicate your involvement.

Keeping them talking

The aim of the interview is to elicit information from the talent and to do this you need to focus on your questioning technique. John Sawatsky is a Canadian investigative reporter and academic who is an expert on the art of interviewing and has been training journalists all over the world. The following is based on his checklist of seven things to avoid while conducting interviews (2000):

- *Avoid closed-ended questions.* Closed questions are questions that contain all the information and invite a simple 'yes' or 'no' response. Open questions, by contrast, invite the interviewee to provide the information. They are the five 'w's and the 'h' questions:

who, what, when, where, why, and how. Start a question with any of these words and you pave the way for narrative—for stories to be told, feelings to be remembered, places to be described. As an example, compare this question, 'Is it true that as a child you used to walk 10 kilometres to school each morning?' with this one, 'As a child, how did you get to school?' The first question will lead to a dead end, while the second question will encourage the talent to expand upon this childhood experience.

- *Don't make a statement instead of asking a question.* A statement will simply give the talent the information you actually want to get from them. By rephrasing as a question you pass the ball to them. For example, instead of saying 'It must have been hard to arrive as a migrant to Australia in the 1950s', say 'What was it like to arrive as a migrant in Australia in the 1950s?'

- *Don't ask double-barrelled questions or two questions at once.* If you ask these sorts of questions the interviewee is likely to answer only the last one, or the one they prefer to answer. Instead of asking, 'Have you been taking this medication for a long time and if so what side effects have you experienced?', divide it into two separate questions.

- *Don't overload questions.* As with double-barrelled questions, overloaded questions pack too much information in, giving the talent the chance to be evasive. Sawatsky gives the following example: 'The reporter asks Bill Clinton: "Was Gennifer Flowers your lover for 12 years?" He answers: "That allegation is false". Which allegation is false? That they were lovers, or that the relationship lasted 12 years?' (2000).

- *Don't put comments into questions.* This is another way of putting words in your talent's mouth. Instead of asking, 'How did you feel after the fire? You must have felt terrible when you saw your house burn down', open the way for them to describe it themselves by saying, 'What went through your mind when you saw your house go up in flames?'

- *Don't use trigger or loaded words in questions.* Sometimes interviewees will react to language they feel passes implied judgment on their actions. If you ask the water resources minister 'How will this scheme for saving water impact industry in the area?' you might get the answer: 'It's not a "scheme"'.

- *Don't use hyperbole in questions.* Overblown questions put the interviewee off and they will compensate by under-rating their achievement. For example, asking Ian Thorpe 'How does it feel to be a national hero after your Olympic performance?' will get less of a response than a simple question: 'How do you feel after your multi-medal win?'

Vox pops

The **vox pop** (from the Latin *vox populi* meaning 'voice of the people') is a special interview format that serves the function of a mini-opinion poll. A series of people randomly selected on the street are asked for their opinion on a particular issue. The aim is to get a variety of short grabs that, when edited together in a package, can be used on air to give an extra dimension to a story. A relatively dry discussion between a local councillor and a property developer on a controversial new building project in the city can be brought to life when we hear what the 'real people' have to say about it.

Despite the simplicity of the idea, all the skills of the interviewer need to be marshalled for this exercise. You need to be clear about why you are doing it (the purpose it will serve in your program) and what outcome you are seeking (the style and content of the final package). Managing the talent is challenging since you are approaching total strangers and asking them to perform—you need to use all your people skills to gain their compliance. Although your interviewing style will be straight informational ('What do you think of the plan to redevelop the city mall?'), you need to direct each exchange carefully to make sure all respondents are answering the same question. When the answers are edited together into the package, that question, rather than being repeated over and over again, will be the unspoken accompaniment to all that is being said.

In this chapter we have looked at the mechanics of human interchange and how these elements can be harnessed to deliver natural results in a controlled situation. Whether the format is a half-hour profile interview or a five-second grab for a vox pop, the central point to remember is: the key to good interviewing is good listening. Focus on your talent, make them feel they are the centre of your universe, involve yourself in what they are saying, and the result will be a piece of absorbing and even gripping radio.

Exercises

CD TRACKS 3 and 4 contain examples of two very different interviewing styles.

CD Track 3 is an example of a confrontational style where the interviewer actively challenges the interviewee. Talkback radio presenter Neil Mitchell of Melbourne station 3AW interviews Assistant Commissioner for Crime for the Victorian Police Simon Overland about documents allegedly leaked from the Police Department that may have been implicated in a crimeland killing. Note the interviewer's assertive and uncompromising style as he challenges the talent to provide the information he seeks.

CD Track 4 is an example of an interview in the confessional style, a more gentle technique where the interviewer empathises with the interviewee. Here Julie McCrossin of Radio National's *Life Matters* program tackles the sensitive issue of losing a child at birth, the subject of a documentary by Vanessa Gorman in which she chronicles her own experience of pregnancy and loss. The segment features Vanessa herself and the baby's father, Michael Shaw. Note the style and questioning technique that the interviewer uses to encourage her guests to open up and talk about a very confronting and emotional matter.

Listen to both interviews and transcribe the interviewer's questions from each.

1 Are the questions open or closed?
2 What technique is each interviewer using to get information from the talent?
3 Compare and contrast the interviewing styles.
4 Can you suggest other questions or ways of questioning to get the required outcome?

Further reading

Beaman, J. 2000, *Interviewing for Radio*, Routledge, London.

Masterton, M. & Patching, R. 1997, 'The Art of It: About Interviewing' in *Now the News in Detail: A Guide to Broadcast Journalism in Australia*, 3rd edn, Deakin University Press, Geelong, pp. 203–37.

Sawatsky, J. 2000, 'What To Avoid', *American Journalism Review*, http://www.ajr.org/article_printable.asp?id=678.

Sedorkin, G. & McGregor, J. 2002, *Interviewing. A Guide for Journalists and Writers*, Allen & Unwin, Sydney.

Wilson, R. 2000, *A Big Ask. Interviews With Interviewers*, New Holland Publishers, Sydney.

Working with Sound

7

Ron Sims, freelance sound recordist

Freelance sound recordist Ron Sims joined the ABC with the idea of being a television producer but after a chance secondment to the sound effects department discovered his true vocation—sound production. He has been involved in every aspect of sound production in radio documentaries, radio dramas, and performance pieces that have included live son et lumière staged productions. Ron left the ABC in 2002 to work as a freelance.

Ron Sims, freelance sound recordist.

The job

Ron says: 'I look for magic, I look for spectacle, I look for giving the audience something that excites them, where possible. This means I am very conscious of the fact that one can heighten reality with sound, be it the way I record a voice, or music, or the way I use FX. For me it's very much like a child playing with a game and exciting the audience, and I don't mind sometimes layering it on pretty thick.

'I'm quite happy to go straight for that heart centre and say, "this is what I want you to feel, this is the information I want you to have" and I have recorded this sound, or mixed it or edited it in such a way that there is no mistake about that. I'm not going to apologise, I put it there as big and as large and as excitingly as I can.'

Working with sound

'The radio feature in its true sense is not planned. You simply go out there with your tape recorder, if you want to call that your camera, and you capture what is going on—you capture the reality of the scene, be it a riot or whatever—and then later on in the studio you sit down with this bulk of material and try and make out of it your final piece with editing and juxtaposing things.

'Wherever possible I will go and get my own sound recorded in my way, and when you do that, when you come to the actual editing stage or the mixing stage suddenly there are no problems, and I think it's because early on in the piece I try to think of the whole thing—the subject, the content, the people I am going to interview or work with, the kind of sounds I am going to need.

'Once you've got good interview material, once you've got great sound and you are coming back with material that you can walk into the studio and say "I've got bloody good material here, this material has got a lot going for it", that next stage you can either make that work and make it better, or unfortunately you can destroy it.

'You can actually see my design before I go into the studio—you will see it on paper. It's not designed as a script where the voice leads with FX dropped in. My design sheets are more like graphic sheets with levels of information, where everything takes equal billing because I try to get the audience very involved in the texture of the story.

'The actual mixing becomes an enormous, very exciting stage—it's like a painter going to a white canvas. The colours are there, the palette is there, the brushes and the palette knives are there, and you've got this white canvas in front of you and that is going to be your program.

'This is an area where really there are no rules—you as the designer of that sound will do it your way.'

It is all very well to say that radio is the medium of sound, but what does this mean in production terms? It means that we not only have to identify the sounds we want to broadcast, but we also have to collect and transmit those sounds so that they reach the listener in as clear and pristine a form as possible. This is the ultimate goal that determines the technique and the technology for the radio broadcaster, both in the studio and on location.

Sound doesn't just happen on radio. It reaches the ear of the listener with the aid of microphones, recording equipment, editing and processing equipment, transmitters, receivers—it is obvious there are a lot of technological intermediaries between the original sound source and the individual ear that eventually hears it. However, even while being the product of complex technology, good sound production renders this technology invisible. The aim is to produce sound as close to natural as possible with no discernible technical interference that might distract the listener from the listening experience. In this chapter we look at what this means for the radio broadcaster, both in the studio and on the road.[1]

1   Given the variety and range of equipment used in broadcasting, it is impossible to include detailed technical instructions in a text of this type. Different radio stations and educational institutions will have different set-ups. Instead, this chapter aims to give an insight into the logic that underpins the technology commonly used, so trainee radio broadcasters can approach each piece of equipment with some knowledge of how it works, what it is used for, and how to use it effectively. The list of readings at the end of the chapter includes texts that go into the technical specifications in greater detail.

What is sound?

The greatest instrument you can have is your ears.

Adam Sallur, promotions producer, 720 ABC Perth

You may have something happen in the foreground right up on the speakers and it may be a door opening so that the lock on that door is recorded very close up. This brings the listener's consciousness right up to the front of the speakers. Now if that is followed by something very distant—there may be in this particular scene an owl outside which has been recorded directly at a great distance—you've developed a line of force in the listener's perception between that upfront sound and the owl, so you have actually painted the size of a scene. Into that scene your character can walk—through the door, through a field which has left, right, and front and back. So you have with stereo replay an enormous facility for creating a field of sound.

Ron Sims, sound recordist

We take sound very much for granted, rarely thinking consciously of what it is and how we actually hear it. Hearing is a very sophisticated sense. We don't just hear sounds—we process them noting such things as:

- Loudness and softness—is the volume high or low?
- Pitch—is it high pitched like a whistle or low pitched like a foghorn?
- Nearness and farness—is it close to us or far away? If far away, how far?
- The position of the sound source—where is it located in relation to ourselves? To the right? To the left? Across the room? Across the street? Where is it located relative to other sounds?
- The quality of the sound—is it clear and clean, or is there **echo** or **reverberation (reverb)**? If there is an echo (the repetition of a whole sound) what does it mean? Are we in a stairwell or at the foot of a canyon? If there is reverberation (the quality given to sound when it reflects off other surfaces in an enclosed space), how much is there and what does it tell us? Are we in a small office (high level of reverb off walls and surfaces) or out in the open air (low level of reverb)?

Our ears are very discriminating. With the help of our eyes and brain we are able to choose to foreground sound, or alternatively to relegate it to the background. In a noisy party with lots of people and music blaring from the CD player, we can concentrate on what our friend is saying despite the background noise. If a favourite CD comes on, we can tune out everything else to concentrate on that.

When, as radio broadcasters or program-makers, we create sound, we are relying on a recording or a reproducing device to replicate these sound experiences. The problem is that the technology is a very blunt instrument indeed compared with the ear-eye-brain combination. The microphone, for example, which is our surrogate ear, does not discriminate when it comes to sound. It can't choose to foreground sound the way we can—it records whatever is there. If we want to reproduce the three-dimensionality of real sound, we have to manipulate our recording conditions accordingly. This means understanding the importance of position and location, of echo and reverb. It also requires that we understand the power of **stereo** to create the physical space our sound will inhabit.

Position

If you think of the microphone as an ear, you can appreciate how its position relative to the sound source can give the listener all sorts of information. The closer the microphone is to the sound, the more that sound stands out. Other sounds drop away and you can actually manipulate the balance between foreground and background to get the effect you want. You can, at one extreme, have someone appear to whisper softly into the listener's ear, or at the other have someone yelling at them from the other side of a room. In a noisy coffee shop, you can choose to have the focus either on two friends having an intimate chat at one of the tables, or on the noisy barista making coffee in the background.

Location

Sound creates pictures in the mind, and location noise, whether we intend it or not, tells a story. Play the sound of car horns, and without further prompting the average listener will imagine a busy city street. Play the sound of thunder, and the image of a stormy day will appear in the mind. Location sound gives you the opportunity to import an entire ready-made setting into your recording—the challenge for you as sound recordist is to harness this power so it enhances rather than detracts from the result. The sound of surf crashing on a beach will work wonders in an interview with a surfer talking about the dangers of shark attack, but will be an irritating distraction if you are interviewing a finance broker on the cost of Telstra shares.

Echo and reverb

All too often echo and reverberation are unintended by-products in a substandard recording. Instead of clear sound, we hear sounds muddied and muffled by the echo effect of nearby surfaces. Once again this is something that can be harnessed deliberately to enhance your recording. Echo is fine if you want to record someone talking from the bottom of a well. Reverb is fine if we are being taken on a tour of a castle and are listening to someone describe the stained glass windows in the main hall.

Stereo

Stereo, or stereophonic sound, is recorded on two channels, either with two microphones or with a stereo microphone, and replayed through two speakers. **Mono**, or monaural, sound is sound recorded with a single microphone on a single channel and replayed through a single speaker. With stereo sound, the microphones are able to act as two surrogate ears instead of one, increasing the capacity of the recording to replicate sound as our ears pick it up naturally—in other words, with an added dimension of space. With the two independent channels, the two strands of sound can be moved both in relation to each other and to the listener. Further tweaking of the balance can be done when the sound is processed at the editing and mixing stage. (See p. 81, 'Creating sound—the edit suite'.)

Having examined the characteristics of sound, let's look now at the different contexts in which radio broadcasters make and manipulate sound: in the live broadcast studio, on location, and in the edit suite.

The live broadcast studio

Seeing a broadcast studio for the first time, you would think you were about to pilot a jumbo jet. As you sit at the **console**, you face a bewildering array of microphones, buttons, **faders**, lights, racks of equipment, and computer screens. It all seems totally confusing, but a closer inspection exposes the method in the apparent madness.

A radio console showing VU meters at the top and banks of faders, where each fader controls a different sound source.

The on-air console

The console is simply a mixing desk—a piece of equipment that allows you to activate, at the touch of a button, all the equipment you will need to use in your broadcast. It is therefore a collection of remote start buttons controlling the **inputs** (sound material brought in from other sources) and the **outputs** (sound material subsequently sent from the studio to the transmitter).

If you lifted the console up you would see beneath its relatively tidy surface a mass of spaghetti-type wiring that connects its buttons and knobs with the other machinery that surrounds you in the studio. A closer look allows the rationale of the desk to become clearer.

It is divided into three sections: studio controls, monitoring controls, and the information panel.

Studio controls

The main bank of buttons, knobs, and faders occupying around two-thirds of the console area controls the equipment used for the on-air broadcast. This includes the output sources (the presenter and guest microphones), the telephone switch, and, through remote start buttons, the input sources (**cassette** decks, **minidisc** players, CD players, and computers) that contain the music, promos, ads, and pre-recorded material you will need for your program.

Monitoring controls

Another bank of buttons, knobs, and faders controls the outlets through which you can listen to your program. This can be done through the on-air and off-air speakers and through your headphones. The controls also allow you to split the signal to the headphones to include a cue channel into one ear through which to preview material or to listen to messages from the producer in the control room.

Live-to-air output is monitored through the studio speakers. You can choose to monitor either the sound from the studio, or the sound from the transmitter. It is wise to monitor the program ex-transmitter as you can keep an ear on sound quality and also get advance warning if there is any interruption to transmission.

When the microphone is on, these speakers will switch off to prevent sound feeding back into the microphone (**feedback**). Monitoring then is done through the headphones, which is why radio presenters always have them on during their programs.

Cued material is monitored through the headphones and through a separate speaker on the console itself.

The information panel

Facing you at the rear of the console is an elevated sill that houses a variety of displays—a VU (volume unit) meter, essential for monitoring levels; a digital clock, essential for keeping track of time and for giving on-air time checks; and a current temperature reading, useful for ad-libbing a weather update. There may also be a **peak meter**, which is more sensitive than the **VU meter** and can warn you about high levels that the VU meter might not pick up.

Buttons, faders, and pan pots

The buttons along the bottom of the console turn equipment 'on' and 'off', and also, via a third **'cue' button**, allow you to listen to each channel without the material going to air. This enables you to cue music or to check content before playing.

There may also be another set of buttons controlling the **'delay'** unit. People say unpredictable things on live radio, and offensive or defamatory statements can have serious legal repercussions for the radio broadcaster and the station. It is therefore normal procedure for live programs to be broadcast in delay. When you press the button to go into delay, 7 seconds of time is unobtrusively collected and stored. If trouble arises, by pressing the **'dump' button**, either in the studio or in the producer's booth, that 7 seconds is erased and the program reverts to real time. The audience will never get to hear the offending statement—in a talkback call, for example, what they will hear is the line appearing to drop out and the presenter (in real time) picking up the program from there, possibly with an apology for having had to interrupt the call.

The faders or **sliders** are sliding knobs that allow you to control sound levels for each piece of equipment. Monitoring sound is a tricky process, but it is an essential duty for the radio broadcaster in order to ensure that sound is not distorted, and that sound from all sources is going out at the same consistent level.

The sound meters are there to help you monitor this, and what you have to watch out for is the indicator going into the red zone. If it is consistently in this area the output will sound fuzzy and distorted. The sound levels should bounce around 0 **decibels** (dB) in analog mode and around the -8 dB to -12 dB zone in the digital mode. This is the level, usually marked both on faders and on the sound meters, which produces the optimum sound output from the radio transmitter. You won't be able to keep your levels consistently at this mark, but it represents the average you should aim for within the range of highs and lows. The faders allow you to tweak levels so they remain even throughout the broadcast, from whatever source. They also allow you to play with the levels of different sound sources so that, for example, you can fade down a music track in order to talk over it. The more complex **cross-fading** technique involves fading one sound down as you fade another sound up, by which the transition from one item to another is made as seamless and smooth-flowing as possible. A row of knobs or **'pan pots'** above the faders allow you to move or 'pan' the sound to ensure a proper sound balance between left and right stereo channels (see p. 83).

It is not surprising that working at the console is described as 'driving the desk' because mastering it is very similar to mastering the controls of a car. With practice, manipulating the controls becomes second nature and it is at that stage that as broadcaster you are fully liberated and can properly focus your full attention on performance and content.

The microphone

Microphones come in various shapes and sizes—these are discussed in more detail on p. 75 ('Location recording'). The kind you are likely to encounter in the studio is a **directional microphone** that has a sound **pick-up pattern** focused towards the front—in other words, it will pick up your voice as you speak into it, but pick up less sound from other parts of the studio. Even the sound of paper rustling as you read your scripts can be minimised by holding them below and to the rear of the microphone, where they are out of range.

Operational skills

When operating the desk as presenter your aim is first to minimise technical 'noise', and second, to have a smooth and seamless flow.

Technical noise comes from various sources and you can minimise this interference simply by being aware that it exists and adapting your studio technique accordingly. Here are some common problems and possible solutions.

- There are audible on-air clicks as you push the buttons to fire CD players and other equipment. By fading your microphone a split second before pressing that CD button, the 'click' will not be heard.
- You are **'popping'** when you are talking into the microphone. 'Popping' is caused when air is blown directly into the microphone, and some people do this when pronouncing the so-called plosive consonants 'p', 'b', and 't'. You can minimise this by positioning the microphone just off centre to your mouth so your breath passes alongside the microphone rather than into it.
- There are thumping and rumbling sounds coming from the microphone. The microphone picks up all noise, including that caused by any sort of handling. This sort of interference can be avoided by moving carefully in the vicinity of the mike to avoid accidentally brushing against it, and by handling it delicately if you need to reposition it for any reason.
- The sound is fuzzy and distorted. This comes from having the levels too high. You can avoid distortion by monitoring the VU meter and peak level meter to ensure you are keeping within the required range.

Having a smooth and seamless flow is the product of careful planning and accurate timing. This is where you juggle sound as cleverly as any musician. You need to be familiar with your material, both spoken word and music. This means knowing how each event begins and ends. This in turn allows you to adopt the right tone in your voice, select the right form of words in your intro and outro, and manipulate levels so fades and cross-fades knit all sound together in an unbroken stream. The listener is thus given no inkling of the technical complexity of the production process that delivers so many sounds from so many different sources.

Live studio checklist

A thorough check prior to broadcast will allow you to set things up to your specification and help to minimise on-air glitches:

1   Check all faders are in the 'off' position.
2   If you are using the telephone, check that the phone and the phone switch into the desk are working (a telephone call to the recorded weather or time services is a useful way of rehearsing).
3   Check the microphone—does it have its **mike sock** (this is a foam cover that fits over the mike head, reducing the flow of air across the microphone and so minimising 'popping')? Is it in the right position for you?
4   Do guest microphones have mike socks? Are they in the right position for the guests?
5   In 'cue' check your levels and levels of any guests. Use faders to set levels from all sources so they are within the optimum range and not distorted.

6   Check other gear (CD players, minidiscs) is in working order. In 'cue' pre-listen to material to set levels.

7   Put scripts in order to avoid last minute searches and unnecessary paper rustle.

8   After your broadcast, leave the studio ready for the next shift with remote start buttons off, faders down, all pan pots at 12 o'clock.

Location recording

When you get into a story and you are getting it on the run, the actors—the people you are working with—are not there for you as in a drama where they will do what you tell them to do, to stand here, to say these lines now. In a radio feature, you're the intruder, but at the end of the day you want the story, you have to get every word, so it's a very tiring business. At the end of that half-hour you're exhausted. Your mind has been working all the time: got to go left, go to the right, go through the crowd this way, put the mike there, is the wind in the way, all that kind of thing. It means you have to have a knowledge of the things that can go wrong to try and overcome them on the run, at a pace that is not your pace—it is the pace of the performance or the happening. And that's a typical day, I think, in that kind of sound recording.

Ron Sims, sound recordist

Location sound recording is for many novice broadcasters the most challenging technical arena since, instead of the relatively stable and safe environment of the studio, they are out in the real world where anything can (and usually does!) happen. Even in such an unpredictable situation, your mission is the same as in the studio—to capture sound uncontaminated by the technology you are using to record it.

Recorded sound should sound like live sound—the recording process should not diminish it in any way. It should come across as crisply and clearly as if the listeners were there themselves. In fact because microphones are less discriminating than our own ears, sometimes recorded sound needs to sound even better than real life for us to get the full 'live' impact. Many a sound recordist has had the experience of doing the perfect recording of a waterfall only to end up with something that sounds more like frying bacon.

All recordings will be susceptible to the sound of the machine itself corrupting the recorded sound. It might be a rumble or an electronic hum. The weaker the recorded audio signal, the more prominent this extraneous noise will be, and the aim of good recording is to reduce what is called the **signal-to-noise ratio** as much as possible.

Monitoring of levels is as vital on location as in the broadcast studio and similar rules apply. Your goal is to avoid distortion and to keep levels even. Just like the studio desk, the portable equipment will have sound meters that will tell you when you are in the danger zones. Again, as with the studio equipment, the aim is to keep the levels bouncing around 0 dB on analog equipment or between -8 to -12 dB on digital equipment, avoiding the red zones. Unless you get good strong sound registering on your sound meter at the time of recording, no amount of pumping up the levels after the event will make it better—all that will happen is that you will simply get louder distorted sound.

Recording equipment

There are many recording devices at your disposal; some are analog, but more and more of them are digital with new formats being introduced all the time. Here are some of the more common ones.

The cassette recorder

This analog recording device uses a magnetised tape to capture and reproduce the sound. The small enclosed cassettes are difficult to cue and to edit, and the recorded material generally needs to be transferred to a digital format (minidisc or computer) to be processed. **Tape hiss** can be a problem when recording, so care needs to be taken with setting audio levels.

The minidisc recorder

This is a lightweight digital recorder that works in a similar way to a CD—it stores compressed digital sound files on a disc which are then 'read' by laser beams. Minidiscs don't suffer from the same 'signal-to-noise' ratio problems as analog recorders—there is no tape hiss to contend with—but there are other challenges. Digitally recorded sound is unforgiving—set the levels too high and you will get distortion and clicks that are equally ruinous to your recording. Careful monitoring of levels is essential to ensure you don't enter these danger zones, especially when the minidisc has automatic level control that prevents you from riding levels manually during recording.

Like CDs, minidisc recordings can be divided into 'tracks', and each one can be given a title that appears on the machine itself. The recordings can be manipulated on the machine so basic editing can be done—cutting, pasting, and rearranging so you can play the tracks in any order. With this digital technology, what you are doing is programming the machine to read the recorded information in a certain order. Unless you physically delete material it is always there for you to retrieve if you need to. More sophisticated sound processing is achieved by downloading material onto a computer where there is the capacity to work in **multi-track** formats (allowing you to incorporate music and other recorded sound) and to insert fades and cross-fades. (See p. 81, 'The edit suite'.)

The DAT recorder

Digital audio tape (**DAT**) recorders record digitally, like minidiscs, but the information is stored on magnetic tape in the form of small cartridges similar to the videocassette. These can record up to two hours of material. As with minidiscs, you can include identification markers to separate recorded material or to mark cue points. Editing is done by downloading digital material onto computer. (See p. 81, 'The edit suite'.) While DAT recorders were considered the next big thing a few years ago, advances in recording technology have left them in a cul de sac as cheaper and more flexible formats have evolved.

Flashcard recorder

This is an example of the sort of developments that have sidelined DAT machines. This technology allows you to record onto a removable card that can later be inserted directly into a desktop or laptop computer for replay or editing. Possessing all the digital features of the minidisc it has the added advantage of instantaneous transfer between recorder and computer. Rather than having to cope with cumbersome conversions from one format to another, and the delays caused by real-time copying, with flashcard recorders the process is a simple matter of transferring a sound file. Possibly the single biggest benefit of flashcard recorders is that they have no moving parts, a great advantage for portable recorders that have to go on location and may occasionally get the odd bump.

Microphones

> In the outside world a great skill when you are coming to record a scene is that you immediately think: 'What are the sounds that I hear? Is there a fridge running? An air conditioner going? Is there wildlife happening? Where do I best put my microphone to negate those things and get the sound I want?' I think it's a learned thing. It's not something you just know—it takes many accidents, many failures, many fluffs before you get it right!
>
> Ron Sims, sound recordist

The purpose of the microphone is to pick up sound and feed it into either an **amplifier** that broadcasts it in a particular location, or a recording device that preserves it in a more permanent form. Though the microphone works like an ear, as noted above, it isn't as clever—it just responds to whatever is around. Getting good sound depends on knowing which microphone will produce the best result in any given situation.

How microphones work

All microphones are based on the same principle: sound enters at one end, passes over a thin diaphragm creating a vibration, the vibration is converted into an electrical signal, and this is passed down a wire into an amplifier or a recording apparatus that allows it to be 'heard'. Sound isn't uniform—it is composed of a range of low, medium, and high tones called audio frequencies. Just as our ears vary—some of us are more sensitive to high-pitched sounds; others to low frequency rumbles—so microphones vary in their sensitivity to different sounds. The better the quality of the microphone, the wider its frequency range is likely to be. This means it will pick up resonances across the entire sonic range, creating a deeper, broader, and more realistic sound reproduction. Lesser quality microphones tend to have a more limited range, favouring either the higher end (leading to sound that is light and tinny) or the lower end (leading to sound that is bassy and muffled).

Microphones can also vary in their power—some give 'more bang for your buck', in other words generate a stronger electrical signal that increases their sensitivity to sound over a distance. With microphones, as with recording devices, the aim is for the lowest signal-to-noise ratio—the least amount of sound corruption from the instrument's own technical noise.

Dynamic versus condenser

There are two main sorts of microphones, representing two variations on the 'sound-diaphragm-electrical charge' concept.

In dynamic microphones, the vibrations are picked up via a magnet and either a metal ribbon (ribbon microphone) or a coil of wire (moving coil microphone).

In condenser microphones, the vibration is picked up and relayed via a battery-powered electrical circuit.

A key difference between them is that where the dynamic microphone requires no external power source, the condenser either relies on its own battery power or else feeds off the 48-volt power supply from the recording equipment or the studio console. This has implications for the user: the power source must be checked! There is nothing worse than being on location with the recorder ready to roll only to find that the battery in the condenser microphone is dead, or that the recording device doesn't supply 48-volt power.

Pros and cons of different microphones

The dynamic microphone

Advantages:
- The coiled wire microphone is robust and withstands field conditions well.
- It has no need for a separate power source.
- It is less susceptible to picking up handling noise.
- It is good for voice recordings.

Disadvantages:
- It may be less successful in picking up ambient sound and low frequencies because of its reduced sensitivity compared to the condenser.

Use for:
- Voice only work.
- Location work where voice is foregrounded.

The condenser microphone

Advantages:
- It is lighter than the dynamic microphone.
- It can be very small and unobtrusive, in the 'bug' or lapel clip versions, which can reduce the stress of the talent in the interview situation.
- It has a wider frequency range, and produces good results in the field where it can pick up ambient noise that gives greater breadth and depth to the sound recording.

Disadvantages:
- It needs its own power source so batteries (and more importantly replacement batteries!) are essential.
- It is more fragile than the dynamic microphone and sensitive to dampness and the wet.
- It is more sensitive to microphone handling noise.

Use for:
- Field work where you need to focus on ambient noise as well as the foreground voice.
- (As a clip microphone) Static, longer-length interviews to help the talent to feel comfortable and relaxed.

Apart from pick-up patterns, dealt with below, the differences between dynamic and condenser microphones in terms of how they record sound can be summarised as shown in the table above.

Pick-up patterns

Like the real ear, the microphone not only picks up sound frequencies, but also does so within a particular range. The specifications of any individual microphone will include not only its frequency range (the high and low sounds) but also the sound field within which it is most effective. The pick-up patterns can be divided into **omni-directional** and directional.

Omni-directional (see figure 1)

This sort of microphone picks up sound indiscriminately from all directions, just as our ears do. In a recording situation, this means it will pick up the sound that you want along with sound you may not want, such as the hum from the fridge or the squeak from a chair. This makes it more challenging for the sound recordist who may want to foreground one sound over another.

Pick-up patterns

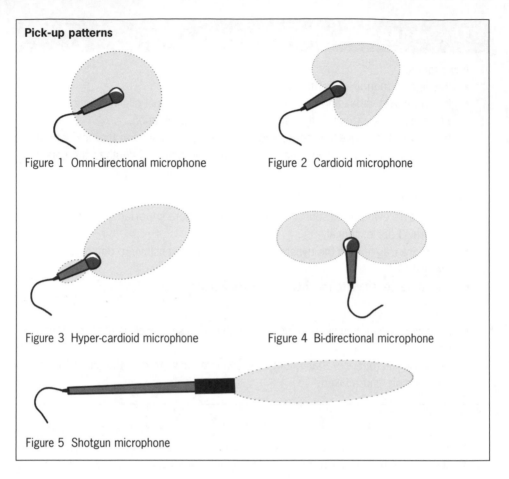

Figure 1 Omni-directional microphone

Figure 2 Cardioid microphone

Figure 3 Hyper-cardioid microphone

Figure 4 Bi-directional microphone

Figure 5 Shotgun microphone

Directional

This is the name given to the group of microphones that are more sensitive to sound from one direction. There is a range of different pick-up patterns that determine the extent to which you can focus on a particular sound.

The unidirectional microphone favours sound directly in front of it and to a lesser or greater extent reduces the amount of ambient noise recorded on the side. Versions of this pick-up pattern include:

*   The **cardioid microphone** (see figure 2), as its name implies, picks up sound in a heart-shaped field favouring the front, with some pick-up at the sides, but virtually no pick-up at the rear. This allows you to foreground a voice while also picking up some ambient noise. It allows some movement of the sound source without it impacting on quality.
*   The **hyper-cardioid** (see figure 3) and **super-cardioid** microphones are more uni-directional versions of the cardioid microphone in which the heart-shaped field is elongated further towards the front. The **shotgun microphone** (see figure 5) is the most **uni-directional** of all, allowing the recordist to home in on a single sound source while picking up the bare minimum of surrounding sound.

- The **bi–directional** or **figure eight microphone** (see figure 4) collects sound from two sides in a figure-of-eight pattern. It enables you to record two speakers simultaneously.

Selecting your microphone

Bearing in mind the characteristics of dynamic and condenser microphones, their respective strengths and weaknesses and their pick-up patterns, when selecting your microphone for any recording situation you will have to consider:

- the type of sound you are recording (voice, music, ambient noise)
- the location (studio, ordinary room, outside location)
- the frequency range—you will get the best results from a microphone that picks up sound evenly across a wide frequency range, as opposed to one that picks up sound unevenly and is skewed too much towards either high or low tones
- the signal-to-noise ratio—you will get best results from a microphone that produces little noise of its own to interfere with the sound being recorded.

Operational skills

Even after you have selected your microphone, taking into account all the technical features you need to look out for, you can still be let down by one unpredictable variable— YOU! Operator error can result in all sorts of problems and the trick is to understand what these problems are so you can solve them on the spot. Let's look at a few.

Popping
This results from the passage of puffs of air across the top of the microphone, which tends to happen when we use the so-called plosive consonants, 'p', 'b', and 't'. Popping is reduced by covering the end of the microphone with a foam shield called a 'mike sock', windsock, or **'pop filter'**. If the problem persists, the position of the microphone can be adjusted so the mouth is further away, or to one side.

Muddy sound
This is usually caused by the microphone being too far away from the talent's mouth so that the higher frequency ranges aren't being picked up, while the bassy **ambient sound** from the rest of the room is.

Fuzzy sound
This is caused by the microphone being held too close to the mouth, so sound is over-recorded and distorted.

Too much bass
Directional microphones have a tendency to emphasise bassy sounds the closer they are to the mouth. This is called the **proximity effect** and can be countered by adjusting the

position of the microphone. Sometimes a bug or lapel microphone can pick up too much of the bassy vibrations from the chest, and here too adjusting its position should alleviate the problem.

Background noise too loud

Microphone positioning will rectify this. A directional microphone will block out much of the peripheral noise. If the noise is still too loud it is best to look for another location as it can pose too much of a strain on the listener.

Too much echo

This is caused by sound reverberating off other surfaces, particularly bare walls where there is nothing to absorb the sound to prevent it from bouncing back (this is why studio walls are padded to provide a deadened neutral area). Select another location.

Microphone handling noise

Microphones pick up sound from being handled. The shifting of your grip on the handle or the movement of the cable can result in clicks and rumbling that are an unwelcome intrusion on your clean sound. When handling a microphone keep your hand still. You can avoid cable noise by looping the cable around your hand as you grip the microphone to prevent it swinging around.

Electronic hum

Assuming you have checked your equipment to ensure it is in good working order and not producing the hum itself, this can be caused by other equipment in the room (fridge, computer). The only solution is to choose another location for your recording.

Troubleshooting for location recording

Symptom	Cause	Remedy
1. Popping	Blowing into mike	Use mike sock or reposition mike
2. Muddy sound	Mike too far from source	Reposition mike closer to source
3. Too much echo	Sound bouncing off bare surfaces	Select another location
4. Distortion	Wind blowing on mike without windsock	Use windsock to cover mike surface
5. Mike clicks	Caused by cable movement against mike	Coil cable around hand to prevent movement

CD TRACK 5: This track contains some examples of bad quality sound. Poor audio of this kind is very hard or impossible to correct afterwards. This highlights the importance of getting high quality clear recordings with no technical interference when you are on location.

Location recording checklist

Preparation is the key to good location recording. Before you go out on the road:

1 Select your recording equipment.
2 Do a thorough check of the kit to make sure batteries are included and are fully charged and that gear is in working order.
3 Check there is an adaptor if you intend to use the local power source, and also collect any cabling you may need for your location.
4 Select your microphone. Will it do the job you want it to do? Does it have a windsock? If it is a condenser, is the battery charged? Is there a spare battery?
5 Check the headphones. Are they in working order? Do they have the right connecting cable for your recording equipment?
6 Do a trial recording before you go—this is a good way of double-checking that you have everything you need and that it is all in good working order.

The edit suite

In addition to the live-to-air studio and location sites, the third place where radio program makers create sound is in the production studio, or edit suite. This ranges in splendour from the elaborate multi-channelled **mixing console** to the more modest live-to-air studio itself (when it is not being used for broadcasting), down to the even more minimalist computer workstation. However complex the facilities, this is the arena where sound is processed—edited and mixed into creative packages for broadcast at some later time.

Edit suite components

The edit suite generally comprises the following facilities.

The mixing console

This is a more elaborate console than the live-to-air console, having more channels and thus the capacity to juggle more inputs. You can work on individual sound tracks separately before mixing them together in a final recording. You can play with the sound, using the pan pots to adjust the balance of left and right stereo channels, or the **EQ (equaliser)** controls to adjust the ratio of low, medium, and high frequencies.

The inputs

Surrounding the mixing desk will be the equipment from which you will download your sound: CD players, cassette players, minidisc players, computers, and microphones. You will also be able to transfer your finished packages as output back onto recording devices (cassette, minidisc, etc.).

Microphone

The console has its own microphone, but can also record sound from microphones in remote studios. Voice links will often be recorded from separate voice-booths located adjacent to the production studio but with a soundproof glass window that allows eye contact between producer and talent. A separate channel on the desk allows for audio contact between the two areas.

Computer workstation

Although it is hard to beat the mixing console for high-quality complex productions, there are digital editing systems available on computer that duplicate many of its functions. Programs such as Adobe Audition, Pro Tools, and Sound Forge give you the capacity to edit and multi-track at a single workstation. Further, they give you access to sophisticated sound processing devices (EQ, echo, reverb and **sound effects**) that previously were the exclusive province of the experienced audio engineer.

Operational skills

As with live broadcasting and location recording, the aim in this production area is to make the technology invisible. You are bringing together sound from a variety of sources:

- location recordings
- music
- sound effects (FX)
- studio recordings (narrative scripts, etc.)

and you are knitting this sound into what you hope will be a seamless coherent whole. This requires meeting the following standards:

- the sound will be of a uniform high quality
- levels will be consistent throughout
- edit points will be inaudible
- edit points will be undetectable in terms of their impact on the coherent flow of the piece
- fades will be well-positioned and of an appropriate duration.

Stereo

The mixing desk gives you the further capacity of manipulating your sound around what is in effect a sound stage. This is where stereo recording comes into its own. As noted above, stereo recording allows you to record sound on two channels, increasing the capacity for your created sound to have the multi-dimensionality of the 'real thing'. When we listen, our left and right ears pick up sound from all around our head. With stereo a similar effect is gained through left and right speakers. The pan pots on the mixing desk allow you to manipulate the channels independently, 'moving' the sound to the left or to the right.

When the pan pots are centred, the sound appears to come from in front of you. If you pan the left channel far to the left and the right channel far to the right, you will get the pingpong effect of sound moving across the room, or people talking across a space. Add this to the near/far effect you get by the position of the voice relative to the microphone and you can appreciate the power that comes from being able to access what is in effect a three-dimensional sound space. The challenge for you as a sound producer is to harness this power to bring your recordings alive.

Edit suite checklist

This sort of sound production requires a lot of pre-preparation, and planning is dealt with in more detail later in the chapters on the radio story, and ads and promos. Suffice it to say that by the time you reach the stage of your final mixdown you will need to have ready:

- pre-recorded interviews, logged, edited, timed, and organised into the order in which they will feature in the piece
- intros and links, scripted, recorded, edited and timed, and slotted into their allocated place in the final piece
- selected sound effects and music.

CD TRACK 6: Sound recordist Ron Sims talks about the nature of sound and the techniques he has used to build sound pictures in his productions.

Exercises

1   This exercise will help you learn to listen. Sit in a crowded and noisy room with your eyes closed. Identify and listen to individual sound sources in the room (two people having a conversation on the right, music playing on a stereo on your left etc.). Move around the room in this fashion, foregrounding certain sounds while ignoring others. Your ears and brain are able to separate out individual sounds whereas a microphone is unable to discriminate in this way—it just records and mixes all the sound sources together. What would you need to do if you wanted to record the individual sounds?

---

2   For this exercise you will need portable recording equipment (cassette or minidisc) and a microphone.
- Record yourself in a room environment and listen back, experimenting with different mike positions to test the impact on sound quality. Which mike position delivers the best result? Why?
- Record yourself in different locations (a tiled bathroom, an outside garden, a noisy café). Using the troubleshooting list in this chapter, identify how the location has affected the sound quality. What do you have to do in each case to ensure that your voice remains clear and distinct?

Further reading

Ahern, S. & Pascoe, R. 2000, 'The Studio', in Ahern, S. (ed.) *Making Radio: A Practical Guide to Working in Radio*, Allen & Unwin, Sydney, pp. 23–69.

Alten, S.R. 2005, *Audio in Media*, 7th edn, Wadsworth, Belmont CA.

McLeish, R. 2005, 'The radio studio', in *Radio Production*, 5th edn, Focal Press, Oxford, pp. 18–38.

McNab, P. & Best, K. 2000, 'Audio Production', in Ahern, S. (ed.), *Making Radio: A Practical Guide to Working in Radio*, Allen & Unwin, Sydney, pp. 139–45.

Starkey, G. 2004, *Radio in Context*, Palgrave MacMillan, Basingstoke, pp. 6–22

PART III

Radio Production Formats

Bill Bunbury, feature producer, ABC Radio National

Bill started his career as a high school teacher. He joined the ABC in the late 1960s to work as a producer in radio for education programs. He transferred to television and worked as an education producer for 3 years, before returning to radio where he has been working ever since as a documentary maker in Radio National's Social History Unit.

Bill gets into work at 7 am and spends the first part of the day reading emails to keep abreast of any departmental requests, and reading newspapers where he is always on the lookout for potential story ideas. The rest of his day is devoted to research on stories he is doing or is planning to do, arranging or recording interviews, and editing any work in progress.

Bill Bunbury, feature producer, ABC Radio National.

The job

Bill says: 'When I was doing television I became aware of the enormous strength in the community of oral history. So I went down and started to record these stories and made them into radio features. The radio gave me a chance to really find out what the audience wanted and I began to take a great interest in the design and the craft of these stories and how they should be told, composite stories, groups of people sharing a story with you, and I got fascinated by the documentary craft—it seemed so rewarding a field to work in.

'I've always seen my work as a kind of evolution, a kind of journey. I think 15 years ago when I was first doing this I was doing what I would call the standard social histories of people who had interesting experiences. Now I think that I am looking at the underlying issues behind those—I think 10 or 15 years ago I didn't understand how important those issues were, I might have interviewed people without understanding the context. Now I'm alive to the fact that those stories are important structurally to an understanding of society, so I guess I am evolving all the time.'

The skills

'You need to be a good listener—to listen to stories, to try and capture what it is that people want to tell you, and ask questions that really show that that person is the most important person in the world to you at the time. Listening intently is the most important thing because you can miss so many cues if you've got this list of questions somewhere that you've got to refer to all the time. You have to submerge yourself in the other person's identity, I think.

'You can ring people up on the telephone and get a feeling of how they respond, and then sometimes that can be disappointing because they can actually prove to have less to say than they thought. On the other hand, sometimes people say "Oh, I don't think I've got very much to add", or "I don't know very much about it", yet often prove to be surprisingly good.

'You have to have a certain element of risk in there—but generally I think you get a sense of the liveliness of tone, the urgency with which people respond to things, the sense of "Oh yes, I'd love to talk about that" or a sense of distancing— "Well, I wasn't really a witness". It's a matter often of just suck it and see.'

Making a feature

'What I am trying to do as I make a documentary is to get that sense of taking the person into an experience as closely as possible. Without the distractions of the visual image, that person can actually, I think, enjoy that story more intimately because they can bring their imagination to it. That's the great beauty of radio. You can imagine the scene the way you want to, clothe it with the images that you want to see, and that frees you. It's why I love working in radio.

'I have this image of a guy driving a truck down the Stuart Highway somewhere in Central Australia with a load of plumbing pipes on the back; he's switching radio stations to find something to listen to—I want him to enjoy what I am doing. Or it could be someone at home washing the dishes—how can you catch them? Are they going to stay with you? That sense of always imagining someone needing to be caught, to be held, and wanting to listen to more.

'There's a sense in which radio is a sound film, an unfolding sequence of ideas, and I've always tried to go for that and used the minimalist narration style. I'm not reluctant to be on the air, but I think if people are telling a story perfectly well themselves my job is to let that story tell itself as naturally as possible.

'You really don't try to make judgments as much as try to seek the truth and see what lies there, and the truth is very rarely simple—it's complex—and the program should reflect that complexity.

'I think you're into that area where you want to translate a total experience, and language with music and with sound is so important. Music is another language and it has to be handled very carefully, I think, for that reason. Natural sound in a documentary—well, I can't think of making a documentary without it. If I go to a place, I collect the sound: I will open station gates, I will sit for several minutes just recording the birdsong in a place, I will go and collect cattle mustering, I will record people outside as much as possible in their own environment.

'When I listen to my material I might log it and my judgment tends to be based on my first hearing because I think that's the only hearing the listener's going to get. Is this story really intriguing? Did that strike you first up as really good? And so I tend to react as much as possible in selecting material like the listener—"Oh I really enjoyed that", or "I was drifting here; was I really concentrating?"—so there's a sense in which you always have to see it from the listener's point of view.'

The news should give people the facts and the background and the current affairs should give them that, but also bring it to life for them so that they can understand, especially places that people have got no reference point for. They have never lived like people have lived in a refugee camp or a starvation area or whatever so take them there, almost like you're writing television without the pictures – you want them to breed the pictures in their mind so that they are with you, and that can be really powerful. You can really have a big impact on people if you get it right.

> Sally Sara, foreign correspondent, ABC News and Current Affairs

Some of what I do is journalism in that you are telling a story, but what I'm after are production values. I'm interested in how the story will actually sound because I'm not doing it in a current affairs way where the important thing is the content. I'm doing it in what I call an affective way. If you make this distinction between cognitive and affective you certainly need to know the facts, but you need to hear them in a way that moves you.

> Bill Bunbury, feature producer, ABC Radio National

In radio, sound is the image. Radio features and drama really are acoustic films—that's what they are.

> Ron Sims, sound recordist

What makes the radio story different from a television or newspaper story? The same thing that distinguishes radio from other media: sound. In this chapter we look at what it takes to transform a story idea into a sound experience. Whether you are creating a 3-minute current affairs report, a long-form documentary, or a specialist feature, you are engaged in a process of hunting and gathering: hunting for the story idea and then gathering together the elements that you will then be assembling into the final product.

Story planning

Selecting your story

Where do we find our radio stories? Anywhere and everywhere (resources for journalists are discussed below, p. 163). As important as the subject itself is the way it is treated—even the most mundane topic can be transformed into a riveting radio piece with the right ingredients. As with any sort of journalism, the more widely you extend your net, through your own exposure to the world at large, the greater your access will be to potential sources for stories. Newspapers, magazines, the Web, other electronic media—all give you a window on the world and the wide variety of people and events that might trigger a story idea. Also, never underestimate the importance of your own personal networks, especially beyond your work sphere. This keeps you in touch with real life outside the media hothouse and can provide ongoing refreshment of your 'story idea' pool.

What makes a good radio story? You need to consider the same elements as for any other part of the radio program:

- Is it interesting? Reporters need to develop a gut feeling for whether stories will work or not. If you find a story interesting, that enthusiasm will help you to draw your audience in. If you find a story boring, then why inflict it on anyone else? A defining characteristic of a good reporter is curiosity—you will be the sort of person who finds the world an intriguing place. Part of your success as a reporter lies in your capacity to convey that sense of intrigue to your audience.
- Is it relevant to the audience? Different audiences require different things. A 20-year-old Triple J listener won't have the same interests, priorities, or world picture as a 35-year-old listener to Radio National or a 55+ listener to talkback radio. People listening at breakfast time will have different needs from those listening at night. When considering story ideas, you therefore have to take into account who will be listening, and when, in order to strike the right chord with your audience.
- Does it suit the program format? This affects not just the way you treat the story but also the style and length of the story. A morning current affairs program will require one sort of treatment, an afternoon light entertainment program another, while a specialist half-hour documentary program will call for yet a third sort of approach.

Selecting the angle

One of the really hard things about reporting is structuring your story, working out what your story is about and getting a focus, because five minutes isn't a huge amount of time and if you have got three voices in there you want to make sure the story has a real focus.

Steve Cannane, radio presenter, ABC Triple J

Having come up with a story idea, the next thing you have to think about is how you are going to develop it. Stories can be told in countless different ways and, just as with story selection, the story angle will be governed by interest value, relevance, and program format. Take the following real-life story as an example:

In December 2004, Adelaide residents were horrified when 18-year-old Nick Peterson was killed in a vicious shark attack at a popular suburban beach. He was being towed behind a boat on a surfboard when he was pulled under the water and torn apart by two white pointers. His three friends who managed to clamber to safety on the boat could only look on helplessly. The attack provoked immediate local debate over whether the shark should be chased and killed.

Now see how this story might be treated in three different programs: a current affairs morning magazine, an afternoon talkback program, and a specialist documentary program.

Current affairs morning magazine

This program deals with the key stories of the day and comprises live interviews with politicians and people in the news, as well as reporter packages, generally around 3 minutes long. The program is a fast-paced news digest aimed at the breakfast audience eager for a news fix as they head in to work. It is serious and authoritative, a must-hear for all news junkies. In this sort of format there is rarely room for extended development, and you will tend to find the story will be confined to the two main yes-and-no sides of any issue.

- Angle: update on the latest developments in the aftermath of the tragedy.
- Talent: reporter at the scene, spokesperson from the South Australian Sea Rescue Squadron.

Afternoon talkback program

This is an easy-listening blend of lifestyle and entertainment stories with lots of opportunity for listener involvement via talkback.

- Angle: to kill or not to kill: does the shark deserve to die?
- Talent: debate between representative of the state government, which is advocating that the shark be destroyed, and the South Australian Conservation Council, which opposes this action.
- Length: 5 minutes.

Specialist documentary program

This is a weekly half-hour program devoted to analysis of key issues of the day. Unlike the shorter news story dealt with above, this format allows you to go beyond the yes-and-no dimension, so you can include expert commentators and other players, allowing you to explore the issues involved.

- Angle: sharks and humans—can they co-exist? A look at shark behaviour and the uneasy relationship Australians have with these predators.
- Talent: social historian on the role sharks have played in the Australian myth of the beach; surf lifesaving representative on the dangers of the surf; CSIRO marine scientist on shark behaviour and how humans should deal with the danger they pose.
- Length: 28 minutes, 50 seconds.

You can see from this example that the selection of the angle is not an arbitrary process, but the careful calibration of a story idea to a specific program context. You as reporter don't have a lot of scope to be self-indulgent. Audience expectations and time constraints very much define the product you are required to produce. However, you are totally in control of how you bring your story together—how you treat it as narrative to exploit its dramatic potential; how you use sound to set up a location or to build a mood. This is the focus of the next phase of feature production.

Doing your research

As a reporter, you have to know your stuff. The better your research, the better your story. You need to go beyond the surface of an issue to fully appreciate its complexities and broader ramifications. Your role isn't to accept facts at face value, but to be alert enough to question them in order to get to the real story. This means that you have to read the relevant documents, check details, go out and speak to the people involved, and make sure that you get all sides of the story. Some of these contacts you will use just for background, but some will appear in your piece, and this is your opportunity to check them out as potential talent. It is also the time when you can go out on location to begin to get ideas for your story's soundscape.

Selecting your talent

What are you looking for when selecting talent for your story? Of course the potential interviewees have to know their subject, but, equally importantly, they have to be able to speak about it clearly and coherently. It also helps if they are interesting to listen to—entertaining rather than boring. Many illustrious experts have had to be bypassed as talent because they stammer or stutter, are too technical, or drone on and on. Through your backgrounding research interviews you can determine who will fit best into the plot of your story.

Avoid committing yourself to the talent too early. It can be awkward and embarrassing to have to back out of an interview commitment once you realise the talent won't work.

Selecting your sound

> The main thing with radio from Africa is a lot of the stories are quite confronting and depressing and you need to find some way to take the audience with you right from the beginning of the story and that can either be powerful writing or more

often than not it's sound. When people are busy in the morning when AM is on—they're taking kids to school or they are in the car or something—if there is some way that you can get sound that will grab them from the start and they will then stay with you for that story, that is my aim, just to keep them with me.

Sally Sara, foreign correspondent, ABC News and Current Affairs

It is sound that gives radio the power to create a theatre in our heads. So vigorous is our imagination that the pictures that sound conjures up in our mind's eye can have as great an impact as anything we see in the physical world. Planning the soundscape is therefore an important part of planning the radio story. What sorts of sounds will you use? Is there an interesting location with sounds that can build a mental image for the audience? Will sound effects—bird calls, the patter of rain, the gunning of a car engine—have a role to play? Will music be useful to set a mood, or can the lyrics of a song help to underscore a theme?

Making your plan

Gradually, as you consider these different elements, you can begin to map out the shape of your story package. This means that even before you set foot outside the studio, you will have a clear sense of how the story will develop, of what you will need to go where. Your fieldwork will not be a random fishing expedition, but a clear-headed exercise to collect quite specific material.

You will need to:

- Set out the storyline, ensuring it has a clear beginning–middle–end that takes greatest advantage of its dramatic potential.
- Work out what sounds and voices you will use and where.
- Decide what sort of scripts you will need to help the story along, remembering that these are a very powerful storytelling tool. What links will be done in the studio? Will any links need to be done on location?
- Work out how obtrusive you need to be as reporter—do you need to play an active role as interrogator, or a more removed one as narrator/commentator, or a bit of both?
- Set out a production schedule, since you will usually be working to a deadline. This means blocking out times for preparation, fieldwork, and studio production in line with the on-air date to ensure you do everything you need to do in the time that you have at your disposal. You may find the following template useful in setting out the plan for your feature story.

Story template

Working Title	Parental leave
Duration	28 minutes
Story	In the light of proposals to increase access to childcare, this documentary aims to highlight the strains on families in balancing work and family pressures.

Issues	Current situation in Australia. Declining birthrate, ageing workforce, need for greater workforce participation. Problems: childcare crisis, 2-year waiting lists, tax disincentives, need for two-parent income. Australia in international perspective: only OECD country without paid parental leave. Proposals for change by Equal Opportunity Commission.

Key questions

- What is the rate of access to childcare currently?
- What factors influence family decisions relating to working versus staying at home?
- How important is it to have a parent at home?
- Long-term benefits of home-based parent versus contribution via working
- Parents' attitudes to childcare—differences between men and women?
- Long-term impact of childcare on children—positive or negative?
- Workplace attitudes towards working mothers versus working fathers
- Family-friendly workplaces.

Interview talent

- Academic expert
- Dads at home
- Mums at home
- Children—range of ages
- Advocacy group
- Union representative
- Employer representative
- Government spokesperson.

Data sources

- ABS or other statistics on numbers of working men; working women; children in childcare; numbers of childcare centres, etc.
- Government reports
- Academic research reports
- Family Assistance Office (administer family allowances)
- Newspaper articles, journals, Web searches.

Sound

- Children playing
- Children singing
- Family environment—making dinner, watching TV
- Childcare environment
- Workplace environment
- The Wiggles theme or other children's TV theme.

Source: Adapted from McLeish, R. 2005, *Radio Production*, 5th edn, Focal Press, Oxford, pp. 266–7

Collecting story material

If you're in some particular place, give them some sound that will make people come with you because, going right back to the old days of having drama and plays on radio, people's minds just open up if you give them some sound—they will create the pictures in their heads. So that might even be, if you are in a place with a lot of echoes, some footsteps and some people talking. Or if you are doing a story where there is an airdrop of food into a starvation area, take the right cables with you so that you can plug into the headphones on the plane and you can hear the pilots talking as they are getting ready to make the airdrop. All those sorts of things—just be prepared and be thinking sideways all the time as to what the opportunities will be. It's not just a case of having drums or music or something like that. Get whatever kind of sound you can get, and let it breathe, and nine times out of ten you've got people—they'll come with you then and they will be prepared to listen to your story.

> Sally Sara, foreign correspondent, ABC News and Current Affairs

Ask questions that really show that that person is the most important person in the world to you at the time.

> Bill Bunbury, feature producer, ABC Radio National

This is the interesting thing with the radio feature—it happens at a pace which is not your pace. It happens at the pace of the story, so it's not like actors where you can actually rehearse them and get them right and put them in front of a microphone.

> Ron Sims, sound recordist

Having prepared your plan, you are ready to go into the field to begin the second stage of feature-reporting—gathering the material.

Doing the interview

You soon learn not to record too much stuff! You can come back with an hour's worth of stuff and you have got to put it into 5 minutes—what a nightmare!

> Steve Cannane, radio presenter, ABC Triple J

Anastasia Michael interviews Tanya Strahan on location for her feature story.

The best interviews bring together a well-informed interviewer with a well-briefed interviewee in an interesting, focused, and entertaining exchange.

Being a well-informed interviewer means that you know enough about the subject to know what questions need asking. Remember the rules for interviewing outlined in chapter 6. It helps to prepare an outline of the planned interview with the questions written out. This gives you the opportunity of running through things in your mind and bringing together the words you may need. Good interviewers may never refer to their question list during the interview—in fact reading from a piece of paper can make the interview sound stilted and unnatural. However, it can act as a safety net if you get lost along the way, providing a reminder of a fact or a name, or an angle you meant to pursue. All this helps to make sure that you sound confident and fluent—essential if your voice is to appear in the final result.

It is often tempting for reporters to resort to re-recording questions afterwards if they feel they haven't expressed themselves well. This is to be avoided for two reasons. First, you may unwittingly distort the result, subtly changing the emphasis of the original question and therefore misrepresenting your interviewee. Second, you may destroy the sound quality—unless you re-record in exactly the same location, the disparity in background sound as you jump from one location to the other will be painfully evident.

Just as you need to prepare yourself, it is equally important for you to prepare your interviewees. This means ensuring that they are briefed about the purpose of the interview, the role they are playing in the development of the story, and the amount of time you expect to take. You don't want to go so far as a full-on rehearsal, which could spoil the spontaneity of the final result, but this sort of preparation will help you to get the information you need in the form that you need it, and in the least amount of recording time.

Collecting location sound ('actuality')

Part of the interview preparation involves deciding where the interview will be held. Should it be done in the studio? On location? In an indoor or outdoor setting? This depends on how relevant the location is to the topic. For example, if you are doing an interview with a sports doctor on sporting injuries in professional basketball, it would make sense to take us to a basketball court during a practice session and have the doctor speak against a background of the sound of players in action. At the same time, the location visit would be a useful foraging exercise for other sorts of location sound, or 'actuality', which could be used—in the changing rooms, in the showers, grabs of the players talking among themselves on and off court. Your story could then evolve against the sound backdrop of a real live game, which would give it far greater impact than it would have if confined to a more neutral office or studio environment.

Bear in mind that location sound can also be distracting. In the case of the basketball story, while the initial introduction of the talent might take place on location to set the scene, you might then shift to a quieter room for the bulk of the interview if you needed the listener to focus on what was being said.

Location sound recording is dealt with in more detail in chapter 7.

Selecting music and sound effects

Music can play a variety of roles in the radio feature:

- It can be used as an introduction to the piece, immediately conveying a mood or setting up a theme.
- It can be used as a break within the piece to provide a resting place or, conversely, to regain the listener's attention.
- It can be brought in periodically to reinforce a mood.
- The words of a song can be used to underscore a theme, providing a lyrical subtext to the feature topic, which can be serious or comic, emotional or ironic.

It is important to ensure that music contributes to, rather than detracts from, your story. If the music you have chosen doesn't connect to the story, help tell the story, or take the story forward, it is better to leave it out. Also if you do use music, bear in mind the rules governing the use of copyright material (see chapter 16). Most radio stations have blanket agreements with the agencies regulating copyright such as the Australian Performing Rights Association and the Australian Record Industry Association. These agreements are likely to cover most of the music or professionally recorded sound effects you may want to access. While this means that you won't necessarily need to write to individual music companies for permission to use their material, you will still have to include all album, track, and composer details on the link script you provide to the station.

Sound effects (FX) also serve several functions:

- They can help to build a sound picture. The call of the magpie will immediately conjure up the wide open spaces of the Australian bush.
- They can be used as an audio code. The sound of coins going into a cash register will prepare us for a story about the retail trade.
- They can provide a humorous commentary. The energetic crowing of a cockerel can give a finishing mocking touch to a feature on people who have trouble getting up in the morning.

Radio isn't all sound. Sometimes the absence of sound can have the greatest impact—the few beats of silence at the end of a highly-charged interview with a parent talking about losing a child to cot death; the pauses and hesitations as a Holocaust victim tries to find words to express the horror of life inside the death camps; the vacuum of silence that gradually fills with the rising song of the dawn chorus as we are led into the depths of a rainforest. These soundless periods can be used for punctuation and emphasis and are as powerful as any sound in conveying atmosphere and mood.

Assembling the story

The radio feature in its true sense is not planned. You simply go out there with your tape recorder—if you want to call that your camera—and you capture what is going on. You capture the reality of the scene, be it a riot or whatever, and then later on in the studio you sit down with this bulk of material and try and make out of it your final piece with editing and juxtaposing things.

Ron Sims, sound recordist

You've always got one deadline—which is whatever time it has got to be on air—but you have got to give yourself some mini-deadlines, like 'I need to get this part of the story done by a certain time, then I need to record all my interviews in this period of time, I need to get into the editing suite by this time, I need to finish the story so I can write my intro by this moment', so you have got to get out your mini deadlines. When you first start a job you don't know that stuff—it just takes experience. You've got to ask people to learn from their experience.

Steve Cannane, radio presenter, ABC Triple J

After you have gathered all your material—the interviews, the location sound, the draft scripts, the music, and the sound effects—the challenge that remains is to bring it all together. Just as preparation was vital throughout the gathering process, so the more thoroughly you organise yourself now, the better the outcome will be. The process is identical for any produced material, from the shortest promo to the longest documentary, and consists of the following steps.

Assemble your material

The edit suite is your workbench. Just like any carpenter or painter, you should have to hand all the tools you need to put your feature together. In the past, access to a studio and mixing desk was vital. Now all you need is a computer with a multi-track digital editing program connected to the various sources from which you will download the raw material—the CD player for music; the recording device you have used for the sound you have recorded. If you follow your story plan and gather all the ingredients together you will minimise the number of last-minute emergencies to fill unforeseen gaps.

Log your material

Having spent all this time gathering your ingredients, you now need to go through it all reminding yourself about what is there, and isolating the bits you are actually going to use. **Logging** involves making notes about what happens where, noting useful **in-** and **out-cues** and the times when they occur in the recording. This can save heaps of time by making it possible for you to go straight to a particular grab without having to listen to the whole piece over and over again. Below is an example of a log, prepared by Radio National's Bill Bunbury, for an ABC Radio National documentary on Federation.

Extract of log from Bill Bunbury's 'Federation' documentary

WA supported idea of Federal Council in first place—kept us in the pic. In the 1880s—also promise of trans-continental railway

Kept us interested.
Ends @ 1'09

Q. NSW and WA both pivotal in this debate—NSW felt itself top dog—and WA felt it could be left out?
Yes—WA further from Sydney than Auckland and WA unaffected by depression of 1890s and booming with gold so why come into union of depressed SE Australian colonies.

Q. Agriculture affected?
Yes—as it happened agriculture did all right in 20th century but worry in 1890s—WA would be flooded with imports from East. Quotes Winthrop Hackett Editor of West Australian—apart from Premier Forrest 'Feeling (against Fed) amounting almost to frenzy'.
Ends @ 2'53

Q. So how does WA come into Federation?
Classic explanation is that t'othersiders swayed the issue (more of them than rest of WA population) that's true in one sense—but not whole story—miners mainly from working class and Victoria and also NSW and Qld Labor movement worried by Fed.—thought bosses would combine more effectively and also Labor people in those states didn't like idea that a Tasmanian or a WA vote in the senate was worth as much as a Victorian's. Fed. described as a racket and yet in WA Labor went other way on the whole.

Q. Smaller states suspected of being Conservative enclaves—and not the case?
Far from it—Labor senators in 1901 came from Qld, SA and WA. Same as who had given the women the vote first, SA followed by WA. A complete misconception of how things were.
Ends @ 4'51

...

Q. Social aspects of Fed? Feeling of awakening of new nation in 1901?
Suspects other way round—we became a people before we became a nation—technology had changed—people wanted to move round their country as one people—rail had helped here not feel restricted. Fed. posed practical problems. Feeling varied from place to place—Vic. enthusiastic, WA voted yes but more soberly, matter of fact.

Ends @ 10'24

Q. In Perth—celebration?
In Perth—people crowded into streets—but emphasis on British Empire—loyalty etc.

Q. Peculiar to WA—this Britishness?
Quite common all through Australia—but most marked in WA—but Advance Australia etc. in Sydney.

Q. Separateness notion in WA
Yes—always been a lot of British-born in WA—hanging on to Mother England is a way of not getting too involved in Federation.

Q. Queen dies within 3 weeks—cast a damper on the celebrations?
Just long enough that they'd taken down the bunting—but gloom was universal—gets into comparison with QE II when she goes.

Q. Role of media?
Many more newspapers 100 years ago—in a large country town you would have 2—often on opposite side—in Perth there were 2 dailies and an evening—orig. all opposed to Fed. West Australian swung round—Sunday Times—thought not democratic enough but came round later. Goldfields press unanimous for Fed.—but threat there of separate independent state of goldfields—thought to have pushed many West Australians into agreeing to Federation—didn't want to lose the gold. The goldfields would have taken in the NW as well—huge area. So did Albany people in SW who were cross at losing their pre-eminence as a port to Fremantle so threat of small states clinging to rest of Australia. My bet is that had that happened—rest of WA would have come into Fed. about 1942—saw economic disadvantages of Fed. in Depression but defence threat from Japan would have brought them back.

Ends @ 16'08

SUMMARY
I suggest we go from **1'09-4'51** to cover WA entry and skip to **12'28**—to cover separate—**Ends 16'08**—perhaps add point @10'24 about the Britishness of WA if we have room. That will give us the WA report. The rest is or probably will be covered by other state reports. My suggestions. Bill

Source: Bill Bunbury, ABC

Do a rough edit

As the term suggests, this is your initial edit of the recorded interview material, when you extract the portions of sound ('sound grabs' or **'grabs'**) you will be using in the final product. Here is where careful planning pays dividends: trying to get a 3-minute grab from a 40-minute interview is much harder than getting the same grab from a 10-minute one. This is also where you feel the benefits of the log—this will have helped you identify the grabs. At this stage you are now concerned with placing the grabs in the order in which they need to be for your story.

Do the fine edit

Having isolated and organised your grabs, you now tidy them up. Remember the art of good radio, whether live or pre-recorded, is to keep the technology out of earshot. This is when you check that the edited sequence retains the sense of the original and that the in-points and out-points are clean and free of any clicks and bumps that betray an awkward edit point. You monitor the flow of speech to make sure it keeps to the pace and rhythm of natural conversation—checking for words clipped off too soon, or pauses going on for too long as a result of the editing process.

Finalise the script

Though you will have been working from a rough script prepared at the planning stage, now is the time when you refine it so that it fits in with the material you have collected. You will check that it guides the audience efficiently through the storyline, giving the right amount of information about where we are, who is talking, and how this fits in to the whole to prevent us getting lost along the way. Your links should lead smoothly into each grab, and pick up just as smoothly out of it so the joins are seamless. Record it and add it to your edited package. Below is an example of a script, in this case one prepared by Bill Bunbury for his Radio National documentary series 'It's not the money—it's the land'.

Feature script: Hindsight 2000/49

```
RRECORD    624      NOV. 6
REPLAY     SUNDAY   DEC. 3    1405
REPEAT     THURS    DEC 7     1105
           FRIDAY   DEC 8     0200
```

IT'S NOT THE MONEY
IT'S THE LAND

THE EQUAL WAGES STORY PART (1)
'AND IN THIS LAND WE PAY THE PRICE'

* *

FX Cattleyard background. Fade under

BILL
Hullo, I'm Bill Bunbury and welcome to Hindsight.
    Today the first of three programs about the effects of an historic legal decision handed down from the bench in 1966, nearly 35 years ago—the decision to grant

Equal Wages to Aboriginal pastoral workers on the cattle stations of Northern Australia.

CUT 1   STOCKMEN MEMORIES
Begins   We grew up in station ...
Ends ... we never even get nothing back.
DUR 00'41

CUT 2   MURRAY—30 YEARS ON
Begins   Well I think the tragedy was ...
Ends ... hands, 30 years down the track.
DUR 00'28

BILL
Former stockman Jacky Dan and pastoralist Peter Murray.

So what was the tragedy thirty years down the track? And was it all a disaster? These are questions I've been trying to ask as I've put together this three-part Hindsight special on the Equal Wage decision of 1966. What I found was that the answers aren't simple and that the questions remain. (And I should warn indigenous listeners that from time to time in this series they may hear the voices of deceased persons.)

When the Equal Wages case, initiated by the NAWU, the Northern Australian Workers Union, on behalf of indigenous workers was heard by the Commonwealth Conciliation and Arbitration Commission, it seemed that only two parties were present—the pastoralists who put up a strong case against the granting of Equal Wages and the NAWU who argued on the other hand that Equal Wages were a matter of social and economic justice.

Aboriginal workers were certainly not in court and not directly cited in evidence by either party.

Ever since white pastoralists had established their runs back in the 1880s in both the Kimberley and the Northern Territory, pay for Aboriginal pastoral workers had been patchy and unregulated.

In Queensland stockmen and drovers were paid almost a full wage and in the Pilbara where Aboriginal workers had struck back in 1946 some pay also existed but in the Northern Territory and in the Kimberley region of North Western Australia, pay was mostly in kind—tea, sugar, flour, blankets and clothes as needed. The upside was that the pastoralist kept the entire community—workers, older people and children—all in rations and looked after their medical needs. It was a way of life—as we'll hear shortly—that had gone on for almost a century.

When the case came up in 1965, lawyer Hal Wootten was junior counsel to John Kerr as advocate for the pastoralists in their case against the Union. But as the case went on he became concerned about the outcome.

CUT 3   HAL WOOTTEN—PERSONAL CONCERN
Begins   My deepest personal feeling ...
Ends   ... and they should have a choice.
DUR   00'29

> **BILL**
>
> Hal Wootten—and we'll come back to the 1965 Equal Wages case later. But it's worth asking how things got this way—why Aboriginal people weren't paid properly for their work and how they became involved with the pastoral industry in the first place.
>
> Historian Geoffrey Bolton believes that in the Kimberley they took up pastoralism themselves almost as soon as the first white cattlemen arrived.
>
> **CUT 4**   BOLTON—ABORIGINAL RUSTLERS
> Begins   The Aborigines in the North ...
> Ends   ... That they hasn't built.
> **DUR 00'37**
>
> **FX CATTLE BELLOWING**
>
> Source: Bill Bunbury, ABC

Mix music and sound effects

The music and sound effects are the last pieces of the puzzle, the finishing touches that polish the feature off, adding colour and flavour to the mix. Here you are literally fine-tuning, monitoring the music to make sure that:

- The grab is the right length. Too short and the listener won't have time to register it; too long and the listener will lose the thread of the story.
- The grab is in the right place. This means developing a feel for when the listener needs a breathing space, or when the story calls for the sort of dramatic reinforcement music can give. When you are using lyrics, there is the extra complication of ensuring the slice of lyric you choose serves its purpose of reinforcing a particular point or theme.
- The sound effects are in the right place. FX require particularly subtle treatment. Compare these two examples:
  (a) "It was a dark and stormy night (FX thunderclap)'
  (b) FX thunderclap, fade-out under: 'It was a dark and stormy night.'
  The first example is leaden and predictable, the script simply introducing the effects. In the second example, the sound is allowed to make its impact on the listener, unleashing the imagination in a wealth of associations before the script leads the already-primed listener further into the story. FX should be selected and placed to maximise their dramatic potential.
- The grab is edited 'to the beat'. All sound including speech has a rhythm—sometimes it is as subtle as the beating of our heart. When integrating music you need to be alert to this rhythm to make sure the music beat picks up where the speech leaves off and vice versa. This adds to the seamless feel of the piece.
- The fades are well judged. Too abrupt a fade-in or fade-out will jar; too extended a fade will slow the pace down.

CD TRACKS 7 and 8: These two tracks illustrate different aspects of radio story production.

TRACK 7: In this track Radio National's Bill Bunbury talks about his approach to feature production using illustrations from his work. He focuses particularly on his interaction with his talent and the techniques he has used to get them to tell their stories with maximum effect.

TRACK 8: This track from the ABC's *The World Today* program is an example of a current affairs story. Sally Sara provides an eye witness account of an encounter with one of the rebel armies fighting the government forces in the brutal war in Southern Dafur. She makes use of sounds directly from the location and the power of her own descriptive language to set the scene for us as the rebels prepare for their next attack. The track begins with presenter David Hardaker introducing the story.

Journalistic challenges in radio story production

Feature production is a format where you have more time to get things right. In contrast to live radio where, as we shall see later, you fly by the seat of your pants, in feature reporting you are working to more extended deadlines. Even with the luxury of more time to reflect, the legal and ethical challenges facing all journalists confront you here as well. These are dealt with in detail later (see chapters 16 and 17), but it is worth looking at the sorts of situations you could encounter as a reporter to see how you might deal with them.

Legal dilemmas

Defamation, bad language, contempt

Example: You are doing a story on a controversial local development that is being built on a nature reserve. While you are recording an interview with a conservationist, she accuses the local Member of Parliament of taking kickbacks from the successful contractor.

This comment is damaging to the reputation of the Member of Parliament and could result in your being sued for defamation if it went to air.

Unless you have strong evidence that would allow you to successfully defend this statement in court, it would be most unwise to leave it in. What can you do? You have two options:

- Because this is a pre-recorded interview, you can interrupt the talent to caution her that she cannot make such a statement on air and take a different tack in your questioning.

- You will have plenty of time to have the station lawyer check the interview to assess the risk of the allegations going to air. If you are advised not to include them you can excise them during the editing stage.

The same procedures can be applied to bad language and potential contempt. When in doubt, seek advice and remove the offending material if necessary.

Copyright

Example: You would like to use the theme from the ABC series *SeaChange* for a story you are doing on the mid-life crisis.

You are likely to want to use material from other sources to spice up your feature. This could be music, audio clips from radio, the Web or film sources, and sound effects.

You will have to check what is covered by the blanket agreements your station has with copyright agencies. For everything else, you will need to get written permission from the copyright holders beforehand.

Ethical dilemmas

You have editing dilemmas where you have to edit something for time but you don't want to take out of context what the person said and change what they've said. That's a really important thing—you should never do that, because in fact you *can*—the technology is there to manipulate what somebody has said—but you just don't do it because it is just not right. You wouldn't want that to be done to yourself.

Steve Cannane, radio presenter, ABC Triple J

In feature reporting, you can't go wrong if you try to live by the four key principles of ethical journalism as defined in the Journalist's Code: honesty, fairness, independence, and respect for the rights of others. Here's how they might apply to you in this context:

Honesty

Example: Local powerworkers have been on strike, leading to severe disruption to power supplies. You are preparing a feature on the background to the dispute and record an interview with the union leader. You keep the tape running after the interview and catch several indiscreet remarks he makes about the Energy Minister and the powerplant management. If you broadcast these remarks they will cause a sensation and give you a scoop.

A good reporter is an honest reporter who can be trusted to do the right thing by the story, and the right thing by the talent. You must avoid misrepresenting the facts, and you must avoid misrepresenting yourself. Since in this case the remarks were made after the talent believed the interview to be over, you acquired them via subterfuge and they are technically 'off the record'.

Let the union leader know that the offending comments have been recorded and ask permission to use them. You will have to take the risk that permission will be refused. Gaining a reputation as a sneaky player won't do your reputation as a journalist any good in the long run.

Fairness

Example: You are doing a story on poor conditions at a local school. The parents are up in arms and the head teacher is under the hammer. You record an interview with her to get her side of the story. Though you get good material, she loses her temper when you suggest she may have been negligent, and she terminates the interview and storms out of the room.

Pre-recorded formats give you a lot of power. At the editing stage you can play with the material in all kinds of ways, and with a little tampering it is easy to present black as white. In this example, technically it would be possible to give your feature more bite by editing the interview to highlight the bad behaviour at the expense of the more accurate but duller material in the rest of the interview. However, to do so would misrepresent the tenor of the whole exchange.

Always edit responsibly in order to convey the meaning of the story as you understand it. Resist any temptation to misrepresent or distort. The head teacher's anger should be seen in the context of the wider exchange rather than highlighted in isolation.

Independence

Example: A local travel agent offers you a free trip to Bali if you promise to do a feature on the resort he is pushing.

The line between journalism and advertorials is becoming increasingly blurred, and the growing popularity of lifestyle programs across the media only makes the situation worse. Your independence as a journalist rests on your capacity to report without fear or favour, and this includes having the freedom to decide what is, and is not, a story.

The only person who should be paying you for a story is your employer. Turn down all other offers. On those occasions where coverage is facilitated by 'freebies' (e.g. reviewing of films, theatrical productions, and computer games; travel writing; restaurant reviews) full disclosure is essential.

Respect for rights of others

Example: You want to do a story on Sudden Infant Death Syndrome and plan to include an interview with a bereaved parent. You are put in touch with one possible contact but she is reluctant to be interviewed.

In the race for a good story, real people often get trampled. With your eyes fixed on your journalistic goal, it is easy to see talent simply as the means to an end, to be used and then discarded with no consideration of the impact on them. It is important to treat people with respect, and this includes respecting their feelings, and respecting their right not to be involved.

Look for someone else. There are numerous ways to cover a story, and if one contact fails you should have the resilience and the resources to find another.

Exercises

Select and listen to a current affairs story from *AM*, *PM*, or *The World Today* on ABC. As you are listening, note down the different elements of the story:

- introduction
- interview grabs
- sound (location and FX)
- voice links by the reporter.

Think about the following:
1 How does this story start and does it grab your attention? Can you suggest a more attention-grabbing way of starting?
2 How visible is the reporter and what role does he or she play in telling the story?
3 If actuality or sound is used, what is it and what does it do?
4 If sound isn't used, what actuality could you use to give the story more life?
5 Every story can be told in different ways. Suggest an alternative story structure for getting the point across.
6 Does the style of script suit the tone of the story?

Further reading

Dancyger, K. 1991, 'Writing a Radio Documentary', in *Broadcast Writing: Dramas, Comedies, and Documentaries*, Focal Press, Boston, Stoneham, pp. 44–52.

Hesse, J. 1987, *The Radio Documentary Handbook: Creating, Producing, and Selling for Broadcast*, Self-Counsel Press, Vancouver.

McLeish, R. 2005, 'Documentary and Feature Programmes' in *Radio Production*, 5th edn, Focal Press, Oxford, pp. 264–75.

Starkey, G. 2004, *Radio in Context*, Palgrave MacMillan, Basingstoke.

Web sites

http://www.insideout.org
http://www.americanradioworks.publicradio.org
http://www.soundportraits.org

Radio Ads and Promos

9

Adam Sallur, promotions producer, 720 ABC Perth

Adam began his career in theatre and went from there to producing the *Evening program* on ABC Radio in Perth. He left the ABC and added to his existing expertise by producing corporate documentaries and working as a radio advertising copywriter. He then rejoined the ABC in his current role as promotions producer.

Adam Sallur, promotions producer, 720 ABC Perth.

Adam begins his day by sorting through the previous day's playlists removing outdated material. He then checks the emailed production schedules from the programs to see what promos they would like produced. He compiles a list, gets the studio ready for his production stint, and begins the creative work on some promo ideas. This will probably involve a trip to the music library in search of music or other sound grabs. The rest of the day is spent writing scripts, recording voices, editing the packages, and compiling the on-air schedules when the promos will be played.

The skills

Adam says: 'In many ways I didn't like it, having to sit down and write 15-minute corporate documentaries, but it was a discipline because I found that having to write, having to do research, to sit down, to go through things and pick out the information and then compress it into a script form, was tough. Often I'd spend two weeks doing a draft. All those experiences drew me to that point where I was able to say I feel confident about writing and producing promotions. When it came down to actually writing radio promotions I suddenly thought, hang on, I've only got 30 to 60 seconds, I can put all the effort into actually eradicating the words and using other elements such as the grabs from the programs. All the effort is going into the thought process as opposed to the writing, whereas in corporate it was more a case of slaving over the words.

'I guess my greatest thing is less is more. The greatest challenge is being able to convey the idea so you are getting the message across, but you are also trying to entwine it into something creative, but you've only got that 30 seconds generally to work in.'

The job

'I tend to take my instructions from my marketing manager or the program director or the programs themselves, and so we will look across the day at the programs we feel need that extra attention.

'Things come in all the time—things suddenly happen. If stories break, we can have something out and on air quickly if need be, especially with the digital system that we use now. Instead of having to record it in one place, **dub** it off in another, and deliver it to yet another place for replay, now it's all recorded once, it's in there, and anybody anywhere else in the building can access it. That saves a lot of time and allows you to be really proactive and really quick to get things on air.

'The real problem is getting a full day just in production, because there are so many other things that happen. If I could get four or five good promos out a day that would be really good.'

Making promos

'It's really a matter of spending a lot of time thinking about ideas and writing.

'You're trying to combat against the fact that people are listening to information all across the day and you've got 30 seconds to actually sell them something, or tell them about something, so therefore I try to make them interesting and dynamic. I think about whether that idea will make people stand up and listen, and then if I've got your attention, I think about how I am going to tell the information.

'First of all the idea will come from the writing. Say I am writing a situation where we are going to be at the zoo, so I'll want these sounds. How I assemble them depends on how the presenter is delivering the words, or what they are saying, and in what context they are saying it, and I will embellish those sound effects around that.

'I guess the FX are more where I feel as though you need to audibly indicate what that surrounding or that scenario is. Or sometimes I might want FX for things like transitions through the promo so they help link or sew it all together, so instead of just going from a voice-over to a scene, to another scene, say from a studio environment to an actuality environment, I actually put little sweeper things through that just to give it that smoothness.

'I use a lot of contemporary music, I use a lot of stuff that's more in the youth networks, but I am able to use that music because it just seems to fit a lot of the style of what I am doing. And so I'll go off to the record library and grab that bit of music and I start looking for the instrumental bits out of it and looking how I can use that. And sometimes I won't even use it that day but it will stay there so that when suddenly something else is happening I'll suddenly think about that piece of music.

'I try to put myself into the listener's point of view. People don't sit glued to the radio, they're doing things, clattering things, so things can be missed. It's all right if it's an FX that they miss, but if it's a vital piece of information you want to hope-fully make sure it just happens to hit at the right point so that they hear it.'

The radio format contains lots of bits and pieces—small pre-produced packages that serve a variety of functions. These include:

- **Stings**—these are short grabs, sometimes just a few seconds long, which are used to give the announcer a bit of breathing space, to fill an awkward gap, or to mark the transition from one program element to the next. Radio is supposed to be a seamless experience, its technology hidden within an unbroken flow of sound. The sting—whether music alone or music and voice—helps to knit the program together.
- Station/program **IDs**—since radio depends on sound alone, the listener needs some audio reminder from time to time of what the station or the program is. Short station or program identification packages repeating the station **call-sign** or the program or presenter name are used as part of the menu, in addition to any information the pre-senter may include live-to-air.
- **Ads and station promos**—ads and station promotional packages have a slightly longer format, averaging 30 seconds, but sometimes going for as long as a minute. Ads are announcements paid for by commercial clients to whom the station sells airtime. Station promos are the station's own promotional material plugging the station, forth-coming programs and promotional events.

Although these miniature packages are much shorter than a radio story, they are assem-bled in a very similar way: you need to start with an idea, do your research and prepara-tion, collect your material, record, edit, and do the final mix. Having seen in the preceding chapter how the radio story comes together, let's now see how these production tech-niques apply to radio ads and promos.

Selecting the story and angle

Whether you are working to a station client's brief or for the station itself, you need to start with a concept. Ads and promos are message bombs. They grab the listeners' atten-tion, detonate the message ('try this', 'listen to that'), and finish with a flourish, all in the space of 30 seconds. You have to decide:

- The message—in such a limited time-span, the message must be brief. You have to decide what aspect of the product or program you are going to highlight.
- The approach—for this, as for any radio product, the starting point has to be the **sta-tion format** and target audience. An ad for a music station with an 18–24 age demo-graphic will have to adopt quite a different approach from one aimed at the 55+ listenership of an adult contemporary station.

- The treatment—a message can be conveyed in a variety of ways. It can be delivered straight or through the use of humour. It can be a simple one-person read or a multi-person mini-drama. It can be voice only, or dressed up with music and sound effects.

Remember, you are working for a client—whether it is a station advertiser or the station itself, you are going to have to take their views into account in putting your concept together.

Selecting the sound

Once you have decided on your approach, you need to think about the ingredients—the sounds you are going to use in your production. These include:

- Voices—you have to consider who the players in this mini-production are going to be, and this depends on the image you want the voices to convey: lively and youthful? Mature and authoritative? Friendly and reassuring? Do you want male or female voices, or a mixture of both? Remember that voices can be altered technically. Echo, reverb, sound filters, and other sound production techniques can add extra creative dimensions.
- Music—music can be worth a thousand words in a format such as this where space is limited. It instantly sets a tone or conveys a mood, while song lyrics can reinforce a theme.
- Sound effects (FX)—radio creates pictures for the ear, and sound effects in a promo can instantly set up a scene or a mood.

Be careful not to overload your production. In ads and promos the message has to be attention-grabbing but simple—and this applies to sound, too. The focus has to be on the information, and anything else you use should add to it rather than distract the audience from it.

Remember the rules governing the use of copyright material (see above p. 97 and chapter 16). If you are working for a broadcasting organisation you may be covered by blanket agreements with the Australian Performing Rights Association and the Australian Record Industry Association. If this is not the case, you will need to seek permission from the music companies in order to use their material. You will also have to provide all album, track, and composer details to the broadcaster.

Writing the copy

Advertising or promo copy shares the characteristics of all radio writing:

- It is written for the voice—it must sound like natural speech.
- It is written for the ear—the content must be clear and concise, easy to digest in a single hearing.
- It is pared to the bare essentials. Keep away from long sentences, long words, and complex facts and figures.

- Stick to language that conjures up pictures and feelings—the appeal should be to the heart, not the head.
- It is well structured. It must grab the attention immediately with the first line, go on to develop the message, and then end with a bang rather than a whimper.

For me, it's always a case of I want the best quality out there each time. Sometimes you just have to sacrifice the concept a little bit about how you're going to execute it—I mean, you won't have all the bells and whistles because they'll take more fine-tuning, but you can still be clever.

It's really odd—I can produce a 30-second promotion in half an hour if I need to, or 15 minutes, but if you want to sit down and do a 7-second ID and you want to make it slick and polished, it takes a heck of a long time. And it's all about getting that right feel.

Adam Sallur, promotions producer, 720 ABC Perth

ABC PROMOTIONS (Perth)
HOPMAN CUP 2000
1 x 30 Radio Promo (National)

Client: ABCTV

Sydney D-Car7 0407

Pan to Voice

V/O:

(Light start – Rising synth pad)

December 31'st is a special day

Because it's the *last* day of the year –

(tempo rises) and the *first* day of the **Hopman Cup**

(smashing fx) — *Hollywood Fx Sampler*

(big fast & ballsy please!)

ABCTV brings *you* 40 Hours of the hottest tennis action!

The Thirteenth Hopman Cup - LIVE from the Burswood Dome in Perth/

The Crème of the tennis world - including World Number One Martina Hingis, and defending champions Amanda Coetzer (Kootsar) and Wayne Ferreira. (Fur-rera)

(fast cut tennis action)

Join Karen Tighe – Steve Robilliard and Glenn Mitchell And our panel of experts..

For the 13th Hopman Cup -

Live and Exclusive to ABCTV

Starts December 31st

Music: "Keep hope Alive" Crystal Method Sampler 8-93

An example of marked-up promo script.

Source: Adam Sallur, ABC Perth

Preparing your plan

Having developed your idea and drafted a script, you then need to put everything on paper in a production plan that contains the instructions for putting it all together. The script will be expanded to include details of which voice will be used and where. Details of the music and sound grabs will be incorporated, allowing you to find the exact grab when the time comes. These include:

- album
- track
- grab intro and outro
- duration.

You will also indicate location and duration of fade-in and fade-out spots to help you achieve a smooth and seamless result.

Recording your sound

With your plan in place, you can record the voices and any specific sounds you need for the package (although you can rely on FX library material, it is often better to make your own sound effects to ensure you get the exact effect that you want).

Whereas in an interview situation the interviewees are expected to be themselves, for ads and promos you require voices to act a particular role. This means that you are in the role of director and it is up to you to get your talent to deliver the performance you need. This requires that you:

- know exactly what you want
- explain it clearly to your talent
- give support and encouragement, especially if things go wrong
- remain calm and be patient
- try to make the recording session fun.

Rely on your ears, not your eyes—the listener won't be able to see the face behind the voice and you need to ensure that the voice says it all in terms of tone, inflexion, pace, and mood.

Assembling your material

At this stage you bring together all the pre-recorded elements, just the way a cook assembles all the ingredients before baking a cake. The better organised you are, the smoother the production process will be.

Michael Spooner, ABC Radio Sydney, working on a promo.

Do a rough edit

This is where you start working on the voice material, cutting it down to size and isolating just the grabs you will be using in the final mix. You can begin to get an idea of how close you are to the prescribed duration.

Do the fine edit

You refine your edit further at this stage, making sure edit points are clean (see p. 101).

Mix music and sound effects

Music and sound effects are always mixed in last as they knit the package together, and they also can be played around with to ensure the final version is exactly to time.

Once again, you are in the role of director, this time in terms of creating a sound stage using sound to create a three-dimensional space. The 'voice' exists not in a void, but in a dining room, or a shopping mall, or a doctor's surgery. It is through sound that the listener will 'see' the character in that setting. This means not only that the sound effects have to be realistic, but also that they have to be balanced in relation to the voice. If you use the sound of a car engine running, its loudness or softness will suggest to us whether the character is on the curb or by an open window looking out at the street. You can even use panning to 'move' sounds around this sound stage. The voice has to be your reference point—the soundscape has to revolve around that.

Technical enhancements

There are many ways you can play around with sound at this stage of the production. You can add reverberation or echo; you can duplicate the voice track to create another sort of echo effect; you can use equalisation (EQ) to smooth the sound out, or at the other end of the scale to create a telephone-voice effect. It is easy to get carried away at this stage, especially when so many tempting possibilities are afforded by digital technology. However, the same rule holds here as for the rest of promo production—simple is best.

CD TRACK 9: On this track ABC promotions producer Adam Sallur talks about the art of promo making and the techniques he uses in bringing music and speech together to make attention-grabbing packages.

Exercises

CD TRACK 10: contains an example of an ad from commercial radio station 2GB in Sydney. Note down the following :
1   Content—what is the message?
2   Style—is it formal? Conversational? Colloquial?
3   Approach—how is the message put across? Simple announcement? Storyline?
4   Use of sound—how does it make use of various sorts of effects?
5   Use of voice—what sort of voices are used and what is their pace, tone, volume?
6   Overall impact—what does the ad tell us about the type of station and audience profile?

Further reading

Aitchison, J. 2003, *Cutting Edge Radio. How To Create the World's Best Radio Ads for Brands in the 21st Century*, Prentice Hall, Singapore.

Best, K. 2000, 'Copywriting', in Ahern, S. (ed.), *Making Radio: A Practical Guide to Working in Radio*, Allen & Unwin, Sydney, pp. 132–8.

McLeish, R. 2005, 'Making Commercials', in *Radio Production*, 5th edn, Focal Press, Oxford, pp. 188–203.

McNab, P. & Best, K. 2000, 'Audio Production', in Ahern, S. (ed.), *Making Radio: A Practical Guide to Working in Radio*, Allen & Unwin, Sydney, pp. 139–45.

Starkey, G. 2004, 'Advertisements and Trails', in *Radio in Context*, Palgrave MacMillan, Basingstoke, pp. 143–64.

Live Radio

10

The thing about this ego-driven business is that when you are seen to have transgressed or said something that some section of the public or individuals don't like, they come looking for you. You can't hide behind being an anonymous newspaper journalist. Here I am, I'm Howard Sattler, I'm exposed three hours every day. I mean they've only got to get on the phone, they could tell the producers anything, 'I want to talk to him about the budget' and they come on and say 'I really want to talk to you about the ABA inquiry and you're a crook, and you took money', and all that sort of stuff, and I don't mind talking about the ABA inquiry, but the point is you are exposed, and that isn't a bad thing.

Howard Sattler, radio talkback presenter, 6PR Perth

When you first abandon yourself to being live to air with no notes and no scripts, it is really like walking down the street with no clothes on, but once you have done it, and you realise that you didn't fall over, it can be quite intoxicating. It took me many years to crack it, but I am now in a position where I think that if everything fell over in the studio and everything failed, leaving me like a shag on a rock, I could talk forever—it's a facility that I have learned.

Margaret Throsby, radio presenter, ABC Classic FM

When you are on air you feel really vulnerable and so every stumble and every dumb question you ask you think is really magnified, and they are really not that bad.

Steve Cannane, radio presenter, Triple J

Live radio is radio without a safety net. It is the most exhilarating production experience you can have, but it is also the most demanding because there is no margin for error. In the live studio, organisation is the key. Presenters and producers live by the clock, their every action determined by the movement of hour and minute hands around the dial, or the digital countdown on the studio consoles. Presenters need to have their brains in gear as they manage equipment, guests, and unexpected ad-libs with a fluency that belies the often frantic scenarios in the control rooms where damage control is a way of life.

In this chapter you will learn about the live radio program and also about the roles of the members of the production teams who make the programs happen.

The Summer Drive program team preparing to go to air on ABC 702 Sydney.

The live radio program

The ABC audience is very loyal, but the commercial audience is much tougher. They expect you to have strong opinions and you have to put yourself on the line. People have sensitive bullshit detectors and they can sense if you don't mean what you say.

Philip Clark, radio talkback presenter, 2GB Sydney

You can't be all things to all people. I've learnt that in radio. No radio station is going to have everybody—impossible—so you have got to go for your niche.

Howard Sattler, radio talkback presenter, 6PR Perth

Radio is really all about continuity and companionship. If there is any popularity, it is not all to do with doing something well—it is being reliably there because you become part of the scene of people's life and I think that is very comfortable for them.

Margaret Throsby, radio presenter, ABC Classic FM

I think the interaction with the audience is something that feeds the program, that drives the program.

Clark Forbes, Program Director, 3AW Melbourne

The radio audience

Without the audience, radio wouldn't exist. This may seem a truism, but it is worth stating because sometimes program-makers can forget about the audience in the excitement of putting programs together. Programs are not made in a vacuum, and we will talk about the broader context in which they exist shortly. However, the starting point has to be the audience—these are the people the program-maker wants and needs to pull in. Who are they?

People listen to radio for a variety of reasons. They want:

- up-to-the-minute news and information
- local traffic or weather information
- the companionship of a friendly voice
- access to the broad world of ideas
- to tune out and relax to the sound of their favourite music
- to have their say in a public forum.

Whoever they are—whatever their gender or age—they access radio, and the rainbow range of radio services aims to cater for their varied needs. This isn't done out of altruism. In Australia, with the exception of the public broadcasters (the ABC and SBS) and the network of community radio stations, most radio services are commercial in nature. This means that they rely on advertising revenue to finance their operations. In this sector, the content is the nectar to attract the bee—the vehicle for attracting specific audiences that can be on-sold to the advertisers.

A whole industry has been set up in an attempt to capture the size and identity of the diverse radio audiences. For many years a radio diary system has been used to record listening habits as well as other details such as age, occupation, and gender in an attempt to capture the demographic (or audience profile) for each radio service. More sophisticated monitoring systems are in the pipeline that will use people meter technology to track the public's listening patterns with even greater precision. Through this sort of monitoring we know that talk stations attract an older audience, while contemporary music stations appeal to the younger end of the market. Listeners tune in longer to music stations, while listeners to talk are more fickle. This contributes to the dominance of music stations in most Australian metropolitan radio markets: younger listeners tend to have a ravenous around-the-clock appetite for the latest sounds, while the older listeners to talk radio are more likely to have less listening time available because of work and family commitments. Melbourne is the exception, with the local market dominated by the commercial talk stations.

This method of audience measurement was set up to serve a specific purpose for commercial stations, but in fact is the prime measurement of success across the entire broadcasting sector. This puts the non-commercial sector at some disadvantage. For example, the ABC, operating as a non-commercial entity, is committed by its Charter to providing a wide variety of niche services (see chapter 1). Although these services taken as a group may, and do, garner up to a quarter of the available audience in any capital city, each service by itself may only attract a smaller audience share in comparison with its commercial competitors. As far as the ratings popularity poll is concerned, the ABC stations tend to lag behind the mass appeal music and commercial talkback stations in the capital cities.

Be this as it may, no matter what the radio service, knowledge of the target audience is a prerequisite for any program-maker. You need to know who your radio station is trying to attract and how far it is succeeding. The audience will determine your program content and approach, and the better you know them the more successful will be your strategies for attracting and holding them.

The radio station menu

Radio programs don't exist in isolation. They are part of an overall station menu that imposes quite specific demands on the program team in terms of content and style. The starting point for live radio is the station format.

When you turn on your radio you have a varied menu of services to choose from. Depending on your mood or your preference you can listen to:

- all music
- all talk
- music and talk (music heavy)
- talk and music (talk heavy).

The blend, or format, is a precise art aimed at capturing as much of the available targeted audience as possible. The variety is theoretically limitless, especially with the development of radio services on the Internet, which has added a global dimension to our listening as well as the capacity to format our own pick-and-mix service to suit our individual taste. So what are we likely to find as we make our way around the radio dial?

As far as music services are concerned, there is something for almost every palate. In the commercial sphere, where competition is intense for listeners and for the advertising revenue they can generate, music stations have tended over the years to focus on niche audiences. Music formats have been developed to target specific age groups (for example, Top 40 for the teenagers, Easy Listening for the 25+, Golden Oldies for the baby boomers) or special interests (such as Country and Western or Classical).

With talk, there is less scope for variety. Talkback has the widest appeal—this is a format where the driving force is the personality of the presenter, and the defining element is direct interaction with the listeners. The focus is local, the subjects topical, and the treatment is aimed at triggering discussion and debate with the listeners themselves as key participants. The commercial 'shock jocks' tend to dominate the field, with their brand of no-holds-barred commentary pulling in large audiences compared to the more restrained programs on the local ABC or community radio talkback stations.

Magazine formats are less interactive and more reflective, and can be all talk or a talk/music mix. Very often they contain pre-produced features as well as live elements. This format is exemplified by the ABC's Radio National (for example, programs such as *Life Matters*, *The Science Show*, and the *Sunday Morning* arts program).

News and current affairs formats are talk-dense, featuring a blend of up-to-the-minute news, sport, weather, stockmarket reports, and news-related features. In Australia, the ABC's NewsRadio is an example of this fast-paced, music-free format.

It is the talk radio formats that we will be focusing on in this chapter as we move on to discuss program production and the role of the program teams.

The radio day

As a potential live radio program-maker, after you have taken account of the radio format in which your program will be embedded, you will have to consider what time of day you will be going to air. The radio day is divided up into clear **'dayparts'**, each with its own style and pace. This hasn't been done in an arbitrary way, rather it is a statistical device that has helped the industry to identify and track listening habits of specific pockets of consumers. The radio day is therefore structured around assumptions about what the target audiences (and hence potential markets for advertisers) are likely to be doing at any particular time and, consequently, what radio service will fit best into that daily routine.

Breakfast

Breakfast runs from 0500 or 0600 until 0830 or 0900. This program is a wake-up call. It will welcome listeners to the new day with a bright and breezy style to wake them up and keep them awake; it will be carefully structured around regular segments at specific times to allow listeners to use them to keep a check on the time; its tone will be light and jokey, but will contain a thread of useful information (news/traffic/weather/stock-market reports) to prepare listeners for the working day. Radio National's *Breakfast* program is the exception to this rule—it is built on news and current affairs and, as a national program, it is limited in the amount of local information it can relay beyond the weather.

Morning

The Morning program follows on from breakfast, starting around 0830 or 0900 and going through until 1100 or 1200. For commercial talk radio and the local ABC stations, this is the domain of the talkback host. Programs tend to be fast-paced, dealing with a variety of topics ranging from politics through to lifestyle and entertainment. The style tends to be more abrasive than easygoing breakfast, aimed at engaging the listener, literally as well as figuratively, through the talkback call.

Afternoon

The Afternoon program occupies the 1200 to 1500 or 1600 slot. Here the pace slows down to a more easy-listening rhythm, the prime audience assumed to be the listener at home, and the presenter now fills the role of friendly companion. Lifestyle and entertainment are the dominant themes.

Drive

The Drive program occupies the early evening slot through to 1800 or 1900. Here the pace picks up again with the program filling the brief of 'afternoon newspaper of the air'. The audience is assumed to be on the move, either picking up children from school or driving home from work, and keen to hear news of what has been happening during the day. Though talkback may be a feature, the focus tends to be more on straight interviews, mixed with information about latest news and sport, weather, traffic, and stockmarket reports.

Evening

The Evening program runs from 1900 until midnight or 0100. Like the afternoon slot, here again the pace slows down. Presenters tend to be approachable and friendly, or witty and amusing, as programs aim to provide light relief, entertaining information, and even on-air counselling as we move into the night when people are apt to feel most isolated and alone.

Mid-dawn

The Mid-dawn shift runs from midnight through to breakfast. This is the most unusual of the shifts—certainly the most antisocial as its audience will be shiftworkers, night-owls, and insomniacs seeking companionship and entertainment at a time when most of the world is asleep. The challenge here is to get the tone just right with a blend of informative and engaging material when the presenter may worry that there may be no one listening at all!

Program ingredients

Steve Cannane from Triple J planning his program.

After you have established what format your program belongs to, the audience you are targeting, and the time of day in which you sit, it is then time to consider the ingredients you will have at your disposal to mix into a coherent whole. The main ingredients are:

- interviews
- music
- news bulletins
- promotional material (station promos, advertisements, station identification stings)
- general information (weather reports, traffic updates, time-calls, community announcements, ad-libs).

Interviews

These are the talk slots around which you will base the program. They can take the form of straight one-on-one live interviews, pre-recorded interviews, studio discussions and debates, pre-recorded feature reports, or listener talkback.

Music

If your station has a talk/music format, you will need to work into the schedule a certain number of music tracks (generally pre-selected for you by the music director who prepares a program playlist). You will usually be given a formula to follow governing the proportion of music to talk. For example a ratio of 60 per cent talk to 40 per cent music will establish the program as talk-based, where the reverse ratio will foreground music over talk as far as the audience is concerned.

News bulletins

Many elements are obligatory, and often immovable, parts of your program format around which you have to fit in the rest of your content. News bulletins are the most important. They constitute key turning-on points for listeners as far as the radio stations are concerned. Radio's credibility in the competitive multimedia news market really hinges on its capacity to provide virtually instantaneous access to up-to-the-minute news, and no matter what the service—talk or music—or what audience it appeals to, radio stations treat the news seriously. It appears promptly in its allocated timeslot (top of the hour, with bulletins or headlines often on the half-hour, especially in peak morning and drive timeslots) and is precisely timed. As program-maker, you need to leave these windows free in your program and have to keep a close eye on the clock to ensure you don't run over time.

Promotional material

Promos, station identification announcements (station IDs), and ads are other elements that the station will require you to play in your program. Sometimes you will be given set times at which to play them; otherwise, they can be used as useful fillers. As we saw in chapter 9, a lot of care goes into the crafting of these mini-productions. They have their own dynamic with a mood and tempo that, like music, can enhance and reinforce (or conversely undermine) the program mood, pace, and flow.

Promos

Running mostly at 30 seconds, rarely more than a minute long, they allow the station to publicise in-house information—other programs, station events, community service announcements, and other station-related material.

Station IDs

Shorter 5 to 10-second 'stings', these punctuate the program as reminders to the listener about the program, station, and frequency they are tuned to.

Ads

In commercial radio, ads need to be treated as seriously as the news as they are the station's bread-and-butter: timeslots bought and paid for by customers whose wishes have to be adhered to precisely. Advertisers are charged on a sliding scale according to the program and timeslot they choose—a popular morning program will attract higher rates than the mid-dawn shift; an ad appearing close to the news will have greater prominence than one tucked away in the middle of a program. These paid-for windows will have to be accommodated in the program **rundown** with interviews, music, and so on timed around them.

General information

As mentioned before, live radio is radio without a safety net. It is an area where Murphy's law definitely applies—what can go wrong will go wrong. Presenters have to keep things going no matter what calamity befalls them. As an example, commercial radio presenter Howard Sattler heroically presented his entire 3-hour program sitting on a milk crate in a dark studio when a city-wide power failure immobilised the station. With the help of emergency generators that got the microphone and transmitter working, and relays of information gathered by the production team working the phones, the presenter ad-libbed his way through what must have seemed the longest program he had ever done.

In less stressful situations, all sorts of information can fill unforeseen gaps, or smooth the transition between items. Listeners rely on radio to provide them with timely information on the world outside, so time-calls and weather reports are a program staple. Traffic reports are essential during peak hours. Other general announcements about community events, public health campaigns, and so on are also useful fillers. Skilled presenters have mastered the art of the ad-lib, relying on a store of anecdotal information they can draw on to fill any unforeseen gaps.

The radio clock

Having assembled all your ingredients, and programmed in the set pieces (news, ads, etc.) that form the skeleton of your show, you then have to fit everything else in. This is where the radio clock comes in. Even in these digital times, the analog clock face is still the most effective way of planning your program. The clock allows you literally to visualise each hour so you can see how the different program elements fit together. More importantly, it allows you to approach your program strategically in an attempt not only to win an audience, but most importantly to keep them listening.

The driving philosophy behind radio (and electronic media generally in fact) is to keep the audience hooked. This derives from the commercial impetus for most media: putting advertisers in touch with mass audiences. The measure of success is how many people access a service and for how long—this is what is tracked by audience research companies who monitor station performance week by week and release periodic league tables showing how the stations rated relative to each other. The audience ratings figures are compiled on the basis of who is listening each quarter-hour, and so the challenge for the program-maker is to structure the program in order to attract the listeners and then entice them to stay across the quarter-hour boundary. This is called quarter-hour mainte-nance. With radio listeners deprived of any physical program rundown, it falls on the pre-senter not only to manage the here-and-now, but also to keep reminding listeners of what is coming up. In the illustration you can see how a program clock would look covering the first hour of the Philip Clark program. The program rundown shows how the infor-mation is presented for the program team to follow when they go to air.

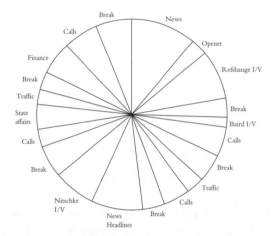

Program clock

Program rundown: Philip Clark Drive Program, 2GB Sydney, 23 March 2005

4.07 Opener
4.09 ANDREW REFSHAUGE, State Treasurer re: meeting today with other Treasurers and Peter Costello about GST and possible stamp duty cuts
————————————————break————————————4.15
4.17 BRUCE BAIRD, Liberal Backbencher re: Immigration rule changes and the new bridging visa
4.18 Calls

————————————————break————————————————4.22
4.24 Traffic report
4.27 Calls
————————————————break————————————————4.28
4.30 News Headlines with Erin Maher
4.35 DR PHILIP NITSCHKE, Euthanasia advocate and author of *Killing Me Softly* re:
new death pill and Terri Schiavo case ph: in studio
————————————————break————————————————4.40
4.43 Calls
4.45 RACHEL STEVENS with state affairs ph:
4.48 Traffic report
————————————————break————————————————4.49
4.51 Finance Report
4.54 Calls
————————————————break————————————————4.57
————————————————5pm NEWS————————————————

Source: 2GB Sydney

Programming tactics

For me a good story is one where we get people to talk. No one wakes up with the aim of calling into a program—we have to grab them. This is a big consideration in our selection of topics. Though we access a whole range of news sources, the best stories come from our audience.

Selby-Lynn Bradford, radio talkback producer, 2GB Sydney

We tend to talk to 'real' people as opposed to correspondents or reporters—we like to get your view of what is going on as a housewife or as a farmer or as a bloke pumping gas—that sort of thing. We'd much rather speak to the person in the street than to a reporter about something and elicit the information in that way.

Clark Forbes, Program Director, 3AW Melbourne

People have just had it up to past their ears with politics and politicians. We can't ignore it because it impacts on our life but we've got to take what they say not too seriously because what it is is politicking—she's trying to score points off him and he wants to get her, and all that sort of thing. But at the end of the day you've got to say to yourself: what impact does that have on my listeners? Is this going to change their life? And most of the time it's not, so it's a waste of time.

Howard Sattler, radio talkback presenter, 6PR Perth

Radio listeners are fickle. Radio may have tremendous advantages in being always accessible, in any and every room of the house, in the car, even carried around on the person. At the same time, however, as a sound-based medium, it has to work hard to keep itself in the foreground when listeners have so much else going on in their daily lives. So what sort of tactics can you use to keep the listener listening?

Be relevant

Whether your program is national or local, its success depends on how much it resonates with its target audience. This is not just a question of subject matter that means something to them—it is also about emotions and shared experiences with which they can identify.

It is worth remembering that programs are always works-in-progress. They may start off as a result of a program director's inspired hunch, but how they evolve depends on the interaction between the program team and the audience. Radio listeners are never backward in providing feedback and their response is vital in helping the program-makers to anticipate their needs.

Successful stories come from having a finger on the audience's pulse, which allows you to pick and present issues they will find interesting and relevant to their lives. This doesn't mean you are restricted to problems with parking meters in the local shopping centre—though these sorts of stories have their place in any program. A discussion on the ethics of euthanasia can be just as thought-provoking, while talkback telephone lines may light up on the issue of bringing fugitive war criminals belatedly to trial. Any story can be made relevant—the trick lies in the treatment. If you start out by thinking about your audience, you can't go far wrong.

Balance light and shade

You need to think about the stories you select to make sure there is a balance between heavy, serious topics and lighter, more entertaining ones. Listeners can get bored quickly by too much of the same thing. Variety is the name of the game in radio.

Balance sound

Although radio is a 'sound' medium, this is actually something that program-makers often seem to forget. When they do, monotonous tedium can be the on-air result. Nothing switches the brain off faster than an unbroken drone of voices, and listeners soon turn off, mentally if not physically, if the same sound goes on for too long. In radio you have a wonderfully versatile raw material to play with, and you need to consider the ways in which you can use sound to its full advantage. While the telephone is very convenient, allowing instant access to people who may not have time to get to the studio, it tends to be overused in the time-challenged world of live radio. It is worth thinking about different environments for interviews: you will get different effects depending on whether the interview is done on location, in the studio, or on the telephone, and playing with this variable will help to inject variety into the final result.

Balance content

Think about how you want to blend all your program ingredients. Having decided on your story rundown with its mix of light and shade, where are you going to place your stories? Will you come out of news with a strong story to hook the audience in immediately, or will you ease them in with something lighter? When is a good time for a music break? What sort of music will suit the mood on the basis of the surrounding talk? If talkback is part of the format, where will you fit that in? When should you use a promo, and which one should you choose in terms of sound, pace, and content? Where is a good time for the presenter to chat to the audience via a general announcement or a time or weather break? In making these decisions before the program goes to air, you are actually rehearsing what the final result will be, using your knowledge of your audience, and radio listening habits generally, to predict what will work best and where.

Vary the story format

Just as you can vary the sound, so can you vary the format, and it is worth experimenting with different ways of approaching stories. Studio discussions allow you to break away from the standard one-on-one interview. Debates allow for an element of drama by bringing opposing sides together. Talkback draws the listeners themselves into the mix, allowing radio to be the forum for community access. Pre-recorded feature reports add a totally new dimension, taking the audience out of the studio altogether and bringing the sounds and voices of real life directly to their waiting ears. Story length also needs to be borne in mind. You may have a half-hour studio discussion followed by a 3-minute film review, then a 10-minute talkback segment followed by a 4-minute straight interview. In this way yet another dimension comes into play that prevents the program from sounding predictable and stale.

Program style

The on-air style of your program is influenced by the same determining factors that impact on format and content.

Who is your audience?

First and foremost, you must take into account the audience you are addressing. A youthful audience will demand a different presentation style from an older audience; a style suited to a 30+ active family-oriented audience will not work so well with a 55+ audience of retirees; the footloose and fancy-free 18–24 age group will respond to something different again.

What is your station format?

Style will also be influenced by the sort of service the station provides. Music programs have their own conventions in presentation, and even these vary depending on the station's music profile. Classical music presenters, even on the 'pop classic' stations, won't approach the material in the same way as their counterparts in more pop-oriented music formats. The pace will be slower, the links more information-laden, the approach, while companionable and friendly, will be less 'high energy'—totally befitting both the subject matter and the older demographic that this format tends to attract. The pop music stations attracting the younger end of the market will favour a lighthearted jokiness, while stations such as the ABC's Triple J will aim a more sophisticated brand of humour at the alternative youth audience it has in its sights.

Talk radio also has a range of distinctive styles. Where commercial talkback radio champions the 'in your face' shock-jock approach, Radio National adopts a more considered, reflective style. Different again is the ABC's NewsRadio whose hybrid newsreaders/announcers try to be friendly without this impinging on their credibility as deliverers of hard-edged news and information.

What time of day are you on air?

Finally you mustn't forget the day part—the time of day the program goes to air. We have already seen how time of day impacts on pace and content. Presentation style needs to fit in too, with breakfast requiring a higher energy approach than an afternoon program, which can be more laid back and relaxed.

Doing talkback

I put the point that I think we're a very honest medium. Now you may say, and a lot of people say, 'Well hang on, aren't you the commercial radio people involved in the "cash-for-comment"?' Yeah, absolutely, we're involved in the inquiry into 'cash-for-comment', but hang on—you can ring me any time for three hours any day, I'm there every day ready to be lined up, and I'm happy about that.

Howard Sattler, radio talkback presenter, 6PR Perth

Sometimes you'll set out with an agenda at the beginning of the day—where you are going, the sort of stories you are going to cover, that sort of thing—and by the end of the morning you'll have done a totally different program because the audience will have picked it up and will have driven you in a different direction altogether.

Clark Forbes, Program Director, 3AW Melbourne

Callers have to be interesting and they have to be concise. We don't censor them unless they are likely to defame someone, but we have to be brutal: we can only let the best go to air.

Selby-Lynn Bradford, radio talkback producer, 2GB Sydney

What a temptation talkback is. Simply open the lines and let the callers do the program for you! Unfortunately it isn't as simple as that. Talkback can bring a program alive, or kill it stone dead. Like any of the other ingredients we have been talking about, it needs careful handling if it is to be a success. There are three main questions to answer: When do you use it? How do you manage it? And how do you handle any problems that arise?

When to use talkback

Although decisions to 'open the talkback lines' are often made spontaneously during the program to capitalise on an interesting topic, the production team will also consider the role of talkback in the daily program meeting. It needs to serve the following two functions:

- To involve local community. By opening the telephone lines you get real people on air who can customise the content to local needs and concerns. This, in turn, encourages audience ownership of the program. It strengthens the bonds between presenter and listener by allowing the normal intimacy of the medium to extend to direct verbal contact.
- To air public opinion. You hear a variety of voices and points of view that give added dimension to both the sound and the content, providing, of course, that the contributions are thoughtful and interesting. A succession of mindless rants will make for a tedious result.

Talkback is not program filler. Like any other program element, it has to have a reason for being there. Does a subject call for listener involvement? Is there an interesting point of debate? Opening the lines because you haven't anything better to do will result in rambling, pointless exchanges that will be boring for both presenter and audience.

How to manage talkback

The producer and the presenter each have a role in the management of talkback.

Management of content

Like everything else in the program, talkback has to be 'produced'. There is a genuine editorial reason for its being there and this means that you expect certain program outcomes from it—the development of a line of argument, or the exposure of a range of opinions. Just like the rest of the content, it requires monitoring to ensure the discussion flows. This is where good planning comes in. If the presenter and the producer are clear on the outcome, the presenter can steer the discussion on air with the contributors delivered by the producer from the control room.

Much live radio talkback is spontaneous and opportunistic, but Radio National's *Australia Talks Back* illustrates the impact that high production values can have on the format. In this nationwide daily program, the presenter moderates an orchestrated discussion on an issue of the day between specialist talent and callers from around the nation.

Management of talent

Good talkback requires a good talent mix, and the way to ensure variety is by vetting callers. This isn't the same thing as censorship. It means that, instead of putting people to air indiscriminately, the producer gets an idea of what point each caller wants to make and selects the best time at which to include them. This results in a range of voices and opinions. It also provides a chance to advise callers of certain do's and don'ts to avoid land-mines such as defamation, obscenity, and blasphemy—always a risk in the live radio environment (see below p. 149. The law for broadcasters is discussed in detail in chapter 16).

Management of tone

This is where the presenter plays a crucial role. For talkback to work, the presenter has to care: to have a genuine interest in the topic, and to have a genuine interest in what the callers have to say. Just as you use your personality to 'sell' your program, so in talkback the level of listener involvement is affected by what you put into the discussion—how well you 'sell' the topic to bring out the issues that have led you to open the lines in the first place. Like any soapbox preacher you lead from your radio pulpit and it is this talent that the so-called shock jocks of talkback radio have exploited so effectively. Sometimes responsibly, sometimes less so, they rev up public sentiment to such an extent that even politicians take note.

Handling problems

Talkback is live radio at its most dangerous. With all your planning you can never predict what the outcome will be and inevitably some tricky situations arise both on and off air.

Abusive callers

Talkback can get very heated, and both producer and presenter will have to cope with abuse from the occasional caller. Forewarned is forearmed in this situation, and it is a good idea to think through different scenarios and the best reaction to them. Try to avoid engaging in debate with the callers—you will never win since the listeners will always want the last word. The best thing, both on and off air, is to thank them for their opinion and move on.

Defamation and bad language

These are an ever-present risk and the program team must be eternally vigilant in monitoring for such transgressions. The 7-second delay and the dump button, which allow you to wipe out the offending piece of the program, give you some scope for reducing this threat (see pp. 70–1 for an explanation of this technology).

Overuse of regulars

Every program has fans, some more fanatical than others. It is easy for them to feel an exaggerated sense of ownership and to call the talkback lines over and over again. This does not mean they need to get to air. It is quite legitimate to impose a limit on how often people can expect to get to air and inform the callers accordingly. This will ensure that you get as varied a spread of contributors as possible.

Alienation of audience

Talkback works when presenters are in tune with their listeners. However, it is easy to hit a wrong note—to come on too strong so listener sympathy switches to the talent. In the false intimacy that is radio, where conversations carried out in public pretend to be like any normal social interaction, listeners expect social conventions to be respected and can become uneasy when they are transgressed. Bullying and haranguing talent may make for exciting radio—it may even win you friends if a hapless politician is the target—but it may also turn the listener off if it is someone more vulnerable.

The production team

The microphone changes people—it makes them larger than life but also more vulnerable. No matter who they are, whether they are a John Laws, or a Neil Mitchell, or a Howard Sattler, or whoever, I am sure they must wake in fright at times and think of those thousands of people out there that they are talking to and how exposed they are to everything in them. They are laying their lives out in front of all these people day in and day out, and I think that's got to have an effect on you. I think they're all like that—all slightly mad probably! And producers have got to be slightly mad to put up with them!

Clark Forbes, Program Director, 3AW Melbourne

Everything we are doing now is dispensable. This is current affairs radio—that's the way it operates. Don't think that just because we've got nine interviews slotted into the next three hours, that's it. It could all go. Be aware.

Howard Sattler, radio talkback presenter, 6PR Perth

The most exciting thing about live radio is that it is live! You are responsible for a living, breathing show—just as structured, dynamic, and unpredictable as any other sort of live performance. When the microphone goes on, it is like going on stage, and the program team will have the adrenalin rush to prove it. Radio is showtime—it is a performance, there is an audience that needs to be entertained, and this holds true even with the most sober and serious of formats. Bore your audience and they will turn you off, no matter how worthy your material.

This makes particular demands on the program team—the producer and presenter who together make it all happen. So what roles do they play? Obviously these vary from program to program and from station to station. In one team the presenter might drive the show, determining the agenda and using the producer as little more than an administrative assistant. In another team, the producer might hold sway, being largely responsible for stories and treatment, and for direction of the program on air. Although roles are very much determined by program routines, personal interaction will obviously have an impact on the division of labour. However, the best result for the program is a partnership of equals who can share the workload and collaborate on the best outcome for the listener. This is reflected in the discussion below.

The presenter

Steve Cannane, radio presenter, Triple J.

Who is the presenter?

> I believe that, while being the conduit between the people I am interviewing and the listener, I am the representative of the listeners, because the sort of people I interview, they would almost never or rarely at the very best get the opportunity to quiz these people about anything. So I say to myself: 'OK, you have been given journalistic skills, now using those skills ask the questions of these people that will evoke the answers that your audience wants'. We've got to put out what is an easily understandable message, try not to complicate the issue—and a lot of the issues are very complicated—but bring it back to the level where your audience understands exactly where you are coming from. I'm not talking about talking in monosyllables or anything like that, I am just saying represent them. That's what you have got to do.
>
> Howard Sattler, radio talkback presenter, 6PR Perth

As far as the public is concerned, the presenter is the program. No matter who is involved behind the scenes, it is the personality of the presenter that is on display and that develops the often powerful bond with the listener. The paradox with radio is that while thousands may be tuning in at the same time, listening tends to be a private affair—as far as the individual listener is concerned it is a one-on-one communication. The presenter's mouth is as close to the microphone as it would be to the listener's ear, creating a sense of closeness and intimacy that easily leads to the presumption that the presenter is a real friend. Listeners are as sensitive to moods and modulations, to tone and style of delivery as they are in normal conversation. They pick up more about presenters than the presenters themselves may even be aware of revealing, and the trick of on-air presentation is to master a safe persona that can be managed and controlled as self-consciously as an actor controls face, voice, and body movements on stage.

What does the presenter do?

Own the program

By this we mean that you need to be familiar with everything that is going to air—music as well as talk—in order to be able to 'sell' it successfully to the listener. Remember that the listener really has no idea of what is coming next—sound just comes out of the ether as far as the audience is concerned. It is up to the presenter to lead the listener through the program, to explain its rationale—why a particular story is being featured, and why now, at this time in the program; why a particular track has been chosen for this moment; what future delights are in store if the listener stays tuned. And from the presenter's perspective, these stories and music are the best they can be, selected for the listener's delectation. A cardinal rule is never to criticise your material on air. Presenters who bag a music track or story put themselves at the centre of a contradiction: if from the listener's viewpoint the presenters are the program, then how can something get to air that the presenters don't like? Why inflict something on the listener that you don't yourself enjoy? It goes against the expectations otherwise so carefully built up that the listeners are the focus of all your efforts and you are there to please them. It suggests that you aren't doing your job properly.

Link with the listener

Though you may in fact be alone in a studio, with at best the producer in the control room as your only witness, you need to keep your listener constantly at the forefront of your mind. Remember that listening to the radio is rarely a group activity—you are speaking at any moment to one person rather than many. Your presentation should reflect that illusion—it is 'you the individual' rather than 'all of you out there' that the presenter should be addressing.

As mentioned before, these listeners haven't a clue about where the program is going. They need and expect to be kept informed about what has just happened, what is happening now, and what is about to happen, so that they are guided through a structured environment rather than one where everything appears to be happening at random.

For example, where you may have announced someone's name at the beginning of an interview, by the end that name will have been forgotten. Without a 'back announce' (repeating the information at the end), the listeners—who may now really want to know who they have been listening to—will be left feeling confused and frustrated. The same goes for music tracks: it isn't enough just to introduce them—people need to be reminded of where they have just been as well as to be told where they are going. Just as television presenters maintain continual eye contact with the viewer via the camera, so the radio presenter addresses the listener continuously—and the challenge is to maintain your focus throughout the program in order to anticipate accurately what information that listener will need and when.

Communicate

The presenter has to communicate using the vehicle of personality. Whatever you are doing in your program, it is you yourself that the listeners are getting to know. If they like your style, you will be able to do no wrong. If they don't, you may never win them over. Station managers take the punt that enough listeners will take to you to boost audience figures to a respectable level. The challenge is to act naturally and spontaneously in a highly artificial situation where intimacy is feigned between two strangers: yourself as presenter and the image of your typical 'listener' that you carry in your head.

As has already been noted, the people listening to you will be applying to this exchange the full range of intuitive responses that people use to 'read' other people. One commercial radio program director relates the story of how one morning she received several calls from concerned listeners who thought the breakfast presenter might have been unwell. When she checked with the presenter she discovered he was indeed under the weather that day, but had thought he had disguised it rather well. So astute are we in picking up subliminal signals from each other that there is little that escapes the listener. It is therefore important for all presenters to be aware of how they use their on-air persona. It needs to be cultivated and nurtured so that you can act naturally and spontaneously while nevertheless not exposing those parts of you that are your private places.

So, to sum up, the art of presentation consists of knowing what to say, when to say it, and how to say it—in other words it is the timely delivery of appropriate information in a style suited to the program and your target audience.

> I am the neighbour that they used to talk to over the fence, the companion they might have lost in a partnership, but someone who is speaking very much one-to-one with his audience. So I believe that I am the audience now, too. I believe that, while being the conduit between the people I am interviewing and the listener, I am the representative of the listeners. I'm not a block, I think my audience want to know that I am a human being and that I've got feelings.
>
> Howard Sattler, radio talkback presenter, 6PR Perth

> You have a huge amount of freedom in commercial radio—you can do anything providing it works well. But you have to know what you are talking about—much more than when you are writing for a newspaper. You can't be a good talk presenter if you are young. You just don't know enough. You have no corporate memory.
>
> Philip Clark, radio talkback presenter, 2GB Sydney

> If you do your research and you are on top of what you want to do, things can go wrong, but they are less likely to go wrong, and the more interviews you do the more

confident you are that you can respond to certain situations. But you also do interviews that fall completely flat and you go 'How painful was that!' But it's part of your job—you are on air and everyone hears them, but you've just got to deal with them.

Steve Cannane, radio presenter, Triple J

The presenter's skills

Journalistic skills

Only rarely in mainstream talk radio do novice broadcasters get the chance to host their own programs. This is because station managers nowadays seek more than just a pretty voice. What they are looking for is someone preferably with an already-established profile—someone the audience will already know, even if from another context—and with a local track record in public affairs that will give them journalistic credibility and authority.

There has been debate in recent times on the degree to which talkback radio is journalism as opposed to entertainment. In 1999 the 'cash-for-comment' affair exposed the extent to which comments by some prominent Australian commercial talkback radio presenters were bought and paid for by advertisers while being presented to the audience as genuine opinion and information (see pp. 289–90). Sydney talkback host John Laws defended himself by saying he wasn't a journalist but an entertainer, and hence wasn't obliged to abide by the journalists' code of ethics covering truth in reporting. Although, as we have already seen, talkback radio is entertaining (in the way all radio must be if it is to capture listener attention), it is also journalism in so far as it involves story research, story selection, story development, and story treatment. Journalistic skills are therefore essential. What sorts of skills are these?

Be curious

Curiosity is the driving force of journalism. This is what motivates journalists to look at the world around them, and to ask questions in order to find out more about it. As a presenter you have the capacity to deal with anything and everything in your program and you need to be as open as possible to potential story ideas, no matter where they may come from. Setting arbitrary boundaries on the basis of your existing likes and dislikes not only limits your growth as an individual, but also imposes limitations on program content that can ultimately restrict its breadth of appeal.

Read widely

Radio journalists, and media industry people generally, often refer to themselves as 'news junkies'. This means that they access all sorts of media in an attempt to keep themselves fully briefed on what is happening and where. The more widely read you are, the greater the range of story ideas you will be exposed to. Equally importantly you will develop a huge mental database of information that you will need to draw on constantly as an interviewer. Knowing the broader issues and background of a story is as vital as knowing the immediate details in lending confidence and authority to your interviews.

Be able to write

As with other forms of journalism, radio is as much about writing as it is about speaking, but it is a special kind of writing aimed at oral delivery. You are scripting for your voice: writing words that are to be spoken as if they aren't being read at all. Once again the audience looms large—your writing has to anticipate the listener's needs in terms of simplicity, clarity, and brevity. For more on writing, see chapter 5.

Love what you do

You have to love what you do. As we have said before, presentation is the art of winning the listener over by sheer force of personality. As a useful antidote to the egomania that invariably accompanies this sort of public role, it is worth remembering that, however good you may be, you aren't the centre of your listeners' universe. Radio is more often than not just background noise to them and it is up to you to draw the listeners' attention away from what they are doing and towards you. This is why commitment and enthusiasm are essential to anyone in an on-air role. It is like listening to a live band in a pub—if the band isn't having a good time the audience won't be either, and won't hang around to give them a second chance.

Voice skills

With the voice being the primary currency of radio, obviously your voice is your primary tool. You need to be able to control its pace, tone, and modulation as carefully as any actor on a stage so that your message is clear and unmistakable to the ever-present but invisible listener. You have to have a high level of verbal skills. This means that you speak well in terms of grammar and articulation, and also that you have superior brain–tongue coordination—that you are able to speak fluently and can maintain your concentration even in the most stressful of situations. (For more on the voice, see chapter 4.)

Communication skills

We have already spoken about the special intimacy of the presenter–listener relationship. Whether you as presenter like it or not, your listeners are going to feel very close to you. They will be relating to you as if you are speaking to them alone, wherever they happen to be listening. They will be responding to you person-to-person and what they will be responding to are your people skills:

- How natural are you?
- Do you have a smile in your voice?
- Is your manner friendly?
- Do you sound as if you enjoy talking to people?
- Are you good at making people feel comfortable with you?
- Are you adept at reading people—picking up on hidden cues and signals that allow you to anticipate what is needed in any given situation?

You need to be all these things not only for the guests with whom you are communicating directly but also for that unseen witness to the exchange, silently listening to you from afar.

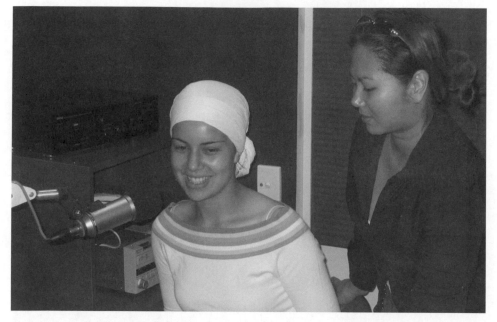

Presenter Faridah Baharuddin is briefed by producer Emerald Tin prior to going to air on community station Radio Fremantle 107.9FM, WA.

Technical skills

At Triple J you have to do your own panelling and it's like when you learn how to drive: you could not have a conversation with a person sitting next to you as you're trying to concentrate on driving the car. When you are first on air and you don't know how to panel you are trying to do both, and so you can't relax and be yourself on air because you are trying to get across the technology. It took me a good 6 months to actually get okay at it and to get familiar with the studio and to be confident on air.

Steve Cannane, radio presenter Triple J

The console is your principal domain as the presenter. This on-air mixing desk allows you to put to air sound from a variety of sources:

- presenter's microphone
- guest microphone(s)
- telephone
- CD player/jukebox
- minidisc player
- computerised playlists.

All are activated at the touch of a button, with faders giving you volume control and the capacity to fade in, fade out, and cross-fade as you go. As presenter you really need three brains—one to control your handling of information, a second to control your voice, and the third to handle the technical challenge of putting your program to air. Running the desk is not unlike driving a car—once you can use the controls, driving the desk becomes automatic, even in emergencies. The better you know and understand the equipment, the smoother your presentation will be. (For more on the console, see chapter 7.)

As presenter, your focus should be on the performance side of things. The better your planning, the better the on-air result. Below is a summary of the presenter's off-air and on-air tasks.

Preparing for talk radio is a 24-hour thing—you have no other life!

Philip Clark, radio talkback presenter, 2GB Sydney

The presenter's checklist

Off-air tasks
1 Know your program. You need to involve yourself in story selection, with the program agenda arrived at via negotiation with the producer, satisfying yourself that the approach and the selected talent will work on air.
2 Know your material. Though time constraints may preclude your writing every script, it is best to do your own preparation as this means that you are fully briefed for each story and can therefore handle it with confidence.
3 Try to listen to all material you will be including so that you know in- and out-cues and can introduce and back announce knowledgeably. This reassures the listener that the program has been a shared experience, with you as the presenter as much involved as the listeners themselves.
4 Make sure you have emergency back-up material—ad-libs and/or reads—which you can use in an emergency should things go wrong. Dead air is the prime enemy on radio and things do go wrong: machines fail, guests don't turn up, interviews are cut off earlier than planned. Numerous unforeseen events require emergency on-air cover by you and a bit of planning goes a long way towards helping you to deal with these stressful circumstances with composure and aplomb.
5 Assemble all ingredients and make sure that they are in proper order for broadcast.
6 Check your equipment to ensure the studio is fault-free.

On-air tasks
1 Keep in constant touch with the producer to pick up important signals regarding pace, flow, and content during the program.

2 Watch the clock to time yourself up to the next music break, promo slot, or news bulletin.
3 Cue the music and promos ready for you to fire at the right time.
4 Keep track of levels to ensure a smooth, even sound throughout.
5 Remember your listener at all times.

The producer

You need a good producer, and good producers are as hard to find as good presenters. A good producer is one who doesn't want to be a presenter! They have to play to the strengths of the presenter in terms of what will work for that person. They have to be knowledgeable with life experience and they don't stop working when they leave the office.

Philip Clark, radio talkback presenter, 2GB Sydney

You have to respect the presenter. You need to be a devil's advocate, to be the audience's ear. You also need to be on the same wavelength, to think in similar ways. To survive as a producer you need to know what the presenter wants so you can act as facilitator.

Selby-Lynn Bradford, radio talkback producer, 2GB Sydney

A day in the life of a producer

Selby-Lynn Bradford is the Executive Producer of the Philip Clark drivetime program on 2GB Sydney and oversees a production team consisting of two production assistants including one who acts as call-vetter when the program is going to air. Selby-Lynn discovered radio while doing a communications degree at university. A period of work experience at Perth's commercial talk station 6PR led to a full-time position as producer of the evening Nightline program, followed by a stint at the other end of the day producing Breakfast. Selby-Lynn then moved to Melbourne where she worked at 6PR's Southern Cross sister station 3AW producing the Drive program, first with Stan Zemanek and then with Derryn Hinch. She was then offered the position of Drive producer at 2GB in Sydney and has been in that job since 2004.

Selby-Lynn Bradford, radio talkback producer, 2GB Sydney

The 2GB Drive program goes to air from 1500 to 1800 Monday to Friday. The program is presented by Philip Clark and aims to be an entertaining and informative story mix aimed at 2GB's main audience demographic, which is skewed towards the older 45+ end of the scale. Audience participation is a key element and talkback is therefore an important ingredient. Because 2GB is a commercial station, stories need to be programmed carefully around pre-determined ad breaks. There are also news bulletins on the hour and half-hour in this key turn-on time as people begin to drive home from work and school.

10.00 am—As soon as the team arrives in the morning they scour all the news sources to get an idea of the agenda for the day. Before leaving for the office, Selby-Lynn will already have read the morning paper and monitored the morning radio and television news services in order to get an idea of what has happened overnight. Once she gets into work she takes a closer look at newspapers, press releases, and other available material with pen in hand ready to jot down potential story ideas in time for the midday program story conference.

The producer's friends! A snapshot of Selby-Lynn's desk gives an idea of the things that make up the producer's survival kit. We see pen and paper for making notes, a highlighter, a telephone and a mobile to make and receive calls from news sources, and, most important of all, her contact file. Here she stores the names and contact numbers of key people (politicians and their media minders; local, state, and federal government representatives and agencies; fire, police, and other services, etc.) as well as contact details for the myriad sources used in past stories. Plus a chicken and avocado wrap in case she has time to grab a bite to eat.

10.30 am—Once across the day's actual and potential news agenda, Selby-Lynn immediately takes to the phones to chase up stories. Her phone calls at this stage will be to get further information in order to establish the details of the story and the possible angle the program may be interested in following. At the same time she is able to check out who she might approach as talent, vetting them for their knowledge, their communication skills and entertainment value, and their availability.

12.30 pm—The program team gets together to discuss the story ideas they have all come up with. Everyone has done their individual research and they pitch their stories to the presenter Philip Clark (centre) to work through how their ideas might work on air in terms of angle, approach, and audience appeal.

The presenter Philip Clark brings a wealth of experience gleaned from a career spanning the law and journalism, including ten years as the presenter of the ABC breakfast program in Sydney. For him, program preparation is a 24/7 affair and the background knowledge and extensive network of contacts built up during his journalistic career come to the fore as the team assembles the day's story list.

1.00 pm— By the end of the program meeting Selby-Lynn has an extensive list of story possibilities. It is generous enough to give her plenty to choose from since there are all sorts of barriers to getting a story up, including: further research indicating there is no story at all; story being superseded by the day's events; lack of research time to do a complex story properly within the tight deadline; inaccessible or unavailable talent.

3.05 pm—Time marches on and the team spends the period up to program time in a flurry of program preparation, researching stories, lining up talent, writing scripts and comment pieces. It all comes together as the 3 o'clock news bulletin finishes. With a flurry of scripts and program rundowns the team settles in to the studio, their home for the next 3 hours.

Philip is in the studio, mike at the ready, as the live broadcast begins. He is apparently cut off from the outside world behind soundproofed windows, however he has three communication channels linking him to Selby-Lynn and the production team: a cue function in his headphones and mike that allows him to talk to the production booth and vice versa; a computer screen on which the production team can relay messages (additional information, talkback caller details, etc.); and visual contact through the studio window. The producers can also go into the studio, usually during ad or news breaks to minimise the risk of on-air disruption or distraction.

The production team occupies the production booth outside the broadcast studio. Story research doesn't stop when the program is on air. With the help of production assistant Andrew Bourke, Selby-Lynn continues to chase stories in order to ensure they cover late-breaking and evolving news. The phones run hot as they chase talent and information and Google is just a click away on their computer screens so they can research online if necessary. At the same time, Selby-Lynn is monitoring what is happening on air in order to anticipate Philip's needs and spring into action if any technical or editorial glitch occurs.

Talkback is an important part of the program format and throughout the program callers are ringing in to comment on the program or to have their say on air. Production assistant Naomi Shivaraman is the call-vetter whose job it is to answer the calls and type up caller's names on the computer and the subject they want to talk about for Philip to access in the studio.

Live programs are always 'work in progress' requiring great flexibility from all the team in order to accommodate things that may go wrong. A talent has gone missing and won't be available for the pre-planned program slot. This means the rundown will have to be re-jigged so something else can be slotted into the gap. Selby-Lynn briefs Philip on the adjustments they will have to make while they try to track the talent down and hopefully fit them in later on.

4.19 pm—Just one hour has passed since the program started—two more to go. For the team the time passes quickly in a blur of phone calls, last-minute briefings, and rundown juggling, all part of the adrenalin-rush that is live radio.

Who is the producer?

Whereas the presenter is the very public voice of the program, the producer lives strictly behind the scenes, but you are far from a silent partner. In fact since, as producer, you are the one in direct contact with the public—talking to talent, dealing with the listeners, liaising with other station personnel (technicians, the sales team, public relations)—your persona is identified with the program just as much as is the presenter's.

As producer, you are the coordinator of all program activities to ensure everything comes together in a smooth on-air result. It is you who keeps the team to the production timetable, ensuring all material is assembled in good time for the broadcast, edited, and ready to go. It is you who puts together the rundown, determining the strongest story order and the mix of talk with music, station IDs, promotions, and so on. However, live radio is full of often unwelcome surprises. No matter how carefully you plan, talent will fail to turn up, telephone lines will drop out, a sudden breaking story will demand instant coverage—all of which require urgent management off air while the presenter maintains a cool focus on air. So the producer is above all the person the presenter should trust most—keeping calm in times of stress, and having an answer for every problem.

What does the producer do?

The producer's tasks can be divided up into off-air and on-air duties.

Off-air duties

- Production coordination. Off-air, the producer has the role of coordinating all the disparate elements that will go into the program. Starting with a blank rundown, you will work out with the presenter what the agenda for that day will be—the shape, form, and content of the program you will be making together. You will discuss and select or discard story ideas both of you will have gleaned from the myriad sources at your disposal, deciding on the story angle and the talent. Then you will have to do the research, find and lock in the talent, and prepare briefing materials and scripts.
- Managing the rundown. Most likely it will be up to you to compile the program rundown—the running sheet that lays out what is going to go where—and you will need to write it up and distribute it to the presenter and others involved in the program transmission. This will range from the receptionist at the front desk who will need it for listener queries, through to the technician in the master control room who may need to deal with specific technical needs the program may have, such as special links or live crosses.
- Crisis planning. Throughout all this you will need to plan defensively—to make allowances for any unforeseen crises that may occur. Working out disaster-coping mechanisms in advance means that you will have an arsenal of tactics at your disposal when you need to call on them in an emergency. These can be as simple as rejigging the rundown, or as complex as having a pre-recorded interview in reserve.

On-air duties

On air, your role is to manage the program so that, as much as possible, things go according to plan.

- You are timekeeper—watching the clock to make sure the presenter keeps to time.
- You are a safety net—keeping a step ahead in order to anticipate anything that may go wrong.

- You are a disaster-manager—resolving potential on-air problems before they become full-fledged disasters.
- You are the content monitor—in effect the presenter's sample listener—maintaining a critical ear on proceedings to give feedback as necessary on what is going on.

You will find that you are in constant communication with the presenter—either via the computer screen or, tactfully, through the headphones, giving off-mike assistance ranging from reassurance that a joke worked to providing serious advice on whether an interview is getting into defamation territory; from suggesting extra questions if an interview stalls to advising on whether to use the dump button if a talkback caller's language is getting too colourful.

> You need to just have the normal skills that any good journalist would have. A bit nosy, a bit pushy at times, a bit of a nose for a story, all those sorts of things that any journalistic text book will tell you.
>
> Clark Forbes, Program Director, 3AW Melbourne

> We have to arrange the program knowing that at any time we could throw the whole program out the door if something bigger happens.
>
> Howard Sattler, radio talkback presenter, 6PR Perth

The producer's skills

Journalistic skills

As noted earlier, even though talk formats are often categorised as entertainment radio, the selection and handling of program material requires strong journalistic skills. We have seen how this applies to the presenter, but what are the journalistic skills required in the producer's role?

News knowledge

The producer needs to know what is happening in the world at large, what is going on where, what is hot, and what is not. It is from this pool of knowledge that you derive the editorial strength to be able to select stories, or to decide whether a suggested story is worth doing. It is also this pool of knowledge that allows you to spot trouble spots, danger zones, or errors of fact.

News sense

Having a news sense means you have to have a feel for what constitutes a 'good' story, or what is needed to make an ordinary story into a good one. It requires an understanding of the elements of a good story (drama, tension, human interest) as well as an appreciation of what will work in radio terms (a straight interview, a recorded package, or a talkback segment, for example). It also means that you have to know your audience and what their expectations are in relation to your program.

Contacts

Contacts can make the difference between an ordinary story and an inspired one. They are what lead you to talent, and the wider and more varied your network of contacts, the more choice you have in selecting talent for any particular story. Contact lists, properly and efficiently maintained by you, lock in the memory of every story you have covered, and can save you a lot of research time down the track.

Research skills

There is precious little time for planning in live radio, so knowing where to go to find information is essential. The Internet is a boon to all researchers and gives you the capacity to access information in record time. It makes it much easier to provide useful background to stories, which before required painstaking sifting through a variety of sources to uncover. Taking time to familiarise yourself with key reliable sites will save you a lot of time in future rapid-response information retrieval (see p. 170 on the Internet as a research tool). Maintaining your own news **archives** also helps if you need to return to a particular story at a later date.

Writing skills

You need to know how to write. Furthermore, you need to be able to write in a variety of styles. One minute you will be writing a straightforward briefing document for the presenter, the next minute you will be crafting a 30-second promo script for a forthcoming program event. Sometimes you will be writing for the eye (briefing notes); most often you will be writing for the voice (scripts). Sometimes you will have time for thought, at other times you may need to get something ready in a matter of seconds. Producers need to be able to write quickly, on demand, and in clear and readable language.

Communication skills

While the presenter is the public voice of the program, behind the scenes the person the public is most likely to have contact with is the producer. As you search for talent, handle talkback callers, and deal with listener queries, you are the program's ambassador, and this role requires highly developed people skills. Your phone voice and manner need to be courteous and amiable, even when confronted by rudeness. When approaching potential talent, you need to be able to show them that you know what you are doing, that you know the issues, and can brief them accurately about what to expect if and when they appear on your program.

Your people skills must extend to dealing with the presenter. Producers have a symbiotic relationship with presenters, but the main goal is to achieve the best on-air performance. The presenter's role is demanding and requires great concentration to make sure that the audience is well served and the program runs smoothly on air no matter what is happening behind the scenes. As producer you serve the program's needs, not your own, and this means you have to understand how your presenter likes to work so that they have what they need when they need it.

Organisational skills

As producer, you have to manage all the moving parts that go into the program quickly, smoothly, and efficiently. You have to organise the talent so they are there at the right time and place; you have to ensure the presenter has everything needed for each story; you have to assemble all the other program-related material; you have to manage the rundown. Above all, you need a sixth sense alerting you to potential traps—situations that might lead to defamatory comments (personal comments that are damaging to reputation and so leave you open to legal action); contempt of court (relating to comments about ongoing court cases, likewise risking legal penalties); blasphemy, and so on. You must not only recognise the potential dangers, but also manage the situation on air.

Technical skills

The producer's domain is the producer's booth or control room. This is a room separated from the main studio, but which nevertheless allows you to communicate with the presenter in three ways:

- visually through a glass window into the studio
- verbally through a computer screen that allows you to write messages onto a screen in the studio
- orally through the presenter's headphones via a microphone on your console.

The equipment you need to manage includes the telephone, which you use constantly as you line up talent and field calls from listeners; the computer screen; and news management programs such as NewsBoss that may be available to you in the control room, allowing you to monitor newsroom output to keep abreast of late-breaking news.

As producer your key role is that of organiser.

The producer's checklist

Off-air tasks
1   Set in place the program content—chase stories, line up interview talent, organise the research material and write scripts as necessary.

2 Check any pre-recorded material before broadcast to ensure that the sound quality is good, the editing is flawless, the piece is an appropriate length. You also need to ensure that each piece has an accompanying script providing a link and all details (first words, last words, time) so the presenter has everything necessary to introduce the piece flawlessly.

3 Set up the format, deciding the **running order** with an eye on the pace and flow, and prepare the rundown.

4 Forewarn the presenter about places that may need to be filled with public announcements, time-calls, and so on.

On-air tasks

1 Keep a step ahead of the presenter, making sure that they are aware of the next event and have the necessary script in place and the minidisc/CD/computer track cued and ready to go.

2 Make sure interview talent is on standby a few minutes before air time.

3 Keep an eye on the clock to check that the program is keeping to time. If you suspect you might run short, find a way to fill the gap, giving the presenter the information about any additional material they may need to play.

4 Keep your ear on the content, checking that live interviews remain interesting and focused, and signalling the presenter when they have gone on long enough. Keep alert for potential legal problems (contempt, defamation, blasphemy, offensive language—see below and also chapter 16).

5 If there are unexpected glitches (for example, a machine malfunctions or an interview talent doesn't turn up), have something in reserve to cover the problem, so you can brief the presenter promptly about what to do next. This means remaining calm, staying a step ahead of the game, and keeping your focus on the outcome for the listener. The program has to sound good, and a cool, composed presenter, briefed by a cool, composed producer, can cover a multitude of sins.

Journalistic challenges in live radio

It is clear from everything that has been said so far in this chapter that the live radio format is radio-on-the-edge. Its fast pace puts tremendous pressure on the production team, who have limited thinking time before the program and precious little reaction time on air. This means they have to deal on the spot with the myriad of ethical and legal dilemmas any journalist faces in chasing stories. Broadcasting law and ethics are dealt with in detail later on (see chapters 16 and 17), but it is worthwhile here to look at some of the implications for live radio production.

Legal dilemmas

Defamation

Example: During a live discussion on the role of the police in the community, a talkback caller suddenly mentions an officer by name and accuses him of taking a bribe.

It is so easy on live radio for someone to say something naughty about someone else. And it is so easy for that person to take serious offence when that happens. This could result in the station and the program team being taken to court, with potentially very expensive outcomes.

When in doubt seek legal advice. If you suspect potential danger points in any story you plan to run, ask the advice of senior station staff or your station's lawyer who will be able to tell you whether there is a problem and how to avoid getting into trouble.

Brief all talent before they go to air. Alert all interviewees including talkback callers about the dangers of referring to people by name in matters of a sensitive nature. This way you provide them with coping mechanisms to keep themselves out of trouble.

Use the dump button. Stations broadcast in delay (see 'The live broadcast studio', p. 70) which means the program is held up for around 7 seconds before being transmitted. The dump button returns you immediately to real time, obliterating the stored 7 seconds, so anything said in that time disappears into the ether—the listener never gets to hear it. This is a useful safety net of last resort, and it means that both presenter and producer need to monitor the program constantly to make sure that on-air talent behaves.

Bad language

Example: A standup comedian who is on air talking about her latest show uses the 'f' word.

This is a more tricky area than defamation because it is difficult to predict what people might say in the heat of the moment. Obscenity and blasphemy on air can actually put your station licence at risk if a complaint is made to the Australian Broadcasting Authority.

Because of the unpredictability of this offence, the dump button is your only option if things go wrong. However, you can minimise the risk by explaining the rules to the talent beforehand to ensure they use appropriate language on air.

Contempt

Example: You are interviewing a reporter about the arrest and charging of a man accused of bashing a taxi driver. The reporter starts to talk about the man's previous record of violent crime.

The concept of a fair trial is central to our legal system and there are strict rules about what can and cannot be said when a case is before the courts. There are many landmines waiting to explode if careless remarks are made on air by either the presenter or an unsuspecting interviewee. In this case a reference to a past criminal record might prejudice the forthcoming trial.

Familiarise yourself with the law of contempt so you are fully aware of the boundaries within which you can operate. Also, make sure talent and talkback callers speaking about sensitive cases are briefed before they go to air about what they can and cannot say.

Copyright

Example: You would like to use an audio grab from the TV satirical series *Frontline* to illustrate a story about gutter journalism.

People have ownership and control over their created works. You may want to use a grab from *Yes Minister* to illustrate a political interview, or the theme from *Desperate Housewives* to introduce a story about modern marriage. Under the Fair Dealing provision of the *Copyright Act*, journalists may use materials for the purpose of review or in news (see below p. 286). It is essential to be aware of the copyright status of any material you intend to use.

Familiarise yourself with the law of copyright, and what is and is not covered by blanket agreements that your station may have with copyright owners or their agents. You will need to get permission for any material falling outside these agreements and may need to acknowledge the source on air.

Ethical dilemmas

Live radio is a constant source of ethical tests for the journalist. Here we will use the four main headings of the journalists' code (reproduced on pp. 293–4) to illustrate how ethics influence the way you need to work.

Honesty

Example: It's a slow news day and you hear about a minor scuffle outside a local nightclub involving some Vietnamese young people. To trigger talkback you use this as an excuse for a high-emotion rant on the problem of Asian gang warfare in the cities.

There can be little doubt that talkback radio is an influence in daily life. Politicians increasingly use it as an unofficial barometer of public sentiment. It is often difficult to gauge how far the talkback programs set, or merely reflect, the current agenda. Either way, it is important that your coverage of issues is a true reflection of how things are. Honesty, both in reportage and in your treatment of talent, always pays higher dividends than shonky practices in the long run.

Keep to the facts. Avoid the temptation to embellish. Pumping up a grey story into shades of black and white can easily result in distortion and misrepresentation of the truth. If the story needs that sort of embellishment, maybe it isn't a story at all.

Keep yourself out of it. Don't let your biases determine your approach—let the story tell itself.

Avoid subterfuge. You should always be straight with your talent, telling them exactly what will be expected of them, even at the risk of them turning you down. To spring an unannounced debate on an unsuspecting interviewee could burn your bridges forever with that talent. Furthermore, it could have more wide-ranging results by giving you the reputation of being untrustworthy.

Fairness

Example: Someone comes to you with a story about the alleged release of pollutants into a local river system by a paint manufacturer. You interview outraged local residents and councillors who tear strips off the company for its irresponsibility, but you are unable to find a representative from the company to answer their concerns.

Time is the enemy in live radio and often time constraints limit the scope for well-rounded coverage of an issue. This may result in only one side getting an airing.

Make it clear that the story will be continued, with other players having their say later in the program or the next day. Facilitate right of reply if in the meantime other relevant parties call in.

Have the presenter adopt a devil's advocate role to represent the alternative views.

Make use of talkback. While you are at the mercy of the callers here, it is good to aim for a spread of views, especially on contentious subjects.

Independence

Example: You are offered the best seats in the house for a local theatre production on condition that you include an interview with one of the stars in your radio program.

Live radio is a magnet for people who want to get their stories on air. Freebies ranging from tickets to the footy to trips to exotic locations are dangled before program teams in exchange for on-air coverage. The 'cash-for-comment' scandal that disclosed secret payments to some commercial radio presenters in exchange for favourable on-air comment (discussed on pp. 289–90) showed the extent to which such pressures can compromise journalistic independence. Even the public broadcasters are susceptible to free film tickets and books for review.

Choose your stories, don't let them choose you. Your morning talkback program might welcome the free copy of Bryce Courtenay's latest book along with the chance to interview the author. His high profile and the popularity of his books would make this a topic of some interest to your listeners. However, it would be difficult to provide similar justification for an all-expenses paid **outside broadcast (OB)** from the Great Barrier Reef, courtesy of a local tourism operator.

Choose your angle, don't let it be chosen for you. While freebies are a fact of life in the entertainment industries, the program content should be your own, not that of a publicist. Don't let the freebie compromise your views.

Respect for rights of others

Example: A young apprentice is electrocuted at work overnight, raising issues about how well he was supervised. The next morning you want to contact his parents to see if they will talk about this tragedy on air.

Radio is a powerful medium, but it can also be a brutal one. It exposes people unmercifully to the public gaze, often against their will. Though there are times when such exposure is warranted, there are others when such an intrusion is less justified. Given that the richest veins for gripping radio stories will involve vulnerable people in sensitive situations, where do you draw the line?

Start with treating your talent with respect. You have no right to intrude on their lives and they are not obliged to talk to you. If they decline an interview, cover the story another way.

Respect people's right to privacy. Some people find relief from grief in telling their stories in the public arena, and even approach trusted radio programs for such a purpose. This is more the exception than the rule, and deathknock requests for interviews do little to enhance the reputations of yourself or your program.

Don't promise what you don't intend to deliver. If you are given someone's silent number on condition you keep it to yourself, don't pass it on to someone else. Likewise don't promise what you can't deliver. Given that there is no legal protection for journalistic sources, there is no way you can guarantee confidentiality—if someone requests such a guarantee you must explain the limitations that exist.

Exercises

1 **CD TRACK 11** is an extract from the Philip Clark drive program on commercial radio station 2GB in Sydney illustrating the talkback radio style of programming and presentation. In this extract Philip Clark interviews Gold coast businessman Ron Bakir about his involvement in the attempt to clear Australian Schapelle Corby of drug smuggling charges in Indonesia. He then takes some talkback callers on the subject. Answer the following questions:

- Compare Philip Clark's style with Steve Cannane's in Track 2. What are the similarities? What are the differences?
- How does each presenter adapt their style to suit his target audience?
- How do their interviewing styles differ?
- What role does talkback play in the Philip Clark segment? What role does the presenter take in talkback interviews?

2 **CD TRACK 12** begins with an extract from a live radio interview Howard Sattler did with the grieving mother of James Annetts, a young jackaroo who died in the bush in tragic circumstances in late 1986, about the failure 15 years later of a compensation claim the parents had pursued through the courts. Howard then comments on the challenges the interview posed for him, not only in terms of handling high emotion on air, but also in the context of navigating carefully around subject matter that might potentially cause legal problems.

List the legal and ethical issues the interview raises and discuss how the presenter dealt with them in preparing this interview to go to air.

Further reading

Ahern, S. 2000b, 'Researching and Producing', in Ahern, S. (ed.), *Making Radio: A Practical Guide to Working in Radio*, Allen & Unwin, Sydney, pp. 112–31.

Hendy, D. 2000, 'Production', in *Radio in the Global Age*, Polity Press, Cambridge, pp. 68–114.

Starkey, G. 2004, 'Live Sequences and Phone-ins', in *Radio in Context*, Palgrave MacMillan, Basingstoke, pp. 58–88.

Wilby, P. & Conroy, A. 1994, 'The Programme', in *The Radio Handbook*, Routledge, London, pp. 193–233.

PART IV

Radio and Television News

Broadcast News

11

News is crucial to 2GB. We're a news/talk station and without news you don't have a station. Some people don't realise the importance of the news because in terms of revenue sometimes it's a big black hole, because you employ journalists and we don't actually bring in any money to the station. It's just money going out—on overseas trips and equipment. But you take news away from a station and then you notice that it's missing.

Justin Kelly, News Director, 2GB, Sydney

News is the beating heart of broadcasting and most radio and television stations offer some sort of news service, be it locally based or networked across the country. The news is the foundation of the station's credibility as it strives to give its audience access to the latest events. Changing digital technologies have given television networks such as CNN and BBC World an immediacy equal to that of radio. Satellite phones, satellite dishes, and video streaming on the Internet have given them an equal capacity to report on the news as it happens.

Though the media may follow similar news agendas, the way reporters handle news changes radically depending on whether it is intended for print, radio, television, or online:

- Newspapers are able to convey complex stories with in-depth analysis assisted by graphs and tables. They have the space for clarifications and backgrounders.
- Radio is best at delivering **breaking news** and spot stories. The live news report of a train collision can reach the listeners as soon as the reporter has reached the location.
- Television is best at delivering action stories with dramatic footage—the attack on the World Trade Center in New York in September 2001 showed the full extent of television's powers in these circumstances. This does not mean that television has to confine itself solely to vision-based stories; however, the medium will have an influence in determining what sort of story the television reporter goes after.
- Online news is a mix of all the above: delivering a range of stories from headline-breaking news to expanded features with links to additional audio, video, photos, graphs, and other related articles.

News is about breaking stories, and media organisations compete to be first to carry a 'yarn'. Through their immediacy and pace, radio and the Web are expected to beat print and television to the news. However, because the four media occupy discrete niches they also complement each other. Reporters know this and accept that a radio listener wanting more information will go online or look to the newspaper for a broader coverage, or will turn the television on to get the more graphic version of the story.

Setting the news agenda

Though technology is a primary influence on the way news is delivered in each medium, there are other more subtle influences at work when it comes to setting the news agenda. While unbiased, objective reporting may be the journalist's goal, personal and institutional pressures can sometimes get in the way.

The impact of the individual

As a news reporter, you need to be sure that your own opinion is never a part of the story—it is the first thing you learn when you start your journalism training. This might sound quite simple and straightforward, but is it really? Does the fact that you are a reporter mean that you are not allowed to have an opinion? Does it mean you can't join a political party, or be an active member of your local council? What is at issue here is the extent to which the viewer or listener can trust you as an impartial observer. Let's look at two examples of how individuals can influence the news agenda.

As part of a study conducted during the 1950s in the United States, a newspaper editor identified only as Mr Gates was asked to record his reasons for choosing the stories for his mid-western newspaper. It was his job to select stories for the front pages from the abundance of copy material coming in from three news agencies. Every day after completing his work, Mr Gates would write down the reasons for his editorial selections. Some copy he dismissed as propaganda, other copy he said suffered from what he called 'poor quality of writing'. His decisions were governed by his view that his readers were '... entitled to news that pleases them' (MacGregor 1997, p. 49).

The second example concerns a broadcast newsroom in Sweden that contained a cohort of journalists in their early to mid 30s. Just like the rest of their age group in the general population, they were at the stage when many of them were having children and raising families, and this had an impact on their news agenda. There were many more stories on family-related issues such as childcare and immunisation arising out of their own areas of current concern. This of course highlights the importance of having a mixed staff in the newsroom. The ideal newsroom would contain a blend of different genders, races, and age groups.

The impact of the institution

Beyond the influence of the individual, the media companies themselves exert an institutional influence on what goes to air.

Different newsrooms have different standards. This becomes clear if, for example, you watch the television news on a single night across all the different networks (commercial, SBS, and ABC) and compare the way news is presented and dealt with. Each service will tackle the news quite differently in terms of story selection, story development, and the order of stories in the bulletin. The public broadcasters (SBS and ABC) are more likely to lead the bulletin with politics, finance, and international affairs. SBS will focus mainly on international stories while the ABC will run with a mix of local, state, national, and international news. The commercial networks will tend to concentrate on local and more emotive stories.) .

These differences are a product of the external influences impacting on the media companies themselves (see chapters 1 and 2). The public broadcasters are answerable to the Australian public and to the government, which holds the purse strings for their operations. They deliver services in accordance with their respective charters, and risk public or government criticism if they appear to stray too far from those remits. The commercial networks are equally constrained, in this case because of pressures from shareholders and commercial clients. Because they are dependent on advertisers for their revenue there is always the risk of news judgment being coloured by extraneous commercial considerations.

Having discussed the often hidden influences that impact on news agendas, we now need to discuss the concept of 'news' itself—just what is it and where do you find it?

What is 'news'?

I think the best news stories often have conflict as a major element of the drama—as any good story does, as any good play does, as any good piece of theatre does. A compelling story has conflict and has strong characters who are interesting and compelling, hopefully who can tell their stories well. The way we do news is almost always about conflict.

Katy Cronin, television journalist

News values

Even news reporters themselves often find it difficult to define 'news'. They may describe it variously as 'something new', 'something that will have an impact on the audience', 'anything people in power don't want you to know'. This can often make news unpredictable: the latest research findings about a new treatment for cancer might appear run-of-the-mill to the medical industry, and yet become a lead story when the journalists get to hear about it. A minor news story about a suburban robbery might, nevertheless, make the headlines on a slow news day.

The concept of 'news' varies depending on the news organisation, the broadcast medium, and the target audience. The BBC defines news like this:

News is new and honestly and accurately reported information which is about current events of any kind anywhere in the world set against a background of other honestly and accurately reported information previously gathered as news; selected fairly but without artificial balancing and without political motive or editorial colouring by trained journalists; included in a bulletin because it is interesting, significant or relevant to the bulletin's audience in the eyes of the journalists; and presented fearlessly and objectively but with respect for the law and the BBC's own rules concerning taste and editorial standards (quoted in Herbert 2000, p. 62).

A regional newsroom will look for local stories of interest to the community, while a national broadcaster will raise the threshold and demand big stories with broader appeal. We might therefore find that a chase through the local shopping centre could make it into the news bulletin of the local radio station, but be ignored by national television where the lack of pictures and limited relevance would kill it as a news story in that medium. By contrast, the debut of a prima ballerina at the Australian Ballet would provide striking visuals suitable for ending the nightly television bulletin, but for precisely this reason might be ignored by radio.

News is also transient. A car crash could lead a radio bulletin while traffic is still jammed, yet the story might disappear by the next bulletin if the road has been cleared.

So in seeking to define news key characteristics emerge:

- It must be timely (the information must be new to the target audience).
- It has to be of interest (the information must have an impact on the target audience).

News may very well be the reporting of planned or unplanned events, but what makes some stories more 'newsworthy' than others? Although details such as the broadcast medium, the size of the newsroom, and the target audience matter, there are also some core news values that journalists share worldwide. A sixty-nine-country survey of journalists and journalism educators produced the following list of top six news values:

- consequence
- proximity
- conflict
- human interest
- novelty
- prominence (Masterton & Patching 1997, p.15).

This might explain why news reporters appear to 'hunt in packs' and why much of the news is the same across many networks.

Let's take a closer look at these criteria using the Asian tsunami disaster on Boxing Day 2004 as an example. When the tsunami struck, the first estimates of the death toll were conservative. It later became clear that the tsunamis triggered by the 9.0-magnitude quake off the coast of Sumatra had left 220,000 dead in eleven Indian Ocean countries. This was, of course, the main story in all media. When applying the criteria for newsworthiness to the catastrophe, it is easy to understand why reports from the tsunami led bulletins for so long.

Consequence

This relates to how many people are affected by the information: the more people affected, the bigger the story.

This was a major regional catastrophe and in addition to foreign casualties there was obviously interest for an Australian audience in the numbers of Australians involved. For weeks it was unclear exactly how many Australians had been killed and there were warnings that the Australian death toll would climb into the hundreds. South-east Asia is a popular tourist destination for Australians and the disaster was on every one's lips. The number of Australians killed was later scaled down and is low compared to the death toll from other countries—twenty-five Australians were confirmed dead in the tsunamis with grave fears for one other Australian.

Proximity

This relates to closeness to and nearness of the event. However, proximity is not just a question of geographical location—it also relates to ethnic or social affinities. The large population of retirees in Queensland's Gold Coast will be interested in stories about mismanagement in retirement homes; the substantial Greek community in Melbourne affects the number of stories from Greece that are picked up by the local media there.

In the case of the tsunamis, proximity was an important factor for news editors. Australia is geographically close to South-east Asia and the waves could be felt along the north-west coastline of WA, with some impact recorded as far south as Busselton where bathers were caught in unnatural tidal rips.

Conflict

The clash of opposites is the most common and classic element of a news story. It is obviously at the very heart of crime and war reporting, but the element of conflict is also exploited in the reporting of the courts, of parliament, of sport, even of the way an individual takes on 'the system'. This pitting of one side against the other is often seen as a trademark of news: the format does not allow for many shades of grey.

The tsunami disaster is a clear example of conflict between man and nature. When footage of the wall of water approaching the shoreline became available, it led every television news bulletin. For weeks newspapers continued to publish photographs from retrieved cameras, like the haunting image of a smiling Canadian couple on the beach that was extracted from the dead pair's digital camera.

Human interest

This is a non-specific term that describes stories involving ordinary people. These are often 'soft' stories about people who would not normally be considered newsworthy, but who make news because of a particular event. In selecting talent for human interest stories, journalists often look for the unusual, the quirky, or the touching; something appealing to the funnybone or to the heart rather than to the head.

There were many heartbreaking stories of ordinary people in the aftermath of the tsunami. One that the media focused on in particular concerned 4-month-old 'Baby 81' found among the debris in Sri Lanka. He was the eighty-first person to be admitted to a local hospital and made international headlines when several distraught couples came forward all claiming to be his parents. Another story involved a young Swedish boy who was thought to have been abducted from hospital in Thailand by a suspected paedophile.

Novelty

Novelty relates to the unusual, most commonly described as 'man bites dog'.

The tsunami story was unusual in that, although quakes are common in the area, there had never been one as powerful and with such far-reaching and devastating consequences.

Prominence

This relates to 'names making news'. The public can't seem to get enough news about the rich and famous, and, in addition to national and international celebrities, each region and each city has its own list of local luminaries.

The death of well-known Melbourne footballer Troy Broadbridge stood out among the tsunami stories. He was celebrating his honeymoon in Thailand with his wife Trisha when the disaster struck. Although Mr Broadbridge was only one of many people killed in the tragedy, his case was a prominent one because of his position as a famous sports person. The photos of Trisha Broadbridge wearing her wedding dress to the funeral were published all around Australia.

A news story need not fulfil all the above criteria, but the general rule is the more criteria it satisfies, the more likely it is to make it into the next news bulletin.

The five 'Ws' and the 'H'

Reporters need to extract the 'Who? What? Where? When? Why? and How?' out of any story and try to get to the heart of the issue in the simplest way because, with radio, the listener is often doing a lot of different things—it's not like a newspaper where you can sit down and concentrate and read. They might be cooking dinner, they might be driving across the Harbour Bridge—so you need to make sure you say things as simply as possible, but you are still delivering the impact of the story which it deserves.

Justin Kelly, News Director, 2GB Sydney

Answering the basic five 'Ws' and the 'H'—What, When, Where, Why, Who, and How—will get you a good news story. All reporters should be armed with these fundamental questions and make sure they get an answer to each one:

- What happened?
- When did it happen?
- Where did it happen?
- Why did it happen?
- Who did what?
- How did it happen?

A further equally important question that could be added to this list concerns 'consequence': what impact will the event have? Even though news is about reporting what happens right now at this very moment, reporters need to look ahead and to draw conclusions about what it will mean to people listening or watching. News reporters seldom have time to go this one step further. They have also been trained to report objectively and to keep themselves aloof from the story. However, with so much information available to us today, the processing of that information is as important as the simple recording of it. If reporters ignore the broader context, they risk leaving the audience with an uneasy feeling that they have only been told part of the story. They will also be left behind by the tough news competition.

Although this sort of analysis could be done as part of general 'news' reporting, in Australia historical institutional conventions have resulted in it becoming the province of 'current affairs'. With more time available, both on air and in production, current affairs programs on radio and television can take stories further than news, asking more questions about 'why' and 'how', and looking at the future impact of the specific event or issue. While a radio news story on a locust plague in regional New South Wales will be 40 seconds long, the same story can be developed into a 2- or 3-minute feature for a current affairs program like the ABC's *AM*.

Finding news

As you work in journalism you do develop layers and layers of experience and knowledge, and you call on them and you begin to understand what the structures are: the organs of politics, for example, and I'm not talking about just parliament and political parties, but trade unions, and business organisations, the corporate sector, and the non-government sector, volunteer organisations, the welfare groups and the media itself, and how these groups bounce off each other and compete against each other, and then sometimes work together on certain things. What I've found, I've sort of begun to have a map in my head of where the pieces fit together, and the interesting stories happen where the conflict happens between those groups. It's those little fracture zones, where the tectonic plates collide, where you get conflict and stories in our society.

Katy Cronin, television journalist

'Where and how do I find the stories?' These are the first questions the novice journalist asks. Journalism is about stories—the 'what is happening'. Stories are about contacts—the 'who is doing it'. As we see from the profiles of the broadcast journalists who feature in this book, stories don't fall out of the sky. They emerge from a process of almost continuous research, which involves trawling through every conceivable source of information to find a topic and an angle appropriate for medium and audience. So where do these news-hunters start their search for stories? Here we look at some common news sources and how they help in the never-ending journalistic quest.

News sources

I guess there are probably two ways in which you source a story and that's got to do with how you discover it. It may either be an organisation or a person who is proactively pushing an idea, by sending out a media release or a media alert or whatever, or it may be purely through your own research on the ground where you are ringing people, cold-calling people, and asking them what's going on, whether there is anything happening, asking them what they've heard around the traps. In either case the way you follow the story through is perhaps to get somebody to be able to talk on the record about it and garner enough information so that you can find an angle into the story and write the story and put it down on paper. And then I guess it is just about following the technical process through to get it to air.

Scott Holdaway, political reporter, ABC News Perth

News can come from a variety of sources. There will always be **'spot news'**—fires, accidents, crime—but any serious newsroom would shy away from relying too much on these action news items. Story leads will also come from a wide-ranging network of contacts: politicians, government agencies, the police, and the public calling in, to mention only a few.

The average newsroom is abuzz with potential stories, and the challenge is to keep track of them. The more efficiently this is done, the more effectively news items can be predicted and planned for way in advance. The newsroom diary is at the heart of the production process as it is where story planning begins. Most newsrooms have both electronic and hard copy files where media releases, newspaper clippings, invitations to exhibitions and so on can be stored. This diary contains dates, times, and background on forthcoming events.

The most common sources for news stories are:

- media releases
- media conferences
- rounds
- council, state and federal government calendars
- **follow-ups** (picking up on previously broadcast news stories)
- other news media (radio, TV, Internet, newspapers, news wires, talk shows on radio)
- specialist journals
- tips from the public
- contacts
- trawling the newspapers; advertisements and letters to the editor
- reporter's own observations.

The media release

Whether you are working in a newsroom or in a program production area, you will find that a lot of material comes to you—without your having to lift a finger—in the form of the media release. Your office will be on the mailing list, email list, and fax list of all the major organisations and public relations companies who have an interest in pushing information out into the public arena. It is information with an agenda—facts or opinions assembled by a sender with the aim of getting them broadcast. It is a convenient way for reporters to be served a pile of information including contact details, suggested interviewees, and background facts. With the pressure of tight deadlines it is tempting for reporters to base their stories on the media release alone (even while they may adapt the script to suit the broadcast format). This gives rise to the often-voiced criticism that news organisations are not as independent or rigorous as they could be. Remember—never take any information that you are given as being the whole story. Always seek corroboration from other relevant sources to make sure you are getting the full picture.

Media Alert frontlineFIRST

Phone: (08) 9222 1217, (08) 9222 1701, (08) 9222 1853 Fax: (08) 9222 1703
Pager: (08) 9480 5311, Email: Media.Section@police.wa.gov.au

PARTY POOPERS CONFERENCE

District Police with members of St Johns Ambulance will hold a joint media conference today, Thursday 23/12/04 to highlight the potential danger with end of season work parties/drinks in the light industrial areas and what action Police will be taking.

The conference will be conducted in the **car park of premises in Guthrie Street Osborne Park near O'Malley Street at 11.30AM (This is a new building right on the corner and opposite number 24 Guthrie Street.**

The representatives will be Superintendent Kevin Looby from the West Metro Police District and Mr Stephen Luke, Team Leader Ambulance Operations.

All media welcome.

Ends alert.

Info contact is Sgt Graham Clifford ▮▮▮▮▮▮.

Graham Clifford APM
Sergeant 3782
Police Media

December 23, 2004

visit our website: www.police.wa.gov.au

Page 1 of 1

Example of a media release.

Source: WA Police

The media conference

This is an organised group briefing for journalists who are able to ask questions from the floor. It is a device that tends to be over-used by government agencies, and, since it is a staged event with minimal opportunity for rigorous cross-examination, it is therefore looked at somewhat cynically by more experienced media representatives. Nevertheless, media conferences can be very useful to both parties. For example, when the Victorian Department of Human Services wanted to inform the media about the causes of an outbreak of Legionnaire's disease in Melbourne, they called a media conference. This was efficient and effective for the department, as the group briefing saved time. It also ensured that the department controlled what information was handed out. The media, meanwhile, had easy access to relevant talent.

However, there is a downside to this format. First, it inevitably gives only one side of the story and that is bound to contain the 'spin' that is least damaging to the agency involved. Second, the format involves sharing the available material with other broadcasting outlets, whereas a reporter would much prefer to do a one-on-one interview. Third, this all-in media event makes it difficult to do anything original. It can be quite depressing to compare your report from a media conference with those done by colleagues in other stations and find they are almost identical in content and structure. This can be avoided with a little extra creativity—enhancing the press conference content with other vision or audio to give it a different look and feel from those of your competitors.

Rounds

These are specialist news beats such as the courts, crime, politics, health, and education, and most big newsrooms have a nominated reporter dedicated to each one. The number of **rounds** depends on the size of the newsroom and how many staff can be spared from general reporting. The advantage of this sort of specialist pool is that reporters are able to build up their expertise in their designated area and deliver more knowledgeable and analytical stories to the audience. They gain a solid network of contacts in their field, while the contacts themselves—the politicians, lawyers, nurses, and union representatives—benefit from having a known quantity on the inside who gives a human face to the media organisation. Again, journalists need to be careful to retain their objectivity. While it is useful having an inside contact, you should not allow this to impede your capacity to question and to probe to ensure you are getting the full story.

Calendars of events

Information about what is happening at federal, state, and local government levels can be found in the local and national newspapers and, more frequently nowadays, on the relevant web site. Though much media attention is given to state and national matters, local councils can also be a good source of news relevant to listeners/viewers living in the area.

Follow-ups

Following up on stories that have already been done can be very rewarding. Listeners often like to keep abreast of the latest developments in an ongoing issue, and a news story can have many different potential permutations during its lifetime. For example, the building of a controversial motor sport complex can take months and give rise to many newsworthy stories:

- the vocal protests organised by the local residents who are worried about noise pollution
- the political tussle between the state government and the opposition over the highhandedness of the planning process
- the plight of the motor sport devotees who fear their sport will go under if they are deprived of a venue.

For many issues, the news doesn't end with a single story, so it is important for reporters to check in with their contacts to keep up with the latest developments. This also gives you a way of ensuring your contact files and personal archives are up to date and ready to be activated the next time the issue enters the headlines.

Other media

It is the name of the game in news that everyone monitors everybody else, and other media are a mine of information for journalists. Broadcast news reporters will monitor print, reading two or three morning newspapers before turning up for work. Print journalists monitor the electronic media, keeping an ear on the radio for news and current affairs across the day, and an eye on the television to compare their news agendas. And everybody monitors what is happening online. The monitoring has a threefold purpose: first, to keep up with what is going on in the wider world; second, to check on what the opposition is doing as all of you race to be first with a breaking story; third, to poach story ideas, a generally accepted practice providing you credit your source accordingly. For novice journalists, such multiple monitoring of news outlets is essential in order to build up the requisite background knowledge about current issues and important people that you will draw on for your stories.

As well as news and current affairs programs, other useful sources include radio talk shows and the various international and national websites and wire services such as Australian Associated Press (AAP), the US Associated Press (AP), the French Agence France Presse (AFP) and the British Reuters. These agencies sell their news to subscribers, and many now are making video and audio clips available as well as words and photographs.

Specialist journals

These publications, especially covering areas such as science, technology, and medicine, are often where important stories first break before finding their way into the mainstream media. Examples are the scientific journal *Nature* and medical journals such as the *Medical Journal of Australia* and the *Lancet*.

Tips from the public

As a journalist, you are in constant touch with members of the public who will often approach you with story ideas. This can be as much a curse as a blessing since it is often very time-consuming to check out these sorts of story leads. When people ring in to say they have a great news story to tell you, it is often hard to judge whether the call will be worth your while—in other words, whether it will result in a broadcastable news story. All media organisations want their audience to 'talk to them', but they seldom have systems in place for following up on those phone calls. Be courteous to callers and open-minded about what they can give you. Take notes and ask for their names and contact details. If they are giving you leaked or sensitive information, get as much information from them as possible to enable you to check whether they are genuine or not. Since journalists can't guarantee protection of their sources, it is also wise to find another source who can corroborate the story if the original source wants to protect their own identity.

Contacts

The importance of a journalist's contact file cannot be overstressed. Your contact file is your professional memory bank, and the more disciplined you are in maintaining it the greater the rewards will be. Your contacts can provide you with stories, or with exclusive comment for other stories, and you won't have to run around and look for phone numbers because you will already have them at your fingertips. On a quiet day in the newsroom your contact file can come in very handy: a ring-around of your contacts is bound to generate at least one story idea.

It takes time to build up useful contacts and it is a tedious task to transfer information from your daily work into the contact file, but it really is worth the effort. There are as many ways of keeping a contact book as there are people, and you have to find a way that suits you. All you need is an indexed notebook or a computer database, and strong motivation. It pays to make sure you include all the information from the start—first name (with correct spelling and pronunciation), mobile phone number, email address, URL to the contact's web site, telephone numbers for the contact's friends and family, and so on. Some reporters like to include story clippings in their contact file as memory refreshers in case a story resurfaces.

Trawling the newspapers

Newspapers are treasure troves of little bits of useful information. The classified advertisements and letters to the editor can be sources for interesting and often quirky news stories. Letters to the editor can make you aware of community concerns that you might not have heard about yet. Advertisements, both commercial and personal, can give you ideas for all sorts of stories. For example, at the beginning of the dot.com boom the abundance of IT job ads caught the eye of a journalist who wondered whether they were evidence of some new trend. With the aid of some statistics and expert comment, this became an interesting and informative story about the way IT was transforming the employment market. Personal advertisements such as births, marriages, and deaths can yield interesting human interest stories.

Reporter's own observation

Because journalists are traditionally trained to be neutral and not to take any active role in the stories they report on, it is easy for reporters to ignore the fact that they can be a source for stories themselves. If the bus you take to work every morning starts running late on a daily basis, maybe it is because the state government has cut the funding to public transport and the bus company does not have enough drivers to keep to schedule. As a journalist you are always on duty, even when your official shift has ended. You need to observe the world around you, to ask questions, and, above all, to talk to the people around you—the people you meet at parties, or outside the school, or on that bus to work.

In addition to these tried, tested, and reliable news sources, reporters have to do a fair share of hunting and gathering themselves, which is why they are often referred to as 'news junkies'. They will read anything that they can get their hands on, constantly monitor radio, television, and the Internet and keep their story antennae working even after the day's shift is over.

Wherever you go for stories as a reporter you mustn't take anything for granted. It is vital that you examine any information for ways that it could be tainted. The most informative source will only be telling you one version of the story—what other versions are there? What motives does the source have for giving you information? Can the information or the person be trusted? The seductive corporate briefing package with all the helpful graphs and profiles might appear to have done all the hard analytical work for you—but what company spin has been put on the data? The government press release announcing a wonderful new health initiative may appear to be the good news story of the week—but would non-government stakeholders share this rosy view? The challenge for journalists is to be sceptical without descending into cynicism—probing and questioning to get to the real story is what your job is all about, but in this process you will uncover the good as well as the bad.

Spot news

Spot news items are unplanned and unpredictable events: no one can foresee when a fire will break out, or when a freak wave will swallow a fisherman. Broadcast media have a fair number of spot news stories in their bulletins. Radio likes them because of its capacity to react quickly to them, with reporters able to file live on-location reports within minutes of an incident occurring. Television likes them because of their visual appeal—fires, storms, accidents, or flooding provide high-impact pictures.

Most of the emergency agencies dealing with these sorts of events (police, fire and rescue, state emergency service, and ambulance) rely on radio communications to control their operations and most newsrooms have electronic facilities to scan this radio traffic and so can constantly monitor what is going on. However, information gathered in this way must be treated with care. Police and other rescue services frequently hold training exercises for their staff and many of these dummy runs can sound like fantastic news stories when taken straight off the emergency radio. As with all other news sources, it is important to double-check all facts before proceeding further with any story.

Some useful 'disaster-sources' are:

- police media—for information about crimes, missing persons, unexpected events, and accidents. They will have statements on their answering service and duty officers to contact. In some ABC newsrooms police have a direct radio link to the newsroom, tagged the 'bat-phone' by the journalists.
- Fire Brigade
- State Emergency Service (SES)
- Australian Search and Rescue and/or the navy (for aviation and maritime rescue operations)
- water police
- hospitals
- ambulance services.

Given that weather is an important source of news stories, newsrooms will also keep in contact with the Bureau of Meteorology, not only for the current forecast, but also for other weather-related items.

Taxi services are a rather more unorthodox story resource. Their big fleets cover a lot of ground and are in contact with lots of people, and the drivers therefore often come across useful information. Many news organisations arrange for the taxi services to get in touch with them if they hear anything that could be newsworthy.

The Internet as a tool and resource

As a communication tool, the Internet is without parallel, with email giving you even better access than the telephone to people anywhere on the planet—although with increased email traffic and the abundance of spam, many people are no longer checking emails as frequently and the old-fashioned telephone has had a revival. The computer on your desk now holds the knowledge of the world and can save you hours of legwork because of the capacity you have to access all sorts of information without leaving the office. This has had a huge impact, not just on how journalists work but on the sort of work they are able to do. Having so much information at your fingertips gives you the chance to delve into databases, to compare and contrast the data, and computer-assisted reporting, or CAR, is transforming investigative journalism.

However, there are both pluses and minuses to cyberspace. The information may be out there, but how do you find it? And once you find it, how do you know you can trust it?

How to find things on the Web

The Web is a moving feast and web sites may be there one day and gone the next. The trick is to find stable ones that bring together the most useful links for you. These can then serve as a first port of call when you are starting to research something from scratch. The list at the end of this chapter contains a few of these catch-all sites. Just as a casual trawl through the phone book can throw up all sorts of interesting contacts, so a familiarisation tour around these sites will allow you to see for yourself how they can assist your research.

Who can you trust in cyberspace?

Because anyone can put anything on the Web, it pays to be very sceptical about what you find there. Just as with any other sort of research, facts need to be verified before you can put them to use in your story. Sites you can trust include government, academic, and major media organisations.

Government sites will be displaying information as part of the public record, so facts and figures will be truthful as far as they go. The devil may lie in the detail, however, and government spin will inevitably affect how much information is included and how it is presented.

The content on academic sites has usually gone through a sifting process to ensure the information has been tested for authenticity and credibility.

Major media organisations carry a lot of public trust and the assumption is that the same editorial rigour is applied to the content on their web sites as to the rest of their product. However, there has been a worrying tendency towards greater recklessness, with rumour sometimes being published as fact—a tendency exacerbated by the Web-induced pressures to be out there with the news first. All this underscores the point that, as a journalist, you can't always believe what you see, hear, and read, and when it comes to doing research there are few ways of cutting corners—you have to get the information by yourself and for yourself rather than relying on others to do the work for you.

So far we have been concentrating on news content, but what about the people responsible for delivering the news to us? In the rest of this chapter we examine the structure of the broadcast newsroom and where and how the reporter fits in to its operations.

The broadcast newsroom

The structure of the broadcast newsroom varies depending on the type of media service and the numbers of people involved.

The radio newsroom is a busy place, with bulletins going to air every hour, 24 hours a day (smaller newsrooms don't broadcast across the midnight to dawn shifts). During the peak times of the morning and afternoon, news headlines are broadcast on the half-hour as well. With a constant turnaround of staff and stories across the day, the working environment of the radio newsroom resembles a factory assembly line.

Channel Seven's newsroom in Perth.

In television, news reporters have the luxury of working towards later deadlines. While most television stations have short news updates during the day, the main bulletin is at night. For that reason, the television newsroom can be a relatively quiet place until late afternoon when the reporters come back from the field, at which point they all want to edit and file their stories at the same time. This routine is changing as new technologies make it possible to escape from the straitjacket of the free-to-air schedule. On the Internet it is possible to put television bulletins to air whenever you like, and as broadband speeds up Internet access television networks will use the new broadcast medium to increase the number of bulletins. ABC Online already runs a television bulletin on broadband for people with access to fast connections.

Historically, radio and television have been seen as separate services, although the expectation has been that reporters will have 'done their time' in radio or print before entering the world of television. This sort of multiskilling, an accidental by-product of career development in the 'old media', is a necessity in the 'new media' environment. Broadcast reporters now are being called on to report for radio, television, and, more and more, for the Internet (for Web skills, see chapter 15). The ABC, for example, operates mixed newsrooms (also referred to as bi-media newsrooms), where reporters are experienced in both radio and television production. While this multiskilling trend has been driven by technology, broadcast managers have been quick to exploit its money-saving potential. Though there is still a call for specialist reporters in the bi-media newsroom, the total number of general reporters will be determined by the financial bottom line. If a reporter from television is covering a hostage drama, they might be expected to provide a live radio report from the scene via mobile phone. This puts extra pressure on the reporter who is expected to be both marathon runner (TV) and sprinter (radio) simultaneously. For television, the reporter needs to grasp the big picture, working across the whole day to get all the information, interviews, and vision needed for a complete story.

For radio, many short updated versions of the story are needed to feed the insatiable appetites of the bulletins across the entire day. For the Web, the journalist adds yet another layer, integrating audio and vision with still pictures and text.

> The way that we operate now is that reporters are sent out on their own with a digi-cam so you literally are operating completely solo. So if you are out in the field you will head out as early as you can, go out filming for the day, get back at four or five, do your radio news from whatever has happened that day—which will be a mixture of what you have seen and having a look on the wires— then around seven you start doing radio current affairs using the sound that you've got from what you have filmed, and then probably by about nine or ten you start television which will involve cutting down your pictures and sending them by satellite phone, and that goes on until the wee hours.
>
> Sally Sara, foreign correspondent, ABC News and Current Affairs

Who does what in the newsroom?

Newsrooms have a clear organisational framework, although the actual job titles may vary from newsroom to newsroom depending on their respective structures and sizes.

At the top of the tree is the news editor (or news director) who has overall responsibility for management of the newsroom and is the ultimate arbiter when editorial issues arise. This editorial control is exercised through daily new conferences and ongoing liaison with news executives. Next in line are the chief of staff (COS) for television and executive producer (EP) for radio, who oversee the day-to-day operation of the newsroom. This is a structure employed by the ABC, but many commercial newsrooms are smaller with the news editor also taking on the role of COS or EP. The COS/EP has to be an organisational wizard doing for the entire newsroom what individual reporters do for themselves, namely sorting and storing the raft of story information that comes in.

The COS/EP will confer with the news editor to determine the issues of the day, and will have ongoing responsibility in deciding whether a story is newsworthy, and what resources are needed to cover it (cars, camera teams, editing facilities, and so on). The COS/EP then will assign stories to reporters, and in some organisations will continue to supervise the story as it is being developed.

At the next level of production, the in-take editor or producer in television, or the subeditor in radio, oversees the editorial side of the production process, providing guidance and advice to reporters. In radio, the subeditor is responsible for script supervision and for producing the bulletin. In television, the team includes a line-up producer, responsible for preparing the rundown and supervision of the bulletin on air; the director, who controls the on-air presentation; and producer's assistant, audio operator, technical producer, and floor manager.

It will fall to the COS or the EP to update the 'daily' and 'future' files, making sure all the information and research materials collected during the day are properly archived, especially in the case of ongoing stories, such as court cases.

While radio news can be organised, supervised, and planned by just one or two staff, television news has a more complex production process requiring more people. The range of support staff includes administrative staff, tape editors, technical operators, and graphic designers. The studio production side of television news is dealt with in more detail in chapter 14, in the section on television news bulletins.

News production is like a spinning wheel that never stops. The news day begins early and ends late. Staff are always working against the clock with little opportunity, or time, to look back or reflect. Organisation and planning is constantly focused on the next production deadline. The newsroom staff, working overlapping shifts, ensure the coverage of stories across the 24-hour news day.

Having looked at how the newsroom hierarchy is organised, let's turn now to the foot soldiers, the news journalists themselves.

The broadcast news reporter

It is not as glamorous or exciting as people might imagine—a lot of it is just hard work so you have got to be really motivated to be up very early in the morning and working right through and to be on the ball when things happen.

Sally Sara, foreign correspondent, ABC News and Current Affairs

You need to be able to be confident in approaching people and talking to them when you may not know them from a bar of soap. It's probably not something that struck me as the primary quality that you would need for a career in journalism, but you need to have that confidence in order to approach people to talk about any subject under the sun, as long as you are not being rude and impinging on their personal life. Interpersonal skills like that are crucial.

Scott Holdaway, political reporter, ABC News Perth

Reporting for radio and television news can often be exciting. The journalist is out there where it is all happening: at the scene of the crime, at the site of an accident, at the hub of political activity. You get to interview famous people. You get access to places that are out of bounds to the ordinary person. All this comes at a price: once your story is filed it is in the public domain and subject to judgment from that most severe of critics, the audience. They will assess how well you represented them in your questions, scripting, and story development, and this can be challenging on a professional as well as a personal level for new reporters.

The skills

So what generic qualities does the broadcast journalist need to have to meet these high public expectations?

Justin Kelly, News Director, 2GB

Justin Kelly is the News Director at commercial radio station 2GB in Sydney. The newsroom at 2GB provides a 24-hour 7 days a week news service with bulletins on the hour throughout the day, and half-hourly bulletins from 4.30 am to 8.30 pm. Most bulletins are around 2 minutes' duration with longer 10-minute bulletins at midday and 10 pm. The staff consists of fifteen journalists rostered across days,

Justin Kelly, News Director, 2GB Sydney.

nights, and weekends, with anywhere between five and ten **stringer**s contributing from interstate. Radio news reporters have to be committed to make it in the industry, says Justin Kelly:

'The first thing they need to have if they are coming from university is the right attitude because we can teach them the skills, but if the attitude is not right it's not worth it. They need to be committed, they need to be dedicated, they need to make sure that they're not coming in expecting to work a Monday to Friday 9–5 job because journalism isn't about that. Journalism is working really odd hours for in some cases very little pay. I mean you can earn more money working in Coles or MacDonald's than as a cadet journalist—it's true—so you really have to have it in your blood to succeed in journalism and we have had a lot of people through here who haven't quite made it because they haven't cut the mustard, so to speak.

'It's different to the ABC because at the ABC you might be given two stories a day to concentrate on and develop, but in commercial radio because we're so thin on the ground you cover one story, you cover it as best you can, and you move on and you do another story. We could write anywhere between 30 to 40 stories a day—more if it's a busy day, particularly if you are working a solo shift such as overnight when there is only one person in the newsroom. So it's a tough job.'

Particularly if you are working on your own, your diary needs to be good, your contacts need to be good, you need to be really disciplined with the way that you plan and the way that you follow up stories because there is no Chief of Staff assigning you or looking out for you. If you miss a story it's because you weren't organised or weren't motivated to get things going.

Sally Sara, foreign correspondent, ABC News and Current Affairs

Some key skills for broadcast journalists are discussed below.

Curiosity

Perhaps the most important trait of a journalist is curiosity. To enjoy journalism you must have an inquisitive mind and a desire to learn. You need to:

- be a 'news junkie'—read as many newspapers as possible, listen to radio, and watch television
- be prepared to ask questions rather than letting information pass you by
- keep your story antennae working, even when you are off duty
- have a passion about wanting to share your knowledge with others.

Knowledge of your beat

Broadcast journalists are always in a hurry. If a story is breaking, there is no time for questions—you jump in the car and do your research on the phone while travelling to the story location. The reporter's general knowledge is crucial, especially when it comes to covering spot news. ABC News's test for potential cadets includes a current affairs quiz. Many universities also run weekly general knowledge tests to encourage students to keep abreast of the news. It pays to study the map of your area of work so you understand its geography. It is essential to compile a comprehensive list of useful phone numbers in your contact book. The more knowledge you have about your 'beat'—the state, the region, the city, and the people—the faster you will be in getting up good, quality stories.

Flexibility

The fast-paced environment of the newsroom demands great flexibility in its workforce. It is unusual for radio and television reporters to know what they will be doing the next day, and with the downsizing of newsrooms they will have to do several stories in a shift. Sometimes they will need to drop a story they are working on to go out on the road to cover a fire or a plane crash. The ability to change tack and to get your head around new issues quickly is therefore essential.

Good communication skills

As a worker in the communication industry you have to be a good communicator yourself. To survive tight deadlines you must also be a fast and concise writer. This requires:

- being a good listener
- having the ability to convey complex issues using words, voice and vision.

Analytical skills

As a journalist you process a lot of information and your job is to interpret and translate it for the listener. You need to be a clear thinker so that you are able to articulate exactly what you want when briefing your interviewees, your newsroom supervisor, and your crew.

Self-confidence

Being a reporter requires self-assuredness so that you can approach people with confidence. This will help you:

- get past gatekeepers
- win the trust of the people whom you want to tell you their stories
- have the courage to ask the obvious questions.

Even the most charismatic public figures can talk nonsense at times and if you don't understand what they are saying, neither will the audience. Trust your own judgment and get them to clarify any points that are obscure or confusing. Don't be impressed or intimidated by jargon like legalese: ask for simple and comprehensible answers.

Toughness

As a reporter you need to be assertive enough to:

- ask difficult questions
- be persistent and, at the same time, patient. Wait for the answer, but don't let go until you get it.
- force your way into the middle of the media pack in an 'all-in interview'. Shrinking violets won't stand a chance when competing with ten camera operators and an equal number of journalists vying for the minister's attention in a doorstop interview.

Creativity

Be innovative and creative in your approach by:

- thinking of novel ways of telling your story to make it stand out from the rest of the media pack
- thinking of creative ways of getting the audio and vision—this might include clever use of ambient sound or sound effects, or unexpected camera angles.

People skills

Be considerate of the people you encounter in your daily work as a reporter:

- make talent feel as relaxed as possible. The measure of a good reporter is the extent to which you can put yourself in your talent's shoes.
- show a genuine interest in the story and what the talent has to say
- listen to your crew and be prepared to learn from their experience
- learn to regard criticism as constructive and positive ('It helps me grow as reporter').

Professionalism

You demonstrate professionalism in the way you act and the way you look. Reporters act professionally by:
- being on time
- being neatly dressed

- being well briefed
- being considerate—don't waste people's time with long-winded interviews.

Good preparation

This means:

- doing your research before the interview. If you know the subject you can quickly pick up errors or inaccuracies during the interview (and you are less likely to have the wool pulled over your eyes by the talent!)
- being clear on what you want and how to get it
- briefing your talent and team about the desired outcome of the interview
- knowing your equipment and ensuring it is in working order.

Organisational skills

The more organised you are, the easier it will be to acquire, retain, and access the knowledge from your accumulated experience. So:

- be methodical and meticulous in transcribing details and facts
- keep clear and accurate notes
- keep a diary
- maintain an efficient and comprehensive contact file
- prepare ways of finding information quickly by labelling, bookmarking, and sorting your material. Keep notes, media releases, previous scripts, articles etc. especially on subjects you are interested in.

Being a broadcast journalist is a great job—it gives you licence to ask anyone questions. But you mustn't forget to listen to the answers! Don't forget the hidden messages conveyed through body language—the way people talk, how they stand, and how they act. A good reporter must be able to stand back, to observe, and to draw conclusions from what they see. This is what helps you develop your own 'nose for the news', that priceless capacity for sniffing out a 'good yarn'.

Exercises

Listen to and record the five o'clock evening bulletin on ABC local radio. Then watch and record the Channel Seven television bulletin and note the stories featured there.

1 Select a radio and a television story from the bulletins and describe each in terms of how they fit the newsworthiness criteria.

2 Count how many stories in each bulletin are 'spot news' and how many are planned events like court cases or protests. Can you determine the sources of the stories just by watching/hearing them?

Further reading

Alysen, B., Sedorkin, G., Oakham, M. & Patching, R. 2003, 'Generating News Stories' in *Reporting in a Multimedia World*, Allen & Unwin, Sydney, pp. 44–72

Conley, D. 2002, 'A "Know" for News', in *The Daily Miracle*, 2nd edn, Oxford University Press, Melbourne, pp. 38–58.

Herbert, J. 2000, 'Working in a Digital Age Newsroom', in *Journalism in the Digital Age: Theory and Practice for Broadcast, Print and On-line*, Focal Press, Oxford, pp. 22–58.

Masterton, M. & Patching, R. 1997, 'Aims: What is Broadcast Journalism Trying to Do?', in *Now the News in Detail: A Guide to Broadcast Journalism in Australia*, 3rd edn, Deakin University Press, Geelong, pp. 5–25.

Randall, D. 2000, 'What Makes a Good Reporter?' in *The Universal Journalist*, 2nd edn, Pluto Press, London, pp. 1–13.

Web sites

The following list is intended to serve as a useful starting point for your web contact file.

Sites with useful links to other sites

Department of Communication, Information Technology and the Arts: http://www.dcita.gov.au: has links to related groups in all three areas, both Australian and international.

Internet Economy Indicators: http://www.internetindicators.com/media.html: has links to many popular and influential publications related to Internet information.

General information sites

Australian Cultural Network: www.acn.net.au: a gateway to Australia's network of cultural organisations.

Consumer World: http://www.consumerworld.org: a US-based site which is a good starting point for consumer-related stories. It provides links to consumer organisations and consumer-related material worldwide.

Sites with useful journalism-related links

ABC NewsRadio: www.abc.net.au/newsradio/links.htm: useful links to other sites in different subject areas including media, science, technology, finance, education, and health.

European Journalism Centre: http://www.ejc.nl

Investigative Reporters and Editors: www.reporter.org/ and http://www.ire.org/datalibrary/: these sites were set up by the group Investigative Reporters and Editors to provide resources for journalists. They contain a wide range of information including databases and articles on journalism issues.

Journalism Net: www.journalismnet.com: the 3000 links on this site are maintained by TV journalist Julian Sher.

Journalist's Guide to the Internet: http://reporter.umd.edu: this extensive site is put together by Professor Christopher Callahan of the University of Maryland's College of Journalism.

Journalists' Toolbox: http://www.americanpressinstitute.org/toolbox: this is a useful web site for journalists and media workers with 2800 links.

Media Entertainment and Arts Alliance: http://www.alliance.org.au: this is the union covering the arts as well as journalists and its link page contains many useful references across government, industrial relations, media, and the arts.

Oz Guide: http://www.journoz.com: Internet Information Sources for Australian Journalists. This University of Queensland site assembles key links for journalists across a vast array of subject areas.

Power Reporting: http://powerreporting.com: this site, which has an international focus, is assembled by Bill Dedman (former Computer Asssisted Reporting director at Associated Press in New York).

Poynter Institute: http://www.poynter.org: an eminent school of journalism in the US with many articles and studies relevant to the practice of journalism.

University of Technology Sydney journalism site: http://www.journalism.uts.edu.au/subjects/jres/index.html: a list of resources for journalists covering media, government, and journalistic practice.

(The authors thank Stephen Quinn for helping us with some of these journalism sites.)

Media sites

Australian Broadcasting Corporation: http://www.abc.net.au

British Broadcasting Corporation: http://www.bbc.co.uk

Bloomberg L.P. (site devoted to finance and stockmarket news and information): http://www.bloomberg.com

Broadcast.Com (Live Online American Radio): http://www.broadcast.com

CNN Online (USA): http://cnn.com

NBC network (USA): http://www.msnbc.com

National Public Radio (USA): http://www.npr.org

Special Broadcasting Service: http://www.sbs.com.au

Sydney Morning Herald newspaper: http://www.smh.com.au

The Age newspaper: http://www.theage.com.au

Australian government sites

Australian Broadcasting Authority: http://www.aba.gov.au

Australian Bureau of Statistics: http://www.abs.gov.au

Australian Communications and Media Authority: http://www.acma.gov.au

Australian Law Reform Commission: http://www.alrc.gov.au

Australian Federal Government site: http://www.fed.gov.au: entry point for links to sites relating to federal and state governments.

The Australian Parliament Home Page: http://www.aph.gov.au

Organisations

Australian Copyright Council: http://www.copyright.org.au

Community Broadcasting Association of Australia: http://www.cbaa.org.au

Commercial Radio Australia: http://www.commercialradio.com.au

Free TV Australia: http://www.ctva.com.au/control.cfm

The Radio News Reporter

12

Scott Holdaway, political reporter, ABC News

Scott was attracted to journalism in his school days, drawn to the profession initially with the idea of becoming a sports reporter. He did a communications degree followed by a post-graduate diploma in journalism, while taking up any opportunity he could to do volunteer or freelance work in journalism in order to gain professional experience. Here the Web provided useful additional opportunities as he was able to file

Scott Holdaway, political reporter, ABC News

sports stories to web sites such as Baggygreen.com and sportal.com. He did an internship with the Perth daily newspaper the *West Australian* during his post-graduate year, but his entry into the industry came via broadcast journalism when he was offered the job of radio reporter with the ABC in Kalgoorlie. He is currently political reporter for ABC News in Perth.

As political reporter Scott's working day is determined by parliamentary hours when Parliament is in session. Otherwise his working day starts at 6.30 in the morning. If he hasn't already read the papers at home, on arriving at the newsroom he will immediately scan the *West Australian* and the *Australian* and begin to follow up stories in preparation for the flagship 7 am and 7.45 am bulletins. He blocks out the day, seeing what the main political players are doing and dividing up jobs between himself and his partner on the political round, and even pulling in other reporters on a particularly busy day. The day is spent sourcing his own stories by cold-calling and checking in to see what is happening around the traps. The rest of the day is spent writing up stories, on a quiet day two or three, on a busy day in excess of seven or eight, with at least two or three versions of each story.

Being a rounds reporter

Scott says: 'With any round—politics, the courts—they've got their own parameters, their own forum, and you are reporting on what happens within there. I think a big difference compared to a round like police or courts is that players in the political game often have a barrow to push as well—you are dealing with people who have a vested interest in pushing a particular line or argument—so it is really a case of enticing them to come to you with that information and then determining what's worthy of putting to air.

'The phrase they use to describe Parliament is "the house up on the hill" and it develops its own persona in a way. Because you are really working in such close confines with people, you have to determine whether how far what happens inside is actually relevant or resonates with people outside.

'It is important to be able to remain impartial. You certainly develop friendships with some politicians, whereas others you may not see or talk to for days on end. But when push comes to shove, and you are writing a story, you have got to treat everybody with the same level of impartiality and respect. Just because you don't have a cup of tea or a beer with them at some stage that doesn't mean that they deserve any different treatment.

'This can be hard sometimes. If, for instance, you have worked in a country town and got to know the local member really well, you have got to push that to one side and really focus and knuckle down on what the message is that they are pushing, why they are pushing it, and if it deserves coverage.'

They need to know how to use their voice, how to write for a commercial radio bulletin, how to get the most out of a story, how to present it in a way that's going to be interesting to listeners, how to make sure that they get and identify the most important issue in a particular story, for instance a news conference. There are so many different facets of the way we do our job—the whole day is a learning process and I don't think you ever stop learning.

Justin Kelly, News Director, 2GB Sydney

In the previous chapter we looked at the generic skills broadcast journalists need. To be a successful reporter in radio news, as the above quote from Justin Kelly indicates, you need a further range of quite specific skills, from being able to write quickly and read for meaning to being stress tolerant and able to work quickly under pressure.

The radio news reporter is often the last to arrive, panting and out of breath, at media conferences because they have had to run straight from a previous job. Reporting for radio news means you are on the go all day trying to get as many stories out as possible. Radio news reporters can expect to do up to fifteen stories per day. As a general reporter you can expect to cover emergencies, courts, parliament, and follow-up stories. You will wait patiently in courtrooms for a specific case to come up, or chase after politicians who refuse to speak. While hunting for stories you will be in contact with a multitude of sources.

And you will spend hours on the telephone, using it for research, for setting up interviews, and for telephone interviews. Of all technology used in the radio newsroom, the telephone is a news reporter's best friend.

Whereas in television you work in teams with a camera operator, and a tape editor, in radio you do everything yourself:

- You research the story.
- You operate the portable recorder, check the microphones, set the levels, and record the sound.
- You work the mobile phone and file a voice report on location based on your notes before heading back to the office.
- Back in the newsroom, you dump the recorded interview from the portable recorder onto the computer.
- You edit the story, write the intro and, in some cases, you even present the news on air.

You can see from this that in the radio newsroom you need to be a jack- and jill-of-all-trades and it is important to quickly become technologically multiskilled.

It is up to you to control all the different storygathering elements, in addition to being able to drive a car and read a map simultaneously.

Planning a radio news story

Newsroom at 2GB Sydney.

So what are the craft skills you need to put a radio news story together?

The angle

I think with radio news it is very easy because you've got such a short time to describe the story, you have really got to stick to the one path and stay on to the one line and the one angle, but what is drummed into you all along the way is that it must be new—I mean, that is what news is about, something that is new and something that hasn't been said before or hasn't been heard before. So finding the angle is probably about finding something that is new.

Scott Holdaway, political reporter, ABC News Perth

A news story can be tackled from many different perspectives. Trying to cover too many sides of an issue can be confusing for the audience, and the small format of news demands a clear and concise storyline. This is done through identifying the story's angle. No matter how big the subject, a story can only have one angle. Andrew Boyd (1997, p. 33) draws an analogy with a diamond:

> A diamond has many facets, and whichever way you hold it, it is impossible to look at them all at once. Some will always be hidden from view ... Each facet represents a different angle. The angle is the part of the story which the reporter chooses to hold up to the light at any one time.

Former Opposition Leader Mark Latham's illness and resignation provides a good example of this. This issue was headline news over several weeks, resulting in many different stories each picking up on a specific aspect of the issue. There was the story about Mark Latham's silence after the tsunami followed by speculations about his future as Opposition Leader. Then there were the stories of his actual resignation and questions about who would take over the leadership from him.

The angle can be determined by asking yourself why the story is being done today—what's new about it? This is crucial in radio news reporting since a news story is seldom longer than one minute. Working in such a small format, there is no room to go off on a tangent. The angle gives you a focal point for the story. It allows you to foreground a small part of an issue in order to highlight and explain a larger issue (the small picture in the big picture). It is useful to write the script early as part of your story planning. This forces you to focus on the one facet of the story to be shown to the audience. Also ask yourself what **topline** or **'hook'** you're going to use to get the audience interested in the story.

Research and background knowledge

Part of me thinks as long as you know how to ask the right questions that's all the knowledge you need, but of course to do that you have got to be backgrounded in whatever it is you are asking about, so being a so-called news junkie is a huge virtue: just being able to soak up information that you read in newspapers or see in television news reports or documentaries or magazines or whatever it might be. You certainly do get trapped in that news junkie-type addiction where you go home and you watch every news bulletin to see how they cover things differently, read every newspaper of a morning, and check out what news is floating around on the Internet. Again, all of that is useless if it goes in one ear and out the other—you have got to be able to store it somewhere and really use your brain as a library so you have got a recollection of it if it pops up again. It is about being able to capitalise on the information so that when you are talking to people you are able to ask the right questions.

Scott Holdaway, political reporter, ABC News Perth

I am covering more than forty [African] countries here and sometimes something can happen somewhere that you haven't had to cover much before and literally within 12 hours you are on a plane to that place to cover some big event. So you try and keep up with things as best you can, and read a lot of historical stuff to put things in perspective too. But sometimes you just get put on that plane and you have pulled something off the net or you've photocopied some other bits and pieces that you have and you just have got to go.

Sally Sara, foreign correspondent, ABC News and Current Affairs

Although time pressures mean that a lot of research in radio has to be crammed into the period when you are waiting for an interviewee to ring back or to arrive at the interview location, the more you know as a reporter the better the interview will be. Research for a radio story also encompasses collecting information about logistics involved in getting the interview.

- Where is it taking place?
- How long will it take to get there?
- Are there restrictions on the use of recording equipment (e.g. in the courts)?
- Can you access equipment?
- Is quality worth more than time, e.g. is it worth going on location or can it be done faster via phone?
- Will you have time to edit or should you file from location?

Based on the above research, the radio reporter can begin to collect the different ingredients of the story.

Finding talent

In broadcast media, interviewees are selected not only because of what they say, but also because of how they say it. A successful 'grab' is clear, concise, short, and snappy, but not everyone is blessed with the gift of speaking in self-contained 15-second grabs (or in the case of television news 6-second grabs). Politicians and other public figures understand the importance of getting the message across in a professional-sounding manner. They also realise that if the message is well packaged and easily accessible, they are more likely to get a spot on the news. This is why most interviewees who feature in broadcast news are trained spokespeople from company or government media offices, or public relations agencies. Even small organisations have staff dedicated to this role who have been trained to speak to the media. In these cases, the reporter isn't given the opportunity to select a talent—it is selected for them.

Journalists should strive to diversify their choice of talent to ensure that multiple opinions and voices are heard. Your contact file can help you, serving as a memory bank in which you record the expertise and broadcast suitability of the range of contacts you meet during the course of your work.

Briefing the talent

All talent, even trained media spokespeople, need to be briefed prior to the interview. They need to be told about the context of the interview and exactly what you want from them. The briefing will cover:

- the outline of the story and specifically the angle you are doing (there is no need to divulge your exact questions, though you can make the line of questioning clear)
- any special information you may require for which the talent may need to prepare
- whether the interview is recorded or 'live' and explaining the implications of each format (for example the former may be edited, while the latter will be going straight to air)
- when and where the interview will be broadcast.

The better prepared the talent, the more likely you are to get the answers and the performance that you are seeking.

Doing the interview

Interviewing is a generic term used to describe the process of extracting information from a person by asking questions. This can be done in many ways and the basics of interviewing have been covered earlier in chapter 6. However, radio news reporters need additional skills because of the very nature of news.

In contrast to the radio program, where the interview talent often wants to tell a story, the news interview can be more adversarial. Politicians are hardly likely to volunteer information about an embarrassing party scandal; a police spokesperson won't relish the prospect of facing the media to discuss corruption in the force. To get the answers, the journalist needs to:

- be prepared with the right background information, so evasive answers can be followed up
- be persistent to ensure they get the answers they want
- keep the audience constantly in mind. The interview isn't a private exchange but one done for their benefit
- be focused on the issue. Maintaining your concentration during a whole interview takes practice, especially when you are dealing with technology, watching the clock, and trying to steer the interview in the direction you want it to go—all at the same time
- make a discreet check of the sound levels as the talent is speaking. While maintaining eye contact is important in an interview, you also need to make sure that there are no technical hitches that might mar the sound quality
- speak confidently and clearly. Timid reporters are often disregarded
- avoid asking double-barrelled questions ('What would it take to change the procedures and how will this ensure it doesn't happen again?') since you risk getting only part of an answer
- nod or use other non-verbal cues instead of audible affirmation to avoid confusing the audience with extraneous sounds.

Many news interviews are conducted at media conferences where it is as important to ensure your microphone is pushed into a good position among all the other mikes as it is to ask the clever question. It is easy for radio reporters to become lazy interviewers because, in fact, their voices rarely feature in the final news story. It is usually just the grab (or **soundbite**) from the talent that is used, not the reporter's question. This makes it all too easy to hide sloppy interviewing techniques. Nevertheless, interviewing skills are vital for getting the result you need. The answers you get from your talent will depend on how you frame your questions and the order in which you ask them. Furthermore, you may have to do the interview live-to-air when the program or bulletin crosses to you on location, as happens with breaking stories. Honing your interviewing technique will ensure you are ready for such impromptu performances.

Filing stories

For radio news you file stories as soon as you can, bearing in mind the hourly or half-hourly bulletin deadlines. It is best to aim to have the story finished no later than quarter to the hour. Having to rewrite the copy 10 minutes before the news bulletin is not a good idea. Give yourself enough time to collect information, write up the story and file it.

Q&A

Radio news reporters can sometimes be on-air talent themselves when covering major events or breaking stories. This is usually done as a question-and-answer (**Q&A**) live into a radio program where a presenter asks the reporter to describe the scene and outline what has happened. Being interviewed live on air can be challenging, and having short bullet-point notes can help you keep track of what you need to say. If possible, try to find out what the program producer wants and prepare for the report as much as possible. In a Q&A, the language is more conversational than in a scripted news report.

Radio news story structure

After the sound grabs have been recorded, the next challenge is to edit them and assemble them into the story. The script will be the thread that weaves everything together. Your story can be told in many ways, but the main thing is it must be clear—and this includes sound quality as well as content. Radio stories must not only make sense; they also have to sound good.

Voice

Every person that we have in the newsroom has to be able to read the news. I could have the best writer, the best reporter, but if they can't use their voice I can't hire them.

Justin Kelly, News Director, 2GB Sydney

I don't mark copy as much as I used to—initially I marked it pretty heavily and a lot of the markings were markings I didn't need to make—they were markings that my brain would automatically pick up on if they weren't there. I still place underlines on words which need to be emphasised, and sometimes cross out words that need to be thrown away and don't need to be emphasised so I know not to dwell on them, to run through them quickly.

Scott Holdaway, political reporter, ABC News Perth

Being in command of your voice is vital when conveying a message on radio. As news reporter your voice may be an essential component of the story in a voice-report or as links in a **wrap**. The tone of the voice will differ depending on the emotion and mood of the story. Think of the difference in tone between a stockmarket report and a **voicer** from a riot or a war zone. A radio news script is concise and succinct and news copy sounds more formal and 'read' compared to other radio scripts. However, it is important to read for meaning and to use the full range of the voice—pace, volume, inflexion, and emphasis—in order to give life to the words used to tell the story.

Many news reporters mark their copy to ensure they emphasise keywords. Getting the breathing right is another important element in gaining a good news voice. More details about voice production and script delivery can be found in chapters 4 and 14.

Actuality

Radio is about sound, and even though in radio news time constraints often mean location sound, or actuality, is not used as much as it could be, it remains a powerful tool to get the message across. Radio takes us to where the action is, allowing us to witness the news as it happens almost instantaneously. Sound married with well-scripted and delivered words can create a powerful radio report and will allow listeners to 'be there'. The horrors of the hostage drama in the Russian school in Beslan were brought home in the radio news stories by letting the audience hear the sounds of grieving parents screaming out their despair.

Format

Stories can be crafted into different formats depending on the length of the bulletin and weight of the story.

Copy or 'words'

This is the smallest news story format. It is a short scripted version of the story written by the reporter, but read by the newsreader. It is called a 'word story', or 'words only', because it doesn't contain any voices from either reporter or talent. Radio copy is seldom longer than four or five paragraphs.

'Words and grab'

This is a piece of copy consisting of a short script read by the newsreader, followed by a recorded grab from the talent. With 'words and grab', the audio grab can be dropped without affecting the integrity of the story itself if the newsreader is short of time. The word copy does not include the reporter's voice or name.

Voicer

This is a news story told by the reporter using their own voice, with or without inserted grab(s) of interviewees. The voicer is a useful device where a summary or background of an issue is needed that requires a lot of facts and information. It consists of an intro, which is the word copy read by the newsreader, followed by a 20- to 30-second recorded report scripted and read by the reporter. The use of reporters' voices has been quite a controversial issue in Australia. In the ABC, for example, reporters were not allowed to file voicers until the 1970s. The public broadcaster was concerned that using the reporter's voice would make it sound as if the reporter were commenting on an issue rather than reporting straight facts.

Wrap

The wrap is the most expanded format in radio news. This is a package summarising a story that has been running over the course of the day. It re-tells the main points of the story, repackaging previously broadcast material. This is a self-contained edited piece comprising the reporter's voice and one or two interview grabs. It begins with the intro—the copy read by the newsreader—and is followed by a narrative integrating the reporter's scripted voice links with the selected grabs. The package can be about a minute long and often includes voices from more than one talent giving the story greater balance. This format allows for more comprehensive coverage of an issue, with room for background information and facts, as well as for different perspectives. Because of its length and complexity, this format is used mainly in the longer bulletins—the main bulletins in the morning and the late afternoon peak periods.

News flash

A **news flash** is used when news is deemed too important to wait for the next bulletin. If the prime minister were killed in a plane crash, the newsreader would break into the radio program with 'news just to hand ...' and read one or two paragraphs. It is used only for major breaking news stories with far-reaching consequences.

CD TRACK 13: This is a news story from Macquarie National News broadcast on 2GB on 20 January 2005 in the one o'clock bulletin. It is an example of the format 'word and grab'. The script could just as easily stand alone as a word copy.

Notice how the script contains most of the necessary information with the audio grab mainly providing colour. You will hear the newsreader reading the following script introducing the interview grab:

New transport minister JOHN WATKINS says he'll be catching trains to work as often as possible—as he begins to improve the system.

MR WATKINS and the Premier have toured SYDNEY's Central station to meet with rail staff—and travellers ... they arrived on a late-running train.

MR WATKINS says he hopes commuters will be patient—as he implements the Government's strategies ...

Multi-versioning

A massive advantage for radio is that you have numerous bulletins throughout the day, so if there is one story you can pick several different angles within that one story and put them to air at different stages of the day. So it generally follows a linear progression: you will have the story in the first bulletin and then perhaps rewrite that story with the same talent for the second version, and then you may be able to go to different talent for reactions to that story, and you can run different reactions throughout the day, and by the end of the day you might be able to wrap them up in a summary story. This is a huge advantage compared to, say, a print story whereby you get the one story to publish of a morning, even though they have much more space.

Scott Holdaway, political reporter, ABC News Perth

Radio news stories have a finite lifespan—the essence of news is that it be 'new' so individual stories die almost as soon as they are born. The expectation is that each bulletin will contain fresh material, and the multiple formats discussed above provide the capacity for **multi-versioning**: reworking story material so it tells the same story in a slightly different way. The best way to develop a story across the day is by using follow-up reactions to the main event.

SLUG		DCART	TALENT	DATE		COPY	
latham beazley		SN2		18/01/2005 13:58:25		0:13	
Dest: NOSE			99:	Writer:	hodgea2x	Subbed:	thompsonj8r
History:							
Headline:							
EX-RN-SYD							

Meanwhile, the man many people believe will stage a comeback to become the next labor leader, Kim Beazley, is due to make a public statement in about an hour.

Mr Beazley will hold a press conference at his home in Perth.

Example of a 'word' story.

SLUG		DCART	TALENT	DATE		COPY	
latham carr		ph863	carr	18/01/2005 7:35:29		0:35	
Dest:	NICE	99:	Writer:	willisl3e	Subbed:	willisl3e	

History:
Headline:

EX-RN-CPH
latham carr
willis

The New South Wales Premier, Bob Carr says he senses the
Federal Opposition is close to sorting out its leadership
crisis, fuelling speculation that Mark Latham may resign
this week due to ill health.

Mr Carr says it's essential that Mr Latham make a statement
on his future, saying he expects the issue to be resolved
this week.

The Labor Leader, who's recovering from severe pancreatitis
at an unknown location, has previously stated he plans to
return to work on Australia Day.

The Queensland Premier says if Mr Latham can't continue in
the job, former leader Kim Beazley should take over, and
Mr Carr agrees.

CART: obviously kim beazley presents the labor party with
an obvious option. i don't diminish the claims that the
younger people in the caucus would make, half a dozen of
them perhaps, but we've got to fill a leadership vacuum,
there'd be no argument with that.

Example of the same story as 'words and grab'. Note that the first four paragraphs make up a **stand-alone** story, which makes sense even if the grab is dropped.

SLUG		DCART	TALENT	DATE		COPY	
latham quits	1500	B 3483	haw/lath	18/01/2005 14:47:05		0:13	
Dest:	NICE	99:	Writer:	hawleys4g	Subbed:	lemaitrej8l	

History:
Headline: improves levels new cart

EX-RN-CPH
latham quits
hawley

Mark Latham has resigned as the Leader of the federal
Opposition and as a member of Parliament.

Mr Latham announced the decision at a press conference in
Sydney saying he wants to put his health and family first.

Samantha Hawley reports.

CART:After increasing pressure Mark Latham finally broke
his silence.//IN RECENT DAYS I HAVE BEEN ABLE TO GET AWAY
REST AND RECOVER AND TALK TO MY FAMILY ABOUT OUR
PRIORITIES FOR THE FUTURE. OUR CONCLUSION IS THAT I
SHOULD LOOK AFTER MY HEALTH AND PIRSUE A NORMAL LIFE
OUTSIDE OF POLITICS// Reading from a statement Mr Latham
said his problem with pancreatitis has been difficult to
overcome.// THIS CONDITION AND THE UNCRETAIN TIMING OF THE
ATTACKS ARE INCOMPATIBLE WITH THE DEMANDS AND STRESSES OF
A PALRIAMENTARY LIFE.// He says he had planned to reassess
his future when he returned from annual leave next week
but ongoing speculation was damaging the party. Mr Latham
has been the Leader of the ALP for just over a year. The
former Leader Kim Beazley is now tipped to take over the
position. Samantha Hawley Palriament House Canberra.

Example of a 'voicer' containing reporter's voice interspersed with talent grabs. It gives a more expanded account of the story.

Source: ABC News

In Australia, grabs are seldom longer than 10 to 20 seconds. A single interview, cleverly edited, may yield any number of short digestible 20-second grabs, each relevant to the story and therefore able to provide the focus of another version of it to carry across the day. Radio reporters can therefore expect to file multiple stories: for example, for a big story a radio news reporter might file a voicer, one 'word and grab', and one or two pieces of word copy. Television reporters, by way of contrast, will file only one or two stories a day, complete and self-contained with both sides represented.

Balance

There is seldom room to develop two sides of a story in a standard radio news item. As important as it is to allow both sides of an issue to have their say, radio producers accept that listeners will have to listen to many bulletins across a day to get the full picture. Much depends on the importance of the story: with some bigger stories, you might be able to present two different slants within the same bulletin.

If a story contains accusations or a controversial statement, a response from the identified person must be included. This can be done in a back announcement or as a separate story (called 'add' in news radio jargon). If the person has been contacted but declines to comment, this can be included as response.

Radio news scripting

You have to use language that you know that your listeners will understand—language that you know people use within their everyday conversation and will be immediately discernable to their ear. If you are talking about a radio news story that may be 40 or 45 seconds long, you don't want to say something that will make the person stop listening and pause for a moment and think 'hang on—what did that mean there?' because that means they have then lost the next 10 seconds of the story. The audience have really got to be able to keep pace and understand everything as it is said because unlike a print article, for example, they can't pause and then keep reading. They have to keep up with the story—they can't rewind and listen to something again.

Scott Holdaway, political reporter, ABC News Perth

The most important feature of any script is accuracy. It doesn't matter how well written your story is—it will lose credibility if the facts are incorrect. The content is the bottom line and the aim is to communicate that content to the listener using scripted words. People want to know what's going on so they can make sense of the world they live in. When you write a news story, make it interesting—find out how events and issues will affect your audience members.

Radio scripts are written for the listener's ear, not the eye, and have to be understood in a single hearing. With only one go at getting the short message across, a radio script has to be whittled down and revised many times to ensure it makes sense despite the restricted word limit.

Although the basic principles of radio writing (covered in chapter 5) hold for news scripting, news has a less conversational style. Just as the tone of voice must be neutral, so the script must be objective rather than personal, delivering fact as opposed to commentary. Some points to remember about news scripting include the following:

- Write for the ear and read the copy aloud to yourself as you write it.
- Keep sentences short—you should be able to read the whole sentence, or paragraph, without having to take a breath. On average, sentences shouldn't be more than about 20 words. Vary the length to create rhythm with some longer sentences and some shorter than 20 words.
- Use transitions to make your script flow between different aspects of the story. Use words like: 'meanwhile', 'however', 'in addition', 'on the other hand', 'also', 'too', 'but', 'and'.
- Make it simple: use 'about' not 'approximately', use 'dead man' instead of 'deceased adult male', use 'cut' not 'laceration'.
- Write tightly. Some adjectives and adverbs can be deleted from the story. 'That' can often be eliminated: 'She says that the plan will destroy the wetlands' becomes 'She says the plan will destroy the wetlands'.
- Watch spelling and punctuation as they are important markers for correct on-air delivery. Make sure your copy is neatly written and includes phonetic pronunciation of difficult names, places, and words.
- Use active voice ('The car crashed into the house' instead of 'The house was crashed into by the car').
- Use the present tense wherever possible. Radio news is about a current event—it is happening now. However, 'has' is commonly used in radio scripts, indicating that something has happened only moments ago: 'The premier has presented the budget ...' rather than 'The premier is presenting the budget ...'. The latter would only be appropriate if the premier were doing the budget presentation live into the bulletin.
- Write in a conversational style using contractions ('she'll' rather than 'she will'; 'he's' rather than 'he is').
- Include the person's title along with the proper name. Titles are generally included before a person's full first and last name: 'State Coroner Alastair Hope says...' This sets the name in context and gives listeners time to prepare themselves to register the name when it comes. A long and complex title might need to be explained to listeners: 'The chairman of a local save-the wetlands group says ...'.
- Use attributions to source information. In radio scripts attribution is usually included in the beginning of a sentence. 'Fremantle Mayor Peter Tagliaferri is urging West Australians to vote *no* and *no* in this weekend's referendum, as he believes extended trading hours will have a negative impact on Fremantle, Perth, and Rockingham.'
- Direct quotes are difficult to use in radio copy. Listeners can't see quotation marks so it's best to paraphrase the words if you don't have a grab: 'Fremantle Mayor Peter Tagliaferri says extended trading hours will have a negative impact on Fremantle, Perth, and Rockingham.'

- Round off complex numbers. Numbers are difficult to absorb when read aloud. Thus the figure of 496,213 would be expressed as 'about half a million' on radio. Write numbers so the newsreader can read them easily. News organisations use different styles, but one common method is to spell out single-digit numbers and use numerals for all two- and three-digit numbers. For numbers that include four or more digits a combination of the rules is used—1,800 becomes 'one-thousand-800',
- Don't begin a sentence with a key detail. Unlike in a newspaper, where articles are clearly separated through the use of layout, radio provides no helpful visual signposts. Instead, the voice is the only indication of where stories begin and end. With no cues other than the voice, listeners can take a moment to get up to speed and they may well miss the first word or two in a sentence. It is better to move the important detail further down and build up to it: 'On the West Bank—10 children are missing after a rocket attack demolished a school'.

								1
WRITER	SOURCE	CART	DUR	Tot.	SLUG		DATE	
EMAHER			00:00	00:10	FINANCE		20/01/2005 12:58	

In Finance...

The All Ords index is UP 17 at 40-38

GOLD trading at 423-U-S-dollars-30 an ounce.

Oil 47-U-S-86 a barrel

One AUSTRALIAN dollar buys 76 point OH-3 U-S cents

Script of finance report from Macquarie National News broadcast on 2GB on 20 January 2005. Note how the numbers are written to facilitate reading and understanding.

Script layout

The basic layout of a piece of radio news copy can tell us a lot about how radio news is written. The copy is made up of three parts: the lead, the background, and the throw or conclusion. Let's look at each section in turn.

Lead

This is the first paragraph of the news script and is its most important element. Just as television uses the best vision to pull viewers in, so in radio you use words in the punchiest way possible to grab the listener's interest. The lead should provide the story focus, and that includes what is new about it, as well as giving an attention-grabbing reason to listen.

Think about how you would tell your friends an important story. If you have seen a car crash, and you come home to tell your family, you wouldn't say: 'When I was coming home today, I saw two cars slowly approaching each other, they collided and caused a major traffic jam, and the road was closed off for hours'.

Instead, you would probably throw your bag on the floor and shout: 'Hey, I saw two cars smash into each other today, and there were cars and debris everywhere, and they had to close off the street for hours!'

You have begun with the most important detail, and the rest of the story follows. The news story follows the same format. The lead is like a headline conveying the essence of the story, and a good lead will stir the interest of the audience and make them want to hear more.

There is seldom room in the lead for more than one aspect of the story. One possible lead for our car crash story might be: 'A car accident on George Street this morning has left five people dead ... '

Later in the day, you could lead with the chaos caused by the blocking of the road during peak hour: 'In the city, traffic is flowing again on George Street. This follows serious disruptions earlier in the day caused by a car pile-up during the morning peak hour ... '

Try not to begin the lead with numbers. As noted above, in radio it takes a second or two for the brain to register what the ear is picking up. If you start with a number, you run the risk of the audience failing to register the information, whereas giving it a bit of a build-up will ensure that its significance is appreciated. Rather than saying 'Five died in a car accident ...' you can try: 'A multi-car pile-up during the morning peak hour has claimed the lives of five people ...'

Background

This part of the copy comprises the second, third, and (sometimes) fourth paragraphs, where the story is fleshed out with more facts and details. The background gives context to the information in the lead and answers many of the 'Ws' and 'H' questions: When was it? Where was it? Why did it happen? How did it happen? What kind of consequences will it have? A background paragraph often points back in time to fill in some of the history and allow listeners to gain an understanding of the bigger picture.

Throw or conclusion

This is the last paragraph of the copy. If the copy has no audio attached, the final paragraph works like a wrap-up, often pointing to the future. For example, 'The International Whaling Commission will present their decision later today ... ' or the classic 'The trial continues ... '.

As with the lead, here too words are important. The last words are the ones that listeners will generally remember, and therefore a news story should end with a bang on a strong and definite note.

If the copy leads in to a recorded grab or a voicer, the last paragraph becomes the 'throw'. The throw is scripted to ensure a smooth transition from the newsreader to the voice on the tape. It must include an introduction to the next voice we will be hearing. It can be short and simple—'Anne Smith reports ...'—or 'Neighbour James Bloggs saw the bomb explode ...'

Alternatively, it can incorporate a summary of the point the talent will be making so that the grab picks up from where the script leaves off. It is important to avoid duplicating what the talent will actually be saying:

Throw: 'RSPCA spokesperson Andy Nightingale says the dogs were in a terrible state.'

Grab of Nightingale: 'They had been without food for three days and were emaciated and distressed when we found them.'

Writing for radio requires you to be a ruthless subeditor of your own work. The difficult part is deciding what to include and what to discard. An average 20-second piece of copy is made up of only sixty words, which leaves no room for unnecessary details. The challenge for the radio news reporter is to condense while retaining the integrity of the information.

Current affairs

> The current affairs story needs to have strong characters; it needs to be more personalised, not in terms of the reporter, but in terms of taking people to where you are. So say if a peace deal is being signed to end a conflict in Sudan, well then your news story is going to be fairly straight about what's happened, why it's happened, maybe a bit of background in the last couple of sentences, whereas for radio current affairs I want to go off and speak to the guy who lost his leg in the conflict, and has been waiting to go home for ten years, to bring it to life.
>
> Sally Sara, foreign correspondent, ABC News and Current Affairs

Current affairs on radio and television became popular in Australia in the late 1970s and early 1980s. It is a format where today's news is explored in greater depth. A current affairs story can be described as a mix between a radio feature and a news story. Whereas radio news covers just one aspect of an issue, the same story presented on, for example, the ABC's *AM* program would have the scope to explore multiple news angles.

The main difference between news and current affairs is the length of the story and this impacts on the way the longer story is developed. An average radio current affairs story runs for about 4 minutes, its length depending on how newsworthy the topic is.

Current affairs reporters have more time to devote to research, gathering, and editing of a story. On the other hand, a longer format demands more in terms of scripting, choice of talents and especially the use of actuality to get the point across. The longer format allows reporters to use less formal and more creative ways of telling the news. Whereas news writing never has a personal touch, a current affairs story can let the listener catch a glimpse of the reporter.

Technical skills for radio reporters

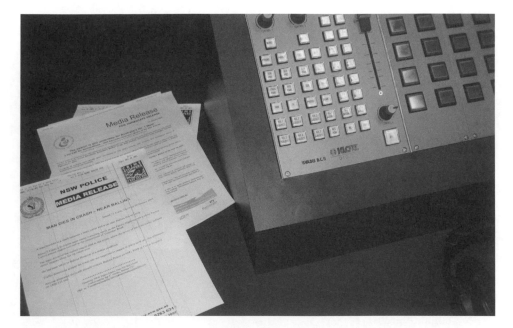

Newsroom desk, 2GB.

> I think to have a go and become really technically switched on is very important. If there's a problem with satellite gear or microphones or cables or whatever, you need to be good at that because you could be the best journalist in the world but if you can't get your story out and get it out on time it doesn't mean a thing.
>
> Sally Sara, foreign correspondent, ABC News and Current Affairs

Radio news reporters use a wide range of technical equipment as daily reporting tools. With no time to practise while on the job, it is important to make sure that you are technically proficient before going into the newsroom. The use of audio equipment for recording and editing is discussed in more detail in chapter 7. However, below is a list of equipment you are likely to encounter in a radio newsroom.

Audio recording

- Minidisc
- Flashcard recorder
- Microphone (mono or stereo; condenser or dynamic).

Audio editing

- Digital audio editing software like: iNEWS, Pro Tools, D-Cart, NewsBoss
- Minidisc editing
- News management systems such as iNEWS, NewsBoss, ENPS, Basys.

Office equipment

- Telephone
- Mobile phone
- Fax machine
- Word processing including email software.

Exercise

Record and transcribe one leading news story from ABC radio news and one from a commercial radio news service. Compare the two stories looking at the following:

- story length
- story development
- scripting style
- length of grabs.

Further reading

Alysen, B. 2000, 'Writing and Narrating', in *The Electronic Reporter: Broadcast Journalism in Australia*, Deakin University Press, Geelong, pp. 73–95.

Boyd, A. 1997, 'The Interview' and 'Setting up the Interview', in *Broadcast Journalism: Techniques of Radio and TV News*, 4th edn, Focal Press, Oxford, pp. 79–91, 92–107.

Dobson, G. 2005, *Better Broadcast Writing, Better Broadcast News*, Pearson Education, Boston, Mass.

Herbert, J. 2000, *Journalism in the Digital Age: Theory and Practice for Broadcast, Print and On-line*, Focal Press, Oxford, pp. 193–212.

Hilliard, R. 2000, 'News' in *Writing for Television, Radio and New Media*, 7th edn, Wadsworth, Belmont, pp. 111–54

McLeish, R. 2005, 'News—Policy and Practice' and 'Newsreading and Presentation', in *Radio Production*, 5th edn, Focal Press, Oxford, pp. 53–79, 115–27.

Masterton, M. & Patching, R. 1997, 'Techniques—Radio', in *Now the News in Detail: A Guide to Broadcast Journalism in Australia*, 3rd edn, Deakin University Press, Geelong, pp. 147–72.

Wulfemeyer, T. 1995, *Radio-TV Newswriting: A Workbook*, Iowa State University Press, Ames, IA.

Web sites

Writing for Radio: http://www.newscript.com. This is a web site about newswriting for radio. It contains links, glossary, and an overview of radio news.

National Public Radio: http://www.npr.org/about/nextgen/howto/. Radio Journalism training online from NPR news (USA).

Poynter Institute: http://www.poynter.org. This is the online site for Poynter Institute for Journalism training. It includes a section on radio and television reporting with online tutorials (USA).

13

The Television
News Reporter

All-in interview

Television I found to be a very ego-driven business and anyone being honest as a reporter on television will admit that for a brief time at least, and sometimes permanently for other people, you fall in love with yourself, and I thought that was pretty tremendous seeing myself on the news that night, and I'll admit to having an ego that couldn't get my head through the door for a time.

Howard Sattler, radio talkback presenter, 6PR Perth

There are many similarities between radio news reporting and reporting for television news. Both produce material for broadcast, with scripts written for the voice rather than the eye. Both require reporters to work within severe time constraints towards multiple strict deadlines.

The television medium, though, is often regarded as the big brother of radio. It is seen as more influential, and its reporters acquire greater fame and earn more money than their radio colleagues. This higher profile looks set to continue in the digital age when the convergence of television and the computer has the potential to give television an even greater role in our lives.

When it comes to the practice of journalism there are distinctive differences between the two media. While a radio news story is put together by the reporter operating as both journalist and technician, the television news story is developed through teamwork at all levels of the production process:

- Vision has to be shot on location, and most newsrooms operate with two-person teams: one reporter and one camera/sound operator. (In some larger productions, a sound recordist may be included for location shoots.)
- The material then has to be edited into the final package, which involves the tape editor who, while following editing instructions given by the reporter, has some freedom in how the vision is joined together.
- Finally the story is checked by a producer and slotted into the rundown of the next bulletin.

Planning a television news story

Katy Cronin: Reflections of a Television Journalist

Katy Cronin has worked for ABC television as foreign correspondent and news and current affairs reporter. She left the ABC in 2001 and here reflects on some key elements of television reporting.

Katy says: 'When you first start in television, there's this awful sort of self-consciousness, that you're on camera—you become, very often, totally preoccupied with the baggage and the performance. You have to enjoy the performance and you have to want to be out there performing and having your voice heard and your face seen. If you don't like that, or if that makes you uncomfortable, then you will

Katy Cronin, television journalist

find the job a bit more difficult. Sometimes I wonder whether in television the reporter becomes too much part of the story because you're expected to put your dial up there in front of the camera. That's a question of styles, and some people are good at it, and flourish, and love it, and do it very well, and other people don't.

'You have to push and ask and wheedle and cajole and plead and try. It's the strategic stuff of just really trying to get what you've got to get that does make you more wound-up and it makes the job more stressful in many ways, and it also requires a certain sort of hard attitude to just going and getting what you've got to get in terms of news, and I'm talking about news here—the daily pressure.

'You can actually do television and know nothing about the process of making it because you have a camera operator, and if you're lucky a sound recordist who know how to make television, and they know what the picture sequence will be, and they know how to edit, so they understand what sort of shots they need to make a story. Now I think it's always extremely helpful as a reporter to know the process too, but you can actually get away with not knowing it.

'It's really hard to do ideas on television. It takes enormous skill and planning and imagination, and by and large what you're doing every day with a news story is just running around and getting what you can get in a day, and that doesn't always mean that you have a mass of fantastic material to work with, so then you have to be a little creative. News is really tough on television. I think you've got to have a fairly strong stomach to do it well on an ongoing basis, particularly in a competitive environment. The need to get those pictures, and to get your talent to say what they need to say on the day, necessarily makes television journalists more aggressive.

'I like the idea of being in the thick of things, that you could have a job where there's an element of performance, there's fantastic intellectual stimulation, creativity, writing, and being where important and interesting things are happening.'

As a TV reporter you have more time allocated to tell the story—both in production and on air. The standard TV news story (excluding the intro) is 1 minute and 20 seconds long while the equivalent story on radio would run for 20 to 30 seconds. This means that in a television format you are able to offer multiple perspectives on an issue. Unlike radio news, where listeners have to catch successive bulletins across the day to get different perspectives on a single issue, the TV version will generally be a complete, balanced account that packages comment from both sides. As with radio news, you never know what story you will be covering. As a general television news reporter it could be business, politics, health, courts, or a follow-up of a previous story.

Before we look at the details of how to craft a television news story, let's go out on the road with a television reporter. Having summarised the process of getting a television news story to air, let's see how it all works in real life.

A day in the life of a TV reporter

Marianne Ellis is a reporter for National Nine News in Perth. She graduated from university in 1998 and worked for ABC and commercial radio in regional and metropolitan WA before moving to television. We follow her on a typical news reporting day (23 December 2004).

8.00 am—Marianne is rostered on the morning shift and has two media conferences lined up. The first is about a police foal being named in a competition. In the second, police warn about a blitz on drink driving after Christmas work parties. It's a slow news day so both police stories will probably end up in tonight's bulletin; the police filly as a reader voice-over (RVO) and the drink driving as a possible package.

10.00 am—The three commercial networks have all sent teams to the Mounted Section stables in Perth. The naming of a young foal will make good vision for a light end-of-bulletin piece.

During the interview about how the horse got its name, the Acting Assistant Commissioner Darryl Lockhart also tells journalists about a P-plate driver who was caught in central Perth speeding at 45 kilometres over the limit. Mr Lockhart informs the journalists about this year's Christmas Road Campaign. He takes some questions on the topic. But there's no vision of the offending driver and for the time being none of the journalists seem really interested in the story.

11.30 am—Time for the next police media conference. Superintendent Kevin Looby warns employees about drink driving after Christmas work parties. The warning is echoed by a spokesperson from St John Ambulance.

12.00 pm—No statistics are presented linking Christmas parties to an increase in accidents, so Marianne has no real facts to put in a news story. But it's early yet and the angle can change. Camera operator Trent Nind goes hunting for cutaways.

12.30 pm—When you're on the road everything happens on the run—the car becomes your office and your dressing room.

Marianne begins to structure her package. It will contain short interview grabs, voice-over links and a piece to camera (PTC).

Marianne and Trent drive around looking for a good spot to record the PTC and after some looking, they decide on a location in a light industrial area with the skyline of Perth as backdrop.

The PTC is a short scripted voice piece that creates a sense of presence in the story. It also saves having to find vision for overlay for that bit of the script.

1.30 pm—Marianne is back at the station. She goes through the raw material (rushes) logging the tape for useful grabs and vision. She does a quick shotlist and writes down timecodes for the sections of the tape she wants to use. The story will probably require some file vision that can be found on the computer system or in the tape library. Once the grabs and vision have been decided on, she can write the draft script.

2.00 pm—Producer Robert Broun wants her to lead the story with the P-plate driver who lost his licence and follow with the police crackdown on drink driving towards the end of the piece.

All stories are subbed by the producer before they're edited. Marianne has to rewrite the script and can now use short interviews from both media conferences.

3.00 pm—Tape editor Lorna Hurst looks through the rushes to get a sense of footage available. In her script, Marianne has written down timecodes for the interview grabs she wants. She has already identified suitable vision, but Lorna's job is to ensure that the story flows well visually. Often the tape editor will edit the story based on script and instructions while the journalist goes off to do another story.

Marianne's package 'Xmas party blitz' ends up being just over a minute long. Later in this chapter (p. 227) you can see the final storyboard of Marianne's story.

The angle

As you can see above, the angle can, and often does, change across the reporting day. In radio, the miniature format and the capacity to do multi-versioned stories across a day enables (or forces) journalists to mould stories into concise and succinct packages with little scope for them to get sidetracked. The longer television format with three layers of information (vision, audio, and script) can make it more difficult to retain a clear and logical storyline. A clearly defined angle prevents you from going off on tangents that detract from the impact of your story. For this reason, it is useful to write the introductory script (the intro) early as part of the planning—this makes you focus on the one facet of the story that you will select to show to the viewers. If you can't tell the story using one or two introductory paragraphs, the angle isn't clear enough.

The challenge for television journalists is not only to tell the story clearly, but also to personalise it so that it makes an impact on the audience. The easiest way to achieve this dual goal is to have a human hook, a 'case' with which viewers can easily identify. A story about cuts in funding to childcare services will have more impact if it includes comments from a parent as well as from a politician and a childcare-centre manager. When using this technique, it is important to use the script to give facts and other information that set the 'case' in context. The parent isn't the whole story, simply an illustrative example to help the audience identify with the issue.

Doing the research

As with radio, basic research for a television news story encompasses collecting information about the issue, such as statistics and other facts; finding suitable talent; and working out the logistics of getting actuality.

For television news 'actuality' is both natural sound and vision and the research component therefore also includes vision research such as:

- Will we be able to get into the building with the camera and tripod?
- What do we do if it's raining?
- Is there ample light in the building for filming (do we need to bring extra camera lights)?
- Are there people involved in the story that shouldn't be on vision (such as in some court cases for example)?

The bulk of the work is done on the phone before leaving the newsroom. Mobile phones make research easier, since you don't have to be office-bound and can make these phone calls on location or while travelling.

If time permits, television news reporters often try to draft a script before leaving the newsroom. This strategy is helpful for deciding what vision is needed for the voice-overs that will join together the interviews in the package. Thinking about vision and words simultaneously can be difficult for inexperienced television reporters. Writing a draft script can make the process less abstract, and it will also make it easier to brief the camera crew about the story.

Finding talent

A lot of time is spent each day setting up interviews, chasing talent, and persuading them to talk on camera. Persistence pays: don't rely on them ringing back—either ask to be put on hold, or ring them back yourself. Sending an interview request by email can be a good way of getting past conscientious minders. The email also allows you to send additional information to the talent such as an outline of the planned interview, time of interview, your contact details, and the interview deadline. However, in a 'same-day' story where a quick answer is needed, the telephone is still the main method of communication. An interviewee is more likely to agree to the interview if they understand the context of the story: what the angle is, what other people will be interviewed, and what program the story will be broadcast in.

As with radio, television demands a high level of performance from its talent—how they appear on camera is as important as what they say. This leads to a frequent criticism of television production: that broadcasters use too much 'tame talent', people who can look good on camera while producing succinct, often entertaining, statements. All too often this can result in issues being presented in terms of black and white, ignoring the shades of grey. This tendency is exacerbated by the need for grabs that are even shorter than in radio—often only a few seconds long. The problems of relying on dedicated media spokespeople have already been discussed (see p. 185). Like their radio colleagues, television journalists should actively work towards diversifying the range of talent to include 'non-professionals'. Almost anyone can answer questions in front of a camera if they are briefed properly.

Briefing the talent

Many journalists wouldn't dare to appear on camera with anything less than full make-up, freshly groomed hair, and a prepared script. Yet we expect talent to perform intelligently when they are comparatively unprepared, and are having to endure a camera lens and microphone shoved at their faces. On television, the interviewees are doubly exposed with both faces and voices on display, so they are even more self-conscious and concerned to present themselves and their case appropriately.

Few things are as intimidating as talking in front of a camera and the journalist should constantly bear this in mind. Most people will feel more comfortable if they understand the process they are part of. This should include both a technical and an editorial briefing explaining:

- the recording process: 'you have to stand still and look at me and not at the camera'
- the editing process: 'don't worry if you make mistakes, we can edit them out later'
- the performance: 'it's better for you to give short answers since we won't then have to edit you down'
- the 'shooting ratio': 'the interview (including **cutaways** and **establishing shots**) may be 5 to 6 minutes long, but will only be used as short grabs of 3–10 seconds length in the final story'
- the topic, which includes a general overview of questions to be asked
- where the talent fits in to the story
- who else will be in the story (if you know)
- where and when the story is going to be broadcast.

While most journalists are reluctant to let talent read their questions before the interview (it invites censorship and reduces spontaneity) a pre-interview briefing is an essential ingredient for a successful outcome. Rather than listing the questions, you can outline the areas or specific issues you will cover. Be honest with the talent and don't waste their time. If you are only going to use a short grab, don't spend 20 minutes doing the interview. It might be enough just to ask two or three questions.

Doing the interview

You have to say: why am I interviewing this person? Why are they important, and what is it that I think that person can contribute to my story, to help explain it to the audience, to help it make sense, to give it life? I find often you're also trying to get the best performance out of your talent, so you try to make them comfortable, but you also try to get them to speak up with energy.

Katy Cronin, television journalist

The principles of interviewing covered in chapters 6 and 12 are equally applicable to television interviews. Every interview has three perspectives—the journalist's, the talent's, and the audience's—and the journalist has to conduct the interview bearing all three perspectives in mind. This includes monitoring the interviewee's answers to ensure they fulfil your requirements for the story. At the same time you have to make sure the talent doesn't overstep legal and/or ethical boundaries. All the while you have to keep the audience in mind: will they understand what is going on? If the talent doesn't make a point clearly enough, you can always stop the interview and ask the question again. Clarity is crucial in broadcast journalism.

In addition to interview content there is the time factor to consider. Most grabs included in television news stories are under 10 seconds, and may sometimes be only 2 to 3 seconds long. This means it is important to frame the questions correctly and cleverly in order to get the answers you want. So how do you ask questions that generate short answers?

- Ask directed questions rather than open ones: 'Why is this road so dangerous?' instead of 'What do you think about this road?'
- Ask questions about the 'why' rather than the 'what': for example 'Why did you decide to close off this street?' instead of 'What have you done here?'

Finally, there is the question of impact. In this sort of story format the journalist carries the narrative and uses grabs from the talent to illustrate a point. The purpose of your questions is to capture emotion. If you are reporting on a save-the-forests protest, for example, asking the protesters an open question such as 'What do you think of the government's new forest policy?' would simply prompt a dry discourse on the political background. On the other hand, a direct approach question such as: 'Why are you protesting?' would very quickly get to the heart of the matter. If you do get a long-winded answer first up, you may then need to rephrase the question or ask the talent to keep the answer short.

Listening is perhaps one of the most important journalism skills. While doing the television interview, reporters need to listen both to what is being said, and to how it is said, to be able to follow up with: 'Why do you say that?'; 'What do you mean by that?'; 'Can you explain further?'

Knowing what you need

As a television journalist, before you embark on the story hunt, you need to be clear about what is expected of you from the newsroom.

- What does the Chief of Staff or producer want in terms of story angle?
- How long should the story be?
- Will there be related stories on the same topic to take into account?
- When does the COS/producer want the story filed?

The 'when' is perhaps the most important question of all for the journalist. Deadlines are sacred and there is no point using up time to get amazing vision if that extra effort means you will miss the evening bulletin. Asking the 'when' question also helps you to establish what else your supervisor needs from you in the form of live phone reports or satellite links on location as updates across the day.

Briefing the team

Channel Nine reporter Marianne Ellis and camera operator Trent Nind check the quality of their footage after a location shoot.

There are great crews who make your life so much easier, and there are crews that make life extremely difficult. I think managing that is something that you really have to think about as a reporter in television.

Katy Cronin, television journalist

Journalism is about communication, and that includes communicating with the people around you who are involved in putting the story together. That is where good journalism starts, and where a lot of people go wrong. The news process in television is complex and involves many people, all of whom need to be briefed about the story in progress: the Chief of Staff (COS), who might need the team back at a specific time; the producer, who wants to know what prominence to give the story in the bulletin; the assistant producer, who has to organise details like titles and edit suite bookings; and so on. The list can get even longer, depending on the newsroom structure.

Getting what you want, in terms of sound, vision, and content, begins with you as the reporter briefing your crew. This often happens while driving to the interview location. Hopefully, you will have had time to begin structuring the story and even to decide on some crucial vision. The camera operator needs to know the following to be able to work as part of a team:

- What is the story about?
- What is the angle of the story (main points of the story)?
- Who is being interviewed?
- Where is the location of the interview (is there a need for extra light or batteries)?
- How much time is allocated for recording?
- How long will the final piece be?
- Is any special vision required to correspond with the script the reporter has in mind?

This briefing isn't a one-way exchange—it is most important to encourage suggestions and input from the crew members. Many inexperienced television journalists rely on and learn from the expertise of the station's camera operators. While the crew may seldom have degrees in journalism, they have an abundance of experience in the field. They know the local issues inside out, they find their way around the locations, they find addresses, and they know the faces of politicians and other frequently interviewed talent. A good camera crew is worth its weight in gold and deserves a bit of pampering from the reporter. Looking after the camera crew is seen as part of the journalist's role, and that can involve planning for a lunchtime break or time out for a quick coffee while chasing the story.

The TV news story

Getting the pictures—the tyranny of the pictures—is what makes television so powerful and at the same time can be so limiting. If you've not got a story with great vision, then it's never going to really work brilliantly on television.

Katy Cronin, television journalist

For radio you can just quietly go and get someone for an interview, but for TV unless you can get the pictures it didn't happen, and that can be difficult.

Sally Sara, foreign correspondent, ABC News and Current Affairs

A well-told story in television terms must not only be informative, but must also make an impact on the audience. It is relatively easy to craft 'spot' news stories because of the natural element of drama in them: the rescue of a swimmer at the local beach, or the search for a missing aeroplane with engine problems. The use of vision is straightforward (the lifesavers struggling in the waves in the first example, and the vision of flight control and a circling helicopter in the second). It is much more challenging to report on, for example, the latest development in gene technology. Dry abstract, or administrative, stories are the ones that put the inexperienced journalist to the test. The most common mistake new reporters make is in telling the story using too many facts and without making it relevant to the audience.

Before looking more closely at story structure and development, we need first to understand the different types of television news stories.

Story formats

There are three main story formats for a television news story, and the main points of difference hinge on the respective roles of newsreader and reporter.

1. '**Live read**' is a word story read by the newsreader on camera. The TV news copy is seldom longer than two to three paragraphs (10 to 15 seconds).
2. RVO (**reader voice-over**) is read by the newsreader, partly on camera and partly as voice-over on vision. The technical director has to make sure that the news presenter's timing is correct and that the words will match with the pictures when the script is being read live-to-air. This is done through rehearsal and altering words to suit. The RVO is generally no more than five paragraphs long (a one- or two-paragraph introduction on camera followed by two or three paragraphs of narration as voice-over; total 35 seconds). If the RVO contains an interview—where the newsreader has to pause to include a pre-recorded grab—the overall length of RVO will be longer. Here, rehearsing reading the script to time is vital for the news presenter.
3. 'Package' is the newsreader's intro followed by a self-contained complete package from the reporter. The package features both reporter and talent, consisting of the reporter's narration edited together with interview segments and possibly a reporter's **stand-up** (a 10- to 15-second 'read' plus a package of 1:10 to 1:50 minutes).

Piece to camera (PTC)

You have to be rather exaggerated on television, I think. Attaining authority on television as a woman is still a hard thing to do consistently—you never rest entirely easy with that and I think your voice level is really crucial. In radio you have to be quite disciplined—it is different to being exaggerated, you just have to find a level and then you have to move within a range of about 20 per cent of that level you're comfortable with.

Geraldine Doogue, radio and television presenter, ABC

Sometimes you can't shoot a piece to camera for two or three days because you are just absolutely filthy, sweaty and disgusting, and you have to set aside a morning where you get up early to wash and you can knock over two or three.

Sally Sara, foreign correspondent,
ABC News and Current Affairs

Writing the script for a piece-to-camera.

The **piece to camera** (also known as the stand-up) is a further variation of the story format, although it is part of the story itself rather than external to it. It involves the reporter addressing the camera directly, looking straight into the lens and speaking a short link. Many networks expect reporters to include a PTC in every story as a way of branding it with both the reporter's and the station's names. It can be a useful component of the story for a variety of reasons:

- It shows the reporter as a physical presence on location and in the story.
- It saves time as it is a quick way of producing a verbal and visual bridge between two grabs.
- It solves the problem of finding suitable shots to cover a voice link.
- It can be used to start a second strand of information halfway through the package or to sum up the story at the end.

A PTC might sound and look as if it is ad-libbed, but it seldom is. Instead, the reporter learns the text off by heart, or finds a way of reading the text without this being obvious on camera. One technique is to write the link on a big piece of paper or cardboard and hang it below the camera lens. Another is to use safety pins to attach the script to the camera operator's shirt, with permission of course! Both tricks will work only if the journalist retains eye contact with the camera lens at all times. Any eye movement to the side will look unprofessional and viewers will be quick to pick it up. Since it is quite challenging to keep your focus on the middle of the lens, memorising the text is the recommended option.

It can be difficult to know what to include in the PTC since it means you have to anticipate what will be required when the rest of the story is assembled in the editing suite. As a rule, the PTC will contain basic information crucial to the story: 'two people were killed here on this road today ...'. Also it will be brief, seldom longer than 15 to 20 seconds, first because it is hard for the reporter to recall a longer text, and second because one person talking straight into the camera can become tedious for the viewers. The PTC tends to be placed in the middle or towards the end of the story. If it is the last ingredient it will also include the reporter signing off on camera: 'This is Susan Staff reporting for ... '

In a PTC, the reporter is on display. This is why television journalists pay more attention to their appearance than their radio colleagues. It is also why they tend to have a higher public profile. Nevertheless, as with all journalism, it is important to remember that whatever the story—be it a short news story or a longer in-depth profile interview—the focus is on the issue and the talent, not the journalist. The journalist is merely 'the person through whom the story is told'.

Building blocks

As with radio news, a television news story consists of many different components. The first thing the reporter has to do is to work out the structure—what building blocks will be used and in which order. The main components are:

- interviews
- script (reporter's own narrative in the form of a voice-over overlaid with vision)
- actuality (called 'natural sound on tape' or **NATSOT** in television)
- graphics
- reporter's PTC.

Structure

Having identified the building blocks, it is now time to focus on how the story is told. The narrative is the basis of any broadcast story and in television the challenge is to deliver this narrative within the limited time at your disposal. There are two main approaches to story-telling:

- *Chronological.* Here the story is told as it happened, from beginning to end. This can be problematic for news since it means that you start with the oldest material: 'the drama started this morning outside the post office on Park Street ... '. News is about bringing the latest information to the audience, and the chronological structure can sometimes work against this.
- *Non-chronological or circular.* Here you start with the latest information, then go back to give background and context, before returning again to the situation as it currently stands: 'volunteers are searching for a couple who went missing while climbing a nearby mountain ... / ...it's the third time this year that people have disappeared in this popular area and locals are urging police to put up warning signs ... / ... both the missing people are described as experienced climbers'. This option allows you to retain the feeling of 'here and now' essential to news. (See pp. 223–5 for an illustration of how this applies to a story.)

Story structuring involves not only how you order the shots and script, but also how you weave together voice, interview, and actuality. Long voice pieces that can be boring to watch can be broken up with a variety of ingredients. For example, you can have a short voice-over/ followed by a grab/ followed by another voice-over/followed by actuality ('natural sound')/ followed by a PTC, and so on. This injects life into the story and makes it much more entertaining for the eye and the ear.

Building the story

Writing a draft script before leaving the newsroom can be useful for a variety of reasons. It makes instructing the crew easier: 'These are my words and I need the vision to match the script'. It also highlights what talent is needed and whether graphics could enhance the story. Most research is done on the phone from the newsroom and the reporter might be able to write the whole story before the interviews are done, based on the information collected from various phone calls.

This is how a first draft of a script might look. The narration is a single piece of text that is chopped up into smaller portions and adapted for insertion between interviews and PTCs.

> Three students were injured in a vicious stabbing at Luke High School in City West late this afternoon. One was seriously injured and rushed to Central Hospital with gashes to his neck and arm. Students at the school say it's gang warfare: two knives and a machete have been confiscated. The police are investigating the stabbing, but no one has yet been charged over the attack. Eyewitnesses saw two 16-year-old boys on the ground. It's unclear who attacked the three teenagers. The police are questioning one of the victims. A friend of one of those injured says there's tension between different gangs at Luke High School, but both police and the school deny there's a problem. The principal says there have been threats before, but never any violence like this. But students who don't want to be named for fear of being attacked themselves say violence is common at the school.

From reading the script, it is clear who the talent could be in this story: students, the principal, and a police officer. After you have done the interviews, the interview grabs you extract might look something like this:

Police officer: 'It's my understanding this is an isolated incident at this school. We won't know whether it's gang-related or not until the investigation's finished.'

Principal: 'We've had threats before, but no real violence like this. It's the first time we have had the police here.'

Student 1: 'We saw them on the ground. They were patching them up.'

Student 2: 'I've seen people get bashed up when there're no teachers around. I saw it last week'

Student 3: 'It's crazy stuff. I've seen all sorts of weapons here before— knives, knuckle-dusters.'

Once the interview soundbites are organised and edited down to size, you can then decide how to tell your story. When it comes to structure there is no right or wrong way of organising the components. As long as the end result makes sense, is interesting, and contains relevant information, the building blocks of your story can be put together in any number of ways. Most of your previously drafted script can be reused when compiling the story, though some sentences will need to be altered so that the building blocks fit together smoothly. One possible structure could be:

Newsreader's intro: *Three students have been injured following a knife attack late this afternoon at Luke High School in City West. One boy was seriously hurt and was rushed to Central Hospital with gashes to his neck and arm.*

STUDENT 1

'We saw them on the ground. They were patching them up.'

REPORTER

Students at the school say it's gang warfare, two knives, and a machete have been confiscated.

STUDENT 3

'It's crazy stuff. I've seen all sorts of weapons here before—knives, knuckledusters.'

REPORTER

A friend of one of those injured says there's tension between different gangs at Luke High School, but both police and the school deny there's a problem.

POLICE OFFICER

'It's my understanding this is an isolated incident at this school. We won't know whether it's gang-related or not until the investigation's finished.'

REPORTER (could be PTC)

But students who don't want to be named for fear of being attacked, say violence is common at the school.

STUDENT 2

'I've seen people get bashed up when there're no teachers around. I saw it last week.'

PRINCIPAL

'We've had threats before, but no real violence like this. It's the first time we have had the police here.'

REPORTER

The police are investigating the stabbing but have yet to charge anyone over the attack.

Scripting for television news

While radio reporters use words as their tool to describe news to listeners, television reporters must learn to minimise the use of words and instead allow the vision to 'speak'. Viewers already have to process two strands of information—audio and vision—so it is necessary for the reporter's script to be as simple as possible. Most of the basic rules below are shared between radio and television scripting:

* Begin the story with clear and precise information using the five 'Ws'. The opening should be a summary of the story pointing out what's new in it ('selling' it to the audience)
* Read the copy aloud to yourself as you write it.
* Write the script to match the vision, not the other way around. When possible, write the script while logging the tape. That way the script can be written and timed to fit exactly into a segment of the vision. Don't script what the viewers can see and hear for themselves: 'The car came to a screeching halt ... '.
* Trust the power of the picture—allow strong vision to run without being cluttered with words.
* Choose words that are familiar to everyone: use 'about' not 'approximately', use 'dead man' instead of 'deceased adult male', use 'cut' not 'laceration'. The viewers will only see the message once. They can't go back and reread as they can a newspaper.
* Use a conversational and informal tone using contractions ('she'll' rather than 'she will'; 'he's' rather than 'he is').
* Use transitions to make your script flow between different aspects of the story. Use words like 'meanwhile', 'however', 'in addition', 'on the other hand', 'also', 'too', 'but', and 'and'.
* Cut out unnecessary words. Some adjectives and adverbs can be deleted from the story. 'That' can often be eliminated: 'She says that the plan will destroy the wetlands' becomes 'She says the plan will destroy the wetlands'.
* Avoid starting every sentence with 'The' and don't use the same word twice in one sentence.
* Watch spelling and punctuation as they are important markers for correct on-air delivery. Make sure your copy is neatly written and includes phonetic pronunciation of difficult names, places, and words.
* Use active voice ('The car crashed into the house ...' instead of 'The house was crashed into by the car').

- Direct quotes are difficult to use in broadcast copy. The audience can't see quotations marks so it's best to paraphrase the words if you don't have a grab: 'Fremantle Mayor Peter Tagliaferri says extended trading hours will have a negative impact on Fremantle, Perth, and Rockingham'.
- Unlike radio, you don't need to 'throw' to the talent. There is no need for 'Prime Minister Elizabeth Hurley says ...' because her name and title will be superimposed using **supers** at the bottom of the screen when she talks. The super can be useful to give the person's location as well.
- Statistics, quotes from court rooms, and important facts may require graphics to get the message across.
- Round off complex numbers. Numbers are difficult to absorb when read aloud. Thus the figure of 496,213 would be expressed as 'about half a million' on television. Write numbers so the newsreader can read them easily. News organisations use different styles but one common method is to spell out single-digit numbers and use numerals for all two- and three-digit numbers. For numbers that include four or more digits a combination of the rules is used: 1,800 becomes 'one-thousand-800'.

Script layout

A television script is traditionally formatted into two columns. These relate to the two strands of information that are combined in the television story: audio and video.

The right-hand side of the page contains a 'map' of the audio part of the story: the reporter's script, interview grabs, and perhaps a PTC.

On the left-hand side the video instructions run parallel with the transcribed audio. The video instructions help editors with details about picture cues—tape number and time-code—so specified vision can be edited to correspond with the scripted text. Since the television news reporter might be off doing another story, the tape editor often has to finalise the cut without the reporter being there and so has to rely on the instructions on the script, like these:

- **UPSOT**—'increase Sound On Tape for duration of the grab'. This reminds the editor to increase sound when talent starts to talk.
- **NATSOT**—'NATural Sound On Tape'. This tells the editor to highlight ambient sound, like gunshots or screams. Ordinarily, ambient sound recorded on location is barely audible under the voice-over. When it is important and needs to be incorporated into the story content, the editor has to be made aware of this.
- **RUNS**—indicates duration of the grab.
- **TIMECODE**—indicates the cue for where grab or NATSOT appears on tape.

The left-hand side of the TV script also includes cues for 'supers'—caption text that is superimposed on the screen to identify names of talent, locations, file tape, and so on.

In television, the newsreader's intro/lead-in is on a separate page from the story script to avoid confusion between the two.

Getting the pictures

Channel Nine camera operator Trent Nind gets the 'horse' shot.

With the advent of smaller hand-held digital video cameras, more and more reporters are finding themselves shooting the vision as well as doing the reporting. This has been a common practice in the USA and the UK for many years. In Australia, radio news reporters working for the ABC in rural districts are trained to file for television as well as radio. A few television reporters covering news for commercial networks from rural areas in Western Australia and Queensland also work as a one-person team. The same applies to some foreign correspondents. Award-winning Australian journalist Mark Davis is an example of a successful one-man band. His unobtrusive equipment has allowed him to report from troublespots such as Afghanistan and Western Sahara. When Sally Sara reported for ABC News and Current Affairs from Africa, she travelled the continent compiling radio and television news reports using a minimum amount of equipment: a digicam, two laptops (one for radio and one with television software), a minidisc, and one satellite phone:

> I could fit most of that into my backpack and then I would have one other bag as well. That's about as light as you can go. A normal crew would be up around 100–110 kilos but I have got it down to 35 or 40 kilos. So it's good because if there is a last seat on a UN plane you'll get it because you don't weigh very much and don't have hangers-on, so that is normally how we go into the field.

This trend towards multiskilling (where reporters do the lot: film, report, and edit) does have its critics, who argue that it is difficult to sustain skills across such diverse areas. The 'split-vision' needed to deal with technical and journalistic issues simultaneously can be challenging at times. This extends beyond the question of whether journalists can learn to edit to more mundane operational matters—for example, traditionally the journalist has to 'watch the camera operator's back' during shots, since the camera operator sees the world through a viewfinder and is not able to look ahead or behind while shooting.

> If you are filming on your own I just don't think you get the best person, whereas if you have got a cameraman he's off getting a few shots and you've got more time to sit and actually talk with people. So you can get kudos for being the jack of all trades, but there is not any Walkley category for a journalist who shoots digicam the best—you can spread yourself maybe a bit too thin.
>
> **Sally Sara, foreign correspondent, ABC News and Current Affairs**

Another difference between the two media is the time it takes to produce a story. A radio reporter can do ten to fifteen stories per day with many versions of the same story going to air. The TV reporter will do one or two stories daily. While radio is a fast-response medium, where an interview can be done via telephone and compiled into a story within minutes, television is more time-consuming at every stage of the process. The need for vision means the television team cannot cover a story by telephone from inside the newsroom. They have to go 'on the road', and that takes up valuable time. The equipment used in television production takes longer to set up, calibrate, and operate compared to radio. Though advanced graphics software used in newsrooms today means that it is possible to do shorter stories with few or no location shots, in most cases the cardinal rule continues to be: no vision, no story.

Whether you are working with a camera operator or operating the camera yourself, it is important for the television reporter to understand what constitutes good vision. This means understanding how the camera sees things and how this can be harnessed to best advantage.

Camera shots

There are three variables to consider in relation to camera shots: where the camera is placed in relation to the subject, whether and how the camera moves, and where the subject is placed within the frame.

Camera position

The distance between the camera and the subject determines how much of the subject actually appears on screen. The range of options includes:

- LS—**long-shot**: includes the subject seen from a distance
- WS—**wide-shot**: includes the subject and the surrounding scene
- MWS—**medium wide-shot**: the subject from knee to head

- MS—**medium-shot**: the subject from thigh to head
- MCU—**medium close-up**: the subject from shoulder to head
- CU—**close-up**: the subject's face and neck
- BCU—**big close-up**: face only
- XCU—**extreme close-up**: eyes only.

In news, the three most commonly used shots are wide-shot, medium-shot, and close-up—though the terminology may vary from newsroom to newsroom. Close-ups draw the interviewee nearer to the viewer, while long-shots show the subject at a distance. Wide-shots are often used as an establishing shot in the beginning of the story as they give an overview of the location, while big close-ups of a face are used to highlight emotion.

Camera movement

The capacity of the camera to move adds to the above range of options. The **zoom** function, either in or out, focuses on details in the shot. The **pan** moves the camera horizontally from one side of the shot to the other. The **tilt** moves the camera vertically from the top of the shot to the bottom, or vice versa. Camera movements are not used much in news footage. First, they take up too much time: with most news shots only lasting 4 to 5 seconds there is no room for lengthy pans across a paddock. Second, they can pose problems at the editing stage: a cut will look incomplete if it occurs in the middle of a zoom or a tilt.

Framing of subject

This relates to how the subject is centred within the frame, and how the talent is placed in relation to other featured speakers. The camera operator will want to avoid too much empty space/air above the talent's head, or too much distance between the talent and the camera. Speakers will be juxtaposed as if they are 'talking to each other' by being placed on the left- and right-hand side of the screen respectively.

When setting up the interview, it is important to make sure that talent and journalist are looking at each other. This sounds simple—of course they are facing each other as they talk—but it needs careful planning to ensure this juxtaposition is captured by the camera. If the talent is facing one way, positioned on the left side of the frame and looking left to right, the reporter should be on the right hand side of the camera, looking right to left. In this way the two will appear to be talking to each other. If the reporter moves to the other side of the camera halfway through the interview, it will appear as if they have crossed the line—that the talent and reporter are suddenly looking away from each other, or, alternatively, that they are both looking at someone else.

Remembering 'the line' is especially important when doing vox pops (see pp. 62–3). When these are done on camera you want to give the impression that the subjects are 'talking to each other' and this is achieved by alternating the speakers on the left- and right-hand side of the frame.

Here the interviewee is looking left while placed at the left-hand side of the frame. This gives the impression that she is looking away from the audience and that she doesn't have 'enough room to look'. It also leaves too much dead-air on her right side.

This interviewee is framed with too much head room, leaving dead-air above his head.

In news interviews the interviewee is usually framed in close-up looking into the picture.

By positioning interviewees on opposite sides of the frame, two subjects can be juxtaposed during the editing (above and above left) creating an impression that they are talking to each other (in news: answering each other's statements).

Using overlays

When you are collecting your vision, it is important to plan ahead so that you have all the ingredients required for a smooth edit later on. Your voice-overs need overlaid vision matching the script, i.e. shots of people walking down the street, someone answering the phone, or a surfer conquering the waves—all depending on the story topic.

Cutaways

Telling stories using vision can be tricky because the 'story' time may not match the duration of the action in 'real' time. Let's take the example of a fire-fighter rescuing someone from a burning house. The time it takes for them to climb down a ladder from the fourth floor would be too long to cover in its entirety in a news story. This problem can be solved by using a **cutaway**—a shot that takes our eyes temporarily away from the main action. (Just as in real life, we accept that people move, and that things change position while we look away.) In this example, if a shot of a spectator is inserted between the two ladder shots, the cut will work perfectly. Another example of this is in a sports package where 90 minutes of action is compressed into 60 seconds. Cutaways to the spectators enable the transitions to be made.

Care needs to be taken in situations like vox pops where interviewees may be filmed against the same background. Because there will inevitably be slight variations in their respective positions, the background will appear to jump in the transition from one to the other, hence the term **jump cut**. This risk is eliminated by alternating their position in relation to the camera (as discussed above in the section on 'framing').

Reverses

Another way of covering edit points in an interview is to **reverse** the camera shot to include vision of the reporter who is doing the interview. This is more common in television current affairs. In some cases, for example in major productions, two cameras are used—one focused on the interviewee and the other on the reporter. Usually in news reporting there is just one camera that will film the reporter after the interview is over either re-asking 'staged' questions or apparently listening attentively to the interviewee (known as the **noddy**). Reverses are also a way of putting the journalist's brand on the story: the more famous the journalists, the more likely it is that their faces will feature on the screen.

A **two-shot** is an example of overlay vision that includes the talent and journalist in shot and is often used over the throw to a grab of the talent to establish them and change tack from previous talent.

File vision

Sometimes you can't get your own vision—either the location is too remote, the subject is too technical, or the talent is unavailable. The story might also be a follow-up for which the main and best vision is days, weeks, or months old. This is where the video archive comes in handy.

Generic **file vision** is non-specific vision that can be used for any number of stories—pictures of sheep grazing in a paddock may be useful for a story on the live sheep trade, or the declining price of wool. File vision is specific vision collected from previous stories that is useful when you are doing a follow-up. However, it has to be used with care for various reasons. First, the audience has a right to know what they are watching. In news, what is seen on the screen is assumed to be 'new', so if you are using archived vision it should be clearly labelled as such. This is why the words 'file vision' will be superimposed on the shot. Second, the old vision may not exactly fit the current story because it was shot under different conditions. A file shot of a sunny Bondi Beach in summer won't necessarily suit the mood or context of a story about a winter oil spill in the same location.

Preparing for editing

The first thing to do once the shooting has stopped is to label the tape (this might be done by the camera operator). Newsrooms have different systems but most will require:

- crew name (reporter and camera operator)
- date
- location
- story name (**slug**)
- tape number.

The next step is to log the **rushes** (the raw material on tape), writing down time codes (the location of the pictures on the tape), shot type, and a brief description. This is essential for two reasons. First, the tight time constraints in television news means that there is no time to fast forward through a tape looking for a specific shot. Second, as mentioned before, the journalist might not be present during the editing process and the shot list will make it easier for the editor to follow the instructions in the journalist's script. This is an example of a log:

Time code	Shot	Shot description
01.00.35	WS	Car approaching
01.01.00	MS	Car door opening
01.01.25	CU	Waiting person
01.02.00	CU	Dog wagging its tail
01.02.35	WS	Man walking away from the car

The editing process

It normally takes me 40 minutes to cut a 1:20 news story, but if it's a breaking news story, I'll do it in 10 minutes. As editor I want journalists to give me the script with relevant time codes and preferably the grabs fully typed out. Reading the grab confirms that I've found the right one. Journalists need to understand the different shots and how you tell a story using vision. I need the 'bread-and-butter shots'—establishing, close-ups and medium shots, for each story. The shot length varies from story to story. Minimum is 2 seconds and if it's a good shot it can last up to 10 seconds. Here at Seven the editors check potential legal and moral issues with vision. We know when people in court cases can't be shown on the news and that we have to be very careful of using vision of violence, death, and blood.

Steve Scott, tape editor at Seven News, Perth

Just as with audio editing, this is the stage when the waste material is discarded and the selected shots are crafted into the finished story. The bulk of the work has already been done during the paper edit; however, now is the time to see if it really works on the screen. As with camera operation, it is important that television journalists understand the process even if they won't necessarily be doing the editing themselves.

Sequence

A story can be told in many different ways. It can be organised chronologically or non-chronologically (see p. 212), and the angle can be approached from any number of different perspectives. These are the sorts of decisions the reporter makes at the scripting and editing stage. In television news, where words and vision are locked together, the story sequence is created by ordering the shots into a logical and clear storyline, in tandem with the accompanying text. Let's look at a sample story.

Linda Kelly is a farmer who is planning to leave the land to make a career in the IT business. You get the following shots on location:

LS	Linda Kelly on the tractor lifting fencing poles
CU	Linda's face while steering the tractor
MS	Linda turns the tractor off and leaves the vehicle
WS	Linda opens door to her house
MS	Linda in her office speaking on the phone and working on her computer
CU	Linda's fingers on computer keyboard
BCU	computer screen with e-commerce company's logo.

Let's see how the story would look if told chronologically, moving from the past into the present/future (the script is in italics):

LS	Linda Kelly on the tractor lifting fencing poles
CU	Linda's face while steering the tractor

'Linda Kelly has been working the farm for years—as her mother and grandmother did before her.'

Followed by an interview.

MS   Linda turns the tractor off and leaves the vehicle

WS   Linda opens door to her house

'But now she's calling it quits and is starting a new career in e-commerce.'

CU   Linda's fingers on computer keyboard

BCU computer screen with e-commerce company's logo

'Her business has been hugely successful since she launched it 6 months ago ...'

Let's now see how it would look if structured in a non–chronological or circular way— beginning and ending on the same note with background information in the middle:

MS   Linda in her office speaking on the phone and working on her computer

BCU computer screen with e-commerce company's logo

'Linda Kelly's e-commerce company has been hugely successful since it was launched 6 months ago.'

Followed by an interview.

LS   Linda Kelly on the tractor lifting fencing poles

CU   Linda's face while steering the tractor

'The farm has been in the family for generations and Linda Kelly had planned to continue the tradition ... '

MS   Linda turns the tractor off and leaves the vehicle

WS   Linda opens door to her house

'But the IT revolution came along and Linda has not looked back since—she's leaving the family farm ...'

MS   Linda in her office speaking on the phone and working on her computer

CU   Linda's fingers on computer keyboard

BCU computer screen with e-commerce company's logo

'For Linda Kelly the new technology has meant an unexpected career change and she's had to quickly learn new skills ...'

The content is the same in both examples, but the order of the shots and grabs is different.

Experienced television reporters tend to structure the story in their heads while collecting material on location. As a general rule, the story should begin with the best and strongest shots available to pull in the viewers. Having said that, many editors like to begin stories with a wide establishing shot to set the story in a physical context. How the rest of the story is told is determined by the reporter's own creativity and the broadcaster's preferred conventions and house-style.

Non-linear editing

Video editing, whether on analog linear equipment or on digital non-linear systems, involves copying raw material from camera tape onto an editing machine, selecting the required shots and grabs, adding voice-over, and finally assembling all the components into a story. Most newsrooms have already switched to, or are in the process of moving to, digital equipment. For that reason, this section will deal with digital editing only. Whatever the technical format, the principle is still the same.

Edit suites come in different shapes and sizes. The suite is generally made up of one or two computers, several monitors, and an audio mixing desk. Unlike the linear systems where editing is done in an orderly sequence from beginning to end on the master tape, non-linear editing is more flexible. It allows editor and reporter to work on any segment at any time, adding new shots, or cutting out unwanted vision.

Non-linear editing of video on a computer screen is a similar process to editing text with word-processing software. The raw material (tape rushes) is copied into the computer and segments are cut up into appropriate grabs. The vision and audio can be highlighted, copied, and moved by simply dragging it and placing it somewhere else along the timeline. The editing process can be described simply like this:

- The reporter records voice-overs on minidisc. This is often done in a small audio booth where each segment of the script is recorded onto a separate minidisc **track**. The voice-over is copied to one of the audio channels on the computer.
- Other vision including grabs is copied from camera tape to computer.
- The individual shots, which appear like thumbnail-sized stamps on the computer screen, are arranged into the desired sequence.
- The editor matches the voice-overs with the designated shots.
- Vision and audio can be edited separately if needed, and shot lengths can be easily adjusted to fit the text.

The television news story is crafted by joining these small segments together seamlessly. This seamlessness is achieved by hiding the transition points, which brings us to the next stage in the editing process.

Cutting and mixing

In television news, the transition between shots should be clear and not distracting. This is done using two basic functions: cutting and mixing.

Cutting simply means cutting from one picture directly to the next. If the sequence is well planned, the transition will pass unnoticed by the viewers. They will not even register the change in shots.

Mixing is where one picture **dissolves** into the next one. This blending can be useful to indicate the passage of time. It can take the form of vision breaking up into little boxes flying across the screen, or one shot slowly fading into the next. It is commonly used in more 'artistically developed' news stories, for example the opening of a new ballet production or museum exhibition.

Putting it all into practice

Earlier in this chapter we went on the road with television news reporter Marianne Ellis. Here you can see her story, which is 1:01 minutes long and is made up of voice-overs, PTC, and two grabs. Below we see the script paired with the corresponding shots as they appeared in the final story. Note how conversational the writing style is and how short the grabs are. Seeing everything transcribed in this way, it is clear how the script serves to map out the story. It begins with the intro read by the newsreader. The layout complies with the house-style of National Nine News (they don't divide scripts into two parts with words on the right and video instructions on the left hand side of the document). Authors' commentary is inserted in italics in the story script.

News story script: 'Xmas Party Blitz' (duration 1:16), National Nine News

Newsreader's script
A P-plate driver has been caught travelling at 45 kilometres an hour over the limit ... just minutes after the official start of the Christmas road campaign.
As Marianne Ellis reports, the teenager has now lost his licence ... after only 4 months on the road.

Story script (duration 1:01)
Police caught the 17-year-old as he sped through the Graham Farmer Tunnel at 125 kilometres an hour ...
Take: UPSOT [*instruction to tape editor to include recorded grab, PTC or actuality in the story*]

NAME: Darryl Lockart [*name of interviewee*]
IN-CUE: OUR MAJOR CRASH PEOPLE RETURNING FROM A SERIOUS CRASH STOPPED THIS FELLOW AND I THINK PROBABLY SAVED A LIFE 20 MINUTES INTO THE CAMPAIGN. [*interview grab transcribed*]
AT: 20'30" [*this indicates where the grab is located on camera tape*]
TO: 20'39"
DURATION: 0'09" [*duration of grab*]
With double demerits in place ... the 17-year-old automatically lost his licence. Meanwhile ... police have launched a crackdown on work Christmas drinks ... hoping to avoid a repeat of scenes like this.
[Notes: file viz of crashes] [*reporter's description of vision to be used as overlays during voice-over*]

Take: UPSOT
NAME: Kevin Looby
IN-CUE: 7:47 A FEW BEERS SORT OF DURING WORK AND AFTER WORK HOURS AND THEY MIGHT NOT REALISE HOW MUCH THEY'VE HAD TO DRINK AND YOU DON'T HAVE TO DRINK A LOT TO GET OVER THE LIMIT. 7:56
AT: 7'47"
TO: 7'56"
DURATION: 0'08"
Officers will patrol the streets looking for those who've over indulged ... in particular employees in industrial areas like Osbourne Park, Kewdale and Canningvale.
[Notes: viz of industrial areas from today trent 10] [*here the description of vision includes the name of camera operator and tape number*]
Take: UPSOT
NAME: PTC [*reporter's piece to camera*]
IN-CUE: POLICE SAY EMPLOYERS HAVE A DUTY OF CARE TO MAKE SURE THOSE THAT ARE DRINKING DON'T GET BEHIND THE WHEEL AND THAT THEY ARRIVE HOME SAFELY [*reporter's PTC transcribed*]
AT: 27'08"
TO: 27'16"
DURATION: 0'08"
The Christmas road blitz continues until January 9.
Marianne Ellis, National Nine News
[Notes: more file viz of police blitz type stuff]

The story can also be 'viewed' with shots and corresponding scripts laid out as a story-board. This storyboard shows how the shots are selected to create a clear and logical sequence with the script correlating to each shot.

Storyboard of 'Xmas Party Blitz' story

Story script	Vision	Shot description
1 [Newsreader] A P-plate driver has been caught travelling at 45 kilometres an hour over the limit just minutes after the official start of the Christmas road campaign. As Marianne Ellis reports, the teenager has now lost his licence... after only four months on the road.		Newsreader Sonia Vinci introduces the story. The role of the introductory script is to grab viewers' attention and to introduce the story angle. In this case the news story foregrounds a 17-year-old driver losing his licence within the broader picture of a police road safety campaign.
2 [Reporter] Police		Story begins with file vision of a car speeding past at night. It is an establishing shot setting the scene of road safety for the viewers.
3 caught the 17-year-old		There were no cameras on location when the 17-year old was caught so the first four shots are file vision from previous police stories.
4 as he sped through the Graham Farmer Tunnel		Night shots of police and police cars are edited into a fast-paced sequence to create a sense of a car chase.
5 at 125 kilometres an hour ...		Shots from inside a police car give the viewers the visual experience of being part of the pursuit.

6	'Our major crash people returning from a serious crash stopped this fellow and I think probably saved a life 20 minutes into the campaign.'		Assistant Commissioner Darryl Lockart describes how the 17-year-old was caught as a result of the Christmas road safety campaign.
7	With double demerits in place ... the 17-year-old		Reporter gives some background information with more file vision night shots of police on the road as overlays.
8	automatically lost his licence.		File vision of rows of drivers waiting at a police check point. The shot is the first of two in a sequence showing a previous road blitz.
9	Meanwhile ... police have launched a crackdown on work Christmas drinks ...		The road blitz vision allows the reporter to change the focus of the story to include information about a police crackdown on drink driving around Christmas. (The word 'meanwhile' is useful when moving into a second part of the story).
10	hoping to avoid a repeat of scenes		File vision of horrific crash scenes is amplified by fast zoom-ins and added sounds of wailing sirens and the crunch of crumpling car bodies.

11	like this.		Each car crash shot is short and the sequence is edited tightly together.
12	'A few beers sort of during work and after work hours and they might not realise how much they've had to drink and you don't have to drink a lot to get over the limit.'		Interview with Superintendent Kevin Looby. Note how he is framed on the opposite side of the previous talent: Looby on left and Lockart on right.
13	Officers will		Camera operator Trent Nind is filming the moving streetscape through the side mirror of the car. It creates a sense of being in a patrolling car.
14	patrol the streets looking for those who've over indulged ...		Real-life bust of driver caught without a licence. The incident is filmed from a distance without identifying the driver.
15	in particular		Example one of employees in light industrial areas.
16	employees in industrial areas		Example two of employees in light industrial areas.

17	like Osbourne Park,		Shot of police car patrolling the areas in question.
18	Kewdale and Canningvale.		Back to the side mirror vision used previously in the story. It creates a little circular vision narrative within the news story. It also indicates that the police continue to keep an eye out for Christmas drink drivers.
19	'Police say employers have a duty of care to make sure those that are drinking don't get behind the wheel and that they arrive home safely.'		Reporter's piece to camera on location in a light industrial area with the skyline of Perth behind her.
20	The Christmas road blitz		In the concluding part of the story, file vision is used to inform viewers the road campaign will continue.
21	continues until January 9.		Medium shot of speed camera to follow up from previous shot.
22	Marianne Ellis, National Nine News		Reporter signs off using easy-to-understand vision that viewers can interpret as a concluding shot (the yellow sign is what you see after going past a speed camera).

Television journalists and the law

Broadcasting law and ethics are covered in detail in chapters 16 and 17; however, there are specific issues to keep in mind when working in the television medium. While radio news reporters have to be careful with what they say in a report, their colleagues in TV have to consider vision as well as words. Sometimes there may be ethical and legal restrictions on the shots that can be used.

Court reporting

Physical identification is the key issue here. You may not use vision of the victims of sexual offences (in Queensland, South Australia and the Northern Territory the accused cannot be identified either until committed for trial).

Children cannot be identified—this applies in the Children's Court as well as general courts where a child might be either a witness or a victim. Remember that by showing shots of a parent, a child can be indirectly identified.

Do not show pictures that would disclose the identity of anyone involved in cases in the Family Court, or of someone accused of a crime where identification may be a central issue in the trial, for example, in cases of murder, sexual assault, and robbery.

Using file vision and general shots

Television journalists need to be careful about unintentionally identifying a person or company when using file footage as background vision to stories about criminal activities. For example, you may be doing a report on a doctor at a local metropolitan hospital who has been charged with rape and you want to use general vision of staff at work inside the hospital. However, you run the risk of being sued for defamation by the staff who appear, since the vision may lead the viewer to associate them with the crime. General vision must be used with caution to ensure that words and vision correlate. Remember to check for copyright clearance if you are using material from external sources (see pp. 286–7).

Permission to film

It is illegal to record a conversation or an interview without the talent's consent, whether it is being done by telephone or in person. However, you can film people without getting their permission. You can also film someone's property, as long as you're not trespassing on it.

Exercise

Record and transcribe the top news story on ABC TV or commercial television. Analyse the story development, structure, and reporter's scripting using the following questions:

- What information is included in the newsreader's intro?

- How does the reporter begin the story? Could you have opened it with a different grab or voice-over for stronger impact?
- Is the story structure chronological or circular or neither?
- Are 'all' sides of the story represented or do you miss anything?
- What do you remember most from the story after watching it?

Further reading

Alysen, B. 2000, 'News Gathering and Packaging', in *The Electronic Reporter: Broadcast Journalism in Australia*, Deakin University Press, Geelong, pp. 33–50.

Block, M. 1997, *Writing Broadcast News; Shorter, Sharper, Stronger*, 2nd edn, Bonus Books, Chicago.

Boyd, A. 1997, 'Camera Shots', in *Broadcast Journalism: Techniques of Radio and TV News*, 4th edn, Focal Press, Oxford, pp. 307–22.

Dobbs, G. 2005, 'Saying it twice', in *Better Broadcast Writing, Better Broadcast News*, Pearson Education, Boston, Mass., pp. 58–71.

Gibson, R. 1991, 'A View of the News', in *Radio and Television Reporting*, Allyn & Bacon, Boston, pp. 209–34.

Griffiths, R. 1998, 'Scriptwriting: The Words' and "Scriptwriting: The Pictures', in *Videojournalism*, Focal Press, Oxford, pp. 51–60 and pp. 61–9.

Herbert, J. 2000, 'Interviewing for Radio and TV', in *Journalism in the Digital Age: Theory and Practice for Broadcast, Print and On-Line,* Focal Press, Oxford, pp. 254–67.

Hilliard, R. 2000, 'News' in *Writing for Television, Radio and New Media*, 7th edn, Thomson Learning, Wadsworth, Belmont, CA, pp. 111–54

Masterton, M. & Patching, R. 1997, 'Techniques—Television', in *Now the News in Detail: A Guide to Broadcast Journalism in Australia*, 3rd edn, Deakin University Press, Geelong, pp. 173–201.

Zettl, H. 2003, *Television Production Handbook*, 8th edn, Thomson Learning, Wadsworth, Belmont, CA.

Web sites

TV Handbook: http://www.tv-handbook.com/. Online handbook covering television production.

Poynter Institute: http://www.poynter.org. This is the online site for Poynter Institute for Journalism training. It includes a section on radio and television reporting with online tutorials (USA).

14 News Bulletins

The news bulletin is what all newsroom journalists work towards—it is the final step in the news production process where their work is finally presented to the audience via radio receiver or television set.

This is the stage at which locally produced stories and imported content from the wire services are mixed and poured into a mould. That mould is defined by the station's news style and is customised to suit its target audience.

For the reporter, seeing or hearing your story go to air along with the work of your newsroom colleagues contributes to a sense of teamwork. It marks the successful completion of your job: the delivery of your story on time and to time, tailored to blend into a smooth and seamless mix that will be beamed out to the invisible listener or viewer.

News bulletin formats

Many people turn to the broadcast media to be informed about the society they live in, and therefore to them radio and television are important suppliers of 'reality'. However, even while the news bulletins appear to deliver snapshots of the real world, this is a mediated reality. What the audience is getting is what journalists select for them, according to set criteria. At every step of the news production chain, decisions will be taken by journalists and news production staff that will affect what eventually hits the transmitters.

News bulletins can be anything from short 3-minute broadcasts on commercial radio to 30 minutes of jam-packed news on public television. Regardless of length and medium, they all conform to specific news bulletin standards. In this chapter, we look at how bulletins on radio and television are organised, what factors govern the content, and how newsreaders get the message across using a microphone or a camera. Let's begin by looking at a generic news bulletin.

Structure

In the linear world of radio and television, where programs start and finish at specified times, news bulletins can be found at the top of the hour (on radio there may also be half-hourly updates across the morning and afternoon). What might appear to be a seamless flow of voices and pictures is, rather, a program built of clearly contained segments linked by one or two newsreaders. These segments are made up of the fundamental building blocks of radio and television journalism: interviews, reporters' voice links, and newsreaders' intros. The following is a list of segments in a typical news bulletin:

- **Opener**/news theme—used as identification of program and station. When Triple J's quirky news theme starts playing on-air, listeners clearly know it's the top of the hour and they have tuned in to Triple J on their receiver.
- Newsreader opens the bulletin, introducing him- or herself and giving a station identification before presenting the headlines of what's coming up.
- Selection of pre-recorded and live news stories introduced by newsreader(s).
- Finance segment (in some bulletins).
- Sport—either as individual stories or as a complete segment read live or recorded by 'sportsreader'.
- Traffic segment (most common on commercial radio stations).
- Weather—read by weather presenter or newsreader.
- **Sign-off** (and in some bulletins, throw to next program).

The structure of a news bulletin is currently more or less static, however, through digital technologies and the promises of interactive television, viewers will have more power over the rundown. Already viewers watching ABC's broadband news bulletin online can select which order they want to watch the television news stories. A bulletin rundown can be varied to accommodate breaking news or a major news event. If the prime minister has a heart attack, the entire bulletin could then be dedicated to that one issue. If a violent cyclone lashes the northern coastline, the weather could become the leading news item. Though sports stories are generally placed towards the end of the bulletin, Australia winning the Davis Cup could be a new and important enough event to bump it up into a lead story. This sort of realignment won't change the generic structure of the bulletin. In the case of the sports story, it will simply feature both as a news story and as part of the 'sports segment' later on.

Though bulletins have a clear structure there's still much scope for variety through what goes into the bulletin (content) and the weighting of stories in the rundown (running order).

Content

> We try to fit in as many stories as we can into a bulletin—during breakfast we've got 2 minutes and 5 seconds of actual news content, with 10 seconds of finance, so it has to be really tight. So the skill is being able to identify a good story no matter what the source, and then rewriting that in a 20-second format and capturing everything that you need to, or as much as you can.
>
> **Justin Kelly, News Editor, 2GB Sydney**

Regardless of how many bulletins a station runs across a day, there is always too much content and some of it must be discarded. Stories can come from local newsroom journalists, wire services, foreign correspondents, stringers (freelancers), and from other networked stations. Line-up producers and subeditors decide on what they think the audience wants and then compile the bulletin accordingly.

Television broadcasters keep a close eye on the daily audience measurement figures to try to ascertain what interests their viewers. The Seven and Nine networks can actually compare their respective products while they are going to air since their bulletins are broadcast simultaneously at 6.00 pm. Each news producer will keep a very close eye on the other's rundown as stories roll off the monitors in the control room.

It is important to remember that bulletins are not elastic. Whatever content is decided on will have to fit into the time restrictions imposed by the bulletin length. The 3-minute radio bulletin can run only for the exact time allocated—no more and no less. There are also other factors determining the bulletin's content.

Supply and demand

Some news days are slow, others busy. A story that gets a run on a slow day might be deemed too insignificant on a busy day when there would be an abundance of stories to choose from.

External influences

External influences include factors such as the 'silly season' in December–January when politics and business close down. News bulletins are more likely to be filled with accident stories, spot news, weather, and lighter material. Weekend bulletins are also more likely to contain a greater proportion of crime, accident, and sports stories since little else may be going on.

International, national, and local input

The ratio of international, national, and local stories will be determined by the news service itself. SBS television news focuses its bulletins on international stories, in contrast to a regional commercial television station that will go for more locally based news.

Running stories

Stories that will develop and be regarded as newsworthy over longer periods have to be factored in. High impact events like the Indian Ocean tsunamis and wars are examples of this sort of story.

Story mix

News is often defined in the negative, as being about bad things such as conflict and catastrophes. However, an unbroken tale of woe unbalanced by good news would be difficult for the audience to take. Producers and subeditors try to create a better balance by including a range of voices, topics, and formats in the bulletin to get the 'right' pace and flow. This is done by building the bulletin from a variety of:

- story formats and lengths. Elements to play with include voicers (reader voice-over in television), word copy, and packages.
- locations. Stories can emanate from different locations both close to and far from the audience.
- new and repeated stories. In radio, top stories and other items regarded as newsworthy will be recycled and reused in consecutive bulletins.

The content of a bulletin is determined by the newsworthiness of each item. Line-up producers and subeditors constantly ask themselves how important the story is to the audience. Stories are weighted against each other and are either thrown out or kept in. As a rule, stories will be thrown out after one or two runs on air and will need to be re-versioned with the incorporation of new material in order to be included again.

Running order

When the bulletin has been filled with a sufficient amount of appropriately mixed stories, the next step is to place them in order. This is where the concept of 'news value' comes in.

If you ask journalists how they weight stories—what goes on top because it is the most important story—many will describe it as 'a gut feeling', or something learnt through years of experience. Whether they are conscious of it or not, their ranking process has a lot to do with the issue of newsworthiness as discussed in chapter 11. A top story must be timely (new to the audience) and be of interest to (have an impact and effect on) listeners and viewers. A story should also contain as many of the news values as possible: consequence, proximity, conflict, human interest, novelty, and prominence.

The broadcasting organisation's house-style will be another factor in determining the running order. As noted above, SBS will prioritise international stories ahead of local items. Commercial television and radio news are more highly formatted with shorter intros and a faster pace compared to public broadcasters. Commercial radio stations can attune their output to their local audience demographic. In contrast the ABC may be broadcasting its bulletins across multiple networks simultaneously, so its style will be honed to suit a wide audience tuning in to services as diverse as local radio, Radio National, and Classic FM.

Other basic rules that will need to be borne in mind include:

- signposting news stories to attract attention. Unlike newspapers, where readers can reread articles or choose which ones to read, audiences of broadcast media have to sit through the whole bulletin to get what they want. (This is changing with on-demand services on the Web, where users can select what news to access and when.)
- taking care with the placement of light and heavy items, as a fluffy story may undermine the seriousness of the heavier one.

Producers and EPs are journalists with many years of newsroom experience coupled with an ability to assist reporters in shaping stories to fit the format and style of the station's bulletin. Since they are the 'hub' of daily news production, they have an overview of all the stories being done and therefore are best placed to determine the running order.

Radio news bulletins

> If it's a particularly big story, we would continually get that reporter to do another version of the same story. If it has been filed once, generally it will have a shelf life of a couple of hours and once it's been on air we don't bring it back. That doesn't mean that in the next half hour we haven't got that same issue reported in another way, or the journo will file 2, 3, 4, 5 different versions. It changes with each bulletin.
>
> Justin Kelly, News Editor, 2GB Sydney

The radio medium encourages a fast turn-around of stories. With simple and relatively inexpensive equipment (compared to television), radio news can be produced and broadcast continuously, around the clock. The ABC, like many other public service broadcasters internationally, has taken advantage of this in its 24-hour parliamentary and news service called NewsRadio.

Radio is good at delivering breaking news, as it happens. Radio is often where listeners hear things first, though they may then go on to other news services such as newspapers, television, or online to get a fuller picture. Radio news bulletins range in length from just a few minutes to a 15-minute full bulletin. No matter what the length, the following points hold true for all radio news:

- All bulletins are restricted by the time-slot allocated to them and each bulletin has to be carefully crafted to fit that time. Running under or over time is unacceptable (10 seconds of 'dead air' on radio seems like an eternity).
- Bulletins are compiled close to airtime to include the latest news.
- Content can be updated during broadcast.
- The newsreader operates all equipment while reading the news.
- News copy is checked and rewritten to ensure it is easy to read and to understand (done by the subeditor or newsreader depending on the organisation).
- Clarity is essential since all information is carried through voice and sound.

Technical skills for radio newsreaders

Since 'driving the desk' is part of presenting the news on radio, journalists need to know how to operate all the equipment in a radio studio. The news booth is a simplified version of a radio studio. It contains a mixing console, microphone(s), telephone connection, a clock, an on-air light, and a computer on which the news stories for broadcast are stored. For a more detailed description of the radio studio see pp. 69–72.

In addition to being technically proficient in the studio, journalists are expected to be computer literate in order to work with the in-house news production system. There are many different software systems used for news in Australian newsrooms: iNEWS, NewsBoss, and ENPS to mention a few. These software programs allow the entire newsroom to work on the same system to produce stories, organise them into bulletins, and archive them afterwards. Word processing makes text editing easy and the use of templates ensures that each copy includes production details such as slug (name of the story), copy

ABC Radio news desk.

length, story length, and transcript of grab. The recorded audio grab is attached to the copy, and both text and audio can be edited using the same computer. Most importantly, the technology makes it possible for both reporter and subeditor to work on the same script simultaneously.

The radio newsreader

I think there are some elements of newsreading which a lot of news readers don't understand— the most fundamental one is that for the listener to listen to a news bulletin it shouldn't take effort to understand what is being said, and if a news bulletin is not read in a way that is easy to understand then it is a waste of time.

Margaret Throsby, former newsreader, current presenter ABC Classic FM

At 2GB we don't read the news as formally as the ABC. Our bulletins are certainly not as long. We don't have three or four paragraph intros to a reporter. We have a one-line intro and then we go to our reporter. And the stories are generally not as long—we try to keep our stories to about 35 seconds for a voice report. I wrote a story this morning that went for 8 seconds—so it was just literally two lines as we needed to fill some space.

Justin Kelly, News Editor, 2GB Sydney

In radio, the voice is what carries the message across and the principles of how to use the voice remain the same whatever the program format (see chapter 4 and CD Track 1). In radio news, the message is often a serious one and therefore the presentation style is more sober and formal compared to, for example, that of a local radio music program. News has to be accurate and the newsreader has to appear trustworthy, and this results in a neutral and formalised delivery. Even so, the radio news delivery style has changed over the years, and newsreaders no longer speak at listeners but to them. Furthermore, different news services adopt different styles: compare Triple J's conversational 'Triple J News, hi I'm ...' with Radio National's more formal 'This is ABC national news ...'.

Using the voice correctly is only part of getting the message across. To be an effective newsreader you have to both understand the script and be able to deliver its meaning live on air.

Understanding the script

Understanding the script is essential to good news presenting. If the meaning is clear to you when you read it, it is an easier task to convey it to someone else. Understanding the script also helps you to determine the appropriate tone, pace, and emphasis. This cognitive process is helped by marking the copy, and pre-reading it before going on air.

Marking the copy

There are different opinions when it comes to how useful it is to mark copy. Some newsreaders say underlining **cue words** or indicating where to breathe in the copy makes you sound unnatural and 'read'. They prefer to familiarise themselves with the content of the script but try to avoid overworking it to ensure it sounds fresh when presented on air. Other presenters say that underlining cue-words corresponding to the news questions 'who, what, where, when, why, and how' will make you get the message across more successfully. The cue-words should identify the skeleton of the story. Stressing these words will help to clarify the meaning and therefore help listeners to understand the text on air. Today many newsreaders read off a computer monitor, which makes marking the copy difficult.

Pre-reading the copy

> The good newsreader will be able to scan the bulletin or read at sight in a way in which they breathe at the right place and pause at the right place and emphasise the right words. There are many ways you can learn how to read fast at sight by skimming your eyes faster along the line so you know what's coming. You learn how to do it by doing it—even now I often just read out loud. This business of reading from the printed page—at sight—reading it and making it interesting and making it sound good—is the sort of thing you can do yourself at home and record and listen to and see what it sounds like.
>
> **Margaret Throsby, former newsreader, current presenter ABC Classic FM**

Pre-read copy before going on air. When reading the script aloud you will pick up mistakes your eye might have missed. Pre-reading the copy will allow you to identify any unfamiliar names or places so you can check pronunciation. Making the content easy to understand and interesting to listen to is essential when presenting such short and concise text as radio news copy.

Breathing

Learning to breathe properly is another important factor in becoming a professional news-reader. A nervous voice becomes unstable and goes up an octave. Breathing with your diaphragm will give you enough air to read the whole paragraph. Push out the air using your stomach muscles to emphasise important words. It helps to sit or stand up straight so you can take in full lungs of air. Some simple deep breaths before entering the news booth will help relax fluttering nerves.

Delivering the message on air

Delivering the news on air can be a frightening experience. It involves having a multiple focus on reading, operating the mixing desk, and monitoring the time, while being flexible enough to cope with last-minute changes to copy to accommodate breaking news. Being well prepared helps to calm the nerves and improve the presentation. Other tips for good news presentation include:

- Remember the three 'Ps': Practise, Prepare, and Pre-read!
- Warm up voice using voice exercises. Yawn to open your voice box.
- Monitor your pace. Serious stories need a slower pace; light stories can be read faster. Important points within a story can be said a touch slower to emphasise them.
- Use inflexion, in other words the modulation of your voice, to help the listener get a feel for the story. Emphasise important cue-words, and distinguish the salient details from background information. An interesting exercise is to record yourself reading and see how far you can go in exaggerating pace and inflexion. What appears abnormal in terms of everyday speech may sound surprisingly normal in an on-air context.
- If necessary, rewrite copy to suit your reading style.
- Don't be afraid of pauses on radio. Pauses between stories indicate that one has finished and the next is about to begin. Pauses also give listeners time to absorb what you have said. They also give you space to take in a breath.
- Think before you speak, and this includes preparing yourself with a range of standard lines to use for different situations that might arise in the studio (for example, if technology fails, or an urgent copy is thrown into the bulletin at the last minute).
- Know your reading speed (average 180 words per minute) and prepare extra copy, or identify what to cut out, to adjust timing to fit the bulletin.
- Know how to deal with mistakes. Make a quick recovery. Don't dwell on a mistake: move on, and think about it when you have left the studio.
- Visualise a listener. Some novice newsreaders find it easier to tell the stories to a listener they can 'see'.
- Enjoy your work. Have a real interest in telling people the latest news.

CD TRACK 1: On this track, which starts with the voices of students attempting to read a news script without any training, retired veteran ABC newsreader Tony Clough talks about the ways of developing good voice production and script-reading skills.

> **CD TRACK 14:** Here you can listen to an example of a commercial radio news bulletin. It features the one o'clock bulletin from Macquarie National News presented by Erin Maher on 2GB Sydney (20 January 2005).

Television news bulletins

Television news rundown.

Producing television news bulletins and broadcasting them to viewers is a huge logistical exercise. Editorial and technical staff start planning for the evening bulletin in the morning. What finally goes out on television that night might bear little resemblance to the morning story list, but the planning needs to begin there nevertheless. Most television stations have short updates across the day and the main bulletin(s) at night. This means that the format can vary from 3 minutes to a full half-hour broadcast.

Unlike radio, where newsreaders link the bulletin items using their voices only, television news involves studio set design, graphics, and vision. One example is the 'above-the-shoulder graphics' that introduce the story visually while the introductory script is read by the newsreader. A lot of this visual enhancement is done using templates to ensure continuity in the look of the bulletin from day to day.

The person who is responsible for 'putting the bulletin to bed' is the line-up producer, assisted by an assistant producer (AP). Since the bulletin may include live crosses from reporters on location, the producer will also be responsible for ensuring that a satellite link is organised. To be able to compile a bulletin, producers need to know some basic information about each news story. They need to know the:

- story development (if the angle is changing across the day)
- story length
- in- and out-cue
- supers (name of reporter, talent, any additional text to be superimposed over vision during broadcast)
- limitations on the use of vision because of copyright or court proceedings
- arrival time for stories coming in from other stations, interstate or internationally.

The final rundown is compiled about an hour before airtime and, as discussed earlier, each news service will have its own generic bulletin structure. Commercial television news has to take the commercial breaks into consideration when compiling the line-up. Rather than ranking the stories in news order from top to bottom, many commercial stations will treat each segment after a commercial break as the beginning of the program, i.e., each segment will begin with a 'hard news' story to pull the viewers in again.

Broadcasters are constantly looking for the ultimate rundown and every structure possible has been tried in the quest for viewers. Some international networks even use stripping newsreaders to get the ratings. Often bulletins will be broken into different segments: a finance report, maybe with a different presenter; a 'world watch' segment for international news. Most television news services try to finish the bulletin on a lighter note, or use spectacular vision as a 'closer' or wallpaper under the final credits. This also allows bulletins to time out to their exact duration.

In larger newsrooms the final rundown is open for amendments in case of breaking news. Once the rundown is set, the technical and broadcast staff can take over. The final sprint before the bulletin begins.

Technical skills for television newsreaders

News update recorded in Seven's newsroom in Perth.

Television newsreaders are not expected to have the same level of technical proficiency as newsreaders on radio. However, they do need to know how to operate in heavily technology-based environments. As in radio, computer literacy is a prerequisite and television newsreaders will work with similar news production software to their colleagues in radio. iNEWS is a bi-media system used by many television and radio newsrooms. Other news software systems are ENPS, Avstar, and Newstar.

The television studio

The television news studio can be an intimidating work environment with its bright lights, cables, and technical equipment everywhere. This is where the newsreaders have to sit, with cameras, microphones, and lights pointing at them as they calmly deliver the news. The newsreader's script rolls off the **autocue** in front of the camera. This enables them to read the text while looking straight into the camera. Hard copy of the script is also provided as back-up. During the bulletin, newsreaders wear hidden earphones so the producer can give them instructions from the control room if necessary. If the bulletin is running over time, newsreaders need to speed up their reading or drop part of a copy.

Graphics or set vision is used as a backdrop behind newsreaders. This can be done using **chroma key**, a special effect where a separately produced background can be projected onto a blue screen behind the newsreader's chair. Some networks use plasma screens with rolling footage behind the newsreader as an advanced version of 'over the shoulder picture' graphics. Most television news studios have three cameras, operated either manually or remotely by robotics, to give the technical producer (see below) different shots to choose from. Where cameras are manually operated, the floor manager in the broadcast studio relays instructions from the control room to the camera operators on the studio floor.

The control room

The control room is where all the components of the bulletin—vision, audio, live links, and pre-recorded stories—are mixed into a live program. The room looks somewhat like space mission control with a wall of monitors, computers, a mixing desk, and other required equipment. Although the producer is still in charge of editorial decisions and timing, the technical director runs the control room and its staff.

Numbers of staff (and what the positions are called) vary with the size of the broadcast operation, but can include a director, technical producer, producer's assistant (PA), audio operator, floor manager and camera operators. Each staff member performs a specific task: the director oversees the whole bulletin and makes sure that all items are cued, and that everything is flowing smoothly and running to time; the PA calls time cues for supers and warns when stories are about to finish; the audio operator mixes the audio, and so on. Ten seconds before airtime, the PA will start counting down to broadcast. Throughout the bulletin, the producer monitors the running time so newsreaders can adjust their reading speed accordingly to ensure the bulletin runs to the exact time.

The television newsreader

Presenting news on television is not everyone's cup of tea. It is nerve-racking enough to broadcast your voice to thousands or millions of people, let alone having them see you as well. Newsreaders are selected for their on-air presence (and in many cases, their looks). As with radio, the television newsreader has to be credible and confident, and therefore broadcasters tend to select mature and experienced people with personalities that can be projected through the lens of a camera.

The same principles of voice delivery covered in the section on the radio newsreader (p. 241) apply to the presentation of news on television. The television newsreader needs to understand the text to be able to convey its content credibly to viewers. This is done by pre-reading the copy, rewriting if necessary, and marking important words. Knowing the content is essential if you are to feel confident on air, and if you feel confident you will be able to look confident and professional.

Delivering the news live-to-air in front of a camera is different from face-to-face contact. The camera restricts body movement and newsreaders have to rely on face and voice alone in delivering their message. Unlike radio, where the newsreader is a disembodied voice delivering information, the television newsreader is a face as well and therefore more of a personality in our homes—a friend we see at the same time every day. Although your audience may number in the hundreds of thousands, through the camera you are making eye contact with one person at a time, and visualising the audience as one viewer could make the experience less daunting for the novice. One technique is to 'see through' the camera to the person you are presenting the news to. It can help to visualise a person you know as the viewer behind the camera. Remember that the broadcast is not about your performance as presenter—it is about you wanting to deliver information to the audience. Shifting the focus from yourself to the audience will make you less self-conscious and therefore a better presenter. Critiquing your own performance should be set aside for afterwards. As with all performances, being well prepared helps to calm nerves and improves the presentation. The list of hints for radio news presenting can also be useful for television, but the medium has its own requirements:

- Know your material and trust yourself to present it to the audience.
- Check that the order of your scripts matches the running order to avoid confusion on air.
- Focus and relax before going to air—a good opportunity is while your make-up and hair is done. Check that your earpiece is secure and sneak the lead behind your ear and under clothing.
- Maintain eye contact with the camera as much as possible. You can look down as a way of indicating the start of a new story. Newsreaders also have to look down when they need to read from hard copy as a result of last-minute changes to the line-up or because of equipment failure.
- Become friendly with the camera—don't talk at it, speak to it. Practise reading in front of a mirror to work out how much you can smile without looking 'too happy' for news. Get to know your face so you know what you can do with it in front of the camera.
- Keep still in front of the camera. The eye movement caused by reading from the autocue can be disguised by small, deliberate head movements.
- Project your personality to the viewers. Think of yourself as a friend informing them at home.
- Be aware of microphones that can be unexpectedly live—don't swear in the studio as it might mistakenly be broadcast to the viewers.
- Have a glass of water near in case you need to lubricate your throat.
- Remember that even very experienced news presenters have adrenalin rushes before a broadcast. Being confident and professional is about taming and using those nerves to create a good performance.

The advent of digital technology has simplified the television production process. The days of having a dozen people to run a control room are gone, and production roles are being filled by smaller numbers of multiskilled staff. The ABC in Melbourne now has news studios that can be operated by two people—the newsreader and one technical operator. Video-editing software enables reporters to edit stories at their own desks. News stories can be broadcast directly from a server instead of going to air from tapes. All this opens up the possibility of more frequent bulletins both on television and on the Internet.

The development of web-TV will encourage journalists to take on other roles: to operate cameras, script the story, edit it, and finally to present it as part of the bulletin. The future is limited only by the rate at which sustainable IT technology is developed, and it is the brave new world of web reporting that we are about to enter in the next chapter.

Exercises

Listen and record a main evening bulletin on ABC local radio and note the stories featured there. Then watch and record the Channel Ten television bulletin listing the stories in the order that they appear.

- Compare and contrast the bulletin rundowns. What story leads each bulletin? Was it a local, national, or international story? Can you explain why the news editors chose the story order that they did? Can you explain any differences between the radio and television line-ups?
- Do the same exercise comparing bulletins from a commercial radio service with ABC local radio (you can use the 2GB bulletin included on the CD track 14). Is the rundown different? Are the types of stories different?

Further reading

Alysen, B. 2000, 'Compiling a News Bulletin', in *The Electronic Reporter: Broadcast Journalism in Australia*, Deakin University Press, Geelong, pp. 149–70.

Boyd, A. 1997, 'On Air!' and 'Newsreading Mechanics', in *Broadcast Journalism: Techniques of Radio and TV News*, 4th edn, Focal Press, Oxford, pp. 146–55 and pp. 156–65.

Day, A., Pattie, M. & Bosly, N. 1998, *Presenting the News On Air. A Self-Paced Program to Develop Your Broadcast Voice*, University of Queensland Press, Brisbane.

Herbert, J. 2000, 'Broadcast Presentation: Looking and Sounding Great!', in *Journalism in the Digital Age: Theory and Practice for Broadcast, Print and On-line*, Focal Press, Oxford, pp. 229–43.

Mills, J. 2004, 'Signposting the Sense (Or How Not To Be a Plonker)' in *The Broadcast Voice*, Focal Press, Oxford, pp. 113–34

Trewin, J. 2003, 'Presenting on Television' and 'Presenting on Radio' in *Presenting on TV and Radio*, Focal Press, Oxford, pp. 94–135

PART V

Working on the Web

The broadcast media online

I think there will always be work for journalists; it just might change in form. But still the fundamentals are the same—you go out, get your story, write it up, and get it out there.

Katy Cronin, television journalist

I think radio and the Internet is one of the great electronic media marriages if it is used correctly. The Web gives radio a visual presence. All of a sudden people are going to see what we look like, you know, cameras in the studio, all that, all happening. It's there now, and it will be a virtual television program with no licence boundaries, so I am really looking forward to it. The new technology is going to make radio fantastic—it will give me a future. I will need a lot more make-up, but there you go.

Howard Sattler, radio talkback presenter, 6PR Perth

As we saw in Chapter 3, online broadcasting is experiencing exponential growth, with traditional broadcasters offering Web services to add value to their conventional broadcasting activities, and with independent operators taking advantage of cheap technology to set up their own individual operations. Most radio and television stations have a Web presence, offering a rainbow of services, some with live broadcasts exclusively for online; some using the Internet to 'retransmit' terrestrial programming; and some storing archived broadcast material to be accessed on demand.

Radio has had a head-start on the Web, though as with other Internet statistics, it is difficult to establish exactly how many stations currently broadcast online globally. Radio-Locator, which claims to be the most comprehensive radio station search engine on the Internet, has links to over 10,000 radio station web pages and 2500 audio streams from stations around the world (most of them in the USA). The web site 'Mike's Radio World' lists almost eighty online radio stations in Australia. Web-TV is also growing, although at a slower pace because of the need for greater bandwidth (the Internet 'pipes' that determine the speed of delivery and amount of content that can be relayed to your home computer). Fast broadband Internet connections and improvements in compression software are now making video almost as accessible as audio.

As the Internet develops, so do media web sites. In the early years most sites were basic, and didn't take full advantage of the opportunity the new technology offered for blending print, audio, and video. This is no longer the case today and media web sites are exploiting convergence to develop online-specific multimedia material. This affects the way content is produced, and is consequently changing how journalists work.

In this chapter we look at the skills broadcast journalists need in this new environment. Before we look at the product, though, we need first to consider the audience. In this medium, no less than in the others, gaining the attention of the elusive, fickle audience is the name of the game, but here the rules have changed. Listeners and viewers now have the power to become players in the game themselves.

The online audience

What makes the Internet unique is the power it gives to the users, or, in media terms, the audience. Audiences are always elusive and we have seen in previous chapters how radio and television producers use ratings and surveys to try to get a handle on what will appeal to their audiences most. Audience-grabbing is as important in new media as in old, perhaps more so as online operations are still really the loss-leaders in the broadcast menu. As long as the public resists paying a fee for access, the industry will struggle with how to turn a profit from online ventures. For now it is still a 'bums-on-seats' game with 'clicks' replacing the ratings book 'ticks' as a way of tallying who is accessing a service at any given time. The new technology makes it more and more difficult for broadcasters to rely on audiences doing their bidding. Audiences can set their own viewing and listening agendas without needing to be locked in to the broadcaster's schedule (see above, p. 26). They can also gain access to a greater variety of services than ever before (though audience research is showing audiences still tend to stick to their favourites—according to one survey of radio audiences in the USA, 52% of online listeners listen to only one station throughout the day (Dardis 2004)).

In news terms, audiences no longer have to sit back and wait for a bulletin to begin, nor even to sit through the whole news bulletin just to get the latest weather report. This flexibility might seem like paradise for listeners and viewers, but the downside of it from a news point of view is that it could tempt broadcasters to produce only what is appealing to the audience, in other words what is 'popular' news. Google News provides an example of an audience-driven approach to news. What Google, the world's most popular search engine, has done is to compile the latest news by trawling through all the news sites on the Web. Items are then aggregated around topics and the site with the latest update becomes the main link to the story. This allows it to benefit most from subsequent 'clickthroughs' as it is likely to be the first place people will go to chase the story. And for web sites, clicks are as important as circulation numbers are for newspapers or ratings numbers are for radio and television.

The increasing tendency to divide news into categories, coupled with an audience-driven agenda, could lead to a situation where people don't access broader news, but only what is of interest to them. This, of course, would have serious implications for journalism, which has until now prided itself on operating on a 'need to know' rather than strictly a 'want to know' basis. The reduced distance between audience and broadcast journalist could change the whole culture of broadcast news. As James Stovall notes: 'Broadcasting is the part of journalism that is the most distant from its audience. It is also the medium with the most immediate impact. Distance and impact have produced a culture of arrogance that has many broadcasters operating as if they had no accountability. Broadcast journalists on the Web will be more within reach of their audiences and more accountable to them'(2004, p. 155). There is also scope for users to be co-opted by the broadcast media to become producers themselves. In the UK, the BBC is trying to activate the online audience to encourage people who have been part of a story (for example, witnesses to a hurricane) to work with BBC journalists to make their experiences part of the BBC's online coverage (Clifton pers. comm. 2004).

Characteristics of online broadcast media

The starting point of any production process is the nature of the medium itself, so let's look at the features that distinguish online broadcast media:

- On-demand access. The ability to archive stories means users can access what they want, when they want it.
- Niche markets. Inexpensive and simple technology allows anyone to publish and broadcast, hence the Internet offers a plethora of sources and web sites catering for people with specific interests.
- Global reach. The potential audience (listeners/readers/viewers) of programs can stretch into millions globally.
- Interactivity. The interactive potential of the Internet allows the audience to take a more active role in the story by being involved in opinion polls, news quizzes, and direct interaction with the journalists.
- Community-building. Interactivity also offers the opportunity to bring people with similar interests together in discussion groups using newsgroups and chatrooms linked to the news story. This can be useful when reporting on specific topics such as health or crime.
- Databases. Searchable databases allow site-users to search for information that relates to their needs.
- Rolling deadlines. With more news media competing online to be the first out with a story, the tradition of hourly or daily deadlines (depending on medium) has vanished. Audiences/users can access information 'as the story happens' without having to wait for tomorrow's newspaper or the next radio bulletin.

These characteristics are forcing media organisations and their journalists to rethink how to produce content for delivery online. How do you design attractive radio programs for a global target audience? What impact does the bandwidth have on the selection of vision used in an online television documentary? It is no longer enough for broadcasters simply to re-transmit content from their terrestrial radio and television operations: the users have learnt to demand more of the product. They want interactivity; they want radio *and* pictures; they want video *and* text.

Continuously developing technology is opening up opportunities for any media organisation to produce content for transmission via a variety of channels: terrestrial radio/TV, newspapers, Web, or email. Systems such as SMS (short message systems) or WAP (wireless application protocol) have made even the mobile phone a transmission

Brett Bugg, Executive Producer, External and Emerging Platforms, ABC.

channel. ABC Online sends some of its Web content as headlines to mobile phone users. While limitations in the technology mean that SMS stories have to be short and concise—only 156 characters long—WAP stories are more or less open-ended and are only governed by the page limit of the particular handset. Some WAP services also now include pictures. The ABC currently publishes a WAP service to four different mobile providers and these stories all contain images and full-length stories. According to Brett Bugg, who oversees content development in this area, during the 2004 federal election subscribers were able to take advantage of the ABC's special SMS service delivering updates on results throughout election night. The opportunities afforded by mobile phone services have got news networks thinking about how to adapt traditional news content to fit. So far, all they have done is to cut the content to mini-versions, but with future increases in bandwidth it will be possible to watch an entire news bulletin on your mobile phone.

The variety of transmission outlets impacts on the way content is produced, opening the way to a range of options illustrated by this example (adapted from Enlund & Lindskog 2000, p. 75):

Think of the story as being on an axis: at one extreme will be the format of the short text-message broadcast to the audience via the display window on mobile phones. At the other extreme, the same story is developed as an exploded news feature, a web page with a library of information embedded in it, including short news texts, pictures, video clips, graphics, audio, comments from the audience, archived stories on the same topic, and links to other sites and perhaps even original source material. The content on such a site is constantly expanding with no real limitations in technology except for space on a server.

Here we see the news story becoming a multi-layered resource for people who want to explore the topic in varying degrees of depth. Instead of the journalist serving up a ready-made story to the audience, the media users can tailor the content to suit their level of interest and the time they have available. (see pp. 266–8 below for an illustration of how an online story develops from short headlines to a full-blown extended news feature with linked audio, video, and text).

The online reporter

This super-flexible job, with creative potential that transcends all media, demands wide-ranging skills. Whereas people in the past specialised in audio, video, or print, the new medium requires an understanding of all three—in fact four if you consider the Internet medium itself that brings them all together. Specialists will not disappear—the more we get to know the new medium the more we appreciate its role as an extra string to the communications bow. However, journalists need to know something about sound, vision, layout, and graphic design to take full advantage of the Web's potential. They also need to think differently about their stories—they no longer have just one lateral dimension (beginning-middle-end), but multiple dimensions through the layers that can be built in. In the online environment, as James Stovall points out, 'The journalist is no longer limited by too little space in print and too little air time in broadcast. An imaginative and highly skilled web journalist can take advantage of the medium to present a wide variety of information in many ways …' (2004, p. 65).

Libby Chow, Content Producer, The Age Online

Libby's studies were in the field of creative film-making and documentary, during which she gained experience across a range of media including video, film, and radio, as well as photography, including Photoshop and 3D computer animation. This multiskilling prepared her well for the new role of multimedia producer that was created as part of the *Age*'s Age Online website. She also produces video content for other Fairfax sites including SMH (*Sydney Morning Herald*) Online.

Libby Chow, content producer, The Age Online

Libby's day starts by logging onto the photographer's diary or having a chat with the picture editor on the newsdesk if she hasn't already lined up a shoot. She also checks in with other production staff such as the entertainment site producer. She keeps an ongoing check on her email and other potential story sources on and off the Web. If there is a story happening she will go out to cover it, otherwise she will work on interviews she may have already set up with special guests such as actors or footballers. She produces one piece a day, dividing the rest of her working day up between shooting, which may take up to 3 hours, and editing, which may take anywhere up to 8 hours depending on the complexity of the piece.

The skills

Libby says: 'Technical skills—I operate a 3 chip mini DV camera, basic lighting and sound. People skills—I need to be able to conduct interviews about any number of subjects from football or finance to film-making and to convince people that they want to talk to me. Research skills—research has become more and more important and I usually dedicate 1 day a week to do that. It also makes the production process easier when you've researched thoroughly. Editing skills—I operate a Final Cut Pro edit suite every day. I have to understand what compression is all about (the video goes through this process so it can fit through the relevant Internet connection i.e. 56K or LAN). I need to be ready to go at a moment's notice and cover big events, which may mean covering a protest or press conference.'

The job

'Online is about immediacy, so with that comes a certain pressure to get the material up ASAP. This can increase the chance of error and reduce the quality of the piece. So there is a constant balance between speed and quality.

'For me, story selection is governed by the locality of the story as I have to get vision, and so local news is what I cover. But it also has to be worth watching, so a train accident or a parade will be more important to cover than a press conference on the new million-dollar budget for roads. I will take footage of the scene and either the journalist or I will interview a spokesperson. I then edit a piece of around a minute-and-a-half. I have also been involved with print journalists in creating video to accompany features that they have written. Sport and entertainment stories are also chosen on the basis of their substance, locality, and visual potential.

'In the case of feature packages, the journalist, editor and I work together. As far as breaking news goes it is pretty much added to the text to give a fuller version of the story.'

Production challenges

'The major production challenge for Web production can be working all by yourself, however, in the last 2 years I have acquired a colleague and we try to help each other on shoots, which has improved the quality of our work. The times when I do work by myself, I have to be aware of lighting, composition, sound levels, all the while communicating with the subject, making them feel comfortable and then interviewing them while filming. This can be quite demanding in that I have to keep eye contact with the subject as well as make sure they don't slip out of the frame and that the audio levels don't start to peak.

'When in a cluster of media, I have to literally fight for a spot because I don't have a sound guy to help me hold the mike close enough to the subject's mouth. There is usually a way around these problems, like conducting another interview separately from the rest if time allows.

'Editing under time pressure is another challenge.

'Being involved in such a new medium that others may be wary of can hamper getting the story at all. The rules and laws are still hazy when it comes to video on the net.

'Being female in such a male-dominated area as news cameramen was a challenge that I enjoyed. The camera guys on the whole are very supportive and keen to give me advice on clothing and shooting etc. For instance, I was told by an ABC cameraman that I shouldn't wear skirts because I might find myself having to climb over a fence and getting stuck, or that I wouldn't be allowed to cover a bushfire story if I wasn't wearing jeans. Helpful tips, like where to buy gloves that allow you to operate the camera.

'The time pressure of getting the video up as quickly as possible has at times not worked and the quality has been low as a result. More recently we have realised that all good things take time and so have changed the way we work by creating more realistic deadlines.

'Who knows where this will lead me! After 5 years I'm still here, which is a good sign I suppose. In terms of this job I want to keep producing engaging content for the online medium. Aside from that, the medium is only a part of what I do and it has already opened so many doors of opportunity for me. I think that online reporting trains you to act quickly and to be flexible because in this world of new technology you just have to be able to adapt to new situations, new ideas, and new ways of doing things.'

When the first online reporters were introduced to the public during a festival in Berlin in 1999 they looked like something out of *Star Trek*. They sported what was called an Urban Jungle Pack, a wearable set of equipment that allowed them to report from the field, streaming audio, video, and text back to the newsroom. The online reporter of today doesn't look quite as eye-catching, but the principle of filing stories on the run using more than one medium is the same. Online reporting is about reconfiguring traditional journalism skills to fit the demanding medium of the Internet. Portable and wireless technologies such as laptops and mobile phones have been used by print journalists for years to file stories from remote locations. Similarly the so-called 'live-cross bag' featuring wireless radio microphones and mini-transmitters has been standard equipment for radio journalists to do live on-location reports back to the studio. Meanwhile, satellite dishes have fulfilled the same function for television journalists, enabling them to do live television reports from outside the station. Technically there is nothing stopping a reporter from filing across all media, however, in Australia few newsrooms have made the leap into fully-fledged multimedia newsrooms. The ABC has co-located radio and television news, but in most cases reporters still file for either radio or television. One explanation is the more time-consuming reporting process of television. Whereas a radio news reporter can do fifteen to twenty stories a day, the television counterpart might do only one. The overall productivity of reporters would go down if they had to do both. In some instances, ABC journalists will report for both media, however, it is far from the vision of integrated tri-media newsrooms (for radio, television, and online) that were envisaged in the beginning of the Internet era.

Web reporting skills

Multiskilling and flexibility are the buzzwords in online journalism. In the digital world it is content that matters, not the distribution platform, and online reporters need to be able to switch effortlessly between different media. And since the audience expects to be able to access information online about an event immediately after it has happened this is an environment where deadlines have been abolished—online it is always deadline time.

Many of the skills used in broadcast journalism transfer easily to online reporting. As we have seen, radio reporters are used to working with technology. They are also accustomed to the demands of reversioning, multiple deadlines, and having to 'think on their feet'. Likewise, television journalists are used to working within a technology-heavy medium and coping with the limitations this imposes on journalistic practice. This gives them a bit of a head start in adapting to journalism online. However, the characteristics of the online medium make different demands on the reporter. Unlike live radio and television coverage where the event is broadcast as it happens, with a commentary as an accompaniment to the live feed, online reporting involves an additional editorial process when the material is captured on a web site. Media audiences can be forgiving when it comes to live broadcasts—the immediacy and urgency will make the occasional fluff allowable—but standards are higher for an edited product and here the values of print journalism come into play. The Web is a print-based medium where the role of the audio and video content is to enhance the text, complementing the words rather than existing as a stand-alone product. In this domain, the writing and layout skills of the print journalist really come to the fore.

Journalists also have to adjust to the fact that their work gains greater permanency on the Web. Instead of radio and television bulletins disappearing into the ether, they are stored and accessible on demand, often indefinitely. This opens journalists to greater scrutiny from and accountability to an audience ready and eager to take advantage of a third defining characteristic of online: interactivity. Journalists are just an email address away from viewers and listeners, and dealing with audience emails has become another task that has to be added to the journalist's day.

The following list summarises some of the core skills needed for online reporting:

- ability to use the Internet and an understanding of the medium
- HTML coding
- server file management
- photo manipulation using Photoshop
- digital audio and video editing software
- basic understanding of design
- ability to write short stories quickly
- teamwork
- basic journalism skills—newsgathering and having a 'news sense'.

It is clear that what we now seek is a breed of super-reporter, although some critics are voicing fears about the impact on quality journalism if reporters also have to take on jobs previously performed by camera operators, sound recordists, graphic designers, and editors. ABC Online's in-house 'survival guide' identifies some skills and attributes, relating to Web news gathering and preparation, that an online journalist should have:

- Be able to find related links for stories/issues
- Be able to use the web for adding details, background or other story extensions.
- Have the ability to select and integrate text, images, graphics, audio, video and other elements (animations, slide shows) to enhance coverage.
- Have awareness of the general legal issues involving news coverage as well as specific issues that apply to online publishing and moderating discussions.

ABC 2004

The focus on the technical aspects of reporting in a multimedia environment foregrounds the role of the journalist as information-gatherer, but we run the risk of forgetting the equally important role of information-processing that the journalist fulfils as well. With the wealth of information available to the public online, now more than ever they need someone who can help guide them through the maze. In the online news world journalists are the 'skilled practitioners who can search, digest, and summarize information for others who are too busy or lack the skills to do so for themselves.' (Gunter 2003, p. ix).

Producing content for the Web

Col Wotherspoon, senior broadband producer, and Kerrin Binnie, journalist/presenter/producer discuss the next broadband news bulletin for ABC Online.

All journalism boils down to the basic tasks of finding, developing, and broadcasting and/or publishing the right mix of stories for a target audience. If a web site is compared to a news bulletin or a radio program, the aim of the editors and producers is to decide what stories to go for and how they will be presented.

The multiple media capacity of the Internet generates new considerations for journalists to keep in mind. What is the most effective way to present the story in terms of text, audio, chats with the audience, and video? What added material should be collected on location? Should the story be developed into a multi-layered feature incorporating backgrounders, links, and archived stories?

What journalists should never forget is their main function, which is to 'tell the story'. Jonathan Dube's (2004) rule of thumb in deciding *how* to tell it may help in deciding what medium to use:

- **Use print to explain.**
- **Use multimedia to show.**
- Use interactives to demonstrate and engage.

http://www.cyberjournalist.net/news/000117.php

The following is a list of elements that media producers have to consider as part of the journalistic process when producing content for the Web.

Editorial issues

Like the news editor or program producer, the site editor (the ABC uses the term 'executive producer') oversees the editorial content of the site as a whole taking the following factors into account.

Story mix

As for other media, the producer/editor tries to find a mix of light and shade.

Treatment of stories

Editorial discussions will cover questions such as: Which will be text-only stories? Which should have pictures and graphs? Which should include audio and/or video? Which should have multiple treatments using different formats: live, feature, interactive, etc?

Multi-layering

Broadcast journalists are constrained by the short formats of a 30-second radio news grab or a 90-second television package. They have to choose one angle and limit the amount of information, comments, and opinions to include in the report. Online reporters have no such limitations. The Web provides the opportunity for stories to be developed 'vertically' as well as 'horizontally'—in other words, they can be developed on a number of different levels.

These range from the short text for breaking news through to the expanded feature that would include timelines, backgrounders, archived material, links to relevant sites, and original source material, and so on. The Mark Latham story on page 266 shows how just one story developed on the Web in a single day. The list of linked audio and video files could be longer if needed. It is more a matter of how many enhancements are available.

Forward planning

Thinking about what might happen and putting packages together before an event happens is standard procedure for journalists. This involves advance preparation of special features on ongoing stories like the Middle East crisis, or one-off events such as the Olympics. These can become news resources themselves because of the wealth of research material (backgrounders, maps, statistics etc) that can be incorporated into them. Editors need to keep an eye out for these opportunities in order to marshal the appropriate information in a timely fashion. This may mean assigning a group of journalists and web designers to a project months beforehand.

Construction of site

This involves decisions about what will be placed where, and any technical considerations such as live talent to be featured in an interactive chat with the audience.

Reporting issues

With the editorial staff overseeing the site as a whole, it is up to the reporter to oversee the development of individual stories, be this covering short breaking news or researching and compiling backgrounders. The following factors will need to be taken into account.

Story enhancement

Reporters doing location interviews will try to get pictures as well as audio (and crop the picture themselves). Enhancements can also include source material such as statistics or background reports that can be scanned in or incorporated by way of links on the web site.

Specialist reporting

Web journalists are generic 'content-gatherers': the way the stories are distributed will be independent of their discipline. However, specialist reporters with superior craft skills might still be necessary for high-quality dedicated content for radio and television. The unlimited capacity of the Web as a journalistic space means there is lots of scope for in-depth and specialist reporting. This kind of story-telling means you have to think ahead so that you can assemble all the material you need for the different ways you will be dealing with the story.

Detailed research

In contrast to radio and television journalism, web reporting offers scope to develop stories in greater depth and detail. This requires thorough research and the collection of sufficient material. Technical feasibility is another issue that has to be considered at the research stage. Just as broadcast journalists have to liaise with editors and technicians in pulling their stories together, so web journalists liaise with their editors and technical site managers to deal with specific technical requirements needed for the story to be properly accessible online.

Writing for the Web

Words, not pictures or electronic media content, are the bread-and-butter for the online journalist. Web language is less formal than newspaper writing. It is closer to the radio script in style—shorter, more conversational and it uses present tense and active voice wherever possible. As a result, wire copy generally needs to be rescripted before being posted on the Web. However, unlike radio and television where the scripts are heard but not seen, you can't afford to be careless with spelling. Here the values of print journalism apply and accuracy—in spelling and grammar as well as in factual details—is essential. Studies conducted by John Morkes and Jacob Nielsen (1997, http://www.useit.com/papers/webwriting/writing.html) have shown that Internet users don't read on the Web; instead they scan pages trying to pick out the information they want. A text written for scanning can contain:

- highlighted keywords
- sub-headings
- bulleted lists
- one idea per paragraph
- concise writing with low word counts.

According to Morkes and Nielsen, users prefer texts to be short and to the point and they also want summaries of topics. Users can decide to follow links to the full article if they want more information. Users are impatient and want information quickly so the inverted news pyramid used in electronic media works well online. That writing technique presents news and conclusion first followed by details and background information.

The ABC Online handbook identifies some important copywriting skills for online journalists:

- Headline writing—headlines that attract readers, identify story content, remain meaningful if they appear alone in a list, and meet metadata requirements for searching.
- Story writing—stories written with clarity, brevity and pace, preferably with some casual flair to match the web's generally informal tone.
- Link writing—hyperlinks that tell the users exactly what they will get if they make the click.

ABC 2004

Subbing

Much of the work online involves refashioning previously broadcast content, so journalists need to have good subbing skills in order to tailor this content to the new medium.

Managing the web site

The ethical principles and legal constraints that apply to traditional journalism are just as important and relevant in the online domain. These are discussed in detail in chapters 16 and 17. However, the Web throws up some issues of its own such as the following.

Balance

The capacity for a story to include information from everywhere adds another dimension to the question of balanced coverage. When enhancing stories by adding links to other web sites, there is a need to ensure that all sides are represented. For example, a story on euthanasia would have to have links to church groups as well as euthanasia societies.

Links policy

Providing links to commercial sites as part of a journalistic story is problematic, since it could be seen as an advertising 'plug' and blur the distinction between journalism and advertorial. Links can be included if there is an editorial reason to do so. For example, after a plane crash, it might be appropriate to include a link to the airline's official web site if it contains information necessary for the public.

Audience interactivity

This can take the form of feedback via email, or comments on stories and issues via chatlines. Many broadcasters feature talent in the studio with whom the audience can 'chat' at a pre-arranged time. Just like talkback on radio, interactivity in whatever form has to be managed. Comments generally aren't posted raw onto the site, but go through an editing process in order to exclude abusive or offensive language, or information that might be considered defamatory or in contempt. Feedback is therefore part of the 'story' and integrated into the overall story production process.

Crediting sources

As with other media, stories from outside sources must be appropriately credited.

Technical aspects of the web site

This covers the technological and design aspects of the Web production process.

Streaming audio and video live and on-demand

Site producers are able to feature both live broadcasts and content generated separately by radio and television. The audience can access the material either in real time (streaming) or later through an audio or video archive (on demand).

Bandwidth

This term relates to the size of the 'pipes' that deliver the data from source to computer. The bandwidth size determines how much data can be transmitted at any one time, and the more complex the site (layout, colour) and the more media-rich the content (audio and video), the more problems potential users will face in accessing the material quickly and easily. After the World Trade Center attack in September 2001, the ABC stripped down its Web site to bare essentials, with some stories offered in a text-only format in order to accommodate the vast increase in 'hits' as people from all over the country, and indeed the world, sought to find out what was happening.

Layout

This is an area where the influence of print is apparent. Just as with newspapers, pictures and headings are judiciously placed to break up the Web page to make it easier on the eye. However, length is an issue since there is not one page but a sequence of pages, each of which takes you further away from the 'headline'. To prevent the readers getting lost, web producers try to keep the number of page clicks to a minimum—three or four at most.

Simple design

This is essential in order to accommodate the broadest audience, including those with less powerful computers.

The mixed media newsroom

The digital revolution and improving Internet technologies are changing the newsrooms. Old production systems are no longer viable in the fast world of web broadcasting. Now newsrooms have a range of media options to select from when compiling a story. While broadcasters add their content to new print-based sites, on the print side newspapers are adding audio and video enhancements to complement their hard copy paper with a faster, more updated multiple-media Web edition. This represents a break with the longstanding tradition of separate radio, television, and print operations. Let's look at two examples in more detail.

The Age Online

In 1995, the Melbourne newspaper the *Age* became the first Australian newspaper to launch an Internet edition and, 10 years later, it can boast that up to 250,000 people log onto its web site each day (Van Niekerk 2005, p. 8). The *Age* is an example of a print-based medium that includes audio and video on its web site The Age Online. It has a small news-room of dedicated online reporters who cover breaking news stories and, where deemed appropriate, they include audio and video with the text story. According to Online Editor Simon Johanson: 'We're increasingly adding audio and video components to sto-ries. We're rapidly moving to convergence in our newsroom between print and online, opening up the possibility of print reporters filing copy to online throughout the day and, if needed, doing pieces to camera or taking audio grabs' (Johanson pers. comm. 2005).

For Simon Johanson the medium presents a wealth of opportunities: 'We often tackle more complex news stories using multimedia story telling, packaging all the compo-nents—video, pictures, audio, text—into one element. This is a popular and successful for-mat with readers, but has also won the site several prestigious awards. The increasing sophistication of the Internet as a news medium and the rapid take up of broadband in Australia is pushing the popularity of news sites like ours. It is also leading towards fuller integration of the various digital streams we use to cover news stories.'

Many of the stories published by The Age Online now also appear on other platforms across Australia. The plethora of PDA (personal digital assistant) devices and digital mobile phones has created new audiences for news. The Age Online articles and video pieces are available on the handsets of all the major telephone companies and on the Web in alter-native systems like RSS (really simple syndication) feeds.

This sophistication is reflected in changing reporting methods. In 2005, the two Fairfax newspapers, the *Age* and *Sydney Morning Herald*, are trialling a new system where reporters and photographers file directly to the newspapers' web sites.

Simon Johanson describes how this works: 'We are sending reporters to cover stories with PDA devices through which they file copy, pictures, and audio reports directly to online. The reporters will file several "takes" of the story, adding information as they go along similar to a wire agency news service. Online editors work with them to add various elements to the story, relevant links to other web sites, images, audio and video compo-nents. We find that readers are also increasingly keen on interacting with the web site, often submitting pictures of big news events, many of which we publish as readers' photo galleries.'

ABC Online

Whereas The Age Online site features audio and video as enhancements to the print text, ABC Online builds text around repackaged material from the radio and television services. Staff constantly trawl the in-house wire services for material to be reworked for

ABC Online newsroom in Brisbane.

the online news site. Because of radio's rolling deadlines, ABC Online has immediate access to the latest news. The marriage between radio and online has proven successful for the online news service. The newsroom in Brisbane has grown from six staff in 1996 to about thirty in 2005 and now includes a specialist graphic designer and other technical specialists.

ABC Online follows a 'broadcast news' model with updates as soon as new information is available.

Although web writing is similar to broadcast copy, quality control is important, and the ABC's online journalists have to rewrite copy from the radio and television newsrooms so that the broadcast writing is brought up to read-only standards. Working with material intended for broadcast can be problematic, especially when transcripts of an interviewee's words can become a verbatim quote online. ABC journalists are becoming more aware that their scripts may be posted on the Web. Scripts from current affairs shows like radio's *AM* can become a feature story online with complementary photos from elsewhere. Wire copy from news agencies is also rewritten to suit the online style.

While ABC News Online has had a policy of employing only journalists, some of those journalists have become, in effect, specialist web developers. More recently the newsroom has employed some traditional craft specialists, such as graphic designers and technical producers.

The ABC Online operation provides news services under licence to a variety of external sources like other web sites, mobile phone carriers, buses and trains and information screens, in accordance with strict editorial guidelines.

Kerrin Binnie, journalist/producer/presenter, prepares for his broadband television bulletin at ABC Online.

The Brisbane newsroom also produces broadband television news bulletins. Eight staff work in the online television unit producing eight bulletins per day covering news, sports, and business. The broadband bulletin contains reworked stories from ABC TV as well as material from wire services like Reuters. Some interested ABC reporters file directly for the online newsroom. A radio voicer can be matched with new vision to make a fresh version of last night's news. Or an audio grab from the morning radio news can be overlaid with graphics to be added to a recut television story. The main aim is to get the latest news to the online viewers. Staff are truly multiskilled—the on-air television studio is designed so the presenter can do the technical work of setting up the camera, checking voice levels, and recording the intros for the news stories. Once recording is done, the presenter edits the bulletin, compresses it, and makes it available as a linear bulletin as well as an interactive version. In the latter, the online viewers can select which order to watch the stories in the bulletin. According to ABC Online, the audience wants longer bulletins with more and shorter stories. Hence, the online broadband bulletin is currently between 7 and 10 minutes long, and the average story is between 2 and 2:30 minutes long.

According to Bob Johnston, manager of ABC New Media News and Information, the past few years have seen the consolidation of new ways of doing journalism: 'We have made huge steps forward in terms of staff multiskilling and in terms of our ability to publish the same story on different platforms. We are now much more able to respond to requests for content to be made available to emerging media' (Johnston pers. comm. 2005).

A day in the life of an online news story

Here you can follow how an online news story evolves from breaking news to a fully developed news feature containing audio and video links.

1. PREVIEW

Like most Australian journalists on 18 January 2005, staff in the ABC News Online newsroom in Brisbane were waiting for Mark Latham's statement about his future as Opposition Leader. Tension had been building over the Christmas break as the Labor leader appeared to drop from public view, failing to emerge even when the disastrous tsunami struck and devastated many countries around the Indian Ocean rim. Then news filtered out that the ALP leader was suffering from a repeat bout of pancreatitis. While this is a painful condition, the credibility of the Labor leader was dented when members of the public began reporting sightings of him in apparent good health relaxing at an upmarket resort. By the third week in January, the pressure on Latham to resign had become irresistible and rumours were circulating that Latham would make a statement today. In advance of any specific development, the leading story on the ABC News Online website contains speculations about whether the leader will stay or go. As can be seen above, the story includes audio and video links. The audio consists of ABC radio interviews with Peter Beattie, Bob Carr, and Kim Beazley and the video is a package from ABC TV that features Labor figures predicting that Mark Latham will step down within 24 hours.

2. HEADLINE

Just before 3.00 pm the online newsroom receives a telephone call from a reporter on the spot that Mark Latham has resigned as Federal Opposition Leader. The story is put on the web site within minutes of the breaking news. At this point it is only a headline story with the information 'full details and reaction to follow' tagged on. The story still links to some of

the

audio grabs included in the previous version of the story. Executive Producer David O'Sullivan keeps a close eye on the in-house ABC wire services and, together with his staff, he looks for suitable images, audio, and video with which to update the story.

3. THE STORY

By 3.07 pm the site has been updated with more information as it comes in. Some frantic journalistic work has resulted in a new picture, an audio grab from Latham's resignation interview, and a much longer and more detailed article. The story does not yet cover all possible angles. It will be updated during the afternoon and will be bulked up with audio and vision covering various aspects of the story as these are fed through.

4. THE FEATURE

The day after the news of Latham's resignation, ABC News Online has built a feature story covering the topic from a rainbow of different angles. The site now contains links to two video packages, eleven audio grabs, and six relating text stories. The focus has moved on from the breaking news of yesterday's resignation to the question mark surrounding the Labor leadership. The main article wraps the story so far with audio and video offering complementary information. Each broadcast grab has a short summary of its content, for example:

- 'Just 13 months after assuming the Labor Party leadership, a sick and frustrated Mark Latham has quit politics entirely.'
- 'Former Labor Party leader Kim Beazley, who says he is fired with ambition for the future, will run for the leadership.'
- 'Labor's foreign affairs spokesman Kevin Rudd has wished Mark Latham well while refusing to rule himself out as a candidate for the leadership.'

Future challenges for Web reporters

As mentioned above, the idea of multiskilled, fast-working journalists who are fluent in all media production skills as well as web design, and file- and server-management, may just be an employer-driven fantasy. Nevertheless, the online medium opens up new opportunities for journalists who want to expand into web reporting.

The Web does give broadcast journalists more scope to develop stories in greater depth, along with the capacity to update information when necessary. A story that gets a 1-minute run on the television news can get a 10-minute slot on the broadcaster's web site.

Journalists crossing media boundaries develop new skills and will be able to use these to devise new techniques to tell stories using more than one medium.

There is a growing demand for journalistic content on web sites and this is opening up a new freelance market for journalists in all media. Audio content, whether interviews or complete stories, can be compressed and emailed as attachments to anywhere in the world. With broadband and faster Internet access, the same is becoming possible for video content.

The Web offers an abundance of data, far more than the average person has time to process. People will need help trawling through the mountain of information available and journalists, with their researching, processing, and communication skills, are perfect for the task. Rather than 'reporter', 'information broker' or 'information architect' may be titles better suited to the new media age.

The online environment is challenging for the journalist. On the one hand it offers many opportunities; on the other it is a world of change and uncertainty. There are several key challenges that journalists have to face.

Change

Ever-changing technology makes forward-planning difficult, and the industry is having to learn as it goes along, with newsrooms cutting down their planning cycles from a year to 6 months. In line with these workplace changes, journalists are finding that they constantly have to retrain just to keep up, and it is even worse for multiple-media reporters who have to master a wider range of skills. Learning is now a life-long enterprise and in this brave new world of digital reporting journalists must be prepared to keep upgrading their skills and knowledge.

Stress

With deadlines abolished and rolling services in place, online journalists are having to work faster and for longer hours. This increases the levels of stress, and the risk of burnout is real.

Resources

Online operations are still not resourced properly, with many reporters expected to take on web reporting duties as well as their ordinary reporting responsibilities. While the media employers may plug their online operations as the place 'where stories are breaking, where background is provided, and where experts are located', at the moment the sites are often run on a comparative shoestring. More money is needed if the services are to live up to their much-vaunted potential.

Public exposure

Where in the old media the journalist collected and processed the raw material with only the final story placed in the public domain, in 'new media' journalism all research material and background information can be included online adjacent to the final story. It makes the process of journalistic enquiry transparent, with the audience easily able to judge for itself whether the journalist got it right or not. And whereas mistakes on radio or television are generally forgotten once the program has gone off air, the Internet allows mistakes to be captured 'forever'.

Audience interaction

The Internet encourages audience interaction with journalists. This extends the life of the story beyond the bulletin and means that online journalists, like talkback hosts, will have to factor engagement with the audience into their working day. This has implications for the time they have available to work on their stories. Chris Masters, investigative journalist for ABC-TV's *Four Corners* program, describes in an interview in the *Bulletin* how the online forums held after the show has gone to air have impacted on his time: 'It used to be that you could have a glass of wine, watch the program, get a call from your mum and go to bed. But now you've got to sit up until 2.30 in the morning talking about it' (Lumby 2001, p. 44).

Law and ethics for Web reporters

The Internet is an egalitarian medium—this is its strength, but for journalists it is also a weakness. If anyone anywhere can access information and put it on to the Web, anyone anywhere can present themselves as a journalist. What are the standards for journalism in this new media age? What is truth and what is rumour? Whom can we trust as an information resource? The simple answer to the question 'what rules apply?' is that the same rules apply—only the temptations to break them are different.

Legal issues

See also chapter 16. While the legal issues remain the same for journalists no matter what medium they work in, the online media often require even greater vigilance to ensure laws aren't transgressed.

Defamation

As mentioned in chapter 3, the global nature of the Web has made journalists and media organisations potentially more vulnerable to defamation action with plaintiffs able to sue anytime and anywhere. The capacity of the Web to capture broadcast material that was previously evanescent means defamatory material can be re-broadcast any number of times to any number of people. Content providers therefore need to be especially careful.

Contempt

In the days of old media it was possible to quarantine information within a given geographical area. Hence, details that might impact on a trial in one state could nevertheless be safely revealed in other states on the basis that the newspaper circulation and even broadcast areas could be controlled. The new media era has eradicated those sorts of boundaries, thereby increasing the threat of contempt for journalists working far away from the story source.

Copyright

The law here is still evolving, and once again the situation is made more complex because of the global reach of the Web. However, the ease with which material can be accessed and duplicated means that journalists have to be sure they follow the appropriate procedures when using material that isn't theirs.

Ethics

See also chapter 17. Journalism ethics has become a real minefield in the online environment. As Peter Preston notes, '…it does, more than ever, become difficult to see the old mantras of fairness, balance and superficial neutrality survive intact. That's not why Fox News is king of US cable channels. That's not why the *Daily Mail* rides high, nor why bloggers are the new champions on the net' (2004, p. 7). Media commentator Paul Carr bemoans the trend towards rumour-based web journalism (pioneered by US-based Matt Drudge with his drudgereport.com web site) and the complicity of journalists who should know better:

> What stinks …is not the glee with which Drudge refuses to let the facts get in the way of a good lie, but that most of those lies…are supplied to him by print journalists who don't have enough evidence to put them into their own pages.
>
> Carr 2004, p.38

The unprecedented access to databases raises parallel concerns about the individual's right to privacy. The versatility and manipulability of the new technology makes digital tampering all the more tempting.

Journalism processes are more streamlined and there just aren't the numbers of checks and balances that the old-style newsrooms had to ensure journalists didn't fall into error, either deliberately or accidentally. Now, more than ever, journalists have to rely on their own moral compasses to chart their route in this complex territory. The media revolution is forcing journalists to examine closely their profession, their work practices, and themselves.

Exercises

Select a story that features on both the Age Online and the ABC Online sites and compare how they are developed.

1 What components are included in the story (audio, video, pictures, graphics, links to external documents/sites)?
2 What is the proportion of audio and video to text?
3 In what way do the components complement each other (is the information given in the text different to that in the video/audio)?
4 How are the sites similar and how do they differ?
5 Are there any elements that betray their respective print and broadcast origins?

Further reading

Dardis, K. 2004, *Radio Online. It's All About the Audience*, Audio Graphics, Inc., Cleveland, Ohio, http://www.audiographics.com/agd/s2121404.htm

Dube, J. 2004, Cyberjournalist.net, http://www.cyberjournalist.net/news/000117.php

Gunter, B. 2003, *News and the Net*, Lawrence Erlbaum Associates, Mahwah, New Jersey.

Morkes, J. & Nielsen, J. 1997, 'Concise, Scannable and Objective: How to Write for the Web', http://www.useit.com/papers/webwriting/writing.html

Pavlik, J.V. 2001, 'Journalism Ethics and New Media', in *Journalism and New Media*, Columbia University Press, New York, pp. 82–100.

Priestman, C. 2002, *Webradio—Radio Production for Internet Streaming*, Focal Press, Oxford.

Randall, D. 2000, 'Journalism on the Net', in *The Universal Journalist*, 2nd edn, Pluto Press, London, pp. 208–17.

Stovall, J. 2004, 'Reporting: Gathering Information for the Web' in *Web Journalism. Practice and Promise of a New Medium*, Pearson Education Inc, Boston, pp. 49–71.

Whittaker, J. 2004, *The Cyberspace Handbook*, Routledge, London.

Web sites

ABC Online: http://abc.net.au/news/

The Age Online: http:// www.theage.com.au

BBC Online: http://bbc.co.uk

Internet Radio Plaza (internet radio directory): http://www.webradiolist.com/

Mike's Radio World (internet radio directory): http://www.mikesradioworld.com/index.html

Radio-Locator (database of online radio stations): http://www.radio-locator.com

PART VI

A Broadcast Journalist's Guide to Law and Ethics

Broadcast Journalists and the Law

16

I have never been sued but I've been threatened to be sued. We have a really good legal section here in the ABC so if in doubt I always go to them, and I have gone to them many times and they've been fantastic.

Steve Cannane, radio presenter, Triple J

You've always got your finger poised on the button and I guess that just comes from years of experience—I mean I have been dealing with lawyers all through my career so you build up experience about what can be said, what can't be said, how far you can push something. It's very grey as you know, it's minefield stuff, and you are never quite sure how far to go.

Clark Forbes, Program Director, 3AW Melbourne

Access to the airwaves is a privilege, not a right. Broadcasters might be accorded unparalleled access to the public, but it is a freedom with legal and ethical strings attached. In these next two chapters we look at the laws and ethical codes that apply to journalists working in the broadcast media.

Journalists work within a legal framework that sets clear limits on how far they can go in pursuit of a story. The law is a strict taskmaster, and even the brightest stars have had their knuckles rapped when they have been judged to have taken things too far. Derryn Hinch at the height of his fame as king of Melbourne's talkback radio scene was sent to jail for broadcasting the details of the criminal record of a man accused of child molestation in advance of his trial—a clear contempt of court. The comedian Max Gillies also saw the inside of a courtroom when Kerry Packer sued him for defamation over a skit on corruption in high places. Meanwhile, the advent of the Internet has given the laws a global dimension. Australian businessman Joe Gutnick successfully sued Dow Jones for defamatory material published in the online version of its *Barron* magazine, thereby establishing that defamation occurs where information is downloaded, not where it is uploaded. Copyright has also become a real headache as journalists feed off other journalists by taking content from the inexhaustible Web pool and passing it off as their own work.

Regulators and judges are constantly having to remind journalists of the boundaries within which they operate. In Australia, the laws limiting free speech are already considered by many to be severe and overly restrictive. It is imperative that journalists know and understand these rules to avoid exposing themselves to situations that not only may have a personal cost in terms of fines or even imprisonment, but may also lead to the laws being tightened even further, to the detriment of society.

So in what way does the law relate to the activities of broadcast journalists? The three areas of greatest concern are defamation, contempt, and copyright.

Defamation

I think in some ways you can get away with a lot more on air. With the printed word it still lies there—someone gets it in front of their corn flakes and they see themselves defamed, or imagine they see themselves defamed, when they're eating their breakfast or when they get to the office, and it's still lying around at 12 o'clock that day. Therefore I think you're likely to get sued a lot more in print—certainly that's been my experience, although we've copped a few writs here over the years. But generally I think you can push the envelope a little further in radio because it's instantaneous: it's out there and it's gone.

Clark Forbes, Program Director, 3AW Melbourne

Broadcasters are in the business of talking about other people. The electronic media are simply a more modern and sophisticated means for transmitting news about someone to someone else. Unlike private conversation, the information goes out to the broader public—to local, statewide, national, or global audiences. What is acceptable in a one-on-one exchange becomes more dubious once it has the potential to spread to a wider audience.

Since the dawn of time, people have put a high price on their honour—indeed some have gone so far as to die in defence of their good name. Damage a person's reputation and you damage, possibly forever, their standing in the community. In other ages, bared fists, drawn swords, or pistols at dawn might have been used to settle the score. Nowadays the more likely weapon is the law, and the battleground is the courtroom.

Yet journalists are in the business of reporting. Their duty is to act as society's recorders, to probe beneath officialdom without fear or favour. This means, more often than not, treading the thin line between the acceptable and the unacceptable, and weighing up whether in particular cases the 'public interest' must take precedence over any individual private interests.

For broadcast journalists, this sort of decision often has to be made on the run, with live-to-air programs allowing little or no time to consider the implications of what is being said, let alone to rectify the damage. Knowledge of the law of defamation is essential to help you navigate this minefield.

What is defamation?

For defamation to occur these things need to have happened:

- Information needs to have been published (and 'published' in this sense includes broadcast transmission).
- The information needs to have related to an identifiable person (the person may have been named, or enough details given about them for people to deduce their identity).

- The information needs to have damaged their reputation either by:
  - leading them to lose esteem in the eyes of reasonable people
  - causing them to be despised, avoided, or ridiculed, or
  - injuring their professional standing.

Types of defamation

Defamation can be either verbal and transient (slander) or published and permanent (libel). It is the latter that is of most concern to journalists since, by definition, they are addressing a wide audience via either the print or the broadcast media.

Defamation can also be subtle—someone may not actually be named, but there is enough evidence in the offending material that would lead a reasonable person to guess their identity. Alternatively, a remark may appear superficially innocuous, but through innuendo may convey a more damaging subtext. No matter how unwitting the transgression, offending journalists may find themselves on the losing side if such imputations can be proven in court.

Who can be defamed?

Defamation applies to any living person (the dead cannot be defamed) or institution (except for governments and local councils). A high-profile example of the latter is the so-called 'McLibel' case in the United Kingdom where the McDonald's fast food company sued two British activists for distributing pamphlets making allegations about the company's practices.

Defamation and the law

In Australia, defamation is considered a tort—a civil wrong—as opposed to a crime, and so comes within the ambit of civil rather than criminal law. This means that individuals can sue for redress in a civil court. (Criminal defamation does exist as an offence, but prosecutions are rare and usually brought by the state in cases where the defamation is so serious as to have potential wider social consequences.) States and territories have adopted different approaches, which means there are variations in the legal treatment of defamation across the country. Western Australia, Victoria, South Australia, the ACT, and the Northern Territory deal with defamation under common law, while Queensland, New South Wales, and Tasmania have devised specific codes to cover defamation.

Who can be sued when things go wrong?

Liability extends to anyone involved in the publication of the offending material. This means journalists, editorial staff, production staff, and management. Even distributors such as newsagents can be pulled into the net if they knowingly sell defamatory material. You can also be prosecuted for repeating defamatory comments first published elsewhere. As noted in chapter 3 and above (p. 275), the Gutnick case has established that if your material is available online you can be sued anywhere in the world where it has been downloaded.

What are the remedies for defamation?

In the hurly-burly of daily broadcasting, most complaints about alleged defamatory material are negotiated fairly amicably. Even when the plaintiff acts through a lawyer, honour may be salved with a rapid on-air correction, an apology, or allowing the plaintiff the right of reply. Always seek the advice of senior management to check the legal implications of any remedial action you may take—for example, an apology might be taken as an admission of guilt and have implications later on if the matter goes to court.

If an aggrieved person was unhappy about dealing directly with the station, they would sue in the courts—usually the state Supreme Court—where one of the following outcomes might occur.

Injunctions

These are orders the courts make to prevent publication of offending material. Courts are generally unwilling to constrain free speech and only rarely prevent publication since the person can always sue subsequently if they believe they have been defamed.

Stop writs

Often journalists may be stopped in their tracks by receiving a writ notifying them of an impending defamation action. The plaintiff's purpose is to impose a media gag, and such is the fear of being taken to court that the device is often successful in cutting off all discussion—the journalist assumes that the matter is now before the courts and sub judice rules may apply (see p. 283). Though it would be wise to seek legal advice before proceeding in these circumstances, the courts have not looked kindly on this ploy, and there is no legal reason for media coverage to cease provided that the journalism is sound and the legal defences for defamation are in place.

Damages

If the matter can't be resolved through person-to-person negotiation, it might then proceed to court where monetary compensation will be sought.

Is there any defence for the journalist?

The main problem for journalists in the area of defamation law is that the usual 'innocent until proven guilty' rule does not apply. Rather than the plaintiff having to show how defamation occurred, the onus is on the journalist as defendant to prove it did not: it is up to you to justify your actions. It is important therefore for journalists to understand just what defences exist, as these will define the boundaries within which they can operate. Though there are variations among the states and territories, defences hinge on the issues of truth and public interest.

Truth

In Victoria, South Australia, Western Australia, and the Northern Territory, truth alone is a complete defence—in other words, a defamatory statement can be published if it is true and its truth is provable in court. This may be easier said than done, since it depends first on whether the journalist possesses information strong enough to stand up to full legal examination—hearsay or circumstantial evidence is not good enough—and second, on whether the journalist or the journalist's employer has the financial resources to cover legal proceedings. Often parties settle out of court rather than risk the potentially greater expense of taking a case to court and then failing.

Truth and the public interest

In New South Wales, you need to show not only that the defamatory comment is true, but also that it relates to a matter of public interest. In Queensland, the ACT, and Tasmania, the test is truth and public benefit. The aim here is to restrain journalists from gratuitously intruding into people's private lives.

Fair report

There are two forums where defamatory comments can be made with impunity—Parliament and the courts. Parliamentarians and participants in court trials have absolute privilege—in other words, they are free to make any statement and have it included in tabled reports of the proceedings without the threat of being sued afterwards. Because of the importance given in democratic societies to the right of the public to be informed about what goes on in these public institutions, as a journalist you are able to report any defamatory comments that occur in these contexts. However, you must do so fairly and accurately. This means you must:

- make it clear that you are reporting what was said in a privileged forum, i.e. in Parliament or in court
- restrict yourself to reports of proceedings—this covers anything that is tabled in Parliament, or that has been admitted as evidence in court. It does not include documents that may have been filed but not yet admitted as evidence
- give an account that is balanced rather than selective
- report on the basis of your own direct experience, rather than relying on second-hand information from others
- in advance of the verdict being handed down, refer to the evidence as 'allegations' rather than fact.

As for other sorts of forums—for example sports association meetings and local council meetings—different rules apply in different states and you will need to check the relevant legislation to see what applies in your own case. Many a journalist has slipped up by being unaware of the differences that apply once you cross state boundaries.

Fair comment

Journalism covers more than the reporting of fact—it also encompasses opinion and commentary that, whether in the form of editorial columns, theatre critiques, or restaurant reviews, can sometimes express strong views. In these areas the defence against defamation depends on:

- the comment being expressed as opinion rather than fact
- the opinion being based on information that is true, or covered by absolute privilege
- the opinion being what a reasonable person might consider fair on the evidence presented
- the opinion being the truly held view of the journalist (given that the aim of this defence is to protect fairly held opinions)
- the comment relating to a matter of public interest.

Qualified privilege

Australian journalists constantly chafe under the legal restrictions that they feel limit their capacity to report freely on matters of public importance. They point to the situation in the USA where the so-called Public Figure test gives their counterparts there considerable latitude to discuss people or issues in the public eye providing they can show absence of malice. In Australia, the closest equivalent is the very limited defence of qualified privilege. This is defined differently, depending on whether the Australian jurisdiction treats defamation under common law or under a separate statute.

Common law qualified privilege

In Western Australia, South Australia, the ACT, and Victoria, the common law defence of qualified privilege exists to cover situations where potentially defamatory material is transmitted from one person to another. This relates to such things as a referee's assessment of a job candidate, a teacher's report on a pupil, or a lawyer's discussion of a client. Comments and judgments conveyed in these contexts might technically defame, but are allowable on the basis that the 'publisher' or 'speaker' has an interest, or a social, moral, or legal duty, to communicate to a person, and that person has a corresponding interest or duty to receive it. Take the example of an employee reference: the employer has a duty to give a future employer a fair and accurate assessment of the employee's capabilities, the bad as well as the good. Likewise the future employer has an interest in receiving this information. The courts would be flooded with cases if communications such as these were the subject of defamation suits. Given that this provision has been crafted with one-on-one communications such as these in mind, the media have not been successful in attempting to extend it to cover print or broadcast material.

There are two exceptions:

- In the interests of protecting the public, the media can, at the request of the police, broadcast the name, description, or picture of a person who is being sought on criminal charges.
- The media can allow someone who has been the victim of a public attack the right of reply, providing they confine themselves to the substance of the original attack.

Statutory qualified privilege

Where defamation is covered by specific laws (New South Wales, Queensland, and Tasmania), legislators have attempted to broaden the common law defence.

In New South Wales a defence of qualified privilege can be made where the publisher:

- believes the audience has a genuine interest in receiving the information to be published
- publishes the defamatory material during the course of satisfying that interest
- has taken reasonable efforts to check the accuracy of the facts.

This defence attempted to give journalists greater leeway in reporting on important matters by releasing them from the burden of having to prove truth. In practice, however, the New South Wales courts have set such stringent tests for 'reasonable' conduct as to make this defence superfluous—to meet the court's standards any journalist would have had to check facts so thoroughly as to meet the 'truth' defence anyway.

In Queensland and Tasmania, there is a defence for the publication of defamatory material if it is published in good faith as part of a public discussion on a matter of importance. This means that journalists don't need to prove truth providing:

- the matter is of importance
- there is a public benefit in its being discussed
- they have no improper motives
- they don't knowingly report an untruth.

Political qualified privilege

1997 was a significant date in the perennial debate over free speech in Australia. In the early 1990s there was an ongoing wrangle over the limits to political reporting that resulted in a High Court ruling that the citizen's right to comment on political matters was implied in the Constitution. There was some discomfort with this constitutional justification and in 1997 the High Court had the opportunity to revisit the matter. Former New Zealand prime minister David Lange brought a suit against the Australian Broadcasting Corporation over allegedly defamatory material in a *Four Corners* program. The High Court ruling in this case acknowledged the community's right of free speech in relation to political and government matters, and created the defence of political qualified privilege. Under this defence, journalists would not be required to prove the truth of a defamatory statement providing they:

- believed the statement to be true
- took all reasonable steps to verify its truth
- had acted without malice
- had sought and published a response from the individual who was defamed.

This gave the media the freedom to publish reasonable and legitimate comment on political figures and their performance.

Preventive measures

Defamation is a tort of strict liability. This means that no matter what justification you might make on your behalf, if the damage to reputation is done, you have to wear the consequences. Despite the high-profile names that figure in some famous defamation cases, it isn't the Mr Bigs that cause journalists most problems. It is the ordinary people who are damaged through simple journalistic carelessness. The best way to avoid the pitfalls is to be diligent.

Check your facts

The best way to avoid the threat of defamation is to make sure you get the facts right. This means checking names, having back-up documentation to substantiate your allegations, taking care with your reporting of legal cases (see the section on Contempt below), and avoiding innuendo.

Keep your notes

Your notebooks, scripts, and program material (recorded and hard copy) are considered legal documents and you may be required to present them if requested by the court. These can be destroyed only if no legal proceedings have been started. Once a court case is underway, destruction of evidence would be considered contempt of court (see below). There is a legal requirement under the Broadcasting Services Act for broadcast material to be logged and retained for 6 weeks after broadcast.

Know the law

Make sure you understand how the law of defamation works (some useful references for further reading are included at the end of this chapter).

Get legal advice

Don't hesitate to consult senior staff or legal advisers—it is better to be safe than sorry. In the first instance, your editorial supervisor, program director, or senior manager are your first port of call. In addition, most broadcasting organisations have legal teams either in-house or on contract available 24 hours a day.

Contempt

We have to be careful with contempt of court. Sometimes with interstate stories we have to negotiate to establish just what we can run with. Once during a siege an eyewitness called through to the program. It was gripping radio listening to the on-the-spot account, but we had to cut it short because you could actually hear the police negotiating in the background and broadcasting that might have had an impact on the outcome.

Selby-Lynn Bradford, radio talkback producer, 2GB Sydney

For all the restrictions imposed on journalists by defamation law, Australian society accepts the right of the public to be informed about what goes on in the institutions responsible for our governance. Thus, in our parliaments and in our courts, privilege protects both freedom of speech from within these institutions, and freedom to report on their proceedings from without. However, certain ground rules are necessary to ensure that the course of justice isn't perverted through careless reporting.

The principle underlying contempt law is the protection of an individual's right to a fair trial. It is the responsibility of the courts alone to determine guilt or innocence, and they do not take kindly to the media taking on this role for themselves. The law sets clear rules for reporters in terms of what can be said, and when.

What is contempt?

Contempt is a criminal offence. Journalists are in contempt of court when, by their actions, they either impede the proper conduct of a trial, or challenge the authority of the court. The sub judice rules cover the former circumstance, while the rules relating to interfering with the administration of justice cover the latter.

Sub judice rules

The expression 'sub judice' literally means 'under the judge' and the sub judice rules cover matters where court proceedings are pending. The aim is to prevent 'trial by media'—the publication of material that might prejudice (literally prejudge) the final outcome. The purpose of a trial, after all, is to give the accused person a fair and impartial hearing, and the rules ensure that during both the pre-trial period and the trial itself no information is reported that might pre-empt a verdict.

The rules apply particularly to criminal trials involving a jury, the assumption being that the jurors, untutored in the law, are more likely to be swayed by public comment. In civil cases that involve a judge sitting alone (for example, commercial, employment, and industrial matters), there is scope for public discussion of the issues involved in the case as long as you don't prejudge the outcome.

The pre-trial period

This covers the period between arrest and charging of the accused and the trial. Journalists must not:

- publish information about a person that might lead to a prejudgment about their guilt (such as any previous criminal history). Such information can only be made public after the verdict has been handed down

- publish photographs of the person if their identity is an issue, as it would be in crimes such as murder, assault, or robbery
- publish details of the crime.

Journalists may:

- publish details of the charges laid and the bare facts of the case, plus anything said in court appearances leading to trial. Beware of following police press releases—journalists have sometimes been trapped by errors in reporting that the police have made themselves
- publish statements about their innocence made by the accused people themselves
- discuss matters of public interest raised by the trial when the trial itself is some months away, on the basis that the comments would be forgotten by that time.

During the trial

Journalists must not:

- publish prejudicial information
- publish evidence before it has been given in open court
- publish information given in court when the jury is absent
- publish information that the court has directed be suppressed.

Note that the sub judice period doesn't always end with the delivery of a verdict—if there is an appeal it is extended to cover the period from the lodging of the appeal until the end of the appeal process.

Other reporting restrictions

Children

Children are given special protection so that in cases in the Children's and Family courts the identities of the parties are not made public. Nor are children identified when appearing as witnesses in other trials.

Victims of sexual offences

Victims of sexual offences must not be identified. This includes publication of any information from which their identity might be deduced. It is for this reason that in some states the identity of the accused may be suppressed.

Interference with administration of justice

This aspect of contempt covers anything that might impede the functioning of the court, threaten its authority, or call it into disrepute. Unlike all other aspects of the law, it doesn't matter if the transgression is unintentional—the fact of the transgression is all that matters. Thus, a surprised 17-year-old man, sitting in on a trial in Perth, found himself jailed for two hours for failing to stand up when the magistrate entered the court. In the magistrate's view he had failed to show respect for the court, and while the hapless subject of the magistrate's wrath was not charged with contempt, he certainly had to suffer a court-imposed period of reflection. There are three sorts of contempt under this heading.

Scandalising the court

This relates to allegations of improper conduct made against the judiciary and the judicial system. Though judges are traditionally tolerant of reasonable criticism, and indeed it is important that no aspect of society be shielded from responsible critique, they nevertheless have the power to take immediate action if accusations are made that damage their authority and reputations, for example allegations that they have acted corruptly or improperly.

Revealing jury deliberations

The main concern here is to shield jurors from harassment both during and after a trial. This is essential to preserve the public's willingness to fulfil its civic function of undertaking jury duty. Though the law varies from state to state, the principal aims are to protect the jurors' identity and to maintain the sanctity of the jury room. While jurors can't be approached for their stories, in some states they are free to come forward under their own volition. In Tasmania, by contrast, jurors are bound by oath to reveal nothing of their deliberations. In Western Australia it is an offence to photograph jurors.

Behaving unacceptably in court

This relates to behaviour that adversely affects the administration of justice in the courtroom. Journalists must adhere to court procedures, and show appropriate respect to the judge and court officials.

Disobedience contempt

This is an area that has affected journalists in cases where they are witnesses and are called upon to provide confidential information or reveal their sources.

Journalists serve the public interest. They are delegated by society to report on the world around us, exposing the good as well as the bad. For this they rely on networks of contacts, but the more sensitive the information, the more exposed those contacts may be, putting their social positions, their jobs, and even their lives at risk. Though the right to protect sources has been enshrined in the journalists' Code of Ethics (discussed on pp. 291–4), it is not recognised in law. As far as the courts are concerned, the law is the ultimate code of conduct that transcends all other codes, and when journalistic public interest is up against legal public interest, the law will reign supreme. Journalists are therefore no different from any other member of the public, and if they are asked to disclose information they must do so. Failure to comply is a contempt of court, and there have been signs in recent years that the courts have been more prepared to take action against this sort of conduct by imposing fines or short terms of imprisonment as punishment. So what preventive action can you take?

Protection of sources

While the two previous versions of the journalists' Code of Ethics made an uncompromising commitment to the protection of sources, they didn't take into account the potential abuse of the legal process by sources who may have lied, or who may have acted with malicious intent. Protection in these instances might compromise the fairness of the trial. Under the latest revised version of the Code, as a journalist you should aim to attribute all information to its source, committing yourself to confidentiality only if you and the source are prepared to face the consequences if tested in court.

Handling of sensitive material

Once a court case is underway, you must obey any requests to hand over relevant material, no matter how sensitive. Destruction of any material from this point on is a contempt of court. The best way of ensuring protection for your source is to keep written documentation to a minimum.

Copyright

Copyright is the law of intellectual property that protects people's ownership and control over their created works. You can't just use an extract from a piece of music or a play—you may have to seek permission first and possibly pay a fee. This area of the law has become a minefield with the growth of the open-access environment of the Internet. The idealistic dream of an intellectual marketplace where anyone in the world can access any item of human knowledge has become a copyright owner's nightmare. Intellectual piracy is rife on the Web and governments and industries are still searching for ways to shackle the monster that has been created. While the law may be struggling to keep up, in the context of journalism plagiarism is an ethical no-no (see chapter 17). Operating in this environment, the issue is clear cut. If as a journalist you need to access the work of others, you have to answer the following questions: When can you use material without permission? When do you need to seek permission? How do you get permission?

When can you use material without permission?

Broadcast journalists don't need permission to use music and sound effects that are covered by the broadcasting agreements that their radio and television stations have already signed. Stations pay performing rights fees to the Australian Performing Rights Association that cover them for access to specified commercial music.

Fair dealing

Under the 'fair dealing' provision of the Copyright Act, journalists are able to reproduce parts of a literary, dramatic, musical, or artistic work without permission if it is for criticism or review purposes, or part of a news report. However, they have to acknowledge the source (in other words, the title of the book and the author; the title of the film and the director; or the radio station from which they have taken a sound grab). This includes material taken from the Internet.

When do you need to seek permission?

In all other circumstances, journalists need to seek permission to use creative works. This includes, for example, using a film grab for other than review purposes, parodying a song, or broadcasting unreleased musical material.

How do you get permission?

If you want to use someone else's work, you will need to get permission from either the copyright owner or someone delegated to act for them. This could be the film distributor, the record company, or the publisher. The following industry bodies also handle copyright issues, permission, and fee schedules on behalf of their clients:

Composers	Australian Performing Rights Association
	Australasian Mechanical Copyright Owners Society
Sound recordings	Australian Record Industry Association
	Phonographic Performance Company of Australia
Literary works	Australian Writers Guild
	Australian Screen Association
Film, television, and radio	Screenrights (The Audio-Visual Copyright Society)
Actors	Actors Equity (part of the Media, Entertainment and Arts Alliance)

Defensive journalism and the importance of note-taking

This chapter has shown how important it is for journalists to get things right when it comes to matters of law. The consequences of not getting it right were dramatically illustrated in the United Kingdom in 2003 when BBC journalist Andrew Gilligan was called to account during the course of the Hutton Inquiry. This inquiry was set up following Gilligan's allegations on the BBC's *Today* program that the UK government had exaggerated the threat posed by Iraq's weapons of mass destruction in order to support its case for war. The anonymous source for these allegations, government intelligence expert David Kelly, committed suicide after his identity was revealed in the media. The inquiry put Gilligan's journalistic practices under intense public scrutiny and the slipshod nature of his notes and his incapacity to corroborate his statements have made journalists painfully aware of the career-damaging consequences of their own laziness.

Media lawyer John Samson is now running training courses for journalists on note-taking practices that can prevent journalists from falling foul of the law. As he points out, 'if you end up in court, what you saw, heard, did etc are the facts to which you can testify, and whether you took a good note, rather than the note itself, is what the judge is interested in ... It is proof, not truth, that counts in court'. He has devised an eight-point checklist for journalists to follow that include the following measures:

- Always bear in mind the secondary function of notes: in the event of proceedings they display your conduct
- Courts are a practical, not philosophical exercise in proving the truth—and your notes must prove the truth of what you have seen, done, heard
- Contemporaneity—take notes at, or close to, the time
- Reliability—make the systematic process of note-keeping a new habit
- Do not lie—if the court is good at one thing, it is exposing lies
- Think clarity, intelligibility, accuracy
- Always distinguish fact from your own opinion
- Practice the two-minute rule after every interview [author note - apply the checklist to your notes within two minutes of finishing them so you can double check them for all relevant details before you forget].

Kerr 2004, p. 6

Exercise

CD TRACK 15 is an example of a court reporting story broadcast on Macquarie National News featuring the newsreader introduction followed by the reporter's voice report. (Source: 2GB Sydney, 20 January 2005).

1 Why is the reporter able to state facts in the way he does without defamation being an issue?
2 What are the two reasons he is not at risk of being in contempt of court?
3 Would the announcement of an appeal against the conviction have made a difference in what he could have reported? Why?

Further reading

Armstrong, M., Lindsay, D. & Watterson, R. 1995, *Media Law in Australia*, 3rd edn, Oxford University Press, Melbourne.

Australian Broadcasting Corporation 1997, *ABC All Media-Law Handbook*, http://www.abc.net.au/corp/pubs/legal/lawgook/links.htm.

Kafcaloudes, P. 1991, *ABC All-Media Court Reporting Handbook*, ABC, Sydney.

Pearson, M. 2004, *The Journalist's Guide to Media Law: Dealing with Legal and Ethical Issues*, Allen & Unwin, Sydney.

Broadcast Journalists and Ethics

17

We give people a fair go, we don't exploit people, we chase wrongdoers in the old fashioned sense of the word, I don't think we have often done anybody a disservice in an ethical sense, and I think that comes from basically years of experience.

You are just hoping it is serving a greater purpose, that if you are upsetting somebody, that if it is causing them hurt to their family or whatever, sometimes these things have to be said.

> Clark Forbes, Program Director, 3AW Melbourne

The biggest challenge is dealing with ethical difficulties: deciding whether to do a death knock, for example. There are ways of getting around the need to do this—and the audience doesn't appreciate you exploiting someone's grief. My exploitation threshold is particularly low!

> Selby-Lynn Bradford, radio talkback producer, 2GB Sydney

I think the media have a real problem with ethics. I think a lot of the media do treat people badly and I think it is really important to think how would I feel if I was in this person's situation, being treated like this, and does this person deserve to be treated in that way?

> Steve Cannane, radio presenter, ABC Triple J

The ones who would say that they're entertainers have probably never been journalists. I think that what I have brought to radio is the fact that I am aware that journalists must have integrity. At the same time it doesn't say that you can't be entertaining, and I like to think that I am never boring. That's probably got me into a bit of trouble over the years, but I don't set out just to entertain.

> Howard Sattler, radio presenter, 6PR

On 12 July 1999, Richard Ackland, then the host of ABC Television's *Media Watch* program, detonated what became known as the 'cash-for-comment' bombshell.

The program had unearthed evidence that some commercial radio talkback hosts, whose high public profile made them respected and feared as powerful opinion-makers, were secretly on the payrolls of some of Australia's biggest business corporations. The talkback hosts were, in effect, allowing their opinions to be bought and controlled by commercial interests without their listeners' (or even their stations') knowledge.

Australian commercial talkback radio has followed in the footsteps of its American counterpart in building formats around forceful opinionated presenters. These figures are the modern-day equivalent of the soapbox preachers. With radio replacing the town square, these orators of the airwaves fulfil a similar role of speaking out on behalf of the silent majority.

Having built themselves up as the voice of the battlers, they have had considerable licence on air, taking liberties with the rich and the influential that their listeners could never dream of taking. Sometimes they have gone too far in their attempts to have a ratings-boosting impact, pushing racist or anti-crime buttons that can cause real damage within society. Whatever the issue, the audience has always assumed, and has been led to assume, that the presenters' agendas were defined by the public interest rather than by private influence. The so-called 'cash-for-comment' affair showed this to be a lie. The presenters were allowing themselves to be bought by commercial entities, and what they were delivering as opinion on air was as likely as not to be a de facto paid sponsorship announcement rather than a genuinely held view.

During the subsequent inquiry conducted by the Australian Broadcasting Authority (ABA), the governing body then overseeing the operations of the commercial radio sector, the issue of ethics was raised. Didn't this sort of conduct transgress the journalists' Code of Ethics, according to which journalists should not have a vested interest in a story, nor be paid by any interest for doing a story? The question was evaded on the basis that talkback hosts were 'entertainers' rather than 'journalists', but the inquiry left no doubt that, even if the journalists' Code of Ethics didn't apply, the industry's own Code of Practice and the terms of the station licence agreements laid down by the ABA established similar points of principle. Ads must not masquerade as factual content, but must be clearly labelled for what they are—messages paid for by clients. There was no hiding place.

This relatively recent public debate, which caused such a furore nationwide, shows that the issue of ethics in broadcasting is not peripheral, but goes to the very heart of the broadcaster's role. Broadcasters have access to the airwaves as part of a bargain with the public. In exchange for their use of a precious public asset, and for their delegated role as the public's eyes and ears on the world, they are expected to maintain certain standards. Even commercial media are subject to rules and regulations aimed at preventing breaches of the public's trust.

Do ethics matter?

Ethics matter in all areas of life, even if people sometimes appear to ignore them. Society acknowledges that there have to be some basic ground rules that govern our behaviour to each other if we are to maintain a civil society. Whether in the form of religious commandments or non-religious ethical codes, they provide us with a moral framework within which to operate. It is to this that we refer as we seek to resolve the dilemmas that we confront in our daily lives. Part of the process of growing up involves determining for ourselves what our moral standards are so that we can rely on them in any emergency.

Journalists have a double burden to bear. They are expected to be trustworthy both professionally and personally—professionally, because the power of having access to the media brings with it the duty of handling information fairly and honestly; personally, because the power of having access to people brings with it the duty to treat them fairly and honestly.

This is as true in our 'cash-for-comment' era as it ever was. As commercial interests increasingly drive the media, ethics become even more crucial to the work of a journalist. Journalistic reputations are hard to build, and easy to destroy. Your work depends on fostering a good relationship with the public on whom you rely as sources for story ideas, information, and talent. You will achieve far more by being known as someone who will deal responsibly with issues presented to you, whose word can be trusted, who is fair and unbiased, and whose judgment is untainted by self-interest than you would from compromising your ethical standards. One false step and your good reputation could be shattered. The bond of trust, once broken, can never be completely restored. If journalists rate just above used car salesmen with the public (Conley 2002, p. 13) they have only their own unethical conduct to blame.

Having said that, there are many temptations. A news story has more impact when recounted in terms of black and white rather than grey. It is so easy to over-simplify, to exaggerate, to omit inconvenient facts. The key question must always be: Am I being fair? This is the cornerstone of ethical journalism and underpins the codes governing journalistic conduct across all media.

Broadcasting codes of ethics

In Australia, ethics is an area where the media industry is expected to regulate itself. This more hands-off approach by government was formalised in the *Broadcasting Services Act* of 1992. Having said that, each sector is obliged to have mechanisms in place to handle complaints from the public when the codes appear to have been transgressed. The journalists' union, the Media Entertainment and Arts Alliance (MEAA), has its own judiciary committees that handle complaints against individual journalists. The Australian Press Council deals with complaints relating to the print media. The Australian Communications and Broadcasting Authority has replaced the ABA as the body which handles complaints in relation to the broadcast media. The Australian Broadcasting Corporation has its own internal Independent Complaints Review Panel that handles complaints in the first instance, passing them on to the ACMA as a last resort.

What are the different ethical codes and what do they mean for broadcasting practice?

The MEAA Code of Ethics

This is the code of conduct that the journalism profession set up for itself. It is administered by the Australian Journalists Association (AJA), now a section of the MEAA.

From its first drafting in 1944 through to the modern version of today, the Journalists' Code of Ethics has sought to capture what ethical journalism means in practical terms.

Given that journalists are often working in situations where they have to make snap decisions—in the face of a tight deadline or in a live-to-air broadcast—the Code of Ethics may often be the only guidance they have in working out what is the right thing to do.

The original code was revised in 1984, and in 1993 the AJA embarked on a second review that resulted in the code as it stands today. The ten standards of the earlier code were increased to twelve and were amended in an attempt to make them better attuned to the pragmatic realities of journalism today. Though this raised concerns among some that this made the code weaker, the importance of ethical standards as the bedrock of good journalism was stressed both in the preamble:

> [Journalists] scrutinise power, but also exercise it, and should be responsible and accountable.

and in a final guidance clause:

> Only substantial advancement of the public interest or risk of substantial harm to people allows any standard to be overridden.

The MEAA Code is reproduced in full on pp. 293–4 , and its twelve standards evolve out of the following four basic principles articulated in its preamble: honesty, fairness, independence, and respect for the rights of others.

Honesty

This covers how you deal with facts and how you present yourself.

How you deal with facts

Facts should be reported as they are, without distortion, artificial embellishment, or the influence of your own personal biases. We live in the age of the 'beat up'—where news is confused with sensation, and where the tendency is to present issues and events in black-and-white terms, with little space for analysis of the shades of grey. Further, each of us is influenced by our personal world picture that inevitably colours our interpretation. Add to this the editorial pressures of the journalism business and it is easy to appreciate the temptation to twist and to distort.

Facts should be free of language that might incite prejudice on the basis of race, gender, religion, or disability. Language is powerful, and its capacity to wound cannot be underestimated. Journalists, as society's storytellers, are charged with interpreting reality for the rest of us, and you should do so in as non-judgmental a way as possible. (The issue of loaded language is discussed in greater detail on pp. 301–4.)

Errors should be corrected efficiently and swiftly. People often complain that the media are all too ready to criticise the specks in the eyes of others while ignoring the motes in their own. It is to be expected that, like all journalists, you will get it wrong on occasion, but you should also rectify the damage as soon as you can.

How you present yourself

As a reporter you should avoid subterfuge. Unless in exceptional circumstances dictated by the public interest you should not attempt to entrap, nor to conceal your true identity.

Fairness

Fairness is the cornerstone of good journalism. It relates to presenting the full picture, giving each side a fair go, and avoiding misrepresentation through careless or deliberate omission. The journalist's power to drag people into the public arena has to be exercised responsibly. You can do no better than to ask yourself before you publish anything, 'Am I being fair?'

Independence

This relates to your own integrity. Journalists should operate freely and independently of any influence that might affect objectivity. This covers everything from personal convictions to monetary payments that might compromise your capacity to report impartially.

Respect for the rights of others

This covers your dealings with the public. Journalists must respect people's right to privacy, especially at times of trauma, and must moderate their approach accordingly. If you are given confidential information, you must respect that confidence—bearing in mind that any assurances you give have no legal authority. The law affords no protection to journalistic sources (see pp. 283–6 on contempt of court).

MEAA Code of Ethics

Respect for truth and the public's right to information are fundamental principles of journalism. Journalists describe society to itself. They convey information, ideas, and opinions. They search, disclose, record, question, entertain, comment, and remember. They inform citizens and animate democracy. They give a practical form to freedom of expression. They scrutinise power, but also exercise it, and should be responsible and accountable.

Journalists commit themselves to:
- Honesty;
- Fairness;
- Independence; and
- Respect for the rights of others.

Journalists will educate themselves about ethics and apply the following standards:

1 Report and interpret honestly, striving for accuracy, fairness, and disclosure of all essential facts. Do not suppress relevant available facts, or give distorting emphasis. Do your utmost to give a fair opportunity for reply.

2 Do not place unnecessary emphasis on personal characteristics including race, ethnicity, nationality, gender, age, sexual orientation, family relationships, religious belief or physical or intellectual disability.

3 Aim to attribute information to its source. Where a source seeks anonymity, do not agree without first considering the source's motives and any alternative attributable source. Where confidences are accepted, respect them in all circumstances.

4 Do not allow personal interest, or any belief, commitment, payment, gift or benefit to undermine your accuracy, fairness or independence.

5 Disclose conflicts of interest that affect, or could be seen to affect, the accuracy, fairness or independence of your journalism. Do not improperly use a journalistic position for personal gain.

6 Do not allow advertising or other commercial considerations to undermine accuracy, fairness or independence.

7 Do your utmost to ensure disclosure of any direct or indirect payment made for interviews, pictures, information or stories.

8 Use fair, responsible and honest means to obtain material. Identify yourself and your employer before obtaining any interview for publication or broadcast. Never exploit a person's vulnerability or ignorance of media practice.

9 Present pictures and sound which are true and accurate. Any manipulation likely to mislead should be disclosed.

10 Do not plagiarise.

11 Respect private grief and personal privacy. Journalists have the right to resist compulsion to intrude.

12 Do your utmost to achieve fair correction of errors.

Guidance Clause

Basic values often need interpretation, and sometimes come into conflict. Ethical journalism requires conscientious decision-making in context. Only substantial advancement of the public interest or risk of substantial harm to people allows any standard to be overridden.

Source: MEAA <http://www.alliance.org.au/>

The CBAA Codes of Practice

The Community Broadcasting Association of Australia is the body that oversees the community broadcasting sector. As discussed in chapter 1, this is the sector operating in a not-for-profit environment on the basis of largely volunteer staff working with the support of local sponsors to provide a service intimately in tune with the local community.

Here the Codes of Practice for radio and television not only embody the core values of honesty, fairness, independence, and respect for the rights of others, they also articulate the particular cultural values and operational parameters that define community broadcasting.

As with all broadcasting, the public interest is paramount, but in this sector more than any other the focus is on diversity and active community involvement. These values have been reinforced in the revised Code for radio (2002) and the newer Community Television code, registered with the ABA in 2004. Community broadcasters aim to offer an alternative to mainstream media by focusing on issues that the big players with their mass audiences may ignore. The codes therefore enshrine not just principles of journalistic practice similar to the MEAA Code, but also principles relating to responsible coverage (e.g. avoiding causing undue alarm to listeners) and inclusiveness (e.g. giving a voice to minority groups). There are separate codes of practice for television and radio and the sections relating to journalism practice are reproduced in Regulations and Codes of Practice at the back of this book.

The ABC Code of Practice and editorial policies

The Australian Broadcasting Corporation, in undertaking the activities defined in its Charter (see chapter 1), has its own editorial policies incorporating codes of practice for its different program strands. The ABC Code of Practice was updated in July 2004 to cover online and emerging new media services. It also now includes factual programming as an additional subset beyond news, current affairs, and information programs. While the Code has always stressed the need for impartiality and balance in reporting, this is an area where the ABC has been particularly vulnerable to attack by successive federal governments. The new Code has attempted to address such concerns by significantly strengthening the precepts relating to editorial bias. The General Program Codes, while acknowledging the need for program-makers to have as much artistic freedom as possible, instruct them to act responsibly in relation to violence, language, sex and sexuality, and discrimination to avoid giving gratuitous offence. The individual's right to privacy is to be respected apart from exceptional cases involving matters of public interest.

The code for News, Current Affairs and Information Programs addresses similar ethical issues to the MEAA and the CBAA codes. Journalists must ensure the accuracy, impartiality, and balance of their reports and must deal sensitively with people in times of trauma. The ABC Code makes explicit reference to the reporting of suicides, stating that if they are reported at all, it should be in moderate terms avoiding reference to the method used.

As far as protection of sources is concerned, the code states that: 'Editorial staff will not be obliged to disclose confidential sources which they are entitled to protect at all times'. This is important, as it indicates that, while protection of sources cannot be guaranteed in law, in this case the employer is prepared to acknowledge this right and by assumption to defend its journalists in court if required. This in no way reduces the onus on the journalist to act defensively—it is far preferable to have something on the record than to find yourself the dupe of an unscrupulous source.

The relevant sections of the ABC Code of Practice are reproduced in Regulations and Codes of Practice at the back of this book.

ABC Editorial Policies (revised July 2002)

This booklet sets out both the ethical values and the editorial principles program-makers are expected to follow in the ABC. The Corporation commits itself to the core values of the AJA Code (honesty, fairness, independence, and respect). The Charter of Editorial Practice for news and current affairs clearly sets out the rules for balanced and impartial reporting. An updated legal section (July 2004) underscores the importance of staff having a good knowledge of the legal parameters within which all media operate. Extracts from the booklet are reproduced in the Regulations and Codes of Practice at the back of this book.

The SBS Code of Practice

Like the ABC's Code, the SBS Code of Practice, revised in 2002 and now covering all media, reflects the brief laid down in its Charter. In delivering programming in accordance with its role as a multilingual, multicultural national broadcaster, it is acknowledged that programming may on occasion be controversial and provocative, even distasteful or offensive to some, but this is permissible as long as reporting is responsible and balanced.

Given the nature of the SBS, it is no surprise that the code puts at the top of its list the dangers of prejudice, racism, and discrimination (2.1). In relation to Aboriginal and Torres Strait Islander peoples, not only has it devised its own protocols for film and television makers, it further emphasises the need for Indigenous people to be part of the production team wherever possible (2.1.2). SBS's Charter commits the broadcaster to foreign language broadcasting, but whereas previously the section on Language and Diversity stressed that language was 'pivotal in the SBS's pursuit of its Charter and Mission objectives' the more recent version is more pragmatic, with the broadcaster now aiming 'to reflect this diversity in its programming, while at the same time remaining consistent with its other Charter responsibilities' (2.2.1). Nevertheless, it confirms that it 'embraces its role as an established medium through which Australia's cultural communities retain and develop their individual languages' and continues to underscore the importance of groups and individuals being able to identify themselves in their own terms rather than having identities imposed on them (2.3).

As for news and current affairs, journalists are advised to abide by the principles of the AJA/MEAA Code, though the SBS will issue its own supplementary guidelines to assist journalists 'in handling controversial issues which could create tensions within the community' (2.4.1). As in the other codes, there are sections on sexual content, violence, suicide, and privacy issues. Relevant sections of the SBS Code are included in Regulations and Codes of Practice at the back of this book.

The codes of practice for commercial radio

The *Broadcasting Services Act* loosened the hand of government on the broadcasting industry, but the quid pro quo was that the industry put its own house in order in relation to
broadcasting standards. As a result, both television and radio devised their own codes of
practice, which came into effect in 1993.

The Federation of Australian Radio Broadcasters, the body representing commercial
radio stations (now known as Commercial Radio Australia), agreed on six codes covering
general programs, news and current affairs programs, advertising, music, complaints handling, and talkback programs. The codes relating to talk content covered similar territory
to the other codes of practice discussed so far: accuracy, fairness, and balance in reporting;
avoidance of sensationalism; avoidance of vilification based on race, gender, religion, or
disability. Additional guidelines, added as revisions in 1993, gave further guidance to
broadcasters on the portrayal of Indigenous Australians and women.

The 'cash-for-comment' case (discussed above) drew public attention to the fact that
there was considerable laxity in the way the codes were being administered. In anticipation
of the outcome of the subsequent 1999 ABA inquiry into commercial radio, the industry
revisited the codes and made adjustments and amendments to ensure that both the spirit and
the letter of the codes would be more diligently observed in future. The 1999 amendments
included measures to ensure compliance, as well as provision for a review every three years.
There was also an additional code relating to the reporting of suicide.

This initiative didn't prevent the ABA from criticising the industry for its past transgressions. It included in its final report in the Commercial Radio Inquiry recommenda-
tions advocating not only a strengthening of the codes, but legislative change that would
give the ABA itself more muscle to enforce industry compliance. In the meantime, in 2001
the ABA brought in three additional 'standards' to tide the industry over until 2003, by
which time CRA was expected to have registered its own amendments ensuring adequate
safeguards against similar transgressions in future. In contrast to the voluntary nature of the
codes, compliance with the standards was obligatory and a condition of the broadcast
licence. These standards toughened up the requirement:

- for full on-air disclosure of commercial agreements that might influence program
  content
- for a clear distinction between program content and paid advertisement
- for measures to ensure compliance by all concerned with these regulations.

In 2003, the ABA extended the standards indefinitely. Further, commercial stations are
now required to inform the Australian Communications and Media Authority (which
superseded the ABA in July 2005) of any commercial agreement entered into by their presenters or other program personnel. Presenters now have to disclose to the licensees any
commercial agreements they enter into, and a register of all such commercial arrangements
must be maintained on the station web site so the public has full access to the information.

ABA Broadcasting Services Standards 2000

Broadcasting Services (Commercial Radio Compliance Program) Standard 2000

This standard requires commercial radio broadcasting licensees to formulate, implement, and maintain a compliance program to ensure compliance with the requirements of the Act, standards and the codes.

Source: ABA, http://www.aba.gov.au/radio/content/compliance.rtf

Broadcasting Services (Commercial Radio Advertising) Standard 2000

This standard requires licensees to ensure that advertisements are distinguishable from other programs.

Source: ABA, http://www.aba.gov.au/radio/content/standards/advertising.rtf

Broadcasting Services (Commercial Radio Current Affairs Disclosure) Standard 2000

This standard requires:

(a) on-air disclosure during current affairs programs of commercial agreements between sponsors and presenters that have the potential to affect the content of those programs; and

(b) on-air disclosure during current affairs programs of the payment of production costs by advertisers and sponsors; and

(c) licensees to keep a register of commercial agreements between sponsors and presenters of current affairs programs and make it available to the ABA and the public; and

(d) licensees to ensure that a condition of employment of presenters of current affairs programs is that they comply with relevant obligations imposed by the Act, the codes and this standard.

Source: ABA, http://www.aba.gov.au/radio/content/standards/disclosure_2.rtf

In September 2004, as part of the scheduled 3-yearly review of the codes, the industry published its revised Code of Practice. It is substantially the same as the previous code, though there are additional restrictions on the invasion of privacy, and compliance with the codes is now something licensees 'must' do, rather than simply 'endeavour' to do. Relevant sections of the code are reproduced in Regulations and Codes of Practice at the back of the book.

The codes of practice for commercial television

At the same time as the Federation of Australian Radio Broadcasters (FARB) was developing its code of practice for the commercial radio industry, the Federation of Australian

Commercial Television Stations (FACTS) was doing the same exercise for commercial television. Though the codes were very similar, the television code was framed to take into account the particular power of televisual images and the way these are transmitted into the family home. It covered five key areas: program classification to protect children from exposure to unsuitable material; amount of advertising time allowed in the schedules; classification and treatment of other material (e.g. community announcements); complaints handling procedures; and, for the news and current affairs area, standards of accuracy, fairness, and protection of privacy. A general code (1.8) covered proscribed material, relating to program matter that might mislead or alarm viewers or cause offence on the grounds of race, gender, religion, disability, or sexual preference. In addition, it warned against illicit use of television technology to induce hypnotic states or to transmit subliminal messages. The codes for news and current affairs (4.3) reinforced these general principles with strictures similar to the other codes already discussed covering fairness, accuracy, and balance in reporting; avoidance of sensationalism; respect for privacy and private grief; and the reporting of suicide. There were also advisory notes covering the portrayal of women, Aboriginal and Torres Strait Islander people, and people with disabilities. The code was revised by FACTS, now renamed Free TV Australia, in 2004 and the amended version incorporates a new advisory note relating to advertisements directed at children (and including the new Australian Association of National Advertisers Code of Advertising to Children). The advisory note relating to privacy has been strengthened and extended to deal specifically with the privacy interests of children. In addition to the existing Television Classification Guidelines, the code has also incorporated the classification guidelines of the Office of Film and Literature Classification into the section dealing with film content. Perhaps taking a leaf out of commercial radio's book, the revised code now requires the disclosure of any commercial arrangements involving product endorsement embedded in factual programming. Relevant extracts from the television code are included in Regulations and Codes of Practice at the back of this book.

Ethics online

Just as the Internet is forcing us to reconfigure the laws relating to broadcasting (see chapter 16) so is it throwing up new ethical challenges. In this environment 'broadcasting' is a global activity and the rules and regulations are still in the process of being established. As lawmakers struggle with the jurisdictional implications of operating beyond national boundaries, so ethicists are challenged by having to set standards in an inherently anarchic environment. Australia has Internet Content Codes, but they are directed more at the Internet Content Hosts and Internet Service Providers than at content developers (http://www.aba.gov.au/internet/codes/documents/IIA_Code.pdf). The codes focus on: protecting children from exposure to unsuitable material; ensuring operations comply with Australian law; and establishing procedures for removing from sites content deemed by the ABA to be 'Prohibited Content' or 'Potential Prohibited Content'. From the journalist's perspective, the digital environment is no different from any other news environment when it comes to ethical standards—it is just that it offers new and tempting ways of transgressing them. The main concerns are in the areas of content and editorial control.

Content

Sources: Content can come from anyone and anywhere on the Web. In fact the new breed of webloggers (bloggers) is bringing people power into the news agenda. Ordinary members of the public with access to information and even established journalists wanting to operate outside the confines of their news organisations are able to have their say online with no editorial oversight. How far can journalists trust them if they wish to use them as sources? The tried and tested rule of checking and double-checking your facts helps you sidestep any pitfalls here.

Treatment: Digital technology allows information to be altered, reassembled, and even forged in undetectable ways. This goes far beyond the sort of processing that was possible in the analog domain. However, the same rules apply: editing is permissible as long as it doesn't distort the original meaning.

Editorial control

Advertising: With the convention of free access on the Web there has been a reluctance from audiences to subscribe to media sites, so industry has had to rely on advertising to make what money it can from Web operations. This has resulted in a further blurring of the already fuzzy lines between news and advertising content. How vulnerable are journalists to pressures to change their sites or their stories to please an advertiser? If you include a link to a commercial site in your story as a way of providing relevant additional information, is it a de facto sponsorship? The ethical principle of editorial independence should apply here, but this is an area where journalists are most likely to confront the realities of business pressures.

Ownership of content: Digital technology has made it possible for journalists to service a variety of media outlets. A single story can be reversioned for radio, television, and online. This means that the media organisation is getting three times the value, but that isn't being reflected in the journalist's wage. This lies more in the realm of business ethics than journalism ethics, but it is an ethical conundrum nonetheless and a headache for organisations such as the MEAA who represent the interests of journalists within each industry.

Avoiding discrimination—protocols for journalists

It is not by accident that all the journalistic codes tackle the issue of discriminatory reporting. When dealing with issues of race, gender, religion, sexual preference, and disability, you have the power through your language and approach to tap into deep emotions, to inflame, to offend, and to encourage prejudice. Discriminatory behaviour contravenes some of journalism's basic principles: you cannot be fair and unbiased if you are favouring one group over another; you can't reflect the truth if your reporting conveys implied value judgments. It is important for journalists to understand the subtleties of discriminatory language and behaviour if they are to avoid these sorts of pitfalls in their practice.

Story selection

Discriminatory reporting begins with the selection of the story. You need to ask yourself the following questions:

Where are you looking for your stories?

Australia is a community renowned the world over for its largely harmonious diversity. If you stick to the world of the mainstream, you run the risk of presenting a distorted view of that society as we actually experience it in our daily lives. Just as multicultural Australia is under-represented in terms of the faces on our television screens and the voices on our radios, so it is largely ignored as a source for stories. We may seek out representatives of a particular community when other matters such as scandal or violence bring them to our attention, but we don't as a matter of routine incorporate them into our newsrounds. This leads to a skewed news agenda that discriminates against the people it ignores.

What is it that makes it a good story?

Is the person's race, gender, or disability relevant? All too often, stories are covered precisely because race, gender, or disability is the issue. Even when they aren't, these details may be mentioned gratuitously anyway. This simply helps to reinforce negative or positive stereotypes.

Who are you using as talent?

Once again, journalists have a tendency to stick to the mainstream, using a relatively shallow pool of commentators, experts, and government representatives who are accessible, media-friendly, and more often than not of Anglo-Celtic background. Expanding your network further into the communities around you will also extend your list of potential contacts. You will gain as a result a larger, and importantly a more diverse, pool of expertise.

What is your approach?

Journalists in the electronic media have a vast array of devices that can put additional inflexion into their material. A camera angle, the selection of pictures, the tone of voice, the way material is edited can, wittingly or unwittingly, create a subtext to your story that can deliver coded messages to the audience. While there may be no trace of prejudice in the words you use, the tone may convey an entirely different message.

Use of language

Just as discrimination can be evident in story selection and tone, so can it be conveyed in the language we use. What is discriminatory language? It is language that excludes or ignores certain groups, or gives unequal treatment to certain groups. It is language that offends or demeans. It is language that is culturally insensitive. Let's look at some common errors:

Gender—things to watch out for

- Irrelevant references to gender. This occurs when gender is highlighted in such a way as to suggest that something goes against an implied norm. Example: woman lawyer.
- Using general terms as if male only. This is another way of conveying the assumption of a male norm. Example: academics and their wives.
- Different modes of address. This imbeds a sense of inequality in status between men and women. Example: Mrs Vanstone and John Howard.

Race—things to watch out for

- Irrelevant references to race. These invite a judgment based on race that is gratuitous and has no bearing on the story. Example: The Aboriginal driver took us to the city.
- Different modes of address. This sets up a sense of hierarchy. Example: Mr Smith demanded an apology that Jones refused to give.
- Labels. This relates to terminology that is demeaning to racial groups. Example: Aboriginal. This word may be offensive when used as a noun. The term 'Aboriginal people', or, better still, the specific name of the group involved is preferred.
- Pejorative references. These are words that groups find demeaning and offensive. Example: black/native/half-caste.

Disability—things to watch out for

- Irrelevant references to disability. These invite a judgment based on a person's physical condition that may have no bearing on the story. Example: John X, a paraplegic, came top of his class.
- Labels. These invite us to define people in terms of their medical conditions alone. Example: 'handicapped'; 'disabled'; 'an epileptic'.
- Value judgments. These bring with them the implication that someone is to be pitied because of a particular physical condition. Example: 'afflicted with'; 'confined to'.
- Stereotypes. This is where stories are crafted in a way that reinforces trite stereotypes. Example: 'the helpless victim'; 'the awesome superachiever'.

You can avoid these pitfalls just by giving some thought to the language that you use. Some examples are given in the following table.

Discriminatory terms and substitutes

Discriminatory term	Substitute
homosexuals	lesbians and gays
mankind	humanity/people
manhood	adulthood
half-caste	part Aboriginal
cleaning lady	cleaner
man the desk	staff the desk

spastic	has cerebral palsy
a man of Lebanese appearance	an olive-skinned man
confined to a wheelchair	uses a wheelchair

Guidelines for journalists have been prepared by various minority, ethnic, and Aboriginal groups and are reflected in all the ethical codes for broadcasters discussed above. The commercial radio guidelines are particularly explicit about reporting on Indigenous and gender issues, and are reproduced in full in Regulations and Codes of Practice at the back of the book. The guidelines relating specifically to preferred terminology in Indigenous reporting appear below.

Indigenous reporting guidelines—terminology

It is preferable to refer to Indigenous Australians or Aboriginal people rather than an Aborigine. It is also acceptable to refer to indigenous Australians by their regional identification: Koori (NSW, Vic, Tas), Murri (Qld), Nungar (SA), Nyungar (WA—southern), Yamayti (WA—northern), Yolngu (Arnhem Land). NOTE: The above regions are not necessarily defined by state borders. Refer to local Aboriginal Media Unit to determine the correct terminology for your region. If there is any doubt, check with a second source, otherwise you could cause offence. Other common terminology:

Aboriginal: The word 'Aboriginal' is an adjective used to describe something associated with Aborigines. See also *Aborigine*.

Aboriginality: The qualities inherent in being an Aborigine relating to Aboriginal heritage and culture.

Aborigine: An indigenous person of Australia. Descendant of the first inhabitants of Australia with a living history spanning more than 40,000 years. The word 'Aborigine' is a noun that also refers to any indigenous person, but is not a popular term (see earlier reference).

Racism: Offensive or aggressive behaviour towards members of another race based on the belief that ones [sic] own race is superior and has the right to rule or dominate others.

Sacred site: A tract of land that has strong religious meaning to all or some Aboriginal people.

Site of significance: A tract of land that has strong meaning to all or some Aboriginal people but may not have strong religious meaning.

Torres Strait Islander: A person of Torres Strait Island descent living in or coming from the group of islands between the northern Australian and New Guinea coasts.

Visitors [sic] permit: A permit to enter designated Aboriginal areas. Obtained from Aboriginal Community Councils or Land Councils.

Unacceptable terminology
The following terms are offensive to Aboriginal people and should be avoided. The alternatives are listed.

Abo, Abbo: Aboriginal person, indigenous Australian, Koori (NSW), Murri (Qld), etc

Boong/Black: See *Abo*.

Gin: Aboriginal woman, Aboriginal person, Koori, etc

Half-caste, quarter-caste: Part Aboriginal.

Full-blood: A concept used by non-Aborigines to divide Aborigines. The definition of Aborigine relates to self-identification and acceptance by the Aboriginal community. Degrees of descent are irrelevant and act against the solidarity of Aboriginal people.

Lubra: See *Gin*.

Native: See *Aborigine*.

Source: ACMA

Exercise

CD TRACK 16 features ABC radio journalist Alison Caldwell describing how she covered the breaking story of the Childers backpackers hostel fire in June 2000 for the *AM* program. This segment includes extracts from her interviews with two survivors on a poor quality mobile phone link the morning after the tragedy, along with her commentary on how she approached interviewing people who had just gone through a highly traumatic experience.

What ethical issues does she take into account in deciding how to approach
- her talent?
- the story?
- her reporting style?

Further reading

Chadwick, P. 1994, 'Creating Codes: Journalism Self-regulation', in J. Schultz (ed.), *Not Just Another Business. Journalists, Citizens and the Media*, Pluto Press, Sydney, pp. 167–87.

Conley, D. 2002, 'Ethical Journalism: Is It an Oxymoron?', in *The Daily Miracle*, 2nd edn, Oxford University Press, South Melbourne, pp. 251–79.

Hartley, J. 2003, 'Their Own Media in Their Own Language', in Lumby, C. & Probyn, E., *Remote Control. New Media, New Ethics*, Cambridge University Press, Cambridge, pp. 42–66.

Hurst, J. & White, S.A. 1994, *Ethics and the Australian News Media*, Macmillan, Melbourne.

Mickler, S. 1997, 'The Robespierre of the Air: Talkback Radio, Globalisation and Indigenous Issues', *Continuum*, vol. 11, no. 3, pp. 1–14.

Pavlik, J.V. 2001, 'Journalism Ethics and New Media', in *Journalism and New Media*, Columbia University Press, New York, pp. 82–100.

Sanders, K. 2003, *Ethics & Journalism*, Sage, London.

Stockwell, S. & Scott, P. 2000, *All-Media Guide to Fair and Cross-Cultural Reporting*, Australian Key Centre for Culture and Media Policy, Nathan.

Tanner, S., Phillips, G., Smyth, C. & Tapsall, S. 2005, *Journalism Ethics At Work*, Pearson Longman, Sydney.

Turner, G. 2003, 'Ethics, Entertainment and the Tabloid: The Case of Talkback Radio in Australia' in Lumby, C. & Probyn, E., *Remote Control. New Media, New Ethics,* Cambridge University Press, Cambridge, pp. 87–99.

Regulations and Codes of Practice

This section contains the relevant sections of the various industry codes of practice for broadcast media (radio, television, and online services) covering both general programming and news and current affairs.

Community sector

Community Broadcasting Codes of Practice (Radio, revised 2002)—extracts

Guiding Principles

There are a number of general principles that unite all community broadcasters across Australia. In pursuing these principles stations endeavour to:

- Promote harmony and diversity in contributing to a cohesive, inclusive and culturally diverse Australian community;
- Pursue the principles of democracy, access and equity, especially to people and issues under-represented in other media;
- Enhance the diversity of programming choices available to the public and present programs which expand the variety of viewpoints broadcast in Australia;
- Demonstrate independence in their programming as well as in their editorial and management decisions;
- Support and develop local and Australian arts, music and culture in the station's programming, to reflect a sense of Australian identity, character and cultural diversity;
- Widen the community's involvement in broadcasting.

    ...

Code No. 1: Responsibilities of Broadcasting to the Community: Principles of Democracy, Diversity and Independence

The purpose of this code is to ensure that the 'Guiding Principles' are reflected in the day to day operations and programming of community broadcasters.

Community broadcasting stations will:

{ Political, regulatory and social }

1.1 Have policies and procedures in place, relating to the licensee's community of interest, which ensure access and equity and encourage participation by those not adequately served by other media.

1.2 Be controlled and operated by an autonomous body which is representative of the licensee's community of interest.

1.3 Have organisational mechanisms to provide for active participation by the licensee's community in its management, development and operations.

1.4 Incorporate policies that apply to all station activities, which oppose and attempt to break down prejudice on the basis of ethnicity, race, chosen language, gender, sexual preference, religion, age, physical or mental ability, occupation, cultural belief or political affiliation.

Code No. 2: Guidelines for all Programming

The purpose of this code is to encourage programming that reflects the principles of community broadcasting; to break down prejudice and discrimination; and to prevent the broadcast of material, which is contrary to community standards.

2.1 Community broadcasting licensees shall not broadcast material which may:
    (a) incite, encourage or present for their own sake violence or brutality;
    (b) simulate news or events in such a way as to mislead or alarm listeners; or
    (c) present as desirable the misuse of drugs including alcohol, narcotics and tobacco.

2.2 Community broadcasting licensees will avoid censorship wherever possible, however, consideration shall be given to the audience; the context; the degree of explicitness; the propensity to alarm, distress or shock; and the social importance of the event.

2.3 Community broadcasting licensees shall not broadcast material which may stereotype, incite, vilify, or perpetuate hatred against, or attempt to demean any person or group on the basis of ethnicity, nationality, race, chosen language, gender, sexual preference, religion, age, physical or mental ability, occupation, cultural belief or political affiliation. The requirement is not intended to prevent the broadcast of material which is factual, or the expression of genuinely held opinion in a news or current affairs program, or in the legitimate context of a humorous, satirical or dramatic work.

2.4 Community broadcasting licensees will establish programming practices which protect children from harmful program material.

2.5 Community broadcasting licensees in observance of privacy laws will:
    (a) respect each person's legitimate right to protection from unjustified use of material, which is obtained without an individual's consent, or other unwarranted and intrusive invasions of privacy;
    (b) not broadcast the words of an identifiable person unless:
        (i) that person has been informed in advance that the words may be transmitted; or

(ii)   in the case of words which have been recorded without the knowledge of the person, the person has subsequently, but prior to the transmission, indicated consent to the transmission of the words; or

(iii)   the manner of the recording has made it manifestly clear that the material may be broadcast.

News and Current Affairs Programming

This code is intended to promote accuracy and fairness in news and current affairs programs.

2.6   News and current affairs programs (including news flashes) programs [sic] should:

(a)   provide access to views under-represented by the mainstream media;

(b)   present factual material accurately and ensure that reasonable efforts are made to correct substantial errors of fact at the earliest possible opportunity;

(c)   clearly distinguish factual material from commentary and analysis;

(d)   not present news in such a way as to create public panic or unnecessary distress to listeners;

(e)   not misrepresent a viewpoint by giving misleading emphasis, editing out of context or withholding relevant available facts.

Indigenous programming and coverage of Indigenous Issues

This code acknowledges Indigenous peoples' special place as the first Australians, and offers a way to demonstrate respect for Indigenous cultures and customs, and to avoid offence with inappropriate words, phrases and actions. In the following section, 'Indigenous Australians' refers to the Aboriginal peoples and Torres Strait Islanders of Australia.

2.7   When reporting on Indigenous people and issues, stations will take care to verify and observe the best way to respect Indigenous cultures and customs by:

(a)   Considering regional differences in the cultural practices and customs of Indigenous Australians.

(b)   Seeking appropriate advice on how to best respect Indigenous bereavement customs on the reporting of people recently deceased.

(c)   Using the appropriate words and phrases for referring to an Indigenous Australian and his/her regional group.

2.8   Broadcasters will seek to involve and take advice from Indigenous Australians, and where possible Indigenous media organisations and/or Indigenous broadcasters, in the production of programs focusing on Indigenous people and issues.

2.9   Broadcasters will avoid prejudicial references to, or undue emphasis on a person who is Aboriginal or Torres Strait Islander.

Practice Notes: The CBAA will support stations in this area of work by providing contact details and referring enquires on to the most relevant indigenous media contacts in Australia.

Source: CBAA

Community Television Code of Practice (registered with the ABA, September 2004)

This Code begins with the same Guiding Principles as radio, with the addition of:

- Demonstrate a commitment to participate in the development of the community-broadcasting sector at a state and national level in order to support continuous improvement across all community television service providers.

Code 3—programming

Community television licensees aim to broadcast material that promotes local and Australian culture, representing diversity in a responsible manner, breaking down prejudice and discrimination, and preventing the broadcast of material that is contrary to community standards.

Community Television stations will:

3.1.   Broadcast programming for entertainment, information and education, with priority being given to matters relating to the local community; and/or of artistic and cultural relevance.

3.2.   Promote freedom of speech and avoid censorship wherever possible, however, consideration shall be given to the audience; the context; the degree of explicitness; the propensity to alarm; distress or shock; and the social importance of the event being broadcast.

3.3.   Ensure no material is broadcast which may:
   (a)   incite, encourage or present for their own sake violence or brutality;
   (b)   simulate news or events in such a way as to mislead or alarm viewers;
   (c)   present as desirable the misuse of drugs including alcohol, narcotics and tobacco; or
   (d)   induce a hypnotic state or use subliminal techniques.

3.4.   Ensure material is not broadcast which may stereotype, incite, vilify, or perpetuate hatred against, or attempt to demean any person or group on the basis of ethnicity, nationality, race, chosen language, gender, sexual preference, religion, age, physical or mental ability, occupation, cultural belief or political affiliation.

   Note: This requirement is not intended to prevent the broadcast of material which is factual, or the expression of genuinely held opinions in a news or current affairs program, or in the legitimate context of a humorous, satirical or dramatic work.

3.5.   Observe an individual's privacy by:
   (a)   respecting each person's legitimate right to protection from unjustified use of material—which is obtained without an individual's consent.
   (b)   not broadcasting the words or appearance of an identifiable person unless:
      (i)   that person has been informed in advance that their words or actions may be transmitted; or
      (ii)   in the case of words or actions having been recorded without the

knowledge of the person, the person has subsequently, but prior to the transmission, indicated consent to the transmission of the material; or

(iii)   the manner of the recording has made it manifestly clear that the material may be broadcast.

(c)   not use material relating to a person's personal or private affairs, or which invades an individual's privacy (in particular when dealing with bereaved relatives and survivors or witnesses of traumatic incidents), other than where there are 'identifiable public interest' reasons for the material to be broadcast.

(d)   taking extra care before using material relating to a child's personal or private affairs in the broadcast of a report of a sensitive matter concerning the child. The consent of a parent or guardian should be obtained before naming or visually identifying the child or a member of the child's immediate family, or a report which discloses sensitive information concerning the health or welfare of a child, unless there are exceptional circumstances or an identifiable public interest reason not to do so.

Definition: 'child' means a person under 16 years.

News and current affairs programming

These codes are in addition to the above programming codes and are intended to promote accuracy and fairness in news and current affairs programs. The likely composition of the audience at the time of broadcast, in particular the presence of children and the personal and cultural composition of a community, will be taken into account.

3.6.   News, current affairs, magazine and opinion programs (including news flashes) will:

(a)   present factual material accurately and ensure that reasonable efforts are made to correct substantial errors of fact at the earliest possible opportunity;

(b)   clearly distinguish factual material from commentary and analysis;

(c)   situate issues in context, identifying all interviewees, not misrepresenting a viewpoint by giving misleading emphasis, editing out of context or withholding relevant available facts;

(d)   not broadcast a news or current affairs program containing visual or aural material which, in the licensee's reasonable opinion, is likely to seriously distress or offend a substantial number of viewers, with the exception of material that is of identifiable public interest and then only if adequate prior warning is given to viewers.

Indigenous programming and coverage of Indigenous issues

This code acknowledges Indigenous peoples' special place as the first Australians, and offers a way to demonstrate respect for Indigenous cultures and customs, and to avoid offence with inappropriate words, phrases and actions.

In the following section, 'Indigenous Australians' refers to the Aboriginal peoples and Torres Strait Islanders of Australia.

3.7. When reporting on Indigenous people and issues, stations will take care to verify and observe the best way to respect Indigenous cultures and customs by:

(a) considering regional differences in the cultural practices and customs of Indigenous Australians.

(b) seeking appropriate advice on how to best respect Indigenous bereavement customs on the reporting of people recently deceased.

(c) using the appropriate words and phrases for referring to an Indigenous Australian and his/her regional group.

3.8. Broadcasters will seek to involve and take advice from Indigenous Australians, and where possible Indigenous media organizations and/or Indigenous broadcasters, in the production of programs focusing on Indigenous people and issues.

3.9. Broadcasters will avoid prejudicial references to, or undue emphasis on, a person who is Aboriginal or Torres Strait Islander.

Practice notes: The CBAA will support stations in this area of work by providing contact details and referring enquires on to the most relevant indigenous media contacts in Australia. Also see the www.CBOnline.org.au_Indigenous almanac.

Source: CBAA

Public broadcasting sector

The ABC Code of Practice (updated July 2004)—extracts

1. Introduction

The ABC's place in the media industry is distinctive. The *Australian Broadcasting Corporation Act 1983* gives the Corporation particular responsibilities such as the provision of an independent news service. The ABC Charter (Section 6 of the Act) sets out the functions of the Corporation and can be found on the Internet at www.abc.net.au/corp/charter.htm. The ABC Act guarantees the editorial independence of the Corporation's programs. The ABC holds the power to make programming decisions on behalf of the people of Australia. By law and convention neither the Government nor Parliament seeks to intervene in those decisions.

This Code of Practice applies to ABC Radio and Television, Online and other emerging new media services. Some parts of the Code apply to a particular medium such as Section 8: Television Program Classifications. Where this is the case material is marked accordingly. The word 'program' is used throughout the Code and covers programs broadcast on ABC Radio and Television, content provided on ABC Online, and through emerging new media services.

This Code of Practice summarises the major principles that guide ABC programs. The ABC Editorial Policies 2004 sets out programming policies and guidelines in full. The ABC's Editorial Policies can be found at www.abc.net.au/corp/edpols.htm.

2. General Program Codes

The guiding principle in the application of the following general program codes is context. What is unacceptable in one context may be appropriate and acceptable in another. However, the use of language and images for no other purpose but to offend is not acceptable.

The code is not intended to ban certain types of language or images from bona fide dramatic or literary treatments, nor is it intended to exclude such references from legitimate reportage, debate, or documentaries. Where appropriate, audiences will be given advance notice of the content of the program.

2.1 Violence. Particular care must be taken in the presentation or portrayal of violence. The presentation or portrayal of violence must be justifiable, or else the material should not be presented. In news, current affairs and information programs, violent events should never be sensationalised or presented for their own sake. In drama programs, the aim is not to see how much violence will be tolerated, but how little is necessary to achieve honest ends without undue dramatic compromise.

2.2 Language. Variations of language favoured by different groups of Australians are valid and have their place in programs. On occasions, the language of one group may be distasteful to another. Use of such language is permitted provided it is not used gratuitously and provided the language can be justified in the context of, for example, news or current affairs reporting, fiction, documentary, dramatisation, comedy or song lyrics.

2.3 Sex and sexuality. Provided it is handled with integrity, any of the following treatments of sex and sexuality may be appropriate and necessary to a program if:
- it can be discussed and reported in the context of news, current affairs, information or documentary programs;
- it can be referred to in drama, comedy, lyrics or fictional programs; and
- it can be depicted, implicitly or explicitly.

2.4 Discrimination. To avoid discrimination, programs should not use language or images in a way which is likely to disparage or discriminate against any person or section of the community on account of race, ethnicity, nationality, sex, marital or parental status, age, disability or illness, social or occupational status, sexual preference or any religious, cultural or political belief or activity. The requirement is not intended to prevent the presentation of material which is factual, or the expression of genuinely held opinion in a news, current affairs, information or factual program, or in the legitimate context of a humorous, satirical or dramatic work.

2.5 Privacy. The rights of individuals to privacy should be respected in all programs. However, in order to provide information which relates to a person's performance of public duties or about other matters of public interest, intrusions upon privacy may, in some circumstances, be justified.

3. Specific program codes

3.1   Children's programs. While the real world should not be concealed from children, special care is to be taken to ensure programs children are likely to access, unsupervised, will not cause alarm or distress.

3.2   Religious programs. Religious programs include coverage, explanation, analysis, debate and reports about major religious traditions, indigenous religions and new spiritual movements, as well as secular perspectives on religious issues. The ABC does not promote any particular belief system or form of religious expression.

3.3   Indigenous programs. Program-makers and journalists should respect Aboriginal and Torres Strait Islander cultures. Particular care should be exercised in the coverage of traditional cultural practices such as the naming or depicting of the deceased.

3.4   Avoidance of stereotypes. Programs should not promote or endorse inaccurate, demeaning or discriminatory stereotypes. Programs will take care to acknowledge the diverse range of roles performed by women and men. Irrelevant references to physical characteristics, marital status or parental status will be avoided. In programs using experts, interviewees and other talent to present opinions, program-makers should ensure a gender balance of commentators and experts where possible.

...

4. News, Current Affairs and Information Programs

This section applies to all programs produced by the News and Current Affairs Division of the ABC and other information programs that comprise both news and information relating to current events. Programs with significant factual content, which do not comprise both news and information relating to current events, are dealt with in Section 5 below.

4.1   Every reasonable effort must be made to ensure that the factual content of news, current affairs and information programs is accurate. Demonstrable errors will be corrected in a timely manner and in a form most suited to the circumstances.

4.2   Every reasonable effort must be made to ensure that programs are balanced and impartial. The commitment to balance and impartiality requires that editorial staff present a wide range of perspectives and not unduly favour one over the others. But it does not require them to be unquestioning, nor to give all sides of an issue the same amount of time.

4.3   Balance will be sought through the presentation, as far as possible, of principal relevant viewpoints on matters of importance. This requirement may not always be reached within a single program or news bulletin but will be achieved as soon as possible.

4.4   Editorial staff will not be obliged to disclose confidential sources which they are entitled to protect at all times.

4.5   Re-enactments of events will be clearly identified as such and presented in a way which will not mislead audiences.

4.6   If reported at all, suicides will be reported in moderate terms and will usually avoid details of method.

4.7   Sensitivity will be exercised in presenting images of or interviews with bereaved relatives and survivors or witnesses of traumatic incidents.

4.8   Television Programs: News Updates. Care will be exercised in the selection of sounds and images used in television news updates and consideration given to the likely composition of the audience.

4.9   Television Programs: News Updates During Children's Viewing Times. News updates should generally not appear during programs directed at children. In exceptional circumstances, news updates may appear during children's viewing times, but must not include any violent content.

4.10   Television Programs: News Flashes. Because the timing and content of news flashes on television are unpredictable, particular care should be exercised in the selection of sounds and images and consideration given to the likely composition of the audience. This should be done, notwithstanding the need to get a news flash to air as quickly as possible. Prior to any news flash during children's and other G classified programs, a visual and audio announcement will be broadcast advising viewers that regular programming will be interrupted with a news flash.

5. Factual Programs

This section applies to all programs with significant factual content which do not comprise both news and information relating to current events.

5.1   The ABC is committed to providing programs of relevance and diversity which reflect a wide range of audience interests, beliefs and perspectives. In order to provide such a range of views, the ABC may provide programs which explore, or are presented from, particular points of view.

5.2   Every effort must be made to ensure that the factual content of such programs is accurate and in context and does not misrepresent viewpoints.

5.3   Demonstrable errors of fact will be corrected in a timely manner and in a form most suited to the circumstances.

5.4   Editorial staff will not be obliged to disclose confidential sources which they are entitled to protect at all times.

Source: ABC

ABC Editorial Policies—extracts

2. Editorial principles

Key values

The ABC aims to follow four key values in all its activities:

- Honesty
- Fairness
- Independence
- Respect.

Honesty requires integrity and accuracy. Program makers should be enterprising and questioning in perceiving, pursuing and presenting issues that affect society and the individual. They must make every effort to ensure that the factual content of programs is correct and in context. If errors occur, the ABC will accept responsibility and respond promptly.

Fairness calls for balance and impartiality in news and current affairs and programs that comprise both news and information relating to current events. All program makers should present a wide range of perspectives, and must not unduly favour one over others. In programs of opinion and comment, every effort must be made to ensure the content does not misrepresent viewpoints.

Independence demands that program makers not allow their judgment to be influenced by pressures from political, commercial or other sectional interests, or by their own personal views or activities. There must be no external interference in the presentation or content of programs. For its part, the ABC accepts legal responsibility for what it publishes, and program makers are responsible for the editorial decisions they make.

Respect for the rights of others is extended to subjects, program participants and audiences. It requires careful handling of sensitive issues such as violence, sex, grief, trauma, privacy and children's programming, and understands the need to avoid stereotypes and other prejudicial content.

...

5.1. The Charter of Editorial Practice

A *Charter of Editorial Practice* for news and current affairs sets the following standards. It should be read in conjunction with the policy of 'upward referral' in Section 5.2 below, which applies to all types of programs.

1. The ABC takes no editorial stand in its programming.
2. Editorial staff will avoid any conflict of interest in performance of their duties.
3. Every reasonable effort must be made to ensure that the factual content of news and current affairs programs is accurate and in context. Demonstrable errors will be corrected in a timely manner and in a form most suited to the circumstances.
4. Balance will be sought through the presentation, as far as possible, of principal relevant viewpoints on matters of importance. This requirement may not always be reached within a single program or news bulletin but will be achieved as soon as possible.
5. The commitment to balance and impartiality requires editorial staff to present a wide range of perspectives and not unduly favour one over the others. But it does not require them to be unquestioning, nor to give all sides of an issue the same amount of time. News values and news judgments are a material consideration in reaching decisions, consistent with these standards.
6. In serving the public's right to know, editorial staff will be enterprising in perceiving, pursuing and presenting issues which affect society and the individual.
7. Editorial staff will respect legitimate rights to privacy of people featuring in the news.
8. Authority for editorial directions and decisions will be vested in editorial staff.
9. Editorial staff will ensure that coverage of newsworthy activity within the Australian community is comprehensive and non-discriminatory.

5.2. Editorial responsibility and 'upward referral'

5.2.1 The ABC's program output through its radio, television and online networks and other outlets is vast. It is the responsibility of individual program makers and editorial staff to ensure that the provisions of the ABC Act, the ABC Code of Practice, laws relating to broadcasting and the philosophies and policies of the Corporation are observed. Subject to normal editorial management and controls, program makers are responsible both for making the program and for exercising editorial judgment. If a problem arises, or there is any doubt, the program maker must consult the next higher level of editorial management for guidance. This process, known as 'upward referral', can extend, through the relevant Executive Director, as far as the Managing Director. If the program maker does not refer the issue upward, he or she will be responsible for the editorial decision made.

...

5.2.5 **ABC Online:** All content published by ABC Online or associated Internet services is subject to editorial lines of responsibility. These are:
  - for web sites directly connected to a particular program or network, the editorial line of responsibility is the same as for the other output of the program area or network;
  - for ABC Online national news and current affairs, the editorial line of responsibility is to the Head of National Coverage via New Media News Editor;
  - for ABC Online Local and State news and current affairs, the editorial line of responsibility is to the Head of Local Coverage via New Media News Editor; and
  - for web sites produced by non-program areas of the ABC, editorial lines of responsibility are through the existing management structure.

  Editorial decisions in the above cases may require consultation with New Media. For other web sites directly managed by or connected to New Media, the editorial line of responsibility is through to Head New Media Content and specialist content areas in radio and television will be consulted where appropriate.

  In addition to the direct editorial lines of responsibility, New Media has responsibility for the presentation and production standards on ABC Online.

  ...

5.3   Legal responsibility (updated July 2004)

5.3.1 The media do not have an unrestricted right to say what they like. Laws relating to copyright, defamation, contempt of court, suppression of publications, tape recording conversations, use of cameras to record or observe private activities, trespass, nuisance, privacy, contract, negligence and racial vilification all apply to the ABC. Particular activities might be governed by state or federal law specific to the circumstances. Editorial and program staff are required to have a good working knowledge of how the law does or might apply to their work. ABC Legal Services is available to provide training about legal issues and Divisions should make arrangements with Legal Services about the delivery of that training.

5.3.2 The law is often difficult to interpret and, with different State or Territory laws often applying to the same program, decisions become even more complex. Program staff have direct access to ABC Legal Services so that legal risk can be minimised. The costs of legal action and awards of damages can be very high.

5.3.3 Program staff are required to refer all matters with legal implications to ABC Legal Services for advice. Legal Services is able to brief external legal Counsel as required. It is important to identify potential legal issues early and to involve ABC Legal Services sooner rather than later. Program staff must ensure that ABC Legal Services has, wherever possible, appropriate time to consider the legal implications of the publication, the facts or opinions upon which the program is based and the risks, if any, for the ABC. Program staff may contact ABC Legal Services at any time of the day or night.

5.3.4 After considering the advice of Legal Services, the final decision on whether to broadcast or publish, or in what form, rests with editorial staff. Upward referral is essential on the rare occasion when program makers consider acting contrary to the advice of ABC Legal Services.

5.3.5 Plagiarism (the use of another person's ideas, words, work etc as one's own) is not tolerated by the ABC. The *Copyright Act 1968* protects original ideas and expressions in a material form such as writing. However a claim of plagiarism can be made in relation to ideas which are not in a material form.

5.3.6 Attributing the source of ideas may overcome claims of plagiarism but will not necessarily satisfy the requirements of the Copyright Act. Except in special circumstances, the use of copyright material is prohibited without the permission of the copyright owner. Fair dealing provisions allow material to be used without permission, for criticism, review and reporting of news, but in the case of criticism and review a 'sufficient acknowledgment' must be made.

...

5.5. Conflict of interest

5.5.1 There should be no conflict between the private interests of ABC employees and their official duties. The outside activities of program makers, including financial, personal and political relationships, must not compromise the editorial integrity of ABC programs. Employees are expected to arrange their affairs in a manner that will prevent conflict of interest.

...

5.5.3 There are three areas to consider: potential, actual, and perceived conflict of interest:

Potential conflict of interest is, for example, where an employee has an interest in or association with an organisation (e.g., being a director or substantial shareholder) or individual that could become a conflict of interest.

Actual conflict of interest is, for example, where an employee has an interest in or association with an organisation or individual to the point where their judgment may be affected; and they are asked to (or are in a position to) enter into negotiations with, or to interview, that individual or someone from that organisation.

A perceived conflict of interest should not be confused with potential or actual conflict of interest, but it may need investigating to see if there is a potential or actual conflict behind the perception.

5.5.4 **Declarations:** To prevent conflict of interest, supervisors must be told about any associations or interests which an individual has that may conflict with editorial responsibilities. Individuals have a duty to declare an actual or potential conflict of interest at the earliest opportunity. They also must declare in advance any proposed activity that might conflict with editorial responsibilities.

...

5.5.9 **Gifts:** The practice of accepting gifts and advantages via work related activity can create both actual and perceived conflicts of interest, and may harm the ABC's credibility. Although some gifts are relatively trivial, such as a token mug or souvenir calendar, others may have substantial value. ... The acceptance of gifts of any substance should be referred upward for a decision. Each division has established a Gift Register which keeps all details of gifts offered, accepted or rejected.

...

Source: ABC

SBS Codes of Practice (revised 2002, covering all media)—extracts

1. Introduction

The SBS Codes of Practice sets out the principles and policies SBS uses to guide its programming. The Codes embrace the principal Charter function of SBS: '... *to provide multilingual and multicultural radio and television services that inform, educate and entertain all Australians, and, in doing so, reflect Australia's multicultural society*'.

SBS's role as a multilingual and multicultural national broadcaster ensures that SBS's services will be distinctive in Australian broadcasting. Across SBS's services, audiences can expect a reflection of the diversity of Australia, and programming which is consistent with SBS's Vision: '*Uniting and enriching our society by creatively communicating the values, the voices and the vision of multicultural Australia and the contemporary world.*'

SBS believes that its audiences are best served by exposure to a wide range of cultures, values and perspectives. As a result, SBS's programming can be controversial and provocative, and may at times be distasteful or offensive to some. SBS will present diversity carefully and responsibly, ensuring a balance of views over time. SBS is for all Australians. Accordingly, SBS aims to represent the different experiences, lifestyles, perspectives, cultures and languages within Australia.

SBS Television and Radio have different priorities and play complementary roles in pursuing SBS's objectives. Nevertheless, the principles and policies of SBS programming are the same for Television and Radio and, except where indicated, these Codes of Practice apply to all SBS broadcasting and datacasting services. SBS's new media content is also selected and developed in accordance with these Codes. Online material is excluded from the jurisdiction of the Australian Broadcasting Authority for the purposes of complaints investigation.

SBS Television

SBS Television emphasises cross-cultural awareness by exposing audiences to a wide range of cultures and perspectives and by presenting the reality of Australia's multicultural society. Most SBS Television programs are either in English or carry English subtitles. This recognises the role of English as Australia's common language and gives SBS Television the widest possible reach across Australian society. In broadcasting programs from non-English-speaking countries, SBS Television provides a medium where people from a non-English-speaking background can watch programming which is in their first language.

SBS Radio

SBS Radio serves Australia's cultural communities by broadcasting in more than sixty languages. Many programs serve audiences from different countries and cultures. Some programs and program segments are in English.

SBS Radio assists communities to participate as fully as possible in Australian society. Where possible, it also supports the maintenance and development of their cultural identities and provides cross-cultural links. While exploring issues relevant to all Australians, SBS Radio fulfils different roles, including information provider, news source, entertainer, educator, cultural vehicle, commentator and a medium for diverse community voices. Language groups endeavour to be responsive to the needs and expectations of community audiences while remaining impartial and objective.

SBS New Media

SBS New Media provides comprehensive text, video and audio services on the SBS website, www.sbs.com.au. The online services extend and enhance SBS Television and Radio programming, providing individual sites for SBS-produced television programs and SBS Radio's language programs. New Media creates original digital content and takes SBS programming into new environments. SBS does not publish material on the Website that it would not be prepared to broadcast.

2. General program codes and policies

2.1   Prejudice, Racism and Discrimination

SBS seeks to counter attitudes of prejudice against any person or group on the basis of their race, ethnicity, nationality, gender, age, sexual preference, religion, physical or mental disability, occupational status, or political beliefs. While remaining consistent with its mandate to portray diversity, SBS will avoid broadcasting programming which clearly condones, tolerates or encourages discrimination on these grounds.

SBS views racism as a serious impediment to achieving a cohesive, equitable and harmonious society, and is committed to its elimination. SBS seeks to correct distorted pictures of cultural communities and issues of race generally. It does this through programming which reflects the reality of Australia's cultural diversity and exposes racist attitudes.

SBS aims to ensure that programs either counter or do not support individual or group stereotyping. SBS strives to eliminate stereotyping by presenting members of different groups in a variety of roles and by avoiding simplistic representations.

2.1.1 Women

SBS aims to promote a greater awareness of the contributions of women through programming which reflects the range of roles in which women are involved in society.

The portrayal of women should not create or reinforce sexual, gender or racial stereotypes. Programs which suggest that the exploitation of women is acceptable will be avoided.

SBS provides opportunities for women to direct, produce and present programs. A high level of involvement from women is sought in all program strands, particularly those dealing with issues of concern to women.

SBS seeks to challenge stereotypes by reflecting a wide variety of cultural mores and roles.

SBS understands that different cultural groups have different perceptions of women. SBS may broadcast programs which directly challenge these accepted cultural views.

2.1.2 Indigenous Australians

'Indigenous Australians' refers to the Aboriginal peoples and Torres Strait Islanders of Australia. SBS recognises the social, cultural and spiritual integrity of Indigenous societies and acknowledges the diversity across and within these societies. SBS aims to promote and facilitate among all Australians an understanding of Indigenous cultures, values and aspirations, and supports the goals of reconciliation.

SBS aims, over time, to provide programming which caters for the diverse and changing needs of all Indigenous peoples and deals with contemporary issues of importance to Indigenous Australians. SBS strives for maximum involvement of Indigenous people in all aspects of the production and presentation of such programs.

In the production, commissioning and presentation of Indigenous programming, SBS will endeavour to ensure that proper regard is paid to the sensitivities, cultural traditions and languages of Indigenous peoples. SBS recognises the need of Indigenous communities to maintain their cultures, languages and traditions, and will seek to provide programs to that end. SBS will be sensitive to the many cultural issues that surround media presentation of Indigenous people and issues.

It is critical that the cultural practices of Aboriginal and Torres Strait Islander peoples are observed in any media programming and news reporting. The bereavement practices of Indigenous people are region specific. It is the responsibility of program makers, news editors and producers to verify and observe local practices when making programs that depict or represent recently deceased Indigenous people or reporting on recently deceased Indigenous people. Where appropriate, footage or sound recordings of deceased Indigenous people will be preceded by a warning.

Program-makers, producers and journalists will refer to the SBS publication *The Greater Perspective* (1997) which contains the Protocol and Guidelines for the Production of Film and Television on Aboriginal and Torres Strait Islander Communities. *The Greater Perspective* sets out six principles which programmakers, producers and journalists should follow when making or producing programs relating to Indigenous Australians. These principles refer to the need for program makers and producers to:

- be aware of and challenge their own prejudices, stereotyped beliefs and perceptions about Indigenous people;
- be aware that an Indigenous view of Indigenous issues may differ from a non-Indigenous view;
- consult with Indigenous people in the making of programs about Indigenous people, particularly with those who are the subject(s) of the program;
- conduct dealings with Indigenous people openly and honestly, which includes informing Indigenous people involved of the consequences of any proposed agreements and of their right to seek independent legal advice;
- respect the lands and cultural property of Indigenous people, as well as the subject(s) of programs; be sensitive to the cultures of Indigenous people and undertake consultation and negotiation with the people concerned prior to and during the making of a program.

2.2   Language and Diversity

2.2.1 Introduction

SBS's Charter responsibilities include contributing to the retention and continuing development of language and other cultural skills and providing programming in people's preferred languages. Many languages are spoken in Australia. As far as practicable, SBS aims to reflect this diversity in its programming, while at the same time remaining consistent with its other Charter responsibilities.

Accordingly, SBS embraces its role as an established medium through which Australia's cultural communities retain and develop their individual languages. On both its Television and Radio networks, SBS seeks to provide programs in which people from a non-English-speaking background can hear their first language. SBS recognises English as the common language of Australia and therefore as a major vehicle through which SBS can promote cross-cultural awareness.

2.2.2 Allocation of Airtime for Community Languages—Radio

SBS Radio is a multilingual and multicultural broadcaster with a direct role in serving Australia's diverse language communities. In recognition of this role, the allocation of airtime to particular languages on SBS Radio is based on the size of the community speaking that language and other criteria which are reviewed from time-to-time on the basis of Census data and in consultation with communities. These may include, for example, age, recency of arrival, English language proficiency and employment rates.

2.2.3 English and Non-English Language and Cultural Content—Television

SBS Television is a multicultural broadcaster serving all Australians. To reach across Australian society, SBS provides:

- English language programming which is readily accessible to a general population;
- English-subtitled non-English language programming which may serve the needs of particular communities and is accessible to a wider audience; and
- non-English language programming which directly serves the needs of particular communities and may be of some interest to other audiences.

SBS seeks in its yearly television schedule to achieve a balance between television programs in English and programs in languages other than English.

SBS aims, as far as possible and over time, to provide programs on SBS Television across all languages spoken in the community and to present programming from a wide variety of cultural perspectives. Program selection will take into account variations in the availability and quality of programming from different television industries around the world, as well as the need to meet the range of SBS's programming objectives.

…

2.3 Self-identification when referring to Groups and Individuals

SBS encourages different groups and individuals to express their cultural identity. Accordingly, SBS does not impose labels on cultural groups, but uses groups' self-identification, if it is freely chosen. SBS is not subject to the desires of any one group as to how any other group is to be identified.

While SBS accepts self-identification of cultural groups, this policy has no implications other than recognition of group identity within the Australian community. It should not be interpreted as recognising any historical or political claims, or conferring official authority on activities counter to the policies or practices of other governments. SBS recognises the nationality of people in accordance with their country of current citizenship.

In the production of programs, SBS will avoid the use of derogatory terms used by one cultural, national or religious group to describe another. In the transmission of purchased programs, SBS will take care not to endorse such usage.

2.4 News and Current Affairs

2.4.1 Introduction

Section 10(1)(c) of the SBS Act makes it a duty of the SBS Board to '… ensure by means of the SBS's programming policies, that the gathering and presentation by the SBS of news and information is accurate and is balanced over time and across the schedule of programs broadcast'.

SBS believes in the right of its audience to make up its own mind after a fair, objective, balanced and professional presentation of the issues. SBS provides a forum for views on important issues to be communicated to audiences and seeks to present the widest range of opinion over time.

From time to time, SBS issues guidelines to assist broadcasters and journalists, particularly in handling controversial issues which could create tensions within the community. SBS journalists are also encouraged to work to the Code of Ethics of the Media Entertainment and Arts Alliance.

Accuracy is the highest priority of news and current affairs and SBS will take all reasonable steps to ensure timely acknowledgment and correction of any errors of fact.

SBS avoids sensationalised and exaggerated treatment of issues and events. In covering murders, accidents, funerals, suicides and disasters, SBS expects its program makers to exercise great sensitivity, particularly when approaching, interviewing and portraying people who are distressed. SBS will report suicides only when such reporting is in the public interest and in accordance with legal restrictions in some States prohibiting the publication of a finding of suicide by a coroner unless the coroner has made an order allowing publication. Any reporting of suicide will be in moderate terms, usually avoiding details of method. …

SBS has a policy of self-identification (see Code 2.3 above) and does not arbitrate on the validity of territorial claims. SBS journalists will identify themselves and SBS before proceeding with an interview for broadcast.

…

2.4.4 Violence in News and Current Affairs

The decision whether to broadcast certain pictures or sounds which portray violence is based on their newsworthiness and reporting value, together with a proper regard for the reasonable susceptibilities of audiences to the detail of what is broadcast. SBS will not sensationalise violent events, or present them for their own sake. Where appropriate, news segments will be preceded by a warning that the material may be distressing to some viewers or listeners. The timing and content of newsflashes are unpredictable. Accordingly, particular care will be exercised in the selection of sounds and images, and consideration given to the likely composition of the audience.

News updates and news promotions portraying elements of violence will not be scheduled during obviously inappropriate programs, especially programs directed at young children.

2.5 Religions

SBS is aware of the need for a responsible examination of the role of religion in society. In broadcasting programs about religion, SBS will not support any particular religion over any other, nor intentionally provide a medium for one religion to denigrate another.

SBS recognises the importance of religion for the many communities that make up Australian society and the potential for programming dealing with religion to cause cross-cultural tensions. Accordingly, SBS will be sensitive and careful in dealing with issues of religion.

2.6   Interviews, talkback and audience responses

SBS will not transmit the words of an identifiable person unless:

- that person has been informed in advance that the words may be transmitted; or
- in the case of words which have been recorded without the knowledge of the person, the person has subsequently, but prior to the transmission, indicated consent to the transmission of the words; or
- the manner of the recording has made it manifestly clear that the material may be broadcast.

2.7   Privacy

The rights of individuals to privacy should be respected in all SBS programs. However, in order to provide information to the public relating to a person's performance of public duties or about other matters of public interest, intrusions upon privacy may, in some circumstances, be justified.

Source: SBS

Commercial sector

Commercial Radio Codes of Practice and guidelines (registered with the ABA, September 2004)— extracts

Code of Practice 1—Programs Unsuitable for Broadcast

Purpose

1.1.   The purpose of this Code is to prevent the broadcast of programs which are unsuitable, having regard to prevailing community standards and attitudes.

Definition

1.2.   In this code 'programs' means all matter broadcast.

Proscribed Matter

1.3.   A licensee must not broadcast a program which:

(a)   is likely to incite, encourage or present for its own sake violence or brutality;

(b)   simulate news or events in such a way as to mislead or alarm listeners;

(c)   present as desirable:

(i)   the misuse of alcoholic liquor; or

(ii)   the use of illegal drugs, narcotics or tobacco.

(d)   depicts suicide favourably or presents suicide as a means of achieving a desired result; or

(e)   is likely to incite or perpetuate hatred against or vilify any person or group on the basis of age, ethnicity, nationality, race, gender, sexual preference, religion or physical or mental disability.

1.4.   Nothing in sub-clauses 1.3(c)(ii), 1.3(d) or 1.3(e) prevents a licensee from broadcasting a program of the kind or kinds referred to in those sub-clauses if the program is presented reasonably and in good faith for academic, artistic (including comedy or satire), religious instruction, scientific or research purposes or for other purposes in the public interest, including discussion or debate about any act or matter.

Social awareness ✗

Program Content and Language, including Sex and Sexual Behaviour

1.5.   (a)   All program content must meet contemporary standards of decency, having regard to the likely characteristics of the audience of the licensee's service.

(b)   The gratuitous use in a program of language likely to offend the anticipated audience for that program must be avoided.

1.6.   Licensees must not broadcast audio of actual sexual acts.

1.7.   Licensees must not broadcast a feature program which has an explicit sexual theme as its core component unless it is broadcast between 9.30 p.m. and 5.00 a.m. and an appropriate warning is made prior to commencement of the program and at hourly intervals during broadcast of the program.

1.8.   Nothing in clause 1.7 prevents a licensee from broadcasting a program at any time, of the kind referred to in that clause, if the program is in the public interest, including discussion or debate about current events.

Code of Practice 2—News and Current Affairs Programs

Purpose: The purpose of this Code is to promote accuracy and fairness in news and current affairs programs.

2.1.   News programs (including news flashes) broadcast by a licensee must:

(a)   present news accurately;

(b)   not present news in such a way as to create public panic, or unnecessary distress to listeners;

(c)   distinguish news from comment;

(d)   not use material relating to a person's personal or private affairs, or which invades an individual's privacy, unless there is a public interest in broadcasting such information.

2.2.   In the preparation and presentation of current affairs programs, a licensee must ensure that:

(a)   factual material is presented accurately and that reasonable efforts are made to correct substantial errors of fact at the earliest possible opportunity;

(b)   the reporting of factual material is clearly distinguishable from commentary and analysis;

(c)   reasonable efforts are made or reasonable opportunities are given to present significant viewpoints when dealing with controversial issues of public importance, either within the same program or similar programs, while the issue has immediate relevance to the community;

(d)   viewpoints expressed to the licensee for broadcast are not misrepresented, and material is not presented in a misleading manner by giving wrong or improper emphasis, by editing out of context;

(e)   respect is given to each person's legitimate right to protection from unjustified use of material which is obtained without an individual's consent or other unwarranted and intrusive invasions of privacy.

...

Code of Practice 3—Advertising

Purpose: The purposes of this Code are to ensure that advertisements comply with others [sic] Codes where applicable ...

3.1   Advertisements broadcast by a licensee must:

(a)   not be presented as news programs or other programs;

(b)   comply with all other Codes of Practice so far as they are applicable.

...

Code of Practice 6—Interviews and Talkback Programs

Purpose: The purpose of this Code is to prevent the unauthorised broadcast of statements by identifiable persons.

6.1.   A licensee must not broadcast the words of an identifiable person unless:

(a)   that person has been informed in advance or a reasonable person would be aware that the words may be broadcast; or

(b)   in the case of words which have been recorded without the knowledge of the person, that person has subsequently, but prior to the broadcast, expressed consent to the broadcast of the words.

Code of Practice 7—Compliance With the Codes

7.1.   Licensees must comply with the Codes, but a failure to comply will not be a breach of the Codes if that failure is due to:

(a)   a reasonable mistake; or

(b)   reasonable reliance on information supplied by another person; or

(c)   an act or default of another person, or to an accident or some other cause beyond the licensee's control

and the licensee took reasonable precautions and exercised due diligence to avoid the failure.

7.2. Each licensee must on at least one occasion in each week during the period that the Codes are in force broadcast on each commercial radio service operated by it an announcement publicising the existence of the Code and a general description of the nature and effect of their operation. Such announcements must be broadcast at different times and in different programs from week to week.

...

Guidelines on the Portrayal of Indigenous Australians on Commercial Radio

The Royal Commission into Aboriginal Deaths in Custody proposed the development of codes of practice and policies relating to the presentation of Aboriginal issues; the establishment of monitoring bodies and the putting into place of training and employment programs for Aboriginal people.

In recognition of those proposals, as a matter of industry policy, members of Commercial Radio Australia are encouraged to adopt the following guidelines in relation to Code of Practice 1 (1.3) of the *Commercial Radio Code of Practice*:

A licensee shall not broadcast a program which:

(e) is likely to incite or perpetuate hatred against [or] vilify any person or group on the basis of age, ethnicity, nationality, race, gender, sexual preference, religion or physical or mental disability.

Guidelines

1. Commercial broadcasters should not transmit material that:
   - is likely to incite or perpetuate hatred against;
   - gratuitously vilifies;
   - is likely to incite serious contempt for; or
   - severely ridicules

   a person or groups of people, for the reason that they are Indigenous Australians.

2. A broadcaster should avoid prejudicial or belittling references to, or undue emphasis on, a person because of their being Aboriginal or Torres Strait Islander peoples.

   Note: It is not up to a broadcaster to question a person's Aboriginality.

   Acceptance of a person's claims of Aboriginality can only come from within the Aboriginal community.

3. Media reports about Aboriginal and Torres Strait Islander peoples should respect the protocols of those people.

4. Care should be exercised in depicting problems encountered by Aboriginal and Torres Strait Islander communities to achieve a balanced approach which does not unduly emphasise negative aspects to the exclusion of positive developments (e.g. descriptions of problems could usefully include efforts being made by the people themselves to resolve them).

5.   As part of this balance, where material is broadcast that:
- reports on a negative aspect of a person, a group of Aboriginal or Torres Strait Islander people, and
- draws attention to the person or group being Aboriginal or Torres Strait Islanders,

the broadcaster of the material should give the person or group an opportunity to reply to the material, and should cause the reply to be broadcast.

6.   The positive portrayal of Indigenous people in programs and news media should ideally assist those communities to:
- maintain and pass on to their descendants their cultures and traditions; and
- facilitate an understanding of Indigenous people's cultures among all Australians.

Explanatory Notes to the Guidelines on the Portrayal of Indigenous Australians on Australian Commercial Radio

The Guidelines can be assisted by the initiation of programs that sensitise non-Indigenous journalists and program-makers to the values of Indigenous people.

Representatives of the National Indigenous Media Association of Australia (NIMAA) may be contacted for advice on an appropriate spokesperson on a news story focusing on the Aboriginal or Torres Strait Islander communities, or simply checking on the sensitivity of broadcasting details of an issue concerning those people.

Of particular offence to Aboriginal people are what they claim to be the myths, allegations, and incidents that reinforce negative stereotypes and generalisations that range from the totally untrue, through the partially untrue, to true statements taken out of context.

Recommended educational material on the portrayal of Indigenous Australians in the media are:

- *Signposts: Guide for Journalists* by Kitty Eggerking and Diana Plater (Australian Centre for Independent Journalism) available from most university bookshops.
- *Rebutting the Myths,* produced by the Office of the Minister for Aboriginal and Torres Strait Islander Affairs (available from Australian Government Bookshops).
- *The Greater Perspective* by Lester Bostock (available through the Special Broadcasting Service—produced principally to assist Television and Film makers, but including general information of use to all involved in presentation of Aboriginal issues).

Guidelines and Explanatory Notes on the Portrayal of Women on Commercial Radio

Women represent 51% of the Australian population and as such are seeking fair and accurate portrayal in the media, which reflects their diversity and recognises the significant and ongoing changes in women's attitudes and their roles in society.

In recognition of this, members of Commercial Radio Australia Limited are encouraged to use the following Guidelines to assist in understanding and meeting the objects of Code 1.3(e) of the *Commercial Radio Codes of Practice*.

Guidelines

In the portrayal of women on commercial radio, broadcasters should avoid promoting or endorsing inaccurate, demeaning or discriminatory descriptions of women by:

1. **Not placing undue emphasis on gender and resisting stereotyping.**

    Sexist language is language that unnecessarily excludes one sex or gives unequal treatment to women and men. Negative or inequitable sex-role portrayal refers to language, attitudes or representations which tend to associate particular roles, modes of behaviour, characteristics, attributes or products to people on the basis of gender, without taking them into consideration as individuals. Negative or inequitable portrayal of women and men can be both explicit and implied. Examples of non-sexist language are: leader/chair not chairman, police officer not policeman, firefighter instead of fireman, sales representatives not salesman, business executive not businessman. Some titles, such as chairman, are considered by some sectors of the community to have become generic through common usage, but should be used with discretion.

    In relation to emphasis on gender, descriptions should endeavour to be relevant, i.e. 'a store manager was attacked and robbed' rather than describing the store manager as 'a single mother of three'. The relevant fact is that the woman was attacked in her capacity of store manager.

2. **Ensuring that reporting and 'on-air' discussions respect the dignity of women and are non-exploitive.**

    Women are as equally intelligent, informed and competent as men and therefore wish to be portrayed in an equivalent manner. Avoid expressions that infer that a person is inferior because she is a woman, or that men have exclusivity, i.e. 'that's a man's job' or 'a woman wouldn't understand that', 'it's a man's world' (the tone of voice can cause more offence than the actual remark). Avoid the use of overt sexual references in relation to a woman's physical characteristics which have no relevance to the issue under discussion.

3. **Recognising the changing roles of women and men in today's society.**

    The roles and opportunities for both sexes are becoming more diverse due to factors such as the elimination of female-only and male-only occupations, changing patterns of parenting and lifestyles. Women and girls are involved in a range of roles as diverse as that for men and boys.

4. **Endeavouring to achieve a balance in the use of women and men as experts and authorities and giving equal prominence to the achievements of women.**

    It is important to recognise the growing female participation in professional life and business so that women are adequately and appropriately represented in responsible roles. Women's achievements have often lacked the same level of recognition as men, i.e. sport.

5. **Not broadcasting material which condones or incites violence against women; and,**

    reporting and discussing appropriate incidences of violence against

women which do not over-emphasise detail, but could include analysis of issues underlying such acts.

Media reports of violence against women generally focus on the issue of stranger violence and ignore the issue of domestic violence because it does not fit the news-worthiness criteria of being unusual. However, almost all family incident reports to the police are lodged by women. This does not mean that all stories of domestic violence should be reported, but that incidents of domestic violence, and the reasons for it, should not be ignored on the basis that 'its [sic] only a domestic'.

Media reports can tend to emphasise violence that occurs in public places and even if it does report violence in the home, it is more likely to be stranger break-in, rather than violence by an acquaintance. Reporting should therefore be balanced to reflect all violence in society and be factual without being sensational.

Care should be taken when reporting instances of violence by men against women which might be seen to offer explanations to diminish men's responsibility for their actions and even shift blame to the victim.

The dignity of a victim can easily be forgotten. Care should be exercised to avoid gratuitous and repetitive detail, such as the state of undress of a victim or description of the crime.

Guidelines on the Portayal of Suicide and Mental Illness on Commercial Radio

Approximately 2500 Australians die by suicide each year and about one in five people will experience a mental illness at some stage in their lives.

Codes of Practice 1.3 (d) and 1.3 (e) of the *Commercial Radio Codes of Practice* are designed to provide appropriate community safeguards by prohibiting licensees from broadcasting programs on suicide that are irresponsible or programs that are derogatory towards or stigmatise people with mental illness.

The following guidelines on the portrayal of suicide and mental illness on commercial radio do not form part of the Codes. However, members of Commercial Radio Australia are encouraged to use these guidelines to assist them in understanding and meeting the obligations of Codes 1.3(d) and (e).

Guidelines

Portrayal of Suicide

In programs about or relating to suicide, stations should avoid depicting suicide favourably or presenting it as a means of achieving a desired result by:

1.   **Checking that the language used does not glamorise or sensationalise suicide, or present suicide as a solution to problems.**

For example, it would be better to use 'non-fatal' rather than 'unsuccessful' when describing a suicide attempt and 'increasing rates' rather than 'suicide epidemic' when describing rates of suicide. Research shows that over-use of the word suicide may normalise the act.

2. **Avoiding an approach which glamorises or sensationalises celebrity suicide.**
   Celebrity suicides usually attract a lot of public attention. Higher rates of suicide have sometimes been recorded after celebrity suicides which received prominent coverage. If a celebrity suicide is reported, care should be taken to ensure that any description of the method used is disclosed only if there is a public interest in providing that information.

3. **Exclude detailed descriptions about method of suicide.**
   Stations should broadcast reports of suicide or attempted suicide only where there is a public interest reason to do so and should exclude any detailed descriptions of the method of suicide or attempted suicide. Such reports should be straightforward and should not include graphic details. Research shows that there may be some correlation between the reporting of methods of suicide and 'copycat suicides'.

Portrayal of Mental Illness

Studies have shown that the negative portrayal of mental illness impacts significantly on people experiencing mental illness and may influence community attitudes, which in turn may lead to stigmatisation and discrimination against people with mental illness.

In the portrayal of mental illness on commercial radio, licensees should avoid broadcasting a program that stigmatises or vilifies people in the community who are living with a mental illness by:

1. **Avoiding the use of certain derogatory terminology.**
   Terms such as 'cracked up', 'nutcase', 'psycho' and 'lunatic asylum' stigmatise and may perpetuate discrimination against people suffering with mental illness. Language that implies mental illness is a life sentence should be avoided—e.g. a person is not 'a schizophrenic' rather they are experiencing or being treated for schizophrenia. In addition, care should be taken to ensure medical terms are not used out of context—e.g. 'psychotic dog', 'schizophrenic economy'.

2. **Remembering that people with a mental illness are not inherently violent, unable to work, weak or unable to get well.**
   There are some negative misconceptions about mental illness in the community and radio programs should avoid reinforcing these misconceptions. Research indicates that people receiving treatment for a mental illness are no more violent or dangerous than the general population and when unwell are more likely to harm themselves than others. In addition, most people with a mental illness recover well with appropriate treatment and support—they work, they have families and contribute to society in many ways.

Source: ACMA

ABA Broadcasting Services Standards 2000

Broadcasting Services (Commercial Radio Compliance Program) Standard 2000

This standard requires commercial radio broadcasting licensees to formulate, implement and maintain a compliance program to ensure compliance with the requirements of the Act, standards and the codes.

Source: ABA

Broadcasting Services (Commercial Radio Advertising) Standard 2000

This standard requires licensees to ensure that advertisements are distinguishable from other programs.

Source: ABA

Broadcasting Services (Commercial Radio Current Affairs Disclosure) Standard 2000—extract

This standard requires:
(a) on-air disclosure during current affairs programs of commercial agreements between sponsors and presenters that have the potential to affect the content of those programs; and
(b) on-air disclosure during current affairs programs of the payment of production costs by advertisers and sponsors; and
(c) licensees to keep a register of commercial agreements between sponsors and presenters of current affairs programs and make it available to the ABA and the public; and
(d) licensees to ensure that a condition of employment of presenters of current affairs programs is that they comply with relevant obligations imposed by the Act, the codes and this standard.

Source: ABA

Code of Practice for Commercial Television (registered with the ABA July 2004)—extracts

Section 1—Introduction

Objectives
1.1   The Code is intended to:
      1.1.1 regulate the content of commercial television in accordance with current community standards;

1.1.2 ensure that viewers are assisted in making informed choices about their own and their children's television viewing;

1.1.3 provide uniform, speedy and effective procedures for the handling of viewer complaints about matters covered by the Code;

1.1.4 be subject to periodic public review of its relevance and effectiveness.

Proscribed Material

1.8. A licensee may not broadcast a program, program promotion, station identification or community service announcement which is likely, in all the circumstances, to:

1.8.1. simulate news or events in such a way as to mislead or alarm viewers;

1.8.2. depict the actual process of putting a subject into a hypnotic state;

1.8.3. be designed to induce a hypnotic state in viewers;

1.8.4. use or involve any technique which attempts to convey information to the viewer by transmitting messages below or near the threshold of normal awareness;

1.8.5. seriously offend the cultural sensitivities of Aboriginal and Torres Strait Islander people or of ethnic groups or racial groups in the Australian community;

1.8.6. provoke or perpetuate intense dislike, serious contempt or severe ridicule against a person or group of persons on the grounds of age, colour, gender, national or ethnic origin, disability, race, religion or sexual preference.

1.9 Except for Clause 1.8.3, none of the matters in Clause 1.8 will be contrary to this Section if:

1.9.1 said or done reasonably and in good faith in broadcasting an artistic work (including comedy or satire); or

1.9.2 said or done reasonably and in good faith in the course of any broadcast of a statement, discussion or debate made or held for an academic, artistic or scientific purpose or any other identifiable public interest purpose; or

1.9.3 said or done in broadcasting a fair report of, or a fair comment on, any event or matter of identifiable public interest.

...

Presentation of Broadcast Material

1.15 A commercial, community service announcement, program promotion or station promotion must be readily distinguishable by viewers from program material.

1.16 Clause 1.15 applies to material broadcast:

1.16.1 between programs;

1.16.2 in a commercial break within a program;

1.16.3 as a visual or audio superimposition over a program.

1.17 Where a licensee receives payment for material that is presented in a program or segment of a program, that material must be distinguishable from other program material, either because it is clearly promoting a product or service, or because of labelling or some other form of differentiation.

...

Section 4—News and Current Affairs Programs

Objectives

4.1.   This Section is intended to ensure that:

      4.1.1.   news and current affairs programs are presented accurately and fairly;

      4.1.2.   news and current affairs programs are presented with care, having regard to the likely composition of the viewing audience and, in particular, the presence of children;

      4.1.3.   news and current affairs take account of personal privacy and of cultural differences in the community;

      4.1.4.   news is presented impartially.

Scope of the Code

4.2.   Except where otherwise indicated, this Section applies to news programs, news flashes, news updates and current affairs programs. A 'current affairs program' means a program focusing on social, economic or political issues of current relevance to the community.

News and Current Affairs Programs

4.3.   In broadcasting news and current affairs programs, licensees:

      4.3.1.   Must present factual material accurately and represent viewpoints fairly, having regard to the circumstances at the time of preparing and broadcasting the program;

      4.3.2.   Must not present material in a manner which creates public panic;

      4.3.3.   Should have appropriate regard to the feelings of relatives and viewers when including images of dead or seriously wounded people. Images of that kind which may seriously distress or seriously offend a substantial number of viewers should be displayed only when there is an identifiable public interest reason for doing so;

      4.3.4.   Must provide the warnings required by Clauses 2.14★ and 2.20★★ of this Code when there is an identifiable public interest reason for selecting and broadcasting visual and/or aural material which may seriously distress or seriously offend a substantial number of viewers;

      4.3.5.   Must not use material relating to a person's personal or private affairs, or which invades an individual's privacy, other than where there is an identifiable public interest reason for the material to be broadcast;

            4.3.5.1   for the purpose of this Clause 4.3.5, licensees must exercise special care before using material relating to a child's personal or private affairs in the broadcast of a report of a sensitive matter concerning the child. The consent of a parent or guardian should be obtained before naming or visually identifying a child in a report on a criminal matter involving a child or a member of a child's immediate family, or a report which discloses sensitive information concerning the health or welfare of a child, unless there are exceptional circumstances or an identifiable public interest reason not to do so;

4.3.5.2 'child' means a person under 16 years.

4.3.6. Must exercise sensitivity in broadcasting images of or interviews with bereaved relatives and survivors or witnesses of traumatic incidents;

4.3.7. Should avoid unfairly identifying a single person or business when commenting on the behaviour of a group of persons or businesses;

4.3.7.1 when commenting on the behaviour of a group of persons or businesses, it is not unfair to correctly identify an individual person or business as part of that group if;

4.3.7.1.1 the licensee can be reasonably satisfied that the individual person or business engages in that behaviour; or

4.3.7.1.2 the licensee discloses that the individual person or business does not engage in that behaviour.

4.3.8. Must take all reasonable steps to ensure that murder and accident victims are not identified directly or, where practicable, indirectly before their immediate families are notified by the authorities;

4.3.9. Should broadcast reports of suicide or attempted suicide only where there is an identifiable public interest reason to do so, and should exclude any detailed description of the method used. The report must be straightforward, and must not include graphic details or images, or glamorise suicide in any way;

4.3.10. Must not portray any person or group of persons in a negative light by placing gratuitous emphasis on age, colour, gender, national or ethnic origin, physical or mental disability, race, religion or sexual preference. Nevertheless, where it is in the public interest, licensees may report events and broadcast comments in which such matters are raised;

4.3.11. Must make reasonable efforts to correct significant errors of fact at the earliest opportunity.

4.4. In broadcasting news programs (including news flashes) licensees:

4.4.1. Must present news fairly and impartially;

4.4.2. Must clearly distinguish the reporting of factual material from commentary and analysis.

4.5. In broadcasting a promotion for a news or current affairs program, a licensee must present factual material accurately and represent featured viewpoints fairly, having regard to the circumstances at the time of preparing and broadcasting the program promotion, and its brevity. A licensee is not required by this clause to portray all aspects or themes of a program or program segment in a program promotion, or to represent all viewpoints contained in the program or program segment.

★ 2.14 **Material which may distress or offend viewers:** Only if there is an identifiable public interest reason may a licensee broadcast a news or current affairs program containing material which, in the licensee's reasonable opinion, is likely to distress or offend a substantial number of viewers.

2.14.1 If such material is likely, in the licensee's reasonable opinion, to seriously distress or seriously offend a substantial number of viewers, then the licensee must provide the adequate prior warning required by Clause 2.26.

✱✱ *Consumer Advice for Certain Programs*

2.20   Consumer advice provides viewers with information about the principal elements that contribute to a program's classification, and indicates their intensity and/or frequency. It is intended to help people to make informed choices about the programs they choose.

...

Warnings Before Certain News, Current Affairs and Other Programs

2.25   A licensee must provide prior warning to viewers when a news, current affairs, or other program which does not carry consumer advice includes, for an identifiable public interest reason, material which in the licensee's reasonable opinion is likely to seriously distress or seriously offend a substantial number of viewers. The warning must precede the relevant item in a news and current affairs program and precede the program in other cases.

2.26   Warnings before the broadcast of material of this nature must be spoken, and may also be written. They must provide an adequate indication of the nature of the material, while avoiding detail which may itself seriously distress or seriously offend viewers.

2.27   If, in a promotion for a program, a licensee includes advice that the program contains material which may seriously distress or seriously offend viewers, that advice must comply with every requirement for program promotions in the period in which it is broadcast.

Source: ACMA

Glossary

actuality

interviews or sounds recorded on location at an event. See also *location sound*.

ad-lib

improvised speech on air without using a written script.

ad

announcement paid for by commercial clients to whom the radio station sells airtime.

ambient sound

background sound at the location of a recording.

amplifier

an electronic device used to make sound louder.

analog

as applied to recording, the recording of sound or pictures by duplicating them onto the recording medium. A cassette recorder is an example of an analog recording device. See also *digital*.

angle

the particular focus of a journalistic story.

archive

a file where previously broadcast material is stored. It can include audio, video, and/or accompanying scripts.

autocue

a piece of equipment that allows scripts to be projected and scrolled in front of the television newsreader to facilitate reading without needing to break eye contact with the camera.

back announce

see *outro*.

bi-directional microphone

see *figure eight microphone*.

big close-up (BCU)

a camera shot featuring face only.

breaking news

a news story reported as it is happening.

broadband

high-capacity digital-delivery technology.

broadcaster

the public or private company licensed to disseminate information over the airwaves.

broadcasting

the transmission of material from a single source to multiple recipients.

call-sign

the identification tag for a radio station.

cardioid microphone

a mike that picks up sound in a heart-shaped field favouring the front, with some pick-up at the sides, but virtually no pick-up at the rear.

cassette

a small twin-spool cartridge of reel-to-reel tape used for analog recording in a cassette player.

chroma key

a special effect for television where a separately produced background can be projected onto a blue screen behind the television presenter's chair.

close-up (CU)

a camera shot featuring the subject's face and neck.

console

see *mixing console*.

copy

a short scripted version of a news story written by the reporter, but read by the news-reader (also known as a 'read' or a 'word only').

cross-fade

the blending of different sound sources whereby the level of one sound source is reduced as the level of another source is raised, allowing the smooth transition from one to the other. See also *fade in/out*.

cue

to line up recorded material at the spot at which you wish play to start. See also *in-cue/out-cue*.

cue button

the control on the radio console that allows you to listen to each channel without the material going to air. This enables you to set music to start at a designated spot, or to check content before playing.

cutaway

a camera shot that takes the eyes temporarily away from the main action, used to compact story time and to mask an edit point.

cutting

in video or film, crossing from one picture directly to the next.

DAT (digital audio tape)

a digital recording format that stores the information on magnetic tape in the form of a small cartridge similar to the video-cassette.

daypart

the way broadcasters divide up the day, based on the assumptions they make about what the target audiences (and hence potential markets for advertisers) are likely to be doing at any particular time, and consequently what service will fit best into that daily routine.

decibel (dB)

the unit used for measuring loudness of sound.

delay

a time storage mechanism that allows for the insertion of a time lag in a radio program between what is said in the studio and its eventual transmission. This gives the program-makers a short interval (usually around 7 seconds) in which they can decide to 'dump' any material that might be offensive to listeners. By using the 'dump' button they return the studio to real time, erasing the lag and any material occurring within it.

demographic

the audience profile in relation to variables such as age, gender, and occupation.

digital

as applied to recording, the translation of sound or pictures into a sequence of numbers that allows for very accurate reproduction with little distortion compared to analog recording.

directional microphone

a mike that is more sensitive to sound from one direction, compared, for example, to an omni-directional mike.

dissolve

in television or film, where one picture fades out as another fades in.

dub

to copy from one recording format to another (e.g. minidisc to computer) or from machine to machine (cassette to cassette, etc.).

dump button

the control on the studio console that returns you immediately to real time, cancelling the stored time lag between broadcast and transmission. See also *delay*.

echo

the sound effect caused by sound reverberating off other surfaces, particularly bare walls, where there is nothing to absorb the sound to prevent it from bouncing back, giving a repetitive effect.

EQ

see *equaliser*.

equaliser (EQ)

a device for processing sound to adjust the ratio of low, medium, and high frequencies.

establishing shot

a wide camera shot that takes in an entire scene, giving the setting for a particular story.

extreme close-up (XCU)

a camera shot focusing on eyes only.

fade in/out

gradually increase an audio signal from nothing to its required level, or vice versa. In video: to fade a picture in from black, or from normal to black.

fader

also called the slider; the sliding control on the mixing console that controls sound levels.

feedback

the high-pitched screech caused during recording when input and output monitors are on at the same time.

figure eight microphone

a mike that collects sound from two sides in a figure-of-eight pattern.

file vision

in television, non-specific vision that can be used for any number of stories.

follow-up

a story that picks up on one that has already been done.

format

see *program format; station format.*

frequency

Each sound has its own characteristic pattern or soundwave. Frequency refers to the number of times per second the soundwave is repeated. The rate differs depending on whether the sound is of high, medium or low pitch. Frequency also refers to the space on the radio spectrum allocated to broadcasting services.

grab (or soundbite)

an edited segment of a recorded piece of speech or sound.

hook (or topline)

the attention-grabbing introductory line to a radio or television story.

hyper-cardioid

a more unidirectional version of the cardioid microphone in which the heart-shaped field is elongated further towards the front.

ID

abbreviation for 'identification', referring, in terms such as 'station ID', to the short tags, jingles, etc. used to remind audiences of the service call sign.

in-cue/out-cue

the first and last few words of a recorded insert, written out to indicate where it begins and ends.

inflexion

    modulation of the voice to convey emphasis or emotion.

input

    the material that is fed into a recording or mixing device.

intro

    the reporter's introduction to a story package.

jumpcut

    a clumsy video edit that leaves the impression of one shot jumping to another.

lead-in (or link)

    the presenter's scripted introduction to a program event or pre-recorded story package. The link is also the term given to the reporter's scripted narrative that binds a pre-recorded story package together.

link

    see *lead-in*.

live liner

    a continuity script promoting a forthcoming program event.

location sound

    sound collected at the site of a recording to convey the sense of place and atmosphere within which a story takes place.

logging

    reviewing recorded material prior to editing to note useful in- and out-cues and the times when they occur in the recording.

long-shot (LS)

    camera shot that focuses on the subject from a distance.

medium close-up (MCU)

    camera shot that focuses on the subject from shoulder to head.

medium-shot (MS)

    camera shot that focuses on the subject from thigh to head.

medium wide-shot (MWS)

    camera shot that focuses on the subject from knee to head.

mike sock

    a foam microphone cover that reduces the flow of air across the microphone and minimises 'popping'.

minidisc (MD)

    a lightweight digital recorder that works in a similar way to a CD, storing compressed digital sound files on a disc that are then 'read' by laser beams.

mixing console (or desk)

    a multi-channelled desk used to blend together sound from a variety of inputs.

mono

    sound recorded as a single track. See also *stereo*.

multi-track

the capacity to record different sound sources simultaneously. For example, a two-track recorder can record in stereo—using a left and right channel that, when played together, create a more life-like, all-round sound.

multi-versioning

reworking story material so it tells the same story in a slightly different way.

NATSOT

'NATural Sound On Tape', a shorthand instruction to the video editor to highlight background sounds.

network

a collection of broadcasting outlets under a common corporate umbrella that transmits common programming to different markets.

news flash

a short news announcement inserted into normal programming when news is deemed too important to wait for the next bulletin.

noddies

cutaways of the reporter, filmed after a recorded interview, to provide footage to alternate with that of the interview subject to mimic real-life conversation patterns and also mask edit points.

omni-directional microphone

mike that picks up sound indiscriminately from all directions.

opener

the opening theme used to identify service and program.

out-cue

see *in-cue/out-cue*.

output

processed sound broadcast from a mixing desk.

outro

the script used to conclude a program event, often summarising the story and reminding the listener of the names of featured talent.

outside broadcast (OB)

a broadcast that takes place away from the studio.

pan

the movement of the camera horizontally from one side of the shot to the other.

pan pot

'panoramic potentiometer'; the control knob on the console of the mixing desk that allows you to adjust the balance of left and right stereo channels.

peak meter

a more sensitive sound meter that gives a more precise reading of levels than the VU meter.

pick-up pattern

the recording range of a microphone.

piece to camera (PTC)

where a reporter addresses the camera directly, looking straight into the lens and speaking a short link. Also known as a stand-up.

pitch

the variations of tone in speech.

pop filter

see *mike sock*.

popping

sound interference caused by the passage of puffs of air across the top of the microphone, occurring most commonly when pronouncing the so-called plosive consonants 'p', 'b', and 't'.

program format

the type and structure of a broadcast program.

promo

a live read or a recorded package that promotes a program segment, program, station, or station event.

proximity effect

a sound distortion that can occur with directional microphones that have a tendency to emphasise bassy sounds the closer they are to the mouth.

Q&A

'question and answer' interview format.

read

see *copy*.

reader voice-over (RVO)

television term referring to a piece read by the newsreader, partly on camera and partly as voice-over on vision.

resonance

the way the sound reverberates within the throat, chest, mouth, and head to gain richness and depth.

reverberation (reverb)

the quality given to sound when it reflects off other surfaces in an enclosed space.

reverse

in a filmed interview this refers to the camera shot that, instead of focusing on the talent, focuses on the journalist who is doing the interview.

round

specialist news beat such as the courts, crime, politics, health, education.

rundown

also known as program log, this is the written record of the program broadcast schedule detailing everything that went to air.

running order

the order of items in a program.

rushes

the raw filmed material on tape prior to editing.

shotgun microphone

the most unidirectional of all mikes, allowing the recordist to home in on a single sound source while picking up the bare minimum of surrounding noise.

sibilance

the hissing sound caused by the so-called sibilant sounds such as 's' or 'ch' that can be picked up and distorted by a microphone.

signal-to-noise ratio

the strength of the recorded sound compared to the technical noise of the recording device itself.

sign-off

the presenter's/newsreader's final words at the end of a program or bulletin.

slider

see *fader*.

slug

the identification tag attached to a broadcast news story. All material relating to that story (audio, vision, scripts) will carry this ID, which will also be attached to any follow-up stories that may be done.

sound effects

actuality sound used to enhance recorded sound by recreating a place, an atmosphere, a mood, etc. Abbreviated to FX in radio, SFX in television/film.

soundbite

see *grab*.

spot news

unplanned and unpredictable news events such as fires, accidents, and other emergencies that occur during the course of a news day.

stand-alone

a short script read by the newsreader, followed by a recorded grab from the talent.

stand-up

see *piece to camera*.

station format

the type of programming and program structure of a broadcasting service.

stereo

abbreviation for stereophonic, meaning sound recorded on two channels, left and right, which creates the potential for spreading and separating the sound.

sting

a short recorded insert (for example a music grab or a brief station ID) that is used to give the announcer a bit of breathing space, to fill an awkward gap, or to mark the transition from one program element to the next.

stringer

a freelance journalist unattached to the mother newsroom who is contracted to provide additional material beyond the capacity of the reporting pool.

super-cardioid

the most unidirectional of the cardioid microphones in which the heart-shaped field is elongated further towards the front.

super

caption that is superimposed on the screen to give information relevant to the story (for example names of reporter or talent, identification of location, picture source of file tape).

talent

the person selected as the subject of an interview.

talkback

interactive program format where listeners are encouraged to phone in to make an on-air contribution.

tape hiss

the sound of reel-to-reel tape as it passes over the tape heads in tape recorders and cassettes. Normally this is unobtrusive, but it can become a distorting factor when recording levels are badly judged, allowing the machine noise to dominate over the recorded sound.

throw

the last sentence of a script that covers the cross from the newsreader or presenter to the voice on a pre-recorded insert, providing information on the next sound and voice the audience will be hearing.

tilt

movement of the camera vertically from the top of the shot to the bottom, or vice versa.

timecode

the timed location of a picture on film or video tape.

topline

see *hook*.

track

an audio channel.

two-shot

a shot that includes both talent and journalist, often used when a new talent is being introduced.

uni-directional microphone

a microphone that favours sound directly in front of it.

UPSOT

in film, this stands for 'increase Sound On Tape for duration of the grab'. This reminds the editor to increase sound when talent starts to talk.

voice-over

voice piece recorded over other sound or pictures. In radio, the voice-over can be the announcer coming in over a piece of music. In television, the voice-over will be a spoken commentary by an unseen presenter recorded over pictures.

voicer

a news story that the reporter tells using his or her own voice plus the newsreader's intro.

vox pop

a series of recorded short responses from randomly selected members of the general public on a current topic (from the Latin *vox populi* meaning 'voice of the people').

VU meter

volume unit meter that provides a guide to sound levels during recording.

wide-shot (WS)

a film shot that includes the subject and the surrounding scene.

windsock

see *mike sock*.

words

see *copy*.

wrap

a package summarising a news story that has been running over the day.

zoom

relates to a camera shot that can focus in on, or retreat away from, the details in the shot.

Bibliography

Adams, P. & Burton, L. 1997, *Talkback: Emperors of Air*, Allen & Unwin, Sydney.

Ahern, S. (ed.), 2000a, *Making Radio: A Practical Guide to Working in Radio*, Allen & Unwin, Sydney.

Ahern, S. 2000b, 'Researching and Producing', in S. Ahern (ed.), *Making Radio: A Practical Guide to Working in Radio*, Allen & Unwin, Sydney, pp. 112–31.

Ahern, S. & Brown, G. 2000, 'Radio Announcing', in S. Ahern (ed.), *Making Radio: A Practical Guide to Working in Radio*, Allen & Unwin, Sydney, pp. 70–84.

Ahern, S. & Pascoe, R. 2000, 'The Studio', in S. Ahern (ed.) 2000, *Making Radio: A Practical Guide to Working in Radio*, Allen & Unwin, Sydney, pp. 23–69.

Aitchison, J. 2003, *Cutting Edge Radio. How to Create the World's Best Radio Ads for Brands in the 21st Century*, Prentice Hall, Singapore.

Allen, Y. & Spencer, S. 1983, *The Broadcasting Chronology 1809–1980*, AFTRS, Sydney.

Alten, S.R. 2005, *Audio in Media*, 7th edn, Wadsworth, Belmont, CA.

Alysen, B. 2000, *The Electronic Reporter: Broadcast Journalism in Australia*, Deakin University Press, Geelong.

Alysen, B., Sedorkin, G., Oakham, M. & Patching, R. 2003, *Reporting in a Multimedia World*, Allen & Unwin, Sydney.

Armstrong, M., Lindsay, D. & Watterson, R. 1995, *Media Law in Australia,* 3rd edn, Oxford University Press, Melbourne.

Australian Broadcasting Authority 2000, *Broadcasting Services (Commercial Radio Compliance Program) Standard 2000*, http://www.aba.gov.au/radio/contents/standards/compliance.rtf, accessed 17 July 2005.

Australian Broadcasting Authority 2000, *Broadcasting Services (Commercial Radio Current Affairs disclosure) Standard 2000*, http://www.aba.gov.au/radio/contents/standards/disclosure.rtf, accessed 17 July 2005.

Australian Broadcasting Authority 2000, *Broadcasting Services (Commercial Radio Advertising) Standard 2000*, http://www.aba.gov.au/radio/content/standards/disclosure_2.rtf, accessed 17 July 2005.

Australian Broadcasting Authority, Internet Content Codes, http://www.aba.gov.au/internet/codes/documents/IIA_Codes.pdf, accessed 21 July 2005.

Australian Broadcasting Corporation Charter, http://www.abc.net.au/corp/charter.htm, accessed 15 March 2005.

Australian Broadcasting Corporation Code of Practice, ABC, http://www.abc.net.au/corp/code-prac04.htm, 8 December 2004.

Australian Broadcasting Corporation Editorial Policies, http://abc.net.au/corp/edpols.htm, accessed 9 December 2004.

Australian Broadcasting Corporation 1997, *ABC All Media-Law Handbook*, http://www.abc.net.au/corp/pubs/legal/lawbook/links.htm

Australian Broadcasting Corporation 2004, 'Music of the Blogospheres', *Background Briefing*, 31 October.

Australian Broadcasting Corporation 2004, Lost in Space, A News Online Survival Guide [unpublished].

Australian Bureau of Statistics (ABS) 2003, 'Measures of a knowledge-based economy and society, Australia, Information and Communications Technology Indicators' http://www.abs.gov.au/ausstats/abs@.nsf/94713ad445ff1425ca25682000192af2/7599f94ffdbadccbca256d97002c8636!OpenDocument, accessed 16 March 2005.

Australian Communications and Media Authority, Code of Practice for Commercial Television, http://www.acma.gov.au/acmainterwr/aba/contentreg/codes/television/documents/codeof-practice-july2004.pdf, accessed 17 July 2005.

Australian Communications and Media Authority, Commercial Radio Codes of Practice and guide-lines, http://www.acma.gov.au/acmainterwr/aba/contentreg/codes/radio/documents/cra-codeofpractice.pdf, accessed 17 July 2005.

Australian Communications and Media Authority, Community Broadcasting Code of Practice, http://www.acma.gov.au/acmainterwr/aba/contentreg/codes/radio/documents/cbaa_code.pdf, accessed 17 July 2005.

Australian Communications and Media Authority, Community Television Code of Practice, http://www.acma.gov.au/acmainterwr/aba/contentreg/codes/television/documents/ctvcodeofpractice.pdf, accessed 17 July 2005.

Barr, T. 2000, *newmedia.com.au: The Changing Face of Australia's Media and Communications*, Allen & Unwin, Sydney.

Beaman, J. 2000, *Interviewing for Radio*, Routledge, London.

Best, K. 2000, 'Copywriting', in Ahern, S. (ed.), *Making Radio: A Practical Guide to Working in Radio*, Allen & Unwin, Sydney, pp. 132–38.

Block, M. 1997, *Writing Broadcast News: Shorter, Sharper, Stronger*, 2nd edn., Bonus Books, Chicago.

Block, M. & Durso, J. Jr 1998, *Writing News for TV and Radio*, Bonus Books, Chicago.

Boyd, A. 1997, *Broadcast Journalism: Techniques of Radio and TV News*, 4th edn, Focal Press, Oxford.

Broadcasting Services Act 1992, http://www.comlaw.gov.au/comlaw/Legislation/ActCompilation1.nsf/framelodgmentattachments/2AEF6979D3CEFED5CA256F71004C5489, accessed 15 March 2005.

Brown, A. 2000, 'Media Ownership in the Digital Age: An Economic Perspective', *Media International Australia*, no. 95, May, pp. 49–61.

Carr, P. 2004, 'Why Drudge is Bad for Online Journalism', *Media Guardian*, 1 March, p. 38.

Chadwick, P. 1994, 'Creating Codes: Journalism Self-regulation', in Schultz, J. (ed.), *Not Just Another Business. Journalists, Citizens and the Media*, Pluto Press, Sydney, pp. 167–87.

Cohler, D. 1994, *Broadcast Journalism: A Guide for the Presentation of Radio and Television News*, 2nd edn, Prentice-Hall, New York.

Community Broadcasting Association of Australia, Community Radio Code of Practice, http://www.cbaa.org.au/content.php/20.html, accessed 9 December 2004.

Community Broadcasting Association of Australia, Community Television Code of Practice, http://www.cbaa.org.au/content.php/16.html, accessed 9 December 2004.

Conley, D. 2002, *The Daily Miracle*, 2nd edn, Oxford University Press, Melbourne.

Cook, T. 2004, 'Here Comes Everything. Can Technology Solve Information Overload?', *Weekend Australian Financial Review*, 29 December 2004–3 January 2005, pp. 20–21.

Craik, J., Bailey, J.J. & Moran, A. (eds) 1995, *Public Voices, Private Interests: Australia's Media Policy*, Allen & Unwin, Sydney.

Crisell, A. 1994, *Understanding Radio*, 2nd edn, Routledge, London.

Cunningham, S. & Turner, G. (eds) 2000, *The Media and Communications in Australia*, Allen & Unwin, Sydney.

Dancyger, K. 1991, *Broadcast Writing: Dramas, Comedies, and Documentaries*, Focal Press, Boston.

Dardis, K. 2004, *Radio Online. It's All About the Audience*, Audio Graphics, Inc., Cleveland, Ohio; http://www.audiographics.com/agd/s2121404.htm, accessed 16 December 2004.

Day, A., Pattie, M. & Bosly, N. 1998, *Presenting the News On Air. A Self-Paced Program to Develop Your Broadcast Voice*, University of Queensland Press, Brisbane.

Dobbs, G. 2005, *Better Broadcast Writing Better Broadcast News*, Pearson Education, Boston, Mass.

Docherty, D. 2004, 'Why Googleworld will beat Murdoch', *Media Guardian*, 9 August, p. 30.

Dube J. 2004, Cyberjournalist.net, http://www.cyberjournalist.net/news/000117.php, accessed 20 December 2004.

Dyke, G. 2004, 'Rise of the Red Button Culture', Media Weekly, *The Independent*, Monday 18 October, p. 9.

Eggerking, K. & Plater, D. (eds) 1993, *Signposts: A Guide to Reporting Aboriginal, Torres Strait Islander and Ethnic Affairs*, Australian Centre for Independent Journalism, University of Technology, Sydney.

Enlund, N. & Lindskog, T. 2000, 'Nya redaktionella processer vid flerkanalspublicering', in Hvitfelt, H. & Nygren, G. (eds), *På väg mot medievärlden 2020*, Studentlitteratur, Lund.

Flew, T. 2002, 'Television and Pay TV', in Cunningham, S. & Turner, G. (eds), *The Media and Communications in Australia*, Allen & Unwin, Sydney, pp. 173–87.

Flew, T. 2002 (repr. 2003), *New Media. An Introduction*, Oxford University Press, Melbourne.

Gibson, O. 2003, 'Pictures in Words', *Media Guardian*, 14 April, p. 34.

Gibson, O. 2004, 'Sharp Rise for On-demand, *Media Guardian*, 22 November, p. 13.

Gibson, R. 1991, 'A View of the News', in *Radio and Television Reporting*, Allyn & Bacon, Boston, pp. 209–34.

Gillmor, D. 2004, *We the Media: Grassroots Journalism By the People for the People*, O'Reilly, Sebastopol, Ca.

Given, J. 1995, 'Commercial TV: Bucks, Blokes, Bureaucrats and the Bird' in Craik, J., Bailey, J.J. & Moran, A. (eds), *Public Voices, Private Interests: Australia's Media Policy*, Allen & Unwin, Sydney, pp. 15–32.

Given, J. 1998, *The Death of Broadcasting? Media's Digital Future*, University of New South Wales Press, Sydney.

Global Radio News, http://217.34.13.11/home/about.asp, accessed 23 December 2004.

Griffiths, R. 1998, *Videojournalism*, Focal Press, Oxford.

Gunter, B. 2003, *News and the Net*, Lawrence Erlbaum Associates, Mahwah, New Jersey.

Hartley, J. 2003, 'Their Own Media in Their Own Language', in Lumby, C. & Probyn, E., *Remote Control. New Media, New Ethics*, Cambridge University Press, Cambridge, pp. 42–66.

Hawke, J. 1995, 'Privatising the Public Interest: The Public and the Broadcasting Services Act 1992', in Craik, J., Bailey, J.J. & Moran, A. (eds), *Public Voices, Private Interests: Australia's Media Policy*, Allen & Unwin, Sydney, pp. 33–50.

Hendy, D. 2000, *Radio in the Global Age*, Polity Press, Cambridge.

Henningham, J. (ed.) 1999a, *Institutions in Australian Society*, 2nd edn, Oxford University Press, Melbourne.

Henningham, J. 1999b, 'Media' in Henningham, J. (ed.), *Institutions in Australian Society*, 2nd edn, Oxford University Press, Melbourne, pp. 274–97.

Herbert, J. 2000, *Journalism in the Digital Age: Theory And Practice for Broadcast, Print and On-Line*, Focal Press, Oxford.

Hesse, J. 1987, *The Radio Documentary Handbook: Creating, Producing, and Selling for Broadcast*, Self-Counsel Press, Vancouver.

Hilliard, R. 2000, *Writing for Television, Radio and New Media*, 7th edn, Thomson Learning, Wadsworth, Belmont.

Hurst, J. & White, S.A. 1994, *Ethics and the Australian News Media*, Macmillan, Melbourne.

Indymedia.org, http://docs.indymedia.org/view/Global/FrequentlyAskedQuestionEn#what, accessed 17 December 2004.

Inside Out: http://www.insideout.org

Inglis, K.S. 1983, *This is the ABC: The Australian Broadcasting Commission 1932–1983*, Melbourne University Press, Melbourne.

Johnson, L. 1988, *The Unseen Voice. A Cultural Study of Early Australian Radio*, Routledge, London.

Kafcaloudes, P. 1991, *ABC All-Media Court Reporting Handbook*, ABC, Sydney.

Katbamna, M. 2004, 'The "World's Best Radio Station" That You've Never Heard', *The Independent Media Weekly*, 11 October 2004, p. 19.

Kerr, J. 2004, 'Writers, Take Note!', *Media Guardian*, 2 August, p. 6.

Lewis, M. 2000, 'Box of Tricks', *Media Guardian*, 28 August, pp. 2–4.

Little, J. 2001, 'Pirate Radio', *The Australian*, Media, 18–24 January, p. 5.

Lumby, C. 2001, 'Chris Masters. Investigative Journalist', *Bulletin*, 16 January, pp. 42–44.

MacGregor, B. 1997, *Live, Direct and Biased? Making Television News in the Satellite Age*, Arnold, London.

MacLean, S. 2004, 'Old Stager Takes Current Affairs to New Dimension', *The Australian*, Media and Marketing, 25 November, p. 20.

McLeish, R. 2005, *Radio Production*, 5th edn, Focal Press, Oxford.

McNab, P. & Best, K. 2000, 'Audio Production', in Ahern, S. (ed.), *Making Radio: A Practical Guide to Working in Radio*, Allen & Unwin, Sydney, pp. 139–45.

Masterton, M. & Patching, R. 1997, *Now the News in Detail: A Guide to Broadcast Journalism in Australia*, 3rd edn, Deakin University Press, Geelong.

Media, Entertainment and Arts Alliance (MEAA) 1999, Journalists' Code of Ethics, http://www.alliance.org.au/, accessed 8 December 2004.

Mickler, S. 1997, 'The Robespierre of the Air: Talkback Radio, Globalisation and Indigenous Issues', *Continuum*, vol. 11, no. 3, pp. 1–14.

Miller, T. & Turner, G. 2002, 'Radio', in Cunningham, S. & Turner, G. (eds), *The Media and Communications in Australia*, Allen & Unwin, Sydney, pp. 133–51.

Mills, J. 2004, *The Broadcast Voice*, Focal Press, Oxford.

Moran, A. (ed) 1992, *Stay Tuned: An Australian Broadcasting Reader*, Allen & Unwin, Sydney.

Morkes, J. & Nielsen, J. 1997 'Concise, Scannable and Objective: How to Write for the Web', http://www.useit.com/papers/webwriting/writing.html, accessed 20 March 2005.

Negroponte, N. 1995, *Being Digital*, Hodder and Stoughton, Sydney.

OECD 2003, Science, Technology and Industry Scoreboard 2003, Towards a knowledge-based economy, http://www1.oecd.org/publications/e-book/92-2003-04-1-7294/PDF/B42.pdf), accessed 17 March 2005.

Passport to Web Radio 1998 2nd edn, International Broadcasting Services, USA.

Pavlik, J.V. 2001, *Journalism and New Media*, Columbia University Press, New York.

Pearson, M. 2004, *The Journalist's Guide to Media Law: Dealing with Legal and Ethical Issues*, Allen & Unwin, Sydney.

Potts, J. 1989, *Radio in Australia*, NSW University Press, Sydney.

Preston, P. 2004, 'Are Newspapers Burnt Out?', *The Observer*, 21 November, p. 7.

PricewaterhouseCoopers 2004, Australian Entertainment & Media Outlook 2004–2008, http://www.pwc.com/Extweb/ncpressrelease.nsf/docid/0BF393874D90DC2ACA256EFB00 23ECD6, accessed 2 December, 2004.

Priestman, C. 2002, *Webradio—Radio Production for Internet Streaming*, Focal Press, Oxford.

Productivity Commission 2000, Broadcasting Inquiry Report, http://www.pc.gov.au/inquiry/broadcst/finalreport/index.html, accessed 15 March 2005.

Quinn, S. & Granato, L. 1998, *Newsgathering on the Net: An Internet Guide for Australian Journalists*, Precision Press, Winchelsea, Vic.

Radio-Locator, http://www.radio-locator.com.

Randall, D. 2000, *The Universal Journalist*, 2nd edn, Pluto Press, London.

Robertson, L. 2001, 'E-mail Avalanche', *American Journalism Review*, January/February 2001, http://ajr.newslink.org/ajrmailan01.html, 2 February.

Sanders, K. 2003, *Ethics & Journalism*, Sage, London.

Sawatsky, J. 2000, 'What to Avoid', *American Journalism Review*, http://www.ajr.org/article_printable.asp?id=678, accessed 18 March 2005.

Sedorkin, G. & McGregor, J. 2002, *Interviewing. A Guide for Journalists and Writers*, Allen & Unwin, Sydney.

Shingler, M. & Wieringa, C. 1998, *On Air: Methods and Meanings of Radio*, Arnold, London.

Special Broadcasting Service Charter, http://www20.sbs.com.au/sbscorporate/index.php?id=378, accessed 21 August 2005.

Special Broadcasting Service Codes of Practice, http://sbs.com.au/media/5418Codes-of-practice.doc, accessed 9 December 2004.

Starkey, G. 2004, *Radio in Context*, Palgrave MacMillan, Basingstoke.

Stockwell, S. & Scott, P. 2000, *All-Media Guide to Fair and Cross-Cultural Reporting*, Australian Key Centre for Culture and Media Policy, Nathan.

Stovall, J.G. 2004, *Web Journalism. Practice and Promise of a New Medium*, Pearson Education Inc., Boston.

Tanner, S., Phillips, G., Smyth, C. & Tapsall, S. 2005, *Journalism Ethics at Work*, Pearson Longman, Sydney.

Tapsall, S. & Varley, C. (eds) 2000, *Journalism Theory in Practice*, Oxford University Press, Melbourne.

The Feedroom.com, http://www.feedroom.com/main_html_img/index.html, accessed 18 March 2005.

Thomas J. 2000, 'It's Later Than You Think: The Productivity Commission's Broadcasting Inquiry and Beyond', *Media International Australia*, no. 95, May, pp. 9–18.

Trewin, J. 2003, *Presenting on TV and Radio*, Focal Press, Oxford.

Turner, G. 2003, 'Ethics, Entertainment and the Tabloid: The Case of Talkback Radio in Australia' in Lumby, C. & Probyn, E., *Remote Control. New Media, New Ethics*, Cambridge University Press, Cambridge, pp. 87–99.

Van Niekerk, M. 2005, 'Online to the Future', *The Age*, 28 January, A3, p. 8.

White, T. 1996, *Broadcast News Writing, Reporting and Producing*, 2nd edn, Focal Press, Oxford.

Whittaker, J. 2004, *The Cyberspace Handbook*, Routledge, London.

Wilby, P. & Conroy, A. 1994, *The Radio Handbook*, Routledge, London.

Wilson, R. 2000, *A Big Ask. Interviews with Interviewers*, New Holland Publishers, Sydney.

Wulfemeyer, T. 1995, *Radio-TV Newswriting: A Workbook*, Iowa State University Press, Ames, IA.

Zettl, H. 2003, *Television Production Handbook*, 8th edn, Thomson Learning, Wadsworth, Belmont, CA.

Web sites

The Age Online: http://www.theage.com.au

American Radioworks: http://americanradioworks.publicradio.org

Australian Broadcasting Authority: http://www.aba.gov.au

Australian Broadcasting Corporation: http://www.abc.net.au

Australian Communications and Radio Authority: http://www.acma.gov.au

ABC Newsradio: www.abc.net.au/newsradio/links.htm

Australian Bureau of Statistics: http://www.abs.gov.au/

Australian Copyright Council: http://www.copyright.org.au

Australian Cultural Network: http://www.acn.net.au/

Australian Federal Government: http://www.fed.gov.au/

Australian Law Reform Commission: http://www.alrc.gov.au

Australian Parliament: http://www.aph.gov.au/

BBC (UK): http://bbc.co.uk

Bloomberg L.P.:http://www.bloomberg.com

Broadcast.Com: http://www.broadcast.com

CNN (USA): http://cnn.com

Commercial Radio Australia: http://www.commercialradio.com.au/

Community Broadcasting Association of Australia: http://www.cbaa.org.au

Consumer World: http://www.consumerworld.org/

Department of Communication, Information Technology and the Arts: http://www.dcita.gov.au/

European Journalism Centre: http://www.ejc.nl

Free TV Australia: http://www.ctva.com.au/control.cfm

Global Radio News: http://globalradionews.com

Indymedia: http://www.indymedia.org/en/index.shtml

Inside Out: http://www.insideout.org

Internet Economy Indicators: http://www.internetindicators.com/media.html

Internet Radio Plaza: http://www.webradiolist.com/

Investigative Reporters and Editors: http://www.ire.org/datalibrary/ and http://www.reporter.org/

Journalism Net: http://www.journalismnet.com

Journalist's Guide to the Internet: http://reporter.umd.edu

Journalists' Toolbox: http://www.americanpressinstitute.org/toolbox/

Live365.com: http://www.live365.com/info/index.html

Media Entertainment and Arts Alliance: http://www.alliance.org.au

Mike's Radio World: http://www.mikesradioworld.com/index.html

NBC (USA): http://www.msnbc.com

National Public Radio (USA): http://www.npr.org/index.html

Newscript: http://www.newscript.com

Oz Guide: http://www.journoz.com

Power Reporting: http://powerreporting.com.

Poynter Institute: http://www.poynter.org

Productivity Commission Broadcasting Inquiry Report: http://www.indcom.gov.au/inquiry/broadcst/finalreport/index.html

Radio-Locator: http://www.radio-locator.com

Special Broadcasting Service: http://www.sbs.com.au

Sofcom: http://www.sofcom.com.au

Sound Portraits: http://soundportraits.org

Sydney Morning Herald: http://www.smh.com.au/index.html

The Age: http://www.theage.com.au

The Feedroom.com: http://www.feedroom.com/main_html_img/index.html

TV Handbook: http://www.tv-handbook.com/

University of Maryland College of Journalism Journalist's Guide to the Internet: http://reporter.umd.edu

University of Queensland Oz Guide: Internet Information Sources for Australian Journalists: http://www.uq.edu.au/jrn/ozguide/

University of Technology Sydney journalism site: http://www.journalism.uts.edu.au/subjects/jres/index.html

Wikipedia: www.wikipedia.org.

World Radio Network: http://www.wrn.com

Writing for Radio: http://www.newscript.com

Yahoo! Events: http://www.broadcast.com/

Interviews

Binnie, Kerrin, journalist/producer/presenter, ABC Online, 18 January 2005.

Bradford, Selby-Lynn, radio talkback producer, 2GB Sydney, 20 January 2005.

Bugg, Brett, Executive Producer, External and Emerging Platforms, ABC Online.

Bunbury, Bill, feature producer, ABC Radio National, 24 November 2000.

Caldwell, Alison, radio journalist, ABC News and Current Affairs, 8 November 2000.

Cannane, Steve, radio presenter, Triple J, 19 January 2005.

Chow, Libby, content producer, The Age Online, 9 November 2000 and 1 March 2005.

Clark, Philip, radio talkback presenter, 2GB Sydney, 20 January 2005.

Clifton, Peter, editor, BBC News Interactive, 24 September 2004.

Clough, Tony, former radio newsreader, ABC Radio, 1 February 2001.

Cronin, Katy, former television journalist, ABC Television, 8 November 2000.

Doogue, Geraldine, radio and television presenter, ABC, 13 December 2004.

Ellis, Marianne, television news journalist, National Nine News, 23 December 2004.

Forbes, Clark, Program Director, 3AW Melbourne, 10 November 2000.

Holdaway, Scott, reporter, ABC News and Current Affairs, Perth, 18 February 2005.

Johanson, Simon, Online Editor, The Age Online, 9 November 2000 and 4 March 2005.

Johnston, Robert, Manager, ABC New Media News and Information, 7 November 2000, 18 January 2005.

Kelly, Justin, News Director, 2GB, Sydney,

O'Sullivan, David, Executive Producer, ABC Online, 18 January 2005.

Sallur, Adam, promotions producer, ABC Radio, 24 November 2000.

Sara, Sally, foreign correspondent, ABC News and Current Affairs, 18 November 2004.

Sattler, Howard, radio talkback presenter, 2WS and 6PR, 8 November 2000.

Scott, Steve, Channel Seven News, Perth.

Sims, Ron, sound recordist, 24 November 2000.

Southgate, Martin, content producer, ABC Online, 18 January 2005.

Throsby, Margaret, radio presenter, ABC Classic FM, 18 February 2005.

Wotherspoon, Col, Senior Broadband Producer, ABC Online, 18 January 2005.

Index

CD Track List

The companion CD provides a series of audio illustrations of different aspects of broadcast production. It features interviews with broadcasters discussing their approach to their craft, as well as examples of their work. Listening to these tracks will help students to gain a better understanding of the theory behind production practice, and teachers may find the examples a useful starting point for further group discussion.

The CD includes material from both the commercial media and the ABC, although the ABC examples predominate because of the public broadcaster's wider range of talk-based programming. All examples are used with the permission of the copyright holders. As some of the stories were recorded off air, sound quality reflects the quality of the original transmission.

TRACK 1: Using the voice, chapters 4 and 14 (time 6:14)

On this track, which starts with the voices of students attempting to read a news script before receiving any training, veteran ABC newsreader Tony Clough talks about voice production techniques and the ways of developing good script-reading skills.

Source: ABC Radio News, Perth, 22 January 2001, noon bulletin

TRACK 2: Interviewing tactics, chapter 6 (time 8:14)

This track illustrates the process that interviewers go through when deciding on their topic, talent, and approach to an interview. Steve Cannane, presenter of Triple J's afternoon current affairs program, *Hack*, takes us through an interview he did with Deputy Leader of the House of Representatives Peter McGauran on how the newly elected Howard government would be meeting its election promises in relation to the parliamentary agenda. He explains the reasons for doing the interview, the story angle he was following, and the rationale for his approach to his talent.

Source: ABC Triple J, 17 November 2004

TRACK 3: Confrontational interview, chapter 6 (time 4:10)

This is an example of a confrontational style where the interviewer actively challenges the interviewee.

Talkback radio presenter Neil Mitchell of Melbourne station 3AW interviews Assistant Commissioner for Crime for the Victorian Police, Simon Overland, about documents allegedly leaked from the Police Department that may have been implicated in a crime-land killing. Note the interviewer's assertive and uncompromising style as he challenges the talent to provide the information he seeks.

Source: 3AW, Melbourne

TRACK 4: Confessional interview, chapter 6 (time 4:33)

Julie McCrossin of Radio National's *Life Matters* program tackles the sensitive issue of losing a child at birth, the subject of a documentary by Vanessa Gorman in which she chronicles her own experience of pregnancy and loss. The segment features Vanessa herself and the baby's father, Michael Shaw. Note the style and questioning technique that the interviewer uses to encourage her guests to open up and talk about a very confronting and emotional issue.

Source: ABC, *Life Matters*, 1 March 2001

TRACK 5: Sound-recording troubleshooting, chapter 7 (time 2:00)

Poor audio is often very hard or impossible to correct afterwards. This highlights the importance of getting high quality clear recordings with no technical interference when you are on location. This track contains the following examples of bad quality sound:

1   popping (mike too close to mouth)
2   muddy sound (talent too far away from mike)
3a too much echo (reverb off walls)
3b same interview with less reverb
4   distorted sound (on location recording without windsock)
5   same on location recording with windsock
6   mike clicks: intermittent interference caused by bad cable connection.

Voices: Chaz Jones and Dominique Pratt
Sound Recordist: Leo Murray, Murdoch University

TRACK 6: Dealing with sound, chapter 7 (time 6:51)

Sound recordist Ron Sims talks about the nature of sound and the techniques he has used to build sound pictures in his productions.

Sources: 'Sarah Island' (copyright R. Sims) and 'Limestone, Iron and Time' featuring voices of Gillian Berry and Murray Dowsett, ABC, *Poetica* 14 March 1998

The next two tracks illustrate different aspects of feature production as described in chapter 8.

TRACK 7: Longer feature, chapter 8 (time 5:04)

Radio National's Bill Bunbury talks about his approach to longer form feature production, using illustrations from his work. He focuses particularly on his interaction with his talent and the techniques he has used to get them to tell their stories with maximum effect.

Source: '"Nowhere to run"—The Meckering Earthquake', ABC, *Talking History*, 15 December 1986

TRACK 8: Current affairs story, chapters 8 and 12 (time 3:32)

This track from the ABC's *The World Today* program is an example of a current affairs story. Sally Sara provides an eye witness account of an encounter with one of the rebel armies fighting the government forces in the brutal war in Southern Dafur. She makes use of sounds directly from the location and the power of her own descriptive language to set the scene for us as the rebels prepare for their next attack. The track begins with presenter David Hardaker introducing the story.

Source: ABC, *The World Today*, 22 September 2004

TRACK 9: ABC promo, chapter 9 (time 4:58)

720 ABC Perth Promotions Producer Adam Sallur talks about the art of promo making and the techniques he uses in bringing music and speech together to make attention-grabbing packages.

Sources: 'Jeffrey Archer' promo, ABC 720 Perth; 'Hank Marvin' promo, ABC 720 Perth; 'Pythagoras' promo, ABC 720 Perth

TRACK 10: Commercial radio ad, chapter 9 (time 0:21)

Here is an example of a commercial radio ad from Sydney commercial radio station 2GB. Note the pace and tone of the ad and how its style, sound, and format are adapted to suit the type of station and audience profile.

Source: 2GB, Sydney

TRACK 11: Talkback radio, chapter 10 (time 6:40)

This is an extract from the Philip Clark drive program on commercial radio station 2GB in Sydney illustrating the talkback radio style of programming and presentation. Philip Clark interviews Gold Coast businessman Ron Bakir about his involvement in the attempt to clear Australian Schapelle Corby of drug smuggling charges in Indonesia. He then takes some talkback callers on the subject. Note the role of the presenter, who involves himself not just as interviewer but as commentator.

Source: 2GB, 23 March 2005

TRACK 12: Challenges in live interviewing on talkback radio, chapter 10 (time 5:42)

This is an insight into story development in the talkback radio format. The track begins with an extract from a live radio interview Howard Sattler did with the grieving mother of James Annetts, a young jackaroo who died in the bush in tragic circumstances in late 1986. The parents had just heard that their claim for compensation had been rejected by the WA Supreme Court. Howard then comments on the challenges the interview posed for him, not only in terms of handling high emotion on air, but also in the context of navigating carefully around subject matter that might potentially cause legal problems.

Source: 'Interview with Sandra Annetts', Radio 6PR

TRACK 13: Commercial radio news story, chapter 12 (time 0:33)

This is a news story from Macquarie National News broadcast on 2GB on 20 January 2005 in the one o'clock bulletin. It is an example of the format 'word and grab'. You will hear the newsreader reading the following script:

New transport minister JOHN WATKINS says he'll be catching trains to work as often as possible—as he begins to improve the system.

MR WATKINS and the Premier have toured SYDNEY's Central station to meet with rail staff—and travellers ... they arrived on a late running train.

MR WATKINS says he hopes commuters will be patient—as he implements the Government's strategies ...

Grab: 0:12

Notice how the script contains most of the necessary information with the audio grab mainly providing colour. The script could just as easily stand alone as a word copy.

Source: 2GB Sydney, 20 January 2005

TRACK 14: Commercial radio news bulletin, chapter 14 (time 5:20)

This is an example of commercial radio news. It features the one o'clock bulletin from Macquarie National News presented by Erin Maher on 2GB Sydney.

Source: 2GB Sydney, 20 January 2005

TRACK 15: Court reporting story, chapter 16 (time 0:45)

This is an example of a court reporting story broadcast on Macquarie National News featuring the newsreader introduction followed by the reporter's voice report. Note how carefully the reporter has to script this report to stay within the boundaries of what is legally allowable.

Source: 2GB Sydney, 20 January 2005

TRACK 16: The ethics of reporting, chapter 17 (time 3:43)

Radio journalist Alison Caldwell describes how she covered the breaking story of the Childers backpackers hostel fire in June 2000 for the ABC *AM* program. This segment includes extracts from her interviews with two survivors on a poor quality mobile phone link the morning after the tragedy, along with her commentary on how she approached interviewing people who had just gone through a highly traumatic experience.

Source: ABC, *AM*, 23 June 2000